LAWRENCE HENRY GIPSON

AUTHOR

JARED INGERSOLL: A STUDY OF AMERICAN LOYALISM IN RELATION TO BRITISH COLONIAL GOVERNMENT

STUDIES IN CONNECTICUT COLONIAL TAXATION

THE MORAVIAN INDIAN MISSION ON WHITE RIVER

LEWIS EVANS

THE COMING OF THE REVOLUTION, 1763–1775

THE BRITISH EMPIRE BEFORE THE AMERICAN REVOLUTION

THE BRITISH EMPIRE
BEFORE THE AMERICAN REVOLUTION
VOLUME II

THE BRITISH ISLES AND THE AMERICAN COLONIES:

THE SOUTHERN PLANTATIONS

1748–1754

THE BRITISH EMPIRE
BEFORE THE AMERICAN REVOLUTION
VOLUME II

THE BRITISH ISLES

AND

THE AMERICAN COLONIES

THE SOUTHERN PLANTATIONS
1748–1754

BY

LAWRENCE HENRY GIPSON

MCMLXVII
ALFRED A. KNOPF
NEW YORK

L. C. catalog card number: 58–9670
© Alfred A. Knopf, Inc., 1960

THIS IS A BORZOI BOOK,
PUBLISHED BY ALFRED A. KNOPF, INC.

FIRST BORZOI EDITION
SECOND PRINTING, JUNE 1967

Originally published in 1936 by The Caxton Printers, Ltd.,
Caldwell, Idaho.

This edition completely revised, reset, and printed from new
plates.

TO THE MEMORY *of* JAMES ALEXANDER MACLEAN, *one time President of the University of Idaho, under whose tuition the author developed an interest in history and political institutions.*

Preface

IN approaching the revised edition of each of the first three volumes of this series on *The British Empire before the American Revolution*, it should be pointed out that all three were originally conceived and written as an entity of one book published simultaneously in three volumes and subtitled at that time "Provincial Characteristics and Sectional Tendencies in the Era Preceding the American Crisis, 1748–1754." Since each of the revised volumes is now appearing separately and under a somewhat changed title, it is well to restate the objectives of the trilogy so that the individual volume shall not appear to be out of the context of its broad purpose.

In the first volume attention was focused on the active forces which affected life and institutions within the British Isles in the middle of the eighteenth century. In so far as these were in evidence at the time, certain important constitutional, political, economic, and social aspects of the more or less distinct civilizations of England, Wales, Scotland, and Ireland were emphasized, along with the degree to which earlier English expansion — in the form of colonies, possessions, and spheres of influence — had laid down the limits by 1750 of what was commonly called the British Empire.

This second volume is chiefly concerned with the characteristics at mid-century of the various British colonies established in the southern part of North America and on islands in the Caribbean Sea and in the Atlantic Ocean to the south of Newfoundland. Broadly speaking, the economy and social institutions of these portions of the Old Empire — with the exception of Georgia, where the Trusteeship period was drawing to a close in 1750 — were based fundamentally upon the existence of slavery and white bondage. Most of their inhabitants also concentrated their energies upon the production of export staples, such as sugar, tobacco, rice, and indigo, under a plantation system of cultivation. These colonies therefore possessed certain unifying features, despite the fact that, outside of the British

West Indies, they had developed little consciousness of this unity. As for the sugar islands, by the middle of the eighteenth century they were welded together, as will be noted, by the common economic problems that seemed to demand a united front against the more northern British continental colonies. To the extent that this was true there therefore existed aspects of sectionalism within the Empire. Thus, while the expression "southerner" was not a term used in 1750 to designate one living to the southward of Pennsylvania on the mainland, that of "West India planter" was commonly applied to those living within the bounds of the Caribbean Sea and in fact set them apart from other colonials also identified with plantation economy. This sectionalism, however, while real enough, was not a serious threat to the integrity of the Empire, such as was to develop between the years 1760 and 1775 within it and was to lead to its disruption.

In beginning the survey of the more southern colonies within the Empire it will be well to start with Virginia, the oldest of them. Thereafter we shall turn to Maryland, created out of a portion of the Old Dominion, and then describe the processes involved in producing and marketing the chief export staple of these two colonies, tobacco. This will be followed by chapters on the Carolinas, Georgia, Jamaica, the lesser British Antilles, the Bermudas, and the Bahamas. The volume will conclude by dealing with the chief export of the British West Indies — sugar — and the slave trade that made possible its production on a large scale as well as that of the other southern colonial plantation staples — rice and tobacco. As to British claims to certain of the West India Windward Islands and to what is now British Honduras, these are dealt with fully in Volumes V and VII respectively of this series. On account of its importance, a consideration of Indian relations is not included in this volume or the next, but is dealt with extensively in subsequent volumes.

Finally, what is attempted in Volume II and Volume III to follow, is not to present all institutional aspects of each colony, but rather to emphasize the salient characteristics that typified each during the years under consideration. However, in Volume X, which is concerned with the colonies at the beginning of the crisis in Anglo-American relations in 1760, a broad survey of the political, economic, and social patterns that characterized the civilization of British North America will be presented in order to indicate the extent to which, both intellectually and in material development, the people of this area had become mature and sufficiently powerful to meet with confidence the problems — both internal and external in nature — that faced them.

The material for the writing of this volume was secured in the following depositories: the Maryland Historical Society and the Enoch Pratt Free Library at Baltimore, the Maryland State Library at Annapolis, the Virginia State Library and the Virginia Historical Society at Richmond, the North Carolina Archives at Raleigh, the Duke University Library at Durham and the University of North Carolina Library on Southern History at Chapel Hill, the South Carolina Archives Department and Caroliniana Library at Columbia, the South Carolina Historical Society and the Reference Library at Charleston, the Georgia Archives at Atlanta, the Institute of Jamaica at Kingston and the Jamaica Archives at Spanish Town, the Bermuda Archives at Hamilton, the Public Record Office and the British Museum in London, the Bristol Reference Library and the Merchant Venturers Hall in Bristol, England, the Public Record Office of Northern Ireland at Belfast, the Huntington Library at San Marino, California, the Clements Library at Ann Arbor, Michigan, and the Library of Congress in Washington. No archival material in usable form has survived climatic and other conditions in the Leeward Islands and in Barbados relating to the period under review. As my project is carried on in the Library at Lehigh University, I have had available its excellent collection, especially those volumes in the Rare Book Room.

To aid in the preparation of the first edition of this volume which appeared in 1936 and the present revision of it, I received important financial support from Lehigh University, the Social Science Research Council, the American Council of Learned Societies, and the Rockefeller Foundation. To these institutions I must express my deep appreciation, also to Jeannette Reed Gipson, my wife, to Mrs. Jere Knight, my Research Assistant, to her small staff, and to the staff of the Lehigh Library, for their aid in a variety of ways in my researches and in the preparation of the manuscript for the press, to my brother, James A. Gipson, for publishing the first edition of it, and to Alfred A. Knopf, my present publisher, for bringing out this revised edition. While I have sought to utilize, in so far as is possible, the most important source materials that would throw light on the southern colonies whether in printed form or in manuscript, I have also greatly benefited by the large and increasing number of more or less spe-

cialized studies that have been published in book form or in periodi-
cals and have sought to give them recognition in the footnotes.

A final word of explanation may be in order. When Mr. Knopf became my publisher in 1939, he recommended that in subsequent volumes of the series, concerned as it is with the British Empire, I should
follow English rather than American usage in spelling. This I have
done, and the present volume, as well as the revised edition of Volume I, conforms to the style of Volumes IV to IX, as will Volume III
when reissued in revised form.

L. H. G.

The Library,
Lehigh University,
Bethlehem, Pennsylvania,
September 15, 1959

Contents

CHAPTER II

AN OLD CATHOLIC REFUGE

CHAPTER III

THE CHESAPEAKE BAY STAPLE

CHAPTER IV

THE REGION OF THE SOUTHERN PINE BARRENS

CHAPTER V

ARISTOCRATS OF THE RICE SWAMPS

CHAPTER VI

AN AMERICAN ARCADIA

CHAPTER VII

THE CARIBBEAN OUTPOST OF THE EMPIRE

CHAPTER VIII

ISLANDS OF CANE. ISLANDS OF CONTENTMENT.
HOME OF THE OLD BUCCANEERS

CHAPTER IX

THE STRUGGLE FOR THE MUSCOVADO MARKETS

Maps

THE BRITISH EMPIRE
BEFORE THE AMERICAN REVOLUTION
VOLUME II

THE BRITISH ISLES AND THE AMERICAN COLONIES:

THE SOUTHERN PLANTATIONS

1748–1754

CHAPTER I

The Empire of the Old Dominion

Oldest of the English colonies, Virginia was likewise the largest. As the first of the royal colonies, its machinery of government, at least at the provincial level, was used as a model in the creation of succeeding royal governments in the New World; its Anglican Church Establishment, dating from the very beginning of settlement at Jamestown, also had its influence in the efforts to spread Anglicanism among the other English American possessions. These aspects of the history of the province, as well as the means whereby its people gained a livelihood and expanded, are of importance to an understanding of the Old British Empire in the middle of the eighteenth century.

"Virginia," declared Colonel Thomas Lee, President of the Council, in his report to the Board of Trade in 1750, "is Bounded by the Great Atlantic Ocean to the East, by North Carolina to the South, by Maryland and Pennsylvania to the North, and by the South Sea to the West including California." [1] In line with this conception of territorial limits based upon the charter of 1609, the people of the Virginia colony in the middle of the eighteenth century were engaged in the tremendous enterprise of making good their claims to that portion of their empire that lay to the eastward of the Mississippi River. Between the years 1743 and 1760 the Council of Virginia was to grant over three million acres of western land to groups and to

---

[1] See his "Answers to Queries," September 29, 1750. Shelburne Papers, 45:84–90, Clements Library.

individuals.[2] This potentiality for westward expansion is one of the most salient features of the Old Dominion during this period.

Up to the middle of the eighteenth century, knowledge of the region west of the Appalachian Mountains was quite imperfect, although hardy men appear to have passed beyond the Appalachians even before 1675, and others, such as John Howard and John Peter Sally, had explored some of the region in the early 1740's,[3] at least to the south of the Ohio. To the north, Pennsylvania and Virginia traders had settled at various Indian villages on the Allegheny and Ohio rivers.[4] In fact, the idea of a vast trans-Appalachian settlement of English-speaking people, supplemented by foreign Protestants, had already taken possession of the minds of Virginia leaders.

President of the Council Lee emphasized in 1750 the importance of the Crown's taking steps "to discover the situation of the Ohio, Alignay [Allegheny] and other Rivers that empty themselves into the Mississippi and the lakes that fall into the River St. Lawrence, and so to make a complete Mapp of Virginia." [5] He declared that a proper encouragement for men to cultivate the lands on the other side of the Great Mountains "will make this the strongest frontier that is to any of the King's Dominions in America; since the Lands are rich on the Aligany and Ohio [and] where I am told more People may conveniently settle than at this time inhabit Pennsylvania, the Jerseys and New York." [6]

The impression seems to prevail among many students that the Ohio Company's tentative grant of trans-Appalachian lands in 1749 represents the first serious attempt by land speculators and potential settlers to lay hands on this region. This is far from the truth. In fact, it was but an incident in the process of the westward pressure of the population of Virginia.

In the late 1720's and during the 1730's and early 1740's the region

---

[2] Archibald Henderson: "A Pre-Revolutionary Revolt in the Old Southwest," *Mississippi Valley Historical Review*, XVII, 191–212.

[3] Fairfax Harrison: "The Virginians on the Ohio and the Mississippi in 1743," *Virginia Magazine of History*, XXX, 203–22. See also C. W. Alvord: "The Daniel Boone Myth," *Journal of the Illinois State Historical Society*, XIX, 16–30, and C. W. Alvord and L. Bidgood: *The First Explorations of the Trans-Allegheny Region by the Virginians, 1650–1674* (Cleveland, 1912).

[4] J. A. Adams: "The Indian Trader of the Upper Ohio Valley," *The Western Pennsylvania Historical Magazine*, XVII, 163–74.

[5] "Answers to Queries," September 29, 1750. Shelburne Papers, 45:84–90.
[6] *Ibid.*

drained by the upper waters of the Staunton, the James, and the Roanoke to the east of the Blue Ridge, as well as the Valley of Virginia were the objects of interest on the part of the seekers of lands.[7] The counties of Brunswick, Lunenburg, Goochland, and Augusta with the boundaries they then possessed [8] are most frequently mentioned in the petitions to the Council by those desiring grants.[9] However, as early as 1743 James Patton, Gentleman, and others presented a petition for 200,000 acres lying "upon Woods River [10] forty or fifty miles to Westward of the head Springs of Roanoke River & 500 East distant from the Great River Mississippi. . . ." This was ordered to lie by for further consideration with the understanding that the petitioners were to be preferred to others desiring to secure the same lands.[11] In April 1745 John Robinson, Sr., Esq., President of the Provincial Council, Thomas Nelson, Jr., Esq., and associates secured an order in council for leave to take up 100,000 acres of land lying on the Greenbrier River, which flows into the Great Kanawha, and were given four years to secure a survey of the same and pay for the rights.[12] At the same time 50,000 acres lying about the same river were granted under similar conditions to Henry Downes and others,[13] while in November of the same year John Blair, Esq., another member of the Council, and his partners received permission to acquire 100,000 acres on the Youghiogheny.[14] Somewhat earlier than this tentative grant James Patton, John Tayloe, and others secured an allotment of equal size "on three Branches of the Mississippi River, the other two to the westward thereof. . . ." [15]

By the year 1747 there had developed so intense a desire on the part of prominent Virginians to parcel out the trans-Appalachian region that on November 6 Lieutenant Governor William Gooch wrote to the Board of Trade acquainting them that many persons in partnership had made application for grants beyond the Great

---

7 See J. W. Wayland: *The German Element of the Shenandoah Valley of Virginia* . . . (Charlottesville, Va., 1907), Chap. 4.

8 The Jefferson and Fry Map of Virginia shows the counties as they existed in 1751.

9 See the *Executive Journals of the Council of Colonial Virginia* (ed. H. R. McIlwaine and W. L. Hall, 5 vols., Richmond, Va., 1925–45), V, 12, *passim*.

10 Woods River or the Great Kanawha.

11 *Executive Journals of the Council*, V, 134.

12 *Ibid.*, V, 172–3.

13 *Ibid.*, V, 173.

14 *Ibid.*, V, 195.

15 *Ibid.*, V, 173. Really the Ohio is the river the applicants had in mind.

Mountains and setting forth the advantages of this plan. The Board referred the matter to the Duke of Newcastle, Secretary of State for the Southern Department,[16] who requested them to turn to consider the questions involved and thereupon to make representation to His Majesty in Council. This was done in September of the following year and proved favourable to western expansion.[17]

Doubtless as a result of this encouragement on the part of the Crown, two petitions were presented by William Gray and others in 1748 asking for grants in Augusta County on the "west side of the Indian Field Mountains running on the Branches of New River or Mississippi." [18] These were read by the Provincial Council and were acted upon favourably. Early the following year the conditional grant to John Robinson, Sr., and associates for lands on the Green Brier approved in 1745 was renewed, as was that to Henry Downes and his partners.[19] In July, "in pursuance of his Majesty's Instructions of March last," leave was given to John Hanbury of London, Merchant, Thomas Lee, provincial councillor, and their associates, who made up the so-called Ohio Company of Virginia, to take up and survey 200,000 acres "betwixt Romanetto's and Buffalo's Creek, on the South Side of the River Alligane, otherwise the Ohio, and betwixt the two Creeks and the Yellow Creek [20] on the North side of the River, or in such other Parts of the West of the Great Mountains as shall be adjudged most proper . . . for making Settlements thereon," with the promise of an additional 300,000 acres should the promotors, within a period of seven years, erect a fort and garrison it and settle a hundred families upon their grant.[21]

---

[16] *Journal of the Commissioners for Trade and Plantations from* . . . *1704 to* . . . *1782, preserved in the Public Record Office* (14 vols., London, 1920–38), 1741–1749, p. 265 (to be referred to hereafter as the Board of Trade Journal).

[17] P.R.O., C.O. 5:1366, pp. 411–17; *Acts of the Privy Council, Col. Ser.*, 1745–1766, pp. 55–8; Board of Trade Journal, 1741–1749, p. 256.

[18] *Executive Journals of the Council*, V, 250, 257–8.

[19] *Ibid.*, V, 282.

[20] Buffalo Creek and Yellow Creek are shown on the Jefferson and Fry Map of 1751.

[21] See *Executive Journals of the Council*, V, 295–6. On February 14, 1748/9, at a meeting of the Board of Trade an order of the Lords of the Committee of the Council of the 9th instant was read referring back to the Lords Commissioners a report they had made on December 13 together with the draft of an additional instruction prepared for Lieutenant Governor Gooch, empowering him to make grants beyond the Great Mountains to persons in partnership who had applied for them. In doing this the Lords of the Committee directed the Board to reconsider the same together with a petition of John Hanbury of London, merchant, and others for a grant of 500,000 acres on the Ohio River. Two days later Hanbury, who had been summoned, appeared before the Board.

The same day that the Ohio Company received its permissive grant from the Virginia Council, leave was given to Bernard Moore and associates to take up 100,000 acres of land "on the Waters of the Mississippi River [22] beginning at ten Trees marked P T G standing in a Fork of a Branch of the said River, known by the Name of New River,[23] and so down the said River and the Waters of the said Mississippi. . . ." John Lewis, Esq., a provincial councillor, Dr. Thomas Walker, and others, members of the Loyal Land Company, were also permitted to take up and survey 800,000 acres in one or more allotments "beginning on the Bounds between this Colony and North Carolina, and running to the Westward and to the North. . . ." Further, Peyton Randolph, the Attorney-General, and associates, likewise at the same session of the Council, obtained leave to survey 400,000 acres "lying on New River commonly call'd Wood's River, and the Waters thereof," and John Tayloe and associates, who previously had applied for 100,000 acres on the same river and two other branches of "the Mississippi," were allowed to renew their earlier conditional grant. Finally, William Winstone, Jr., and associates received permission to survey "fifty thousand Acres of Land, beginning at Old Fort between Ohio and the Mississippi Rivers, running up the Western Side of Ohio, and Eastern side of Mississippi. . . ." [24]

These great grants of trans-Appalachian land made by the provincial Council on July 12, 1749, represent the last significant work of that body before the departure of Lieutenant Governor Gooch for England. There were present at this meeting: the Governor, John Robinson, senior councillor, Thomas Lee, Lewis Burwell, John Blair, the Rev. William Dawson, and John Lewis, with Philip Grymes and John Custis absent. The grants in each instance were purely conditional to be based upon a survey of the proposed lands, and, with the exception of the Ohio Company, all applicants were obliged to

---

He stated that he had no other proposals to make than were contained in the petition. See the Board of Trade *Journal,* 1741–1749, pp. 380–2; see also C.O. 5:1366, pp. 427–37, and *Acts of the Privy Council, Col. Ser.,* 1745–1766, pp. 55–8.

[22] The petitioners really meant the Ohio.

[23] The Kanawha or New, known also as Woods River.

[24] *Executive Journals of the Council,* V, 296–7. This description taken literally would have placed the Winstone tract in what is now Pulaski County, Illinois, right in the heart of the region of effective French control. It is apparent that the petitioners had in mind a grant within the elbow formed by the Allegheny and the Ohio rivers, embracing roughly lands within what is now Allegheny County, Pennsylvania, a region well known to the Indian traders.

deposit this survey at the Secretary's office and to pay for the rights within a period of four years. The Ohio Company, on the other hand, was not only expressly exempted from the payment of these rights but of quit-rent for a period of ten years, and thereafter payments were to be made only on such lands as were actually placed under cultivation. The Crown, to guard against the possible loss of revenue as the result of the granting of this permit to patent, provided in the instructions to the Governor that no person already owning land within the colony should be admitted to settle on any of the Company's lands without giving security for continuing the payment of the quit-rents on what he already possessed.[25]

To encourage those who had taken these preliminary steps toward the actual settlement of the trans-Appalachian West it was ordered by the Council later in 1749 that an advertisement be inserted in the *Virginia Gazette* signifying that the surveyors were at liberty to proceed with the surveying of lands beyond the Great Mountains, in so far as they did not interfere with the grants to the Ohio Company.[26] There was, however, no great rush of surveyors into this region. Indeed, in August, the year of the grants, disturbing news came from beyond the mountains: the Indians had heard of the Ohio Company's plan to build a fort on the Ohio and were determined to offer resistance.[27] Nevertheless, in the following year Dr. Thomas Walker and a small party, acting for the Loyal Land Company, penetrated the region beyond the Holston up to the Kentucky River.[28] Somewhat later the same year Christopher Gist and a Negro boy went down the Ohio as far as the Miami River, seeking a favourable location for the Ohio Company reserve.[29] As a result of suitable gifts, Gist subsequently secured permission from the Indians for the Company to

---

[25] *Ibid.*; see also *Acts of the Privy Council, Col. Ser., 1745–1766,* pp. 55–8. For the beginnings of the Ohio Company see K. P. Bailey: *The Ohio Company of Virginia and the Westward Movement, 1748–1792* (Glendale, Calif., 1939), pp. 17–31; *George Mercer Papers relating to the Ohio Company of Virginia* (ed. Lois Mulkearn, Pittsburgh, 1954), pp. 1–7, 246–8; and Desmond Clark: *Arthur Dobbs, Esquire, 1689–1765* . . . (Chapel Hill, 1957), pp. 90–4.

[26] *Executive Journal of the Council,* V, 306.

[27] *Ibid.,* V, 302–3.

[28] For Walker's "Journal" see L. P. Summers: *The Annals of Southwest Virginia, 1769–1800* (Abingdon, Va., 1929); see also J. S. Johnston: *First Explorations of Kentucky* . . . (Louisville, 1898).

[29] Gist's first "Journal," also printed by Summers and by Johnston, has been carefully edited by Miss Mulkearn; see her *George Mercer Papers* . . . , pp. 7–31.

settle a stretch of land located between the mountains, the Monongahela, and the mouth of the Youghiogheny.[30]

The Ohio Company approached the task of settlement with caution and apparently little was done in that direction for the next two years. Undoubtedly the death in 1750 of Thomas Lee, President of the Council, who had been the most influential among the Virginians promoting this enterprise, was a serious blow to the Company, especially in light of the fact that he already had connections with the trans-Appalachian West as the result of his fur-trading interests on the Ohio.[31] These connections had been maintained for Lee by the trader Hugh Parker, who was greatly beloved by the Indians on the Ohio and by those living in the direction of Lake Erie. Parker also died in 1750.

Matthew Rowan of North Carolina in a letter to a friend written in the fall of 1751 stated that he had been in Virginia and, upon inquiring as to "what was doing in the Ohio concern," could get no information.[32] In fact, the Company had come to realize that the settlement of its grant could not easily be provided for, as a result of the critical state of affairs on the Ohio, unless the fort that it had agreed to erect was sufficiently strong to resist attack by either the Indians or the French. For the latter had appeared in force on the Ohio under Céleron de Blainville in 1749 and, before returning to Canada, had in the most formal manner taken possession of the country in the name of the King of France and had warned away the English traders as intruders.[33]

To those interested in promoting trans-Appalachian settlement it now seemed that no mere blockhouse would do. One or more forts supplied with cannon must be provided. Therefore, application was made by the new Lieutenant Governor, Robert Dinwiddie, to the home government for twenty or thirty three-pound cannon, with the result that in August 1753 it was agreed to send these with proper supplies.[34] Soon after this, the Ohio Company group, having become

---

[30] *Christopher Gist's Journals with Historical, Geographical and Ethnological Notes* . . . (ed. W. McC. Darlington, Pittsburgh, 1893), p. 78.

[31] See [Captain] Rowan to S[amuel] S[mith] from North Carolina, September 19, 1751, Dobbs Papers, Public Record Office of Northern Ireland, Belfast.

[32] *Ibid.*

[33] An account of the activities of the French in the Ohio Valley is presented in Volume IV of this series.

[34] See *Acts of the Privy Council, Col. Ser.*, 1745–1766, pp. 201–3. Four-pounders, however, were sent instead of the three-pounders.

convinced that a weak settlement would not be apt to flourish, decided to petition the Crown for an enlargement of their grant under
condition that 300 families would be settled there instead of but 100,
and that two forts would be erected, "one at Shurtees Creek, and the
other at the Fork, where the Great Conhaway enters the Ohio." [35]
This was apparently approved but was never properly implemented
in the face of pending international events.[36]

By 1753, the year that young George Washington departed for the
French posts on the Allegheny to warn their garrisons that they were
intruding upon Virginia territory, there was but a handful of English-speaking people living beyond the summit of the Appalachians,
mostly concentrated around the present sites of Mount Braddock
and Connellsville, both in Pennsylvania, but then supposed to be
within the Old Dominion.[37] Of the companies, it would appear that
only the Ohio [38] and the Loyal [39] took the initial step of exploring
for suitable lands, and only the former seems to have undertaken the
work of blazing a trail to its grant and of erecting a storehouse. In
1754 it also started the construction of a fort on the forks of the Ohio,
but the workers were overwhelmed by a French force descending
the Allegheny River. With the last of the intercolonial wars breaking
out in that year, the energies of the Virginia empire-builders were
absorbed in trying to defend themselves to the east of the mountains

---

[35] The request was that the bounds of the grant be fixed running "from Romanetto
or Kiskominetto Creek, on the South East Side of the Ohio, to the Fork, at the Entrance of the great Conhaway River, and from thence along the North side of the said
Conhaway River, to the entrance of Green Brier River, and from thence in a Strait Line
or Lines, to, and along the Mountains, to the South East Spring of Mohongaly River
and from thence Northwards along the Mountains, to the North East Springs of Romanetto or Kiskominetto Creek, or till a West Line from the Mountains intersects the
said Spring, and along it to its entrance into the Ohio . . ." (Acts of the Privy Council,
Col. Ser., 1745–1766, pp. 244–5). For the part played by Arthur Dobbs in the petition
of the Ohio Company for the enlargement of its grant see Desmond Clarke: Arthur
Dobbs, Esquire, 1689–1765 . . . , p. 93.

[36] See Shaw Livermore: Early American Land Companies (London, 1939), p. 79.

[37] See A. P. James: "The First English-Speaking Trans-Appalachian Frontier," The
Mississippi Valley Historical Review, XVII, 55–71.

[38] For a detailed account of the Ohio Company activities in 1753 and 1754 see
Chapter 8 of Volume IV of this series; see also Mrs. Mulkearn's George Mercer Papers
relating to the Ohio Company; K. P. Bailey: The Ohio Company of Virginia and the
Westward Movement, 1748–1792; and H. T. Leyland: The Ohio Company: A Colonial
Corporation (Cincinnati, 1921).

[39] See Archibald Henderson: Dr. Thomas Walker and the Loyal Company of Virginia (Worcester, Mass., 1931).

from the savage thrusts of the hostile French and their Indian allies. That the trans-Appalachian region would have received a large accession of population during this period had it not been for the outbreak of hostilities is indicated by an address of the House of Burgesses which came before the Lords of the Committee of the Privy Council early in 1754, praying that small grants free from payment of the rights, amounting to five shillings per fifty acres, and from quit-rents for a period of ten years, be permitted. Later in the year this was agreed to by the Privy Council, and the Earl of Albemarle, who was Governor of Virginia and acting through the Lieutenant Governor, was instructed to act accordingly. The same condition was attached to these grants as to that of the Ohio Company, that those owning quit-rents on other lands in the province must give proper security for these payments.[40]

The most important fact to stress in viewing that part of the province directly to the east of the Appalachians is that by 1750 there was a rather large body of settlers — mostly Ulster Scots and Germans who had come from the north during the preceding twenty years — gathered together in small communities. They were engaged in general farming and stock-raising much after the fashion of their kinsmen and neighbours dwelling along the banks of the Susquehanna in Pennsylvania.[41] To meet the needs of the inhabitants of this section the counties of Frederick and Augusta had been organized, as had parishes bearing the same names and with boundaries corresponding to those of these counties. Thus, legally, the region was made to conform in most respects to the older-settled part of the Old Dominion, but beyond that fact there was little enough in common between the two areas. Indeed, the people of the Valley, although varying among themselves, were, by reason of their non-English extraction and the consequent inheritance of non-English ideas and practices, dominated by habits that set them quite apart from the planter group. Their very existence along the fringes of civilization contributed to broadening the differentiation between them and

---

[40] See Acts of the Privy Council, Col. Ser., 1745–1766, pp. 235–8.

[41] For the movement from Lancaster County, Pennsylvania, into the Shenandoah Valley, see C. E. Kemper: "Historical Notes from the Records of Augusta County, Virginia," Lancaster County Hist. Soc. Proceedings, XXV, 89–93, 147–55; for migration from Pennsylvania southward see also W. F. Dunaway: "Pennsylvania as an Early Distributing Center of Population," Pennsylvania Magazine of History and Biography, LV, 134–69.

those living in the old tidewater counties with respect to such institutions as the Established Church, slavery, primogeniture, and entail.[42]

Eastward from the Blue Ridge Mountains lies the Piedmont. A study of the history of Virginia land grants during the 1740's shows that much of the land, at least in the western portion of this rolling plateau, was without inhabitants in 1750. Nevertheless, men from the Valley were pressing eastward, while up from the Tidewater came a corresponding movement toward the west which established contact with the other at certain points. What is now southwest Virginia still awaited settlement, although it is true that Lunenburg County had been organized to the west of the counties of Amelia, Prince George, and Brunswick. The area covered by Lunenburg was enormous, but apparently only the eastern portion possessed any appreciable number of people.[43] The Piedmont, as well as the Valley of Virginia, was given over largely to general farming. While slavery existed in this region, it was the exception rather than the rule in 1750, at least in those portions isolated from the coastal plain.[44]

On the one hand, many of the older, established Virginia families had acquired titles to lands well to the west of the fall-line, with the result that some of their members had firmly entrenched themselves in the Piedmont on tobacco plantations worked by slaves after the manner of the Tidewater; on the other hand, thousands of other people were living under rude frontier conditions, having made but a beginning to the conquest of the lands which they were occupying. There was, it seems, a good deal of restlessness on the part of many of these people who, failing to attach themselves firmly to any locality, tended rather to shift from place to place according to circumstances. James Maury, writing to Philip Ludwell after the beginning of the French and Indian War, complained that hundreds of families living along the upper waters of the Potomac, the James, and the Roanoke had deserted their habitations within the period of a few months to remove themselves to other colonies, especially

[42] See F. H. Hart: The Valley of Virginia in the American Revolution, 1763–1789 (Chapel Hill, N.C., 1942); C. H. Ambler: Sectionalism in Virginia . . . (Chicago, 1910), p. 13.

[43] See Jefferson and Fry Map of Virginia in 1751; see also Fulmer Mood: "Studies in the History of American Settled Areas and Frontier Lines: . . . 1625–1790," Agricultural History, XXVI, 30–2.

[44] A list of tithables for the period, one of seven lists for the county of Lunenburg, shows that out of 310 property-holders only 27 possessed slaves, and these mostly but one or two slaves apiece. See William and Mary Quarterly, 2nd ser., XI, 55–8.

to the Carolinas. "And I have it from good authors," he declared, "that no later in autumn than October, five thousand more had crossed James River only at one ferry . . . journeying toward the same place." [45] The lure of the lower South was only less insistent in time of peace. All accounts agree that in the early 1750's Virginians were pouring into the back regions of North Carolina.

Within the tidewater region of Virginia, where modes of life were much more firmly established, naturally no such restlessness on the part of the population was manifested. However, one characteristic the Piedmont and the Tidewater had in common. Everywhere people dwelt in the open country, and this was so in spite of the great efforts at the very beginning of settlement on the James to induce the Virginians to build towns and cities.

Although by 1756 the estimated population of the Old Dominion was something over 290,000 people, a little over half of whom were whites,[46] Richmond, established as a town in 1742 with the privilege of holding fairs, was still the merest village in 1750, the year it became a county seat. The creation of Virginia towns, in fact, was not favourably regarded by the Crown. It was felt that this would lead to the manufacturing of goods which were customarily imported from the mother country and also to a lessening in the importance of tobacco as the staple export from the colony. As a result, acts passed in the early part of the century to encourage the growth of towns by according the inhabitants great privileges were disallowed in 1709.[47] Andrew Burnaby, writing in 1759, declared that though by the acts of Assembly there should have been forty-five towns within Virginia, one half of these had no more than five houses and the other half were but inconsiderable places.[48] He attributed the tendency toward dispersion rather than concentration of the population to the fact that, due to the cheapness of land and the ease of transportation by means of the numerous rivers, almost everyone could establish

---

[45] See Ann Maury: *Memoirs of a Huguenot Family* . . . (New York, 1853), pp. 421–3.

[46] E. B. Greene and V. D. Harrington: *American Population before* . . . *1790* (New York, 1932), pp. 140–1. For a further discussion of population in Virginia see Chapter 3 of this volume.

[47] See Order in Council, December 15, 1709, P.R.O., C.O. 5:1316, No. 42; see also C. P. Nettels: *The Money Supply of the American Colonies before 1720* (Madison, 1934), p. 139, for comment on the order in council.

[48] Andrew Burnaby: *Travels through the Middle Settlements in North America, in the Years 1759 and 1760* (London, 1775), p. 12.

himself upon a small plantation and ship his tobacco from his own door without difficulty, and could thereby live independently.[49] Although Burnaby was incorrect in part, since hundreds of plantations were located away from any navigable stream with the result that tobacco hogsheads had to be rolled to some landing or otherwise transported to a public warehouse, the opportunity to become an independent planter, however small, did exist. This, it goes without saying, was preferable to dwelling in a town as an artisan, depending upon the will of another and working long hours much of the year under climatic conditions less satisfactory than in England. Another thing that drew men to the land was the prospect held out to every small tobacco-grower that by good management he would be able to provide himself with indentured white or slave labour and by that process could hope to elevate himself gradually from the economic and social position of a poor, independent landholder to that of a wealthy, aristocratic planter.[50]

As a result of these influences upon the population, it is not surprising that Williamsburg could boast of hardly 1,000 people, including blacks, and of not more than 200 houses. Burnaby regarded it "as far from being a place of any consequence," although the provincial capital. He affirmed that it had as constant residents, besides the household of the Governor or his deputy, the families of but ten or twelve gentlemen, with some few merchants and tradesmen. During the Assembly sessions and those of the courts of law which were held four times a year, however, it was the scene of great animation with the crowding in of the gentry from far and near. Then much private business was transacted, bills of exchange were purchased, and current tobacco prices agreed upon by those prepared to buy and sell.[51] Moreover, William and Mary College, the only institution that pretended to care for the higher education of the youth

---

[49] Ibid.

[50] Even some of the tobacco-planters opposed to slavery felt impelled to strive to acquire slaves. Referring to the import tax on slaves and the export, Peter Fontaine, writing from Westover, Virginia, on March 30, 1757, declared: "This is part of our grievance, but to live in Virginia without slaves is morally impossible" (Ann Maury: Memoirs of a Huguenot Family [New York, 1953], pp. 351–2). The members of the Society of Friends who dwelt in the South, despite the testimony of many leading Quakers against slavery, were faced by the same problem. See S. B. Weeks: Southern Quakers and Slavery (Baltimore, 1896), Chap. 9.

[51] See J. H. Soltow: "The Role of Williamsburg in the Virginia Economy, 1750–1775," William and Mary Quarterly, 3rd ser. XV, 467–82.

of the South, was established there.[52] As a town Williamsburg was laid out in a regular manner, with an attractive public square and a leading street, impressive for its breadth, at the end of which was situated the college building, where the Assembly met from 1748 to 1755.[53] It was because of the steady growth of population in the Piedmont and the creation of new western counties that a demand arose in the 1740's for the capital of the province to be removed to a more central location — a demand which became insistent after the burning of the state house in 1748. The House of Burgesses strongly favoured a site on the Pamunkey, but the Council, dominated by people living in the lower tidewater area, succeeded in defeating the proposal; consequently, after the year 1749, although the question was subsequently raised,[54] the government continued at Williamsburg until the year 1779, when it was shifted to Richmond.

In 1749 Governor Gooch terminated an administration in Virginia that covered a period of twenty-two years. He had grown old and infirm in office, but throughout his career as Governor he had distinguished himself as a man of courage and of military capacity. Further, in fulfilling the civil functions of his office he had shown a rare combination of tact and firmness. Between all branches of the government during his governorship there had been unusual harmony. Lewis Burwell, who became President of the Council in November 1750, referred to the "Wise and Prudent Government of Sr William Gooch, the happy Influence of which we enjoy'd for above

---

[52] Lieutenant Governor Gooch, in an address to the Virginia Assembly in 1745, referred to the College of William and Mary as that "Seminary of Learning and Ornament of Virginia." He went on to say "that there is not in any Part of the world a College where good order, Decency and Discipline are better maintained, where God Almighty is more constantly and devoutedly worshipped, and where greater care is taken to train up young students in the rudiments of Religion, Loyalty, Science and good manners and carrying them toward Perfection than in this." See Council Journal, February 20, 1745, C.O. 5:1423.

[53] See Carl Bridenbaugh: Seat of Empire: The Political Role of Eighteenth-Century Williamsburg (Williamsburg, 1950), which is, however, largely concerned with political developments after 1763.

[54] In 1750 Colonel Thomas Lee, President of the Council, wrote to the Board of Trade that the removal of the government to Newcastle on the York would greatly further the work of western settlement. See Lee's letter of September 29, 1750, Shelburne Papers, 45:84–90. On April 9, 1752, it was voted in the House of Burgesses, 44 to 34, that a town more convenient to the inhabitants of the colony be established. See Journals of the House of Burgesses of Virginia (eds. J. P. Kennedy and H. R. McIlwaine, 13 vols., Richmond, 1905–13), 1752–1758, pp. 80–1. In the early 1760's this issue again arose.

Twenty Years." [55] The secret of his influence undoubtedly lay in his intimate relations with the great planter group. As previously pointed out, he had strongly approved western expansion, and during the last ten years of his administration numerous land companies came into existence, many of which received very large grants.

Technically Gooch was never Governor, as already indicated, but the Deputy or Lieutenant first for George Hamilton Douglas, Earl of Orkney, and later for William Anne Keppel, Earl of Albemarle, both of them absentees. The latter, upon Gooch's return to England in 1749, was led to favour the appointment of Robert Dinwiddie, who for many years had acted as the Surveyor-General of His Majesty's Customs for the Southern District and who had distinguished himself in detecting frauds in His Majesty's revenues in the West Indies.

The new appointee was far from being a stranger to Virginia: in 1741 he had been admitted to the Council as a councillor extraordinary [56] and in 1743 as a councillor ordinary. [57] When he finally arrived at his post he therefore brought with him an intimate knowledge of the affairs of the province; he also enjoyed by then the acquaintance and good will of many Virginians of first standing. His commission as Lieutenant Governor bore the date of July 4, 1751; [58] the following September he entered into a bond to pay to Albemarle, as the price of receiving the office, the sum of £3,500 and thereafter each six months the sum of £1,665, estimated to be one half of the value of the salary and perquisites. [59] In November he appeared before the

---

[55] *Executive Journals of the Council*, V, 345. See also P. S. Flippin: "William Gooch: Successful Royal Governor of Virginia," *William and Mary Quarterly*, 2nd ser., V, 225–58; VI, 1–38.

[56] *Executive Journals of the Council*, V, 70. For Dinwiddie's American career see L. K. Koontz: *Robert Dinwiddie* . . . (Glendale, Calif., 1941).

[57] *Executive Journals of the Council*, V, 115. The King's sign manual was dated July 10, 1742. The distinction between councillor extraordinary and councillor ordinary was that the former was not allowed to sit as a member of the upper house of the Assembly nor to act either as judge of the General Court or of that of oyer and terminer. It does not appear, moreover, that the councillor extraordinary was entitled to a salary, or to any portion of the £600 allotted to the Council.

[58] For Dinwiddie's commission under the signet and sign manual constituting him Lieutenant Governor of Virginia see C.O. 324:38, pp. 287–9. If he had been appointed Governor his commission would have carried the Great Seal. His commission as Vice Admiral of Virginia was issued July 24, 1751.

[59] Dinwiddie's bond, dated September 7, 1751, is among the Loudoun Papers, Doc. 310, Huntington Library. John Hanbury and Edward Clarke Paris signed the bond

Virginia Council and took the necessary oaths; thereupon the Council authorized a committee to negotiate for the purchase of a suitable governor's mansion and in December voted to present him with £400 sterling to cover his expenses between the time of his appointment and his arrival in the province. In the following spring, the latter part of February, he met his first Assembly, on which occasion he declared: "It was with great Joy I landed here, invested with Power of doing Good to a people, among whom I have formerly mingled in Scenes of domestic Felicity, and experienced the endearing Reciprocations of Friendship."

Here was the beginning of the administration of one of the most capable governors that Virginia has ever possessed — the last of three great Virginia governors of the eighteenth century preceding the Revolution, all of whom were Scots. Unfortunately, the harmony existing between the branches of the government was soon marred by the controversy that arose over Dinwiddie's demand of a fee, quite generally received by royal governors for granting patents to land under the seals of their provinces, but one that had never been levied in Virginia previous to this except during the governorship of Lord Howard of Effingham while James II was King of England.[60] The Governor now began to collect this fee on the larger grants of land, many of which, totalling as much as a million acres, it was asserted, had already, owing to lack of the proper formalities, escaped the payment of quit-rents to His Majesty.[61] The fee, a pistole, equal to a quarter of a Spanish doubloon, was equivalent to sixteen shillings and was therefore not exorbitant, although it was asserted in 1753 in a memorial from the inhabitants of Dinwiddie, the new county named in honour of the Governor, that they laboured under many hardships in being obliged to make this payment over and above the

---

with Dinwiddie. The indenture, made out at the same time as the bond, is also among the Loudoun Papers, Doc. 311.

[60] *Journals of the House of Burgesses, 1752–1758*, pp. 143–4.

[61] For the pistole fee controversy see G. C. Smith: "The Affair of the Pistole Fee, Virginia, 1752–1755," *Virginia Magazine of History and Biography*, XLVIII, 209–21; H. L. Osgood: *The American Colonies in the Eighteenth Century* (New York, 1925), IV, 226–30; L. K. Koontz: *Robert Dinwiddie . . .* , pp. 201–35; and J. P. Greene: "Landon Carter and the Pistole Fee Dispute," *William and Mary Quarterly*, 3rd ser., XIV, 66–9, and especially, by the same author, "The Case of the Pistole Fee: The Report of a Hearing on the Pistole Fee Dispute Before the Privy Council, June 18, 1754," *Virginia Magazine of History and Biography*, LXVI, 399–422. The decision of the Privy Council, while favourable to Dinwiddie, was pleasing to the House of Burgesses in that certain land patents were exempted. See *ibid.*, p. 405.

other fees formerly demanded and recieved.[62] It was doubtless un-popular with all who sought to take up lands. However, John Blair, a member of the Council, in a letter to the Bishop of London, pointed out the reason for a good deal of the opposition. The most noted stickler against the fee, he declared, had unsigned patents for about 60,000 acres and, by opposing the collection of the pistole, was thus able to save sixty pounds a year.[63]

The Burgesses, however, took high grounds in resisting the pistole fee for the use of the public seal, declaring that the demand for it was not warranted by any known and established law and was, as they conceived, "an Infringement of the Rights of the people and a Greivance [sic] highly to be complained of." [64] The whole issue was referred to England, where, as might be anticipated in light of the fact that this was considered a proper perquisite of a colonial gover-nor, Dinwiddie was upheld. He, nevertheless, was requested by the Board of Trade not to levy any fee upon small grants west of the mountains, on grants the orders for which had passed the Council before the date of issuance of his own order for the collection of the pistole, or on grants the certificates of which had been lodged at the secretary's office preceding this date.[65] In permitting the Governor to take this fee, the Board of Trade undoubtedly felt the proper col-lection of quit-rents would be facilitated, unquestionably an impor-tant consideration.

The quit-rents, a small annual sum payable on lands, characterized

---

[62] The petition from Dinwiddie County was read November 21, 1753; see *Journals of the House of Burgesses, 1752–1758*, p. 129.

[63] For an extract of the above letter see P. S. Flippin: *The Royal Government in Virginia, 1624–1775* (New York, 1919), p. 129, note 1.

[64] *Journals of the House of Burgesses, 1752–1758*, p. 143.

Dinwiddie laid the chief blame for the agitation on the Rev. Mr. Stith, President of William and Mary. He declared that Stith, "by his insinuations, and turbulent temper raised so great a heat and animosity in the House of Burgesses, that they have addressed His Majesty by way of Complaint against me. . . . His acrimony against me was be-cause I did not recommend him to your Lordship to be your Commissary, which he knows he had no right to expect" (Robert Dinwiddie to the Bishop of London, Janu-ary 29, 1753, *Historical Collections relating to the American Colonial Church* [ed. W. S. Perry, 5 vols., Hartford, 1870–8], I, 402. Cited subsequently as W. S. Perry: *Historical Collections*).

[65] See *The Official Records of Robert Dinwiddie, Lieutenant-Governor of the Col-ony of Virginia, 1751–1758* (ed. B. A. Brock, 2 vols., Richmond, 1783–4), I, 139, 362–3, hereinafter referred to as the *Dinwiddie Papers*; see also *Acts of the Privy Coun-cil, Col. Ser., 1745–1766*, pp. 232–5.

the land systems of all colonies to the south of New England and were introduced also into New Hampshire.[66] The quit-rent demanded on lands by the Crown in Virginia was put upon the basis of an English shilling for every fifty acres. Before 1750 an indulgence had been granted whereby these rents could be paid in silver at the rate of seventeen and one half pennyweight for five shillings, or in tobacco at one penny per pound. However, in that year, as the result of a report of the Auditor General of the Plantations of May 1, which was based upon a memorial from John Roberts, joint Receiver-General of quit-rents in Virginia, it was decided by the Privy Council to alter the basis of payment. Hereafter, the receivers of quit-rents within the province were to demand English shillings, as were stipulated in the grant; it was also provided that if through the scarcity of English money this could not be had — something, incidentally, that must have been taken for granted in light of the policy of the government respecting the exportation of English specie out of the Kingdom — then they were to demand payment in Spanish-coined silver at the rate of nineteen pennyweight for every five shillings, or in tobacco at the rate of three farthings per pound, which would be at the rate of sixteen pounds of tobacco for every shilling.

The justification for this alteration in the method of money payments lay, according to Roberts, in the fact that not only was nineteen pennyweight more nearly the value of five English shillings but that quit-rents were settled upon this basis by the tenants of Lord Fairfax in the Northern Neck. The alteration in the tobacco payments appearing in the same memorial was necessary, according to the Receiver-General, in order to prevent people from making a habit of discharging their quit-rents in tobacco because of the increase in the amount of Spanish money required. Further, tobacco payments had proved to be undesirable to the Crown, which suffered great losses in disposing of it since little or no tobacco was offered, as a rule, except in counties where large allowances made it convenient for shipping or where the crop was of poor quality.[67]

These changes undoubtedly had a certain effect on the quit-rent collection in 1751 reaching the total of £16,433, including arrears,

---

[66] The standard work on British colonial quit-rents is by B. W. Bond, Jr.: *The Quit-Rent System in the American Colonies* (New Haven, 1919).

[67] *Acts of the Privy Council, Col. Ser., 1745–1766*, pp. 104–5.

in contrast to £3,500 in 1740.[68] In 1760, however, they dropped to a total of £6,000.[69] These sums, paid annually into the receipt of His Majesty's exchequer, were available for meeting the general expense of administering the colony. Certain officials were regularly paid out of the fund and it was also utilized when unusual demands arose, such as those occasioned by Indian treaties and the running of the boundary line between Virginia and North Carolina.

The quit-rent was but one source of royal revenue in Virginia. From 1657/8 to the close of the colonial period there was an export duty of two shillings per hogshead collected on all tobacco, which in 1750 amounted to £5,000.[70] Out of this the Governor's salary was paid, as well as those of some other officials and other charges of government.[71] In addition, there were revenues from fees for taking up land, from escheated land, and from fines and forfeitures, so that toward the middle of the eighteenth century the amount drawn from all sources was as great as £20,000, with the average revenue totalling about £13,000 for the period under consideration. In fact Governor Dinwiddie declared in 1756 that "this Dominion pays more to the Crown than all the others." [72]

An analysis of the system of government applied to Virginia — the oldest of all the overseas possessions — shows that as a royal colony its constitution was based primarily upon the King's commission under the Great Seal to the Governor, supplemented by formal instructions.[73] It was also based upon certain acts of the Assembly — which comprehended the House of Burgesses, the Council, and the Governor or his Deputy — that had, of course, received royal sanction. The Governor (likewise his deputy, and to a limited extent the President of the Council when acting temporarily as head of the government) was responsible for the execution of the royal commis-

---

[68] *Journals of the House of Burgesses, 1752–1758*, pp. 511–13; see also P. S. Flippin: *The Financial Administration of the Colony of Virginia* (Baltimore, 1915), p. 12. It appears that out of this total but £5,230.6 reached the receipt of the Exchequer. See B. W. Bond, Jr.: op. cit., p. 248, n.

[69] P. S. Flippin: *Financial Administration . . .* , p. 12.

[70] *Ibid.*, p. 10.

[71] *Dinwiddie Papers*, I, 353.

[72] *Ibid.*, II, 437.

[73] For an exhaustive study of the structure of the government of Virginia see P. S. Flippin: *The Royal Government in Virginia*, previously cited; see also L. W. Labaree: *Royal Government in America: A Study of the British Colonial System before 1783* (New Haven, 1930).

sion. He held office during the pleasure of the King and was subject to recall and removal. His responsibilities were multifarious, for he was expected to look after the varied civil interests of the colony, to foster and protect the Anglican Church established by law, and, as commander in chief of the militia, to defend the province from attack and from domestic disorder. Under a separate commission as Vice-Admiral [74] he also had many duties to perform from time to time with respect to naval defence and other admiralty matters, and, in addition, he received a special commission for the trial of pirates. His powers of appointment were very broad. Not only did he designate the colonels of the militia regiments and other officers above the rank of lieutenant, but with the advice of the Council he appointed such officials as the justices of the peace, the sheriffs, the coroners, and the provincial naval officers. Nor were his powers limited to administrative functions. He possessed the right of pardon and reprieve except in the instances of murder and treason, and, with the Council, constituted the General Court — the highest tribunal of the province — which heard cases on appeal from the county courts and also enjoyed an original jurisdiction over issues that involved a consideration above £20 current money. Further, he had the authority to summon, prorogue, and dissolve the General Assembly, with an absolute veto over the bills passed, and no act could have even temporary force without his signature. Lastly, sitting with the Council, he was able to dispose of the King's land, under limitations provided by his instructions, and he was expected to see that the King's revenue, derived from such sources as the quit-rents and the export tax of two shillings on each hogshead of tobacco, was collected and paid into the receipt of the royal exchequer. In view of his position and the social requirements attached to it, especially during the meetings of the Council and the House of Burgesses, he was provided with an income from all sources that permitted him to dispense hospitality. This seems to have amounted to a total of some £3,000 sterling.[75]

In his royal administration the Governor of Virginia was assisted

---

[74] For Lieutenant Governor Dinwiddie's commission as Vice-Admiral under date of July 24, 1751, see P.R.O., Adm. Reg. Mun. Books, 9:78. For the office of Vice-Admiral see L. W. Labaree: op. cit., pp. 25–7.

[75] See Beverly McAnear: "The Income of Royal Governors of Virginia," Journal of Southern History, XVI, 197–211.

by a secretary [76] and an auditor, each appointed under the Great Seal, as he was. He was also assisted by a surveyor-general, who with the county surveyors was responsible for land surveys; by four escheators, who with their deputies protected the Crown interest in lapsed lands; by the Surveyor-General of customs for the Southern District, assisted by some six local collectors of customs on exports and imports and an equal number of naval officers, and by at least two searchers of concealed goods. There were also collectors of duty on skins and furs and on liquors, tobacco inspectors, a provincial postmaster, together with county and parish officials, all of whom played a part in the execution not only of the laws of Parliament and of the General Assembly, but also of the Governor's commission and instructions issued under the royal prerogative.

The Council was the next most important branch of the government. It consisted of less than twelve members, who were recommended by the Lieutenant Governor and appointed under the sign manual of the King, and, although generally allowed to remain for life, they were subject to suspension and dismissal. The responsibilities of the Council were very great, although it cannot be said to have enjoyed concurrent authority with the Governor in the exercise of administrative and general executive powers. Nevertheless, its importance is indicated in the royal instructions, which provided that — except in extraordinary emergencies — the Governor could not act in those matters requiring its concurrence without having present at least five members.[77] To the Governor alone, however, were addressed all instructions, and he could refuse to communicate to his advisers whatever seemed best to withhold from their knowledge. It appears, by a reading of the memorials of the Council sitting as an administrative body under the presidency of the Governor, that most matters concerning which he had received instructions were allowed to come up for discussion; although it is by no means clear that it was customary for him to permit to be read before the councillors the exact words of direction, whether from the King's Council, or from

---

[76] The office of Secretary of Virginia was one of real importance. It retained the seal of the province, from which issued all land patents; likewise it had custodianship of most of the official records. The Secretary was always a member of the Council.

[77] Dinwiddie's commission declared that three councillors would constitute a quorum, but his instructions placed the number at five under the circumstances given above. For Dinwiddie's commission see P.R.O., C.O. 324:38, pp. 287–9; for his instructions see C.O. 5:211, pp. 33–40, and C.O. 5:1344.

the Secretary of State for the Southern Department, or from the Board of Trade.

As previously stated, the members of the Council made up the bench of judges of the General Court, and the judges of oyer and terminer were also selected from among them.[78] From the latter part of the seventeenth century they also constituted a distinct house — the upper chamber of the Assembly — although their clerk was still styled the Clerk of the General Assembly. When they were serving in this capacity the Governor was not present except in so far as he would appear to address the entire Assembly and thereupon withdraw.[79] Although the Council could negative the measures of the House of Burgesses, and in 1749 resisted the demand of the latter to search its journal, it lacked the power to initiate legislation. This inferiority as a law-making body is also indicated by the fact that when bills had been passed by the two bodies and were acceptable to the Governor, they received the signature of the Governor and the Speaker of the House of Burgesses but not that of the President of the Council. However, the time that each bill passed the upper chamber had to be indicated, as did the fact that all laws were enacted in the name of the Governor, the Council, and the Burgesses.

When Dinwiddie was appointed to office, the membership of the Council consisted of President Lewis Burwell of Gloucester, a great planter but infirm, who had held office since 1744 and had succeeded to this position by virtue of the rule of seniority; William Fairfax, representing the vast landed interests of Thomas, Lord Fairfax, in northern Virginia; John Blair; William Nelson; Dr. William Dawson, who was Commissary for the Bishop of London; John Lewis; Thomas Nelson; Philip Grymes; Richard Corbin; Peter Randolph; and Philip

---

[78] In 1752 the members of the Council petitioned the King to increase the compensation granted to them from £600 to £1,200 out of the revenue of two shillings export tax on tobacco, the former sum being apportioned among them according to the extent of their services, especially those of a judicial nature. In this petition, which the Governor approved, they urged the great increase in business of the General Court that had compelled them to add six days to every term, so that they were obliged to meet as judges for at least two months every year. Many of them, it was stated, lived far removed from the seat of government, which meant not only a considerable expense in travelling but no small loss by reason of their absence from their estates. See *Executive Journals of the Council*, V, 379–80. The petition was favourably acted upon and the Treasurer ordered to pay the sum of £1,200 per annum from the two-shillings-a-hogshead fund. See *Acts of the Privy Council, Col. Ser.*, 1745–1766, pp. 175–6.

[79] See E. I. Miller: *The Legislature of the Province of Virginia: Its Internal Development* (New York, 1907), p. 140.

Ludwell. They were soon joined by William Beverley.[80] These men represented the wealth and social prestige of the province and many of them belonged to families that had enjoyed, almost for generations, the highest recognition and favours that the government could bestow.[81]

The House of Burgesses in 1748 was made up of eighty-four members. The number was increased to ninety-two in the course of the session of the Assembly which lasted until May of the following year. This was owing to the creation of Chesterfield, Culpeper, Cumberland, and Southampton counties, raising the number of counties to forty-four. Each of them was entitled to two representatives, while Jamestown, Norfolk Borough, Williamsburg, and William and Mary College were each entitled to one. These burgesses were chosen in each instance by the freeholders, whose exact number it is difficult to determine. Dinwiddie, writing to the Board of Trade early in 1756, declared rather ungrammatically that since "most of the People are Freeholders, [they] in course have votes for choosing Assembly Men on wch they strenuously insist on their Privileges." [82] Certainly the legal requirement of ownership of one hundred acres of uncultivated land or of twenty-five acres with a house on it, irrespective of the quality of the land, could hardly have been a serious barrier to those white males who had attained the age of of twenty-one years and who were not "recusants" — that is, Roman Catholics.[83]

---

[80] In the case of Beverley an interesting question arose as to priority of place on the Council. Although his mandamus was issued in 1749, before it reached Virginia he had embarked for England, where he resided until February 1751 by virtue of a leave of absence secured from His Majesty. As a result, he was not sworn of the Council until May of that year. In the meantime Philip Ludwell, who was admitted to the Council in 1750, claimed precedence. Upon reference of the dispute to the Privy Council it was decided that Beverley should take rank from the date of the mandamus. See *Acts of the Privy Council, Col. Ser., 1745–1766*, pp. 285–6.

[81] For the position of the aristocracy in the political and social life of eighteenth-century Virginia see C. S. Sydnor: *Political Leadership in Eighteenth Century Virginia* (Oxford, 1951), and his *Gentlemen Freeholders: Political Practices in Washington's Virginia* (Chapel Hill, N.C., 1952), Chap. 5; see also Carl Bridenbaugh: *Seat of Empire: The Political Role of Eighteenth-Century Williamsburg* (Williamsburg, 1950); L. B. Wright: *The Cultural Life of the American Colonies, 1607–1763* (New York, 1957), Chap. 7; and D. S. Freeman: *George Washington: A Biography* (7 vols., New York, 1948–58), I, Chap. 4.

[82] Dinwiddie to the Board of Trade, February 23, 1756, *Dinwiddie Papers*, II, 345.

[83] *The Statutes at Large; being a Collection of all the Laws of Virginia, from . . . 1619* (ed. W. W. Hening, 13 vols., Richmond, 1809–23), IV, 475–8. This series will be referred to in subsequent pages as Hening's *Laws of Virginia*. See also J. A. C. Chandler: *History of Suffrage in Virginia* (Baltimore, 1901) for an account of the legal re-

It would appear that most of the voters had modest holdings during the period under consideration. Professor Sydnor, after making a survey of the tax lists of a number of typical counties for the year 1785, arrived at the conclusion that three fourths of the voters possessed 300 acres of land or less and that but one in twenty owned over 1,000 acres; also that among the voters a third owned no slaves.[84] The total number of those enjoying the right of franchise, he estimated, was between 35,000 and 40,000.[85]

It is clear that had there been hostility between the great mass of the small planters and the leading families the latter would have been politically submerged when it came to elections to the House of Burgesses. But this was not the case. In fact, the poor man could ill afford the expense of election and the cost of residence at Williamsburg for protracted periods. Further, his small plantation and the care of his family required his continuous presence at home. He therefore was inclined to vote for some large landowner in whom he had confidence as a man of cultivation and of experience in the affairs of the world.

In view of this situation it is not surprising that socially and by standards of wealth there was no distinction to be made between the members of the Council and a large proportion of the burgesses. If none of the Carters, Byrds, Diggses, Harrisons, and Pages were to be found in the Council in 1752, they were in the lower house. Indeed, its seats were generally occupied by the most powerful of the county families, who tended to perpetuate their own power. Almost one half of the burgesses who were elected in 1748 to the Assembly also sat in that body in the spring meeting of 1752. Moreover, several members newly elected to this Assembly bore the family name of the individual whom he replaced as a representative for a particular county. Similarly, old names were prominent in the representation from the new counties.[86] The manner in which families continued in power may be illustrated by the relationship of the Robinsons to the government. For many years before 1750 John Robinson had been Presi-

---

strictions on voting. For the number exercising the right of franchise see C. S. Sydnor: *Gentlemen Freeholders*, Chap. 2 and Appendix 1, and L. G. Tyler: "Virginians Voting in the Colonial Period," *William and Mary Quarterly*, 1st ser., VI, 7–14.

   [84] C. S. Sydnor: *op. cit.*, p. 37.

   [85] *Ibid.*, p. 119.

   [86] In this connection it is noteworthy that planters with land in more than one county could vote in every county where their freeholds met the legal requirements.

dent of the Council; at the same time his son was both the Speaker of the House of Burgesses and Treasurer of the colony. Next to the Governor, the younger Robinson was undoubtedly the most powerful figure in Virginia at that period.

As previously seen, all bills, to become law, had to be approved by the Governor, the Council, and the Burgesses.[87] Thus enacted, measures went into effect immediately and remained in force until disapproved by the royal authority, unless they happened to touch upon some reserved matter. In this case, their operation was suspended by a clause until the King's pleasure could be known.[88] Once a law had met with the royal approval, however, it could not be altered and become effective without first securing the Crown's sanction of the amendment.[89]

The question may well arise here as to how active was the interference of the Crown in the law-making processes of the government of Virginia in the first half of the eighteenth century. From 1703 to 1748 some 128 acts passed by the provincial legislature were examined and reported on by the Board of Trade to the Lords of the Committee of the Privy Council.[90] Of this number 102 were recommended for confirmation, seventeen for disallowance, eight for repeal, and one, an act for the amendment of the staple of tobacco, passed in 1730, "to lie by probationary." The eight recommended by the Board for repeal by the General Assembly related to the public revenue, to land grants, to the establishment of posts and towns, to limitations on legal actions, to import duties on liquors, to restrictions on the importation of North Carolina tobacco, and to the disposition of an estate. Three of these acts were passed in the year 1705, two in 1706, one in each of the years 1726, 1736, and 1742, respectively. There was considerable delay in reporting on two of the acts recommended for repeal, both of the year 1705; that on the limitations on legal actions was not reported on until 1729, while that on restrictions on the importation of North Carolina tobacco not until

---

[87] For a detailed study of the machinery of legislation in colonial Virginia see E. I. Miller: *The Legislature of the Province of Virginia*, a work already cited.

[88] The Governor was expected to see that all laws were sent to the Privy Council at least within three months after being passed.

[89] The Committee of Correspondence to Edward Montague, London agent, December 12, 1759, *Virginia Magazine of History and Biography*, X, 348.

[90] See "List of such Acts passed in the Colony of Virginia as have been reported on by the Board of Trade between the year 1703 and the present time [1748]," *Shelburne Papers*, 49:117–36.

1731. As for the seven acts recommended for disallowance before 1748: one related to office-holding, others to the prohibiting of Quaker meetings, to the payment of foreign debts, to quit-rents, to the government of slaves, servants, and convicts, and to duties on liquors and slaves.[91] These acts were passed between the years 1663 and 1728: two in 1663, one in 1715, two in 1720 and one in 1723, and the last in 1728. Concerning the seventeenth-century acts relating to Quakers and foreign debts, it was not until some fifty-four years after they were placed in the statute books that they were reported for disallowance by the Board, February 3, 1717/8.[92]

In 1748 the Virginia Assembly determined to revise its laws. As a result, between December of that year and May of the following, eighty-nine acts were passed which in turn were submitted to His Majesty for acceptance or rejection. In 1751 the Board of Trade recommended fifty-seven of them for approval, fifteen to lie by probationary, three to be sent to the Commissioners of the Treasury for further consideration, and ten for disallowance.[93] As to the ten, a very brief analysis of the basis for each disapproval may perhaps help to indicate the limits within which the provincial legislature was expected to function.

Two acts, each allowing fairs to be held in particular towns, were found to be objectionable as encroachments upon the royal prerogative, since this power was specifically granted by commission to the Governor. Further, the exemption from arrest or attachments in civil causes of all persons going to and returning from these fairs was held to be not only extraordinary but contrary to the laws of the mother country. The act declaring slaves to be personal estate was disallowed because it repealed two earlier acts declaring slaves to be real estate which ex-Lieutenant Governor Gooch affirmed had answered well the purposes of keeping estates in families by annexing Negroes to land and also because it carried no clause suspending its operation until His Majesty's pleasure was known. A fourth act, having to do with intestate estates and passed in consequence of the preceding act declaring slaves to be personal property, was considered to be undesirable in light of the disposition of the former statute. A fifth, for regulating proceedings in the General Court, was held to place serious limitations upon those who might

---

[91] *Ibid.* Two acts related to duties on slaves, those of 1723 and 1728.
[92] *Ibid.*
[93] Board of Trade *Journal*, 1749–1753, pp. 198–202.

seek to have actions tried in the General Court either directly or on appeal from the county courts, and it was feared that this would be detrimental to those carrying on trade. A sixth, for limitation of actions and avoiding of suits, was objected to upon the ground that, in repealing an earlier act that had been confirmed, it carried no suspending clause, as was also true of a seventh concerned with second-growth tobacco and an eighth for the better support of William and Mary College. A ninth, having to do with servants and slaves, was held contrary to the law of England relating to felons. Finally, a law involving the community of Walkerton was considered extraordinary and likely to produce many inconveniences, since it permitted any person to kill swine going at large within the town.[94]

From this survey it may be concluded that during the first half of the eighteenth century the King's advisers, as a rule, found little to complain of in the law-making activities of Virginia. However, after 1750 the Privy Council felt impelled to give the most careful scrutiny to all new legislation emanating from Williamsburg, for reasons that will be considered in some detail in a later volume of this series.

Below the central government came that of the counties, the civil affairs of which were cared for by justices of the peace, assisted by the sheriffs and other local officials.[95] The number of justices of the peace varied from county to county. For example, in Louisa in 1752 there were eighteen; in Amelia, twelve; and in Fairfax and Accomack, ten each.[96] In the 1720's the total number had reached 404. With the growth of counties, the number of justices of the peace increased until before the period of the American Revolution they numbered almost 1,200.[97] These men were drawn, virtually without exception, from the three or four hundred families that constituted the Virginia gentry.[98] Even men of the first importance sought ap-

---

[94] Acts of the Privy Council, Col. Ser., 1745–1766, pp. 131–41.

[95] For county government see Isabel Ferguson: "County Court in Virginia, 1700–1830," North Carolina Historical Review, VIII, 14–40; see also A. G. Porter: County Government in Virginia: A Legislative History, 1607–1904 (New York, 1947), based largely on Hening's Laws of Virginia for the period under consideration.

[96] Executive Journals of the Council, V, 388–95.

[97] See "Justices of the Peace of Colonial Virginia, 1757–1775," Virginia State Library Bulletin (Richmond, 1922); see also O. P. Chitwood: Justice in Colonial Virginia (Johns Hopkins University Studies, Baltimore, 1905), pp. 74–95, and P. S. Flippin: The Royal Government in Virginia, p. 317.

[98] C. S. Sydnor: Gentlemen Freeholders, p. 119.

pointment to this office. In 1749, for example, a special commission was issued to Lord Fairfax to act in this capacity in each of the counties of the Northern Neck.[99] Within Fairfax County, Lawrence Washington and George William Fairfax enjoyed commissions; within Henrico were William and Richard Randolph; within Charles City, William Lightfoot, William Byrd, and Benjamin Harrison.[100]

The duties of the justices of the peace were varied in their nature.[101] When assembled as a county court, which met four times a year, they could determine any cause in chancery or at common law, with right of appeal to the General Court on the part of the aggrieved party if the decision were for over £5.[102] When sitting in the capacity of what was later generally known in American local government as a board of county commissioners, they could provide for such public improvements as roads, bridges, dams, and causeways within the county;[103] they could levy taxes upon the inhabitants for these purposes; in general, they were entrusted with the good government of the counties. Almost without exception these men were owners of considerable bodies of land and slaves in proportion. It has been estimated that before the outbreak of the War for American Independence,[104] one fourth of the justices of the peace were recruited from some fifty-five leading families and three fourths of them from less than four hundred families. To enforce the responsibilities placed upon them they were made liable to suit in their corporate capacity. During the period under consideration there was considerable criticism of the county courts, principally because of delays in granting justice. The Virginia Council took the matter under consideration and declared that this situation was chiefly owing "to the too great Numbers and Neglect of Justices" and, early in 1752, ordered the

---

[99] *Executive Journals of the Council*, V, 301.

[100] On October 13, 1749, the Council passed the following order: "That a new Commission of the Peace issue for Charles City County and that William Lightfoot, William Byrd, and Benjamin Harrison, Gent: be added, that Mr. Lightfoot be placed according to his Rank in York, that Mr. Byrd be of the Quorum, and Mr. Harrison last in the Commission" (*ibid.*, V, 302).

[101] See Hening: *Laws of Virginia*, VI, 201–10, for the act of 1748 regulating the county courts of Brunswick, Fairfax, etc.

[102] See Thomas Lee to the Board of Trade, September 29, 1750, Shelburne Papers, 45:84–90. The £5 limitation had been changed in 1749 to £10, but the act was disallowed; in 1753, however, it passed into law. See Hening: *Laws of Virginia*, VI, 327.

[103] *Ibid.*, VI, 64–9. The term "county commissioners" was used in Maryland at this period and also in Pennsylvania.

[104] C. S. Sydnor: *Political Leadership in Eighteenth-Century Virginia*, p. 7.

county-court clerks to attend the Governor with a list of justices who had qualified themselves, as well as those who had refused to do so.[105]

The sheriff [106] carried out the orders of the county court involving arrests and punishments and was responsible for the collection of taxes and amercements; he also communicated royal proclamations to the people of the county on court days and performed a number of important ministerial duties, such as the suppression of unlawful assemblages of slaves. To be appointed to this post under the provisions of the law of 1748 it was necessary for a man to be in the commission of the peace — in other words, to be a justice of the peace of the county in question. Out of three nominations submitted by the county court the Governor would appoint the sheriff, who, on the one hand, was compelled to serve for a period of one year on pain of fine and, on the other hand, was limited to two successive years in this office.[107]

Beneath the county, or coterminous with it, was the parish, a civil and ecclesiastical unit of administration.[108] The governing body of this was the vestry, the twelve members of which were elected in the first instance by the freeholders and housekeepers for an indefinite period of time. Once established, the vestry became a closed corporation, the members of which thereafter enjoyed the right to fill vacancies arising from death or other causes.[109] Entrenched in their

---

[105] *Executive Journals of the Council,* V, 378–9.

[106] An act of 1748 prescribing the method of appointing sheriffs and the duties they should perform covers this matter fully. See Hening: *Laws of Virginia,* VI, 515–23. P. S. Flippin's *The Royal Government in Virginia* (pp. 313–16) provides an excellent account of the work of the sheriff.

[107] In 1748 Governor Gooch appointed sixteen persons to this office; in 1750 nineteen appointments were made. The number of counties at that period was forty-one. See *Executive Journals of the Council,* V, 259, 348–9.

[108] In 1755 out of fifty counties thirty had but one parish, the boundaries of which were identical with that of the county; seventeen were divided into two parishes; two, Caroline and York, into three; and Gloucester into four. Many of the older counties, such as James City and Charles City, as well as all of the newer counties, contained only one parish. For a list of parishes as of June 10, 1755, see W. S. Perry: *Historical Collections,* I, 429–30. In order to maintain the boundary lines of the parishes, the vestry was required by law to divide them up into precincts, the boundaries of each of which were to be traversed annually by parishioners conveniently located for that purpose. See Hening: *op. cit.,* II, 102, and III, 82; see also W. H. Seiler: "Land Processioning in Colonial Virginia," *William and Mary Quarterly,* 3rd ser., VI, 416–36.

[109] On occasion the vestry itself might request that a new one be elected. For example, in 1745 the General Assembly received a petition from the vestrymen of the parish of Newport in the county of the Isle of Wight representing that they had become old and infirm in office and were no longer able to perform their duties. They prayed to be

positions, they were normally beyond the interference of the rest of the inhabitants of the parish, although in case dissatisfaction arose the parishioners could appeal to the House of Burgesses to dissolve the vestry and order new elections.[110] Further, the elections to the vestry were subject to the confirmation of the General Assembly.[111] As a result of its quality of permanence and the opportunities thus afforded to exert a decisive influence upon parish affairs, a seat in the vestry was held in high honour and representatives of the leading families of the parish were, as a rule, chosen to it. For example, not only was John Grymes a member of the Provincial Council and a vestryman of Christ Church Parish in Middlesex County in 1745, but Philip Grymes, who later was called to the Council, was also a member of the vestry.[112] Landon Carter was the leading vestryman within Lunenburg Parish in Richmond County.

Along with other responsibilities vestrymen of a parish enjoyed the right of presentation of the pastorate, provided this was done within a period of twelve months;[113] they also elected the two churchwardens, made proper disposition of lands that belonged to the parish, and disbursed the parish funds, including those raised by

dissolved as a corporate body. This was done. In like manner, in 1755 the vestry of "the upper parish" of Nansemond County, by reason of the age of the members, asked to be dissolved. See Hening: Laws of Virginia, V, 381, and VI, 518–19.

[110] C. M. Brydon: "New Light upon the History of the Church in Colonial Virginia," Historical Magazine of the Protestant Episcopal Church, X, 84.

[111] In 1745 the elections of vestrymen for the parishes of St. Anne in Albemarle County and Truro in Fairfax were confirmed, but that for St. Margaret's of Caroline County was laid aside because of the fact that it was carried on in both a disorderly and an illegal manner. In 1752 the vestry of Frederick Parish in Frederick County was dissolved for misconduct. See Hening's Laws of Virginia, V, 380, and VI, 257–60. For a careful study of the Virginia vestry see W. H. Seiler: "The Anglican Parish Vestry in Colonial Virginia," Journal of Southern History, XXII, 310–37.

[112] See The Vestry Book of Christ Church Parish, Middlesex County, Virginia, 1663–1767 (ed. C. G. Chamberlayne, Richmond, 1927), p. 264.

[113] See Hening: Laws of Virginia, VI, 88–90. In referring to this authority, Commissary William Dawson, writing to the Bishop of London, July 15, 1751, called it "an extraordinary Clause in our Laws." In a letter to the Bishop written in 1752, Dinwiddie went into detail about the difficulties that this statute created. "The established Church," he declared, "always flourished in this Colony, and I have reason to think it always would, if kept up in due discipline and regular order, but the regulation by the aforesaid Law, curbs and restrains, nay, I may say, quite destroys the Governor's and Commissary's power, and I am much afraid, unless your Lordship's [sic] interferes, in having that act repealed and the prerogative of the Crown and your Lordship's Jurisdiction restored, It will end in great confusion and give great encouragement to defection and the Dissenters which begin greatly to increase." For these letters see W. S. Perry: Historical Collections, I, 377, 393–6.

taxation and those in form of charitable donations. The care of the poor and otherwise helpless and the maintenance of the parish church, including the proper provision for the rector, were among the chief responsibilities of the vestry.[114]

A few items from the vestry book of Christ Church Parish in Middlesex County covering the period under consideration will illustrate the nature of the work of the vestrymen. On October 12, 1745, Philip Grymes, Gentleman, was sworn to the vestry. This body then proceeded to make certain grants in terms of pounds of tobacco. Among these was one to Bartholomew Yates, minister, of 16,000 pounds;[115] another, of 200 pounds, was made to William Guthry for burying one Okaney Paulo; a third, of 800 pounds, was made to Edward Smith for keeping five orphan children; a fourth, of 468 pounds, to William Kidd for nursing a child of William Wallas during seven months. To the churchwardens for repairing the gates of the several churchyards and making a well at the glebe 3,000 pounds was also appropriated. The total amount allotted at the session of the vestry was 35,883 pounds of tobacco.[116] Within the parish were 1,329 tithables. These were thereupon assessed at the rate of twenty-seven pounds of tobacco per poll to produce the above amount. The minister's salary, it will be noticed, was almost equal to all other claims combined. In 1749, 53,976 pounds were required to meet the charges of the same parish.[117] By this date the number of tithables had increased to 1,384, with the result that each tithable was rated at thirty-nine pounds per poll.

One of the most important responsibilities placed upon the vestry was the maintenance within the parish of the legally established Anglican Church. [118] Since upon this body devolved the choice of the minister, it was expected to satisfy itself as to his fitness for the

---

[114] See M. W. Jernegan: "The Development of Poor Relief in Colonial Virginia," *Social Science Review*, III, 1–19.

[115] According to law a minister "received into any parish" was to be paid 16,000 pounds of tobacco. This provision was retained in the revision of the statutes made in 1748. See Hening: *Laws of Virginia*, VI, 88.

[116] *Vestry Book of Christ Church Parish* . . . , pp. 264–5.

[117] Minutes of October 2, 1749, *ibid.*, pp. 274–6.

[118] See G. M. Brydon: *Virginia's Mother Church* (Richmond, Va., 1947), and Elizabeth H. Davidson: *The Establishment of the English Church in Continental American Colonies* (Durham, N.C., 1936), Chap. 1. For an account of the church and clergy in the early part of the eighteenth century see also Hugh Jones: *The Present State of Virginia* . . . (London, 1724), Part 3. This has recently been edited by R. L. Morton and was republished in 1956 by the University of North Carolina Press.

charge. It, however, was not always fortunate in its choice of a pastor. As a result, parishes occasionally became involved in bitter controversies. Sometimes indeed the minister was guilty of conduct that placed him far below the level of recognized respectability. To illustrate: in 1742 the vestry of North Farnham Parish appealed to the Council against the Rev. Mr. Bluett (Blewit), charging him with drunkenness, profane swearing, and "other Immoralities & Misdemeanors." The latter body upheld the vestry, declaring Bluett "a Scandal to his Function." [119] The same year it also upheld the Nottaway Parish vestry, which was compelled to dismiss the Rev. James Pedin for "lewd and Debauched Actions." [120] In 1754 the Bishop of London received an anonymous letter; in this the writer charged that the Rev. Mungo Marshall of St. Thomas's Parish, Culpeper County, "is one of the most ignorant men (not to say Clergymen), I ever conversed with." The same writer also asserted that the Rev. George Purdie of St. Andrew's Parish, Brunswick County, and the Rev. Robert McLaurin of Southam Parish, Cumberland County, were totally unfit, the former "ignorant & immoral to a Scandalous degree," the latter "remarkable only for his ignorance & folly. . . . We have indeed men of Piety & literature in the Chh here," he also added, "but those I have named with some others, I might take notice of, are a reproach to religion in general as well as to the order to which they belong." [121]

It is probably true that, after all allowances have been made for exaggeration, most of the clergy at this period were too much engaged in material pursuits and pleasures. ". . . it gives me a great deal of uneasiness to see the greatest part of our Brethren taken up in farming and buying slaves which in my humble opinion is unlawful for any Christian and in particular for a clergyman," affirmed a devoted supporter of the Church in 1738.[122] Nevertheless, there were some who gave offence by leaning backward in their strictness. In 1743 the vestry of Charles Parish, in York County, appealed for the removal of the Rev. Theodosius Stage because he was opposed to the singing of the new version of the Psalms and had refused to

---

[119] Executive Journals of the Council, V, 95, 100.

[120] Ibid., p. 86.

[121] See W. S. Perry: Historical Collections, I, 408.

[122] Ibid., I, 360–1. The student in studying the history of the church in Virginia in the eighteenth century should consult a standard book by J. S. M. Anderson: The History of the Church of England in the Colonies and Foreign Dependencies (3 vols., London, 1856), III, 196–279.

christen a child owing to his suspicions that it was illegitimate.[123] As between extremes, one may perhaps take the judgement of the Rev. Andrew Burnaby, who, in travelling through Virginia in 1759, found the clergymen in general living sober and exemplary lives.[124] There were doubtless others among them whose devotion to their high calling equalled that of the saintly Rev. Anthony Gavin of St. James Parish, Goochland. In a touching letter to the Bishop of London, he declared:

> "I have 3 Churches, 23 and 24 miles from the glebe, in which I offi-
> ciate every third Sunday, and besides these three I have seven
> places of service up in the mountains where the clerks read prayers,
> 4 clerks in the seven places. I go twice a year to preach in 12 places,
> and I reckon better than 400 miles backwards and forwards, and
> ford 19 times the North and South Rivers. . . . In my first Journey
> I baptized White people, 229; Blacks, 172; Quakers, 15; Annabap-
> tists, 2. . . . I found at my first coming into this Parish but 6 persons
> that received the sacrament which my predecessors never adminis-
> tered but in the Lower Church, and, blessed be God, I have now
> 136 that receive twice a year, and in the lower part 3 times a year,
> which fills my heart with joy and makes all my pains and fatigues
> very agreeable to me." [125]

Before the middle of the century there had set in a strong drift away from the Established Church.[126] The dissenting element was already in the ascendancy in the Valley of Virginia and had penetrated into the Piedmont. As early as 1736 two Presbyterian churches were in existence to the west of the Blue Ridge and by the early 1740's two more had been erected.[127] Lieutenant Governor Gooch, interested in the settlement of the frontier, had welcomed the Ulster

---

[123] *Executive Journals of the Council*, V, 118–19.

[124] *Travels through the Middle Settlements*, p. 14.

[125] Mr. Gavin to the Bishop of London, August 5, 1738, W. S. Perry: *Historical Collections*, I, 360.

[126] "There is one thing that grieves my heart, viz.: to see Episcopacy so little regarded in this colony," lamented the Rev. Mr. Gavin in 1738. *Ibid.*

[127] See Samuel Kercheval: *A History of the Valley of Virginia* (3rd edn., Woodstock, Va., 1902), p. 59; see also Alton B. Altfather: "Early Presbyterianism in Virginia," *The Journal of the Presbyterian Historical Society*, XIII, 267–81. It may be noted in passing that the activities of the Presbyterian ministers in the Valley of Virginia were directed by the Synod of Philadelphia; those working in the area east of the Blue Ridge Mountains were under the control of the Synod of New York. However, these two synods were united in 1758. See "Early Minutes of Hanover Presbytery" (ed. W. M. E. Rachal), *Virginia Magazine of History and Biography*, LXIII, 53–75, 161-85.

Scots and had agreed to allow them to enjoy their own religion under condition that they would conform themselves to the requirements of the English Act of Toleration in taking the prescribed oaths, in registering their meeting houses, and in conducting themselves peaceably toward the government.[128] He had also been favourably disposed toward the Germans who had passed from the Valley of the Susquehanna into that of the Shenandoah and who, according to the Moravian missionary Gottschalk, had established by 1748 some eleven settlements.[129] Although a number of the more influential among the Germans were led to conform to the Established Church and to become vestrymen, it appears that a majority remained, at least at heart, either Lutheran or Reformed. Actually, the influence of the Established Church penetrated but slightly into the Valley before the middle of the century. It is true that by 1746 a vestry was created for the parish of Augusta in Augusta County,[130] but the loyalty to the Anglican communion of the majority of its members may be questioned.[131] In 1748 these vestrymen actually took steps to purchase land as a glebe for the support of a dissenting minister. This in turn led the Virginia Provincial Council to call upon the justices of the peace of that county not to suffer any to preach who did not conform themselves "to the Directions of the Law." [132] It is, however, unlikely that the justices of the peace were either able or greatly desired to exert themselves effectively in behalf of conformity.

Indeed, it is a fact that by 1750 some of the county courts, as well as some of the vestries even of the Tidewater, had fallen under the influences of the newer religious forces playing upon the colony. Before that year, for example, the Rev. Samuel Davies, a Presbyterian preacher of great power and "adorned with piety & virtue," had entrenched himself in Hanover County and was drawing away from

---

128 See Wesley M. Gewehr: *The Great Awakening in Virginia, 1740–1790* (Durham, N.C., 1930), pp. 40–3.

129 J. W. Wayland: *The German Element of the Shenandoah Valley of Virginia* (Charlottesville, 1907), pp. 105, 108–9.

130 See J. L. Peyton: *History of Augusta County, Virginia* (Staunton, Va., 1882), pp. 95–6.

131 See H. R. McIlwaine: *The Struggle of Protestant Dissenters for Religious Toleration* (Johns Hopkins University Studies, Baltimore, 1894), pp. 40–1. F. H. Hart (*The Valley of Virginia in the American Revolution*, p. 65) affirms that "these dissenting frontiersmen turned local governmental units into almost independent states."

132 *Executive Journals of the Council*, V, 249.

their churches the parishioners of the Rev. Patrick Henry, uncle of the more famous American of the same name, of St. Paul's Parish, and of the Rev. Robert Barrett of St. Martin's Parish. Davies's influence also had spread into Henrico, Louisa, Goochland, Caroline, Cumberland, King William, and New Kent counties. He was, in fact, obliged to minister to some seven meeting houses in an area where, he asserted, there could not have been found seven dissenters six years previous. "The nearest of these Meeting houses," he stated in a letter written in 1750, "are 12 or 15 Miles apart and at each of them large Congregations are wont to assemble who generally hear with eager attention. . . ." [133] The Rev. Mr. Cennick, "well known in England by his strict Intimacy with the Rev[d] Mr. Whitefield," was similarly entrenched in Albemarle and Amelia counties. [134]

Hanover County might be called the centre of the Great Awakening movement in Virginia. About 1744 a layman, one Samuel Morris, living within its borders, attracted a group of neighbours to his home for serious conversation and the reading of religious books. When his home became too small for the numbers who came, a series of "Morris's Reading Houses" were erected as the need arose, and Morris began to go abroad to read to other congregations. Meanwhile, the Rev. William Robinson, a Presbyterian minister, was having a flourishing success as he travelled southward through Virginia. He was invited to visit the people of Hanover County, and his advent there — although "he preached but four days successively" [135] — had the effect of causing the Hanover dissenters to adopt the name Presbyterian and attach themselves to the Presbytery of New Castle. After his departure, a succession of transient Presbyterian preachers followed until Samuel Davies accepted the pastorate there in 1748. [136]

The extent to which Hanover County had drifted away from its

---

[133] Rev. Samuel Davies to Dr. Doddridge, October 2, 1750, W. S. Perry: *Historical Collections*, I, 368–71.

[134] "Address to the Burgesses. The humble Petition of some of the Clergy," 1751, *ibid.*, I, 381–3.

[135] Rev. Samuel Davies to Dr. Doddridge, October 2, 1750, W. S. Perry: *Historical Collections*, I, 368–9.

[136] The activities of Morris, Robinson, and Davies in supporting the evangelistic work of the New Side Presbyterian Synod of New York in Virginia in opposition to the Philadelphia Synod is well worked out by W. M. Gewehr in his *The Great Awakening in Virginia*, pp. 43–99. For the division of feeling among the relatives of Patrick Henry in Hanover County over the preaching of Whitefield and the Presbyterian Samuel Davies, see R. D. Meade: *Patrick Henry, Patriot in the Making* (Philadelphia & New York, 1957), pp. 66–9.

old orthodox moorings is indicated by the action of the county court in 1750 when its judges gave a licence to preach to the radical, itinerant evangelist James Davenport, against whom many New England towns had figuratively slammed their gates. This same court was later to gain great notoriety when the so-called Parson's Cause — relating to the Two-penny Acts of the Assembly that had the effect of depriving the clergy of their dues — was argued before it. In its action favouring Davenport the court aroused the provincial government, which in June of that year ordered an advertisement to be inserted in the next issue of the *Virginia Gazette* forbidding any minister to preach within any county until he had appeared before the chief administrative officer of the colony and had qualified himself according to law.[137] This pronouncement, however, was in vain.

The forces of dissent, in fact, were busily engaged in sapping the foundations of the Established Church. This was manifested in many ways. In 1752 the Rev. George Samuel Klug, minister to a German settlement in Culpeper County, was publicly rewarded out of the provincial treasury. Among his claims upon the public gratitude was a certificate of his services covering a period of many years among the neighbouring English inhabitants of the region.[138] In that same year, it is true, the Council made a show of firmness in the case of the Rev. Alexander Creaghead, who was brought before it charged not only with having "preached and published pernicious Doctrines within the County of Augusta," but of teaching and maintaining "treasonable positions" there. At the same time Richard Woods, a magistrate of the same county, was accused of allowing Creaghead, to whom he had administered the oaths of allegiance, to omit what parts of them he saw fit. However, after the accused preacher was able to produce testimonials of loyalty and fidelity from two Philadelphia ministers, joined by a certificate from the Governor of Pennsylvania, the Board agreed to permit him to preach whenever, after taking the oaths, he should fully recant the disloyal principles and the doctrines contained in a book, apparently his property, that had been turned over to the Governor.[139]

The most striking testimony of what was taking place in parts of Virginia was soon to come in the Act of 1759 for dissolving the vestries of Antrim in Halifax, of Cameron in Loudoun, of Bath in Din-

---

137 *Executive Journals of the Council*, V, 249, 318.
138 *Ibid.*, V, 385.
139 *Ibid.*, V, 399, 407–8.

widdie, of St. Patrick's in Prince Edward, of St. Anne in Albemarle, and of Christ Church in Lancaster. Each of these parishes had become the scene of disorders and strife. The statute in question, which was concerned with the general religious situation within the province, declared that many vestrymen had, after their election, separated from the communion of the Church of England and had actually formed a dissenting congregation while still continuing to act in the vestry. It therefore laid down rules for proceeding in connection with such cases and, significantly, declared that when the number of vestrymen who were not dissenters in any parish should be less than seven, or less than a majority, they should not have power to proceed against those who were dissenters, but that the vestry should continue until the matters were represented to the General Assembly.[140]

In analysing the causes of this drift away from Anglicanism it may be said that the settlement of the Valley of Virginia and the eastern slopes of the Blue Ridge by thousands of Ulster Scots and German dissenters and the penetration of the influence of these frontier settlements into the older-settled counties of the Piedmont and even into the Tidewater were doubtless factors of the greatest significance in the decline in prestige of the church Establishment.[141] Further, one of the fruits of the Great Awakening in North America was the weakening of the official church, whether that church were Congregational, as was the case in Connecticut, or Anglican, as was the case in Virginia.

The Anglican Establishment in Virginia was a part of the English heritage from the seventeenth century.[142] Other parts of that heritage were the closely related institutions of primogeniture and the entail of lands, both of which existed from the beginning of the colony. The great planters of the Tidewater of the eighteenth century sought to preserve these foundations of their own social and economic prestige.[143] At first they had relied upon the English law of real property,

---

[140] Hening: *Laws of Virginia*, VII, 301–3.

[141] See H. J. Eckenrode: *Separation of Church and State in Virginia* (Richmond, Va., 1910) for a discussion of the various factors involved.

[142] For a criticism of the aristocratic concept of seventeenth-century Virginia aristocracy see T. J. Wertenbaker: *Planters of Colonial Virginia* (Princeton, 1922), also reprinted in his volume *The Shaping of Colonial Virginia* (New York, 1958).

[143] See Clarence R. Keim's important unpublished doctoral thesis: "Influence of Primogeniture and Entail on the Development of Virginia," University of Chicago Library.

but in 1705 these principles were embodied in a formal statute which with some modifications remained the law of the province until the close of the colonial period.[144] Not until 1776 were entails abolished [145] and not until 1785 did the rule of primogeniture cease in case of intestacy.[146]

It must not be implied, however, that all Virginia planters entailed their lands, which was done either by will or by deed, or allowed their great estates to pass intact to the eldest male heir. Indeed, the latter practice would seem to have been the rare exception.[147] One peculiarity of the law of Virginia was that after 1705 slaves were, for most purposes, considered real property [148] and after 1727 they could be entailed with the lands.[149] This was the rule in 1750 despite the passage of the act of 1748 declaring them to be personal property,[150] for the latter law failed to secure the royal approval.

Although lands once entailed would ordinarily descend from father to son until the line of entail was exhausted — whereupon they would escheat to the Crown — yet these entails could be docked. Under the English law this was done by means of fines and common recovery, and under the Virginia law of 1705, by special act of the Assembly. A law of the year 1734 further aided the release of lands entailed that were intact by providing that an estate valued at less than £ 200 might be alienated by the fairly simple process of securing a writ at the Secretary's office returnable to the sheriff of the county in which the lands in question were located. The latter thereupon was to summon a jury of recognition, which was expected to determine the value of the lands and also to satisfy itself that such lands were not contiguous to other lands entailed to the same party. When these conditions were fulfilled the entail was to be broken.[151] These elaborate precautions show the solicitude of the law-makers

---

144 Hening: *Laws of Virginia*, III, 320.

145 *Ibid.*, IX, 226–7.

146 For "An act directing the course of descents," passed in 1785, see *ibid.*, XII, 138–40.

147 Dr. Keim established the above point after examining large numbers of deeds and wills; see his study previously cited.

148 However, slaves did not, as in the case of land, escheat. They could also be taken in execution for debt, which was not true of entailed land. See Hening: *op. cit.*, III, 333–4.

149 *Ibid.*, IV, 224–5.

150 *Ibid.*, V, 432.

151 *Ibid.*, IV, 400; see also *ibid.*, V, 414–15.

that this easement of the law of entail should not serve to undermine the institution.

The explanation for the survival of the laws of entail and primogeniture in Virginia throughout the colonial period undoubtedly lies in the control of the law-making process held by people of English ancestry, influenced as they were by the aristocratic traditions of the Tidewater.[152] For it is certain that the Ulster Scots and those of German stock in the western part of the province were just as unsympathetic toward both the entail of lands and primogeniture as they were toward the Anglican Establishment and Negro slavery. During a period of twenty-five years, from 1738 to 1763, the forty-odd cases involving lands held in fee tail which came before the Assembly related exclusively to lands in tidewater counties, with the exception of one case involving Fairfax County and another involving Goochland and Henrico counties, which cases affected the entailed estates respectively of Robert Alexander of Stafford County, Henry Cary of Warwick County, and former Lieutenant Governor Alexander Spotswood.[153]

While it is true that the entailing of property was a means of holding together a great estate and of guaranteeing the future importance of a family, the disadvantages involved in this process were many. An owner was legally subject to quit-rent after the land had become unproductive through soil exhaustion. This was also true of fee-simple land. However, in the case of the latter, the proprietor was free to dispose of it should it become unprofitable to hold. But the entailed estate that had seen its best days as a tobacco plantation might seriously impoverish him. This not infrequently happened, especially when the slaves were also entailed with the land upon which they worked. By natural increase they might overstock the impoverished lands, but they could not be transferred to fresh fee-simple lands without legal difficulties arising.[154] Again, and more

---

[152] See C. M. Andrews: *The South in the Building of the Nation* . . . (12 vols., Richmond, Va., 1909–13), V, 30.

[153] See Hening: *Laws of Virginia*, indexes to Volumes V, VI, and VII under "fee-tail" for references to cases. This is not to imply that there were not many entails in all the counties, but rather that they spread into the back country with the western movement of men from the Tidewater.

[154] In defending the act of 1748 making slaves personal estate, the Assembly stressed the point that when treated as part of an entailed estate, in time they "overstocked" it. See *ibid.*, V, 440–2. While this argument was employed by the Burgesses, Dr. Keim

frequently, the holder of an estate found himself burdened with lands without the necessary capital for applying labour to them profitably. With freedom of sale he could dispose of portions of his estate and invest the proceeds in Negroes for exploiting the remainder of the land. Consequently, as has already been pointed out, the General Assembly was called upon from time to time to frame special legislation designed to dock entails or portions of them on the petition of the inheritors.

The truth is that, irrespective of the drift of political conceptions of the frontiersmen in the direction of hostility to the institution of entail, the experience of those affected by it was not such as to warrant its perpetuation under the conditions that existed in Virginia, where new and highly productive lands were being constantly placed in competition with older lands in connection with tobacco culture. Nevertheless, in 1748 the Assembly reaffirmed in strongest terms its adherence to the general principles of the law of entail in passing the statute for settling the titles and bounds of land.[155] In spite of this stand there is significance in the fact that about twenty years later — that is, in 1767 — a method was devised and ratified by an act of the legislature which substantially defeated the aims of those responsible for the statute of 1705. This was the legalization of leases of entailed land for three lives or for a lesser period.[156]

The plantation system was the basis of aristocracy in Virginia. At its best it operated in such a manner as to allow the owner and his family the wealth and leisure to cultivate the amenities and niceties of life. The author of *American Husbandry* declared:

> "The tobacco planters live more like country gentlemen of fortune than any other settlers in America; all of them are spread about the country, their labour being mostly by slaves, who are left to overseers; and the masters live in a state of emulation with one another in buildings, (many of their houses would make no slight figure in the English counties) furniture, wines, dress, diversions, etc., and this to a degree that it is rather amazing they should be able to go

---

(*op. cit.*) has shown that the tendency was rather in the direction of the decrease of slaves — insofar as the history of docking entails could furnish a clue to the actual situation.

[155] See Hening: *op. cit.*, V, 414.

[156] *Ibid.*, VIII, 183–4; see also R. B. Morris: *Studies in the History of American Law . . .* (New York, 1930), p. 91.

on with their plantations at all, than they should not make additions to them. . . ." [157]

This manner of life produced a body of superior people who dominated the province politically, religiously, and socially by sheer merit and innate capacity, men who, according to Burnaby, "are haughty and jealous of their liberties, impatient of restraint and can scarcely bear the thought of being controuled by any superior power." [158]

The planter aristocracy of the middle of the eighteenth century was supreme because the strongest, most vigorous and enterprising elements of good English stock living in Virginia had naturally come to the forefront in the seventeenth century and early part of the eighteenth and by a process of intermarriage succeeded in producing a generation or two of men and women that for ability and capacity for leadership would be hard to match in any other part of the Old British Empire. [159] Those lordly Georgian mansions that still grace the slopes about the Virginia tidewaters are evidence of the splendour of their ways. [160]

The life of a great plantation-owner was something far beyond building mansions and engaging in cavalcades, house parties, gaming, horse-racing, and fox-hunting. [161] It included these pastimes as a rule, it is true, together with books from London for those of literary inclinations [162] and the other delights of a sumptuously fur-

---

[157] *American Husbandry . . . By an American* (2 vols., London, 1775, reprinted and edited by H. J. Carman, New York, 1939), p. 170.

[158] *Travels through the Middle Settlements*, p. 20.

[159] See L. W. Labaree: *Conservatism in Early American History* (New York & London, 1948), pp. 7–10, 29–31; see also Carl Bridenbaugh: *Myths and Realities: Societies of the Colonial South* (Baton Rouge, La., 1952), pp. 10–18, 51–2; C. S. Sydnor: *Gentlemen Freeholders*, pp. 62–77, 91–3; and D. J. Boorstin: *The Americans: The Colonial Experience* (New York, 1958), Chaps. 17, 18, and 19.

[160] For Georgian architecture in colonial Virginia see T. T. Waterman: *The Mansions of Virginia, 1706–1776* (Chapel Hill, N.C., 1945). The author divides the Georgian mansions into three groups the first, built between 1706–1750 under the influence of the great English architect Wren; the second, built between 1750–1765 in the Palladian monumental style; and the third, built between 1765–1775, in Palladio's Roman-villa style. See *ibid.*, pp. 413–24, for a list of Virginia mansions with dates of construction. For a broad survey of early Virginia architecture see T. J. Wertenbaker: *The Old South . . .* (New York, 1942), pp. 71–117.

[161] For a brief but excellent account of Virginia home life see E. S. Morgan: *Virginians at Home* (Williamsburg, 1952).

[162] William Byrd II collected at "Westover" a library of over 3,000 titles. See L. B. Wright: *The First Gentlemen of Virginia* (San Marino, Calif., 1940), p. 333.

nished home. More importantly, it also meant management of lands and men on a large scale in such a way that the plantation, much like the mediaeval manor, would be as self-contained as possible while at the same time producing its maximum return of the export staple — good-quality tobacco. Provision had to be made for new lands to take the place of those that were showing signs of exhaustion. The supply of slave labour had to be maintained both by preserving the health of the blacks and by due encouragement for them to propagate, or, failing this, by purchase. This labour had to be trained not only to field work but to a variety of tasks so as to provide itself food, clothing, and shelter, as well as many other articles of utility about the plantation. Such a largely self-contained plantation was "Gunston Hall," the property of George Mason, where his five hundred slaves grew tobacco, corn, and other field crops, and also engaged in horse-, cattle-, sheep-, and hog-raising. Among the Gunston slaves were skilled artisans, such as carpenters, coopers, sawyers, blacksmiths, tanners, curriers, shoemakers, spinners, weavers, knitters, and distillers. [163]

There seems to have been a real gulf separating the Virginia aristocracy from the lower-middle-class group of small farmers and artisans, at least in the area of the Tidewater. This has nowhere been better illustrated than in *The Life of the Reverend Devereux Jarratt, Rector of Bath Parish, Dinwiddie County, Virginia: Written by Himself* . . . , which was published in Baltimore in 1806, after his death, by a former student, the Rev. John Coleman, to whom it had been addressed as a series of letters. This humble parish priest was born in New Kent County in 1732. Although his grandfather Jarratt possessed 1,200 acres of land, he and his family were described as "poor people, but industrious, and rather rough in their manners." Devereux's father was a carpenter and was able to provide his family with plenty of plain food. His mother made all the boy's clothing except his hat and shoes, and he recorded that this last article was never worn except in the winter season. The autobiog-

---

[163] For an account of "Gunston Hall" by the son of George Mason, General John Mason, see Kate Mason Rowland's *Life of George Mason, 1725–1792* (2 vols., New York, 1892), I, 94–102. For studies relating to the slave as a skilled labourer in eighteenth-century America see M. W. Jernegan: "Slavery and Industrialism in the American Colonies," *American Historical Review*, XXV, 220–40, and R. B. Pinchbeck: *The Virginia Negro Artisan and Tradesman* (Richmond, 1926), Chap 3.

raphy, which was begun in 1794, makes the following interesting comment on the relations with the aristocracy of the Jarratt family and people of their station in life·

> "We were accustomed to look upon, what were called *gentle folks*, as beings of a superior order. . . . A *periwig*, in those days, was a distinguishing badge of *gentle* folk — when I saw a man riding the road . . . with a wig on, it would so alarm my fears . . . that, I dare say, I would run off, as for my life. Such ideas of the difference between *gentle* and *simple*, were, I believe, universal among all of my rank and age. But I have lived to see, a vast alteration, in this respect, and the contrary extreme prevail." [164]

If the seventeenth century represents the period of growth of extremely aristocratic tendencies on the part of the leading families, the eighteenth century represents the period of the acquisition of their wealth as the result of the enormous extension of Negro slavery. This wealth, as has been suggested, came largely through the exploitation of their lands in the production of tobacco. As will be stressed in the chapter bearing on this crop, it was eagerly sought by British merchants, among whom there was sharp competition. The result was the granting of credit on a vast scale to Virginians. The merchants were only too willing to furnish this credit, for, among other results, it had the effect of binding the planters to provide them with definite amounts of tobacco each year — something highly advantageous especially to those who were engaged in supplying the European market.

One serious drawback inevitably arose from the credit-debtor relationship associated with the eagerness of the British merchants to get colonial tobacco. Many of those planters who were living the rather luxurious and extravagant life [165] that has been suggested permitted themselves and their families to become so deeply involved by accepting the easy credit offered for tobacco that the way of escape was not apparent under the inefficient and wasteful meth-

---

[164] For the first portion of this autobiography, covering the years 1732–63, edited by Douglass Adair, see the *William and Mary Quarterly*, 3rd ser., IX, 346–93. For a general discussion of the colonial craftsmen and artisans in the southern colonies see Carl Bridenbaugh: *The Colonial Craftsman* (New York & London, 1950), especially Chap. 1.

[165] See Burnaby: *Travels through the Middle Settlements*, pp. 11–14.

ods of cultivation which, according to Burnaby, prevailed.[166] Moreover, there must have been many who, while not pretending to live beyond their means, were indifferent business managers or were faced with misfortune. For them it would have been increasingly difficult to meet their obligations from working land that was declining in productiveness, particularly in the face of tobacco prices fluctuating generally at fairly low levels.[167] There is indeed evidence that with the approach of the middle of the eighteenth century numbers of planters were at last beginning to writhe under the weight of accumulated debts. The steps taken by the General Assembly to relieve this situation are closely connected with the beginnings of the revolutionary movement. Because of their great importance it seems best to reserve detailed consideration of these laws to a later volume of this series.

Meanwhile, it may be pointed out that tobacco remained the most profitable export and therefore the greatest wealth-producing commodity of the Virginia province throughout the colonial period. To illustrate, in 1775 some 96,000 hogsheads containing about 100,000,-000 pounds of it, valued at £768,000, were shipped to Great Britain, most of it from the Chesapeake area,[168] with Virginia providing the bulk of the export.

During the period under consideration and throughout its colonial days Virginia was also an exporter of grain, especially maize and wheat, with other foodstuffs such as flour and barrelled pork and beef, as well as skins, iron, ship masting, timber, hempen products, and small vessels built for disposal abroad. The sale of these exports

---

[166] Ibid. "The poverty of the planters here, many of them at least, is much talked of, and from thence there has arisen a notion that their husbandry is not profitable: this false idea I have endeavoured to obviate, and to shew that the cause of it has little or no reference to their culture, but to the general luxury, and extravagant way of living which obtains among the planters — a circumstance which ought rather to occasion a contrary conclusion — a supposition that their agriculture was very valuable; for men without some rich article cannot afford, even with the assistance of credit, to live in such a manner: it must be upon the face of it a profitable culture, that will support such luxury, and pay eight per cent. interest on their debts. What common culture in Europe will do this?" (American Husbandry, 1939 edn., p. 175).

[167] However, money could be made raising tobacco, even at low prices. Washington, who was an excellent business man, was able to pay some £1,200 sterling for "Clifton Neck" in 1760. Diaries of George Washington, 1748–1799 (ed. J. C. Fitzpatrick, 4 vols., Boston and New York, 1925), I, 163.

[168] See American Husbandry (1939 edn.), p. 183.

added materially to the income of the colony.[169] These articles were carried not only to neighbouring colonies, but also to Spain, Portugal, the Madeiras, the Azores, the Cape Verde Islands, and the West Indies in exchange for their own products — a commerce all the more advantageous in view of the fact that the vessels used were in large measure built and owned by Chesapeake Bay men.[170] It is clear that as one views the economic development of Virginia in the middle of the eighteenth century, there is presented impressive evidence of the productiveness of its soil and the enterprise of its inhabitants.

In summarizing the Old Dominion at mid-century it is well to re-emphasize one thing. Virginia in 1750 was an aristocracy buttressed by such institutions as primogeniture and entail. It was an aristocracy in much the same sense that Great Britain was at the same period. As we have seen, the actual machinery of the government of the parish with its closed vestry was in the hands of an *élite*, as was that of the county and the province, with officials appointed for life or good behaviour and with the Governor, capping it all, representing not the people but the Crown. However, in both Virginia and in Great Britain there existed a representative institution that depended upon the franchise of a body of voters most of whom were outside the ranks of the *élite* — the House of Burgesses, on the one hand, and the House of Commons, on the other. This provided an opportunity, both in the Old Dominion and in the mother country, for the electorate to choose between men who hoped to represent them. Further, in each the force of public opinion could be brought to bear upon government at all levels. As a consequence all regulation — even imperial regulation — whether by central or local authority, in each case was apt to conform to the sentiments of the electorate, if not to those of the disfranchised.

Finally, the aristocratic form of government in both Virginia and Great Britain was not unpopular in the middle of the eighteenth

---

[169] *Ibid.* It should be pointed out that in most of the figures covering exports and imports Virginia and Maryland are lumped together, as in the case of tobacco exports. The value of exports on articles other than tobacco for the two colonies in 1775 reached £272,000.

[170] For an excellent account of Chesapeake Bay trade to southern Europe and the West Indies see A. P. Middleton: *Tobacco Coast: A Maritime History of Chesapeake Bay in the Colonial Era* (Newport News, Va., 1953), Chap. 6. See also C. B. Coulter, Jr.: "The Import Trade of Colonial Virginia," *William and Mary Quarterly*, 3rd ser., II, 296–314.

century — nor did any strong movement exist at the time directed toward introducing a more democratic character into the constitution. Such a movement was indeed to develop at a later period in each. For reasons that are not hard to determine, it had its beginnings much earlier in Virginia than in Great Britain.[171]

---

[171] The words "aristocracy" and "democracy" carry various connotations. In the sense that political scientists use the terms, Virginia was neither an aristocracy nor a democracy, since "sovereignty" did not rest in the Virginia élite or in the widely distributed Virginia electorate that was outside of it. However, when applied to such a dependency of Great Britain as was Virginia in 1750, the term "aristocracy" in its generally accepted meaning indicates that — even granting the existence of a representative branch of the government at the provincial level, although not at the local level — the administration of both provincial and local affairs rested in the hands of those of superior fortune, talent, or social station, who were regarded by the generality of people as constituting a social class.

CHAPTER II

An Old Catholic Refuge

To the north of the Old Dominion, skirting the southern shore of the Potomac River, was the Province of Maryland.[1] Although its economic life, like that of Virginia, depended upon tobacco, its uniqueness among the southern colonies in 1750 rests on the fact it had acquired the dubious distinction of being the chief receptacle for those Englishmen transported to America as a penalty for criminal acts. Also, of all the colonies planted by the English in the New World in the seventeenth century, none had departed more fundamentally from one of the chief purposes of its founders than had Maryland.

When Cecilius Calvert established his colony in 1634 he little realized the day would come when the inhabitants would be busy passing laws against the descendants of those fellow religionists whom he sought to succour by offering them asylum in the New World. Nevertheless, during the last years of the seventeenth century and especially in the early years of the eighteenth, when the fifth Lord Baltimore, Charles, became a Protestant, the Anglicans and dissenters, in the majority and secure in their control of the government of this colony, placed on the statute books various acts which seriously discriminated against Roman Catholics. Indeed, of all the British plantations in North America, Maryland had the severest anti-Catholic laws. No Roman Catholic church could legally be erected. No one professing the religion of this church could instruct the youth or purchase lands, and the children of a Protestant could

---

[1] The most important book concerned with Maryland for the period under consideration is C. A. Barker's *The Background of the Revolution in Maryland* (New Haven, 1940).

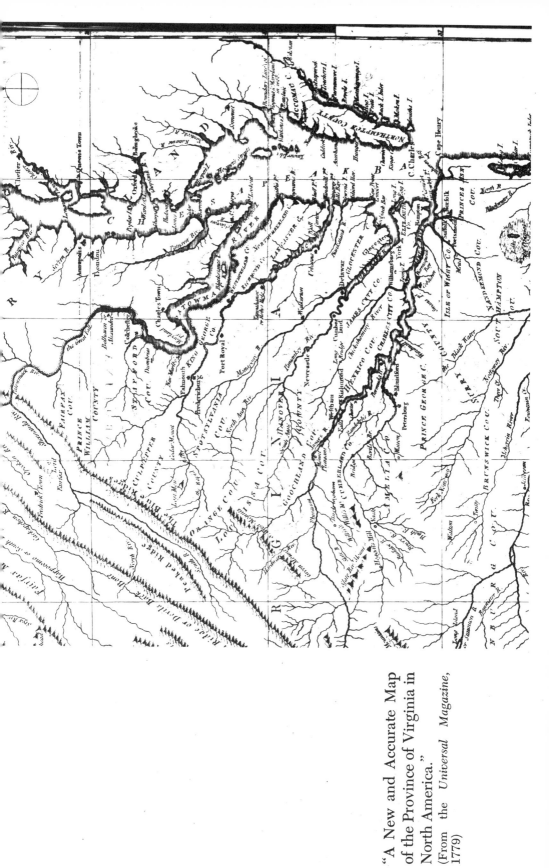

"A New and Accurate Map of the Province of Virginia in North America." (From the *Universal Magazine*, 1779)

A map of Maryland.

(From *The Political Magazine . . . and Literary Journal*, 1780)

be taken away from his widow to be placed under Protestant care, were she to become a Catholic or marry a Catholic. Further, on attaining his majority the child of a Catholic was expected to take the oaths of allegiance, abhorrency, and abjuration in order to be entitled not only to inherit lands but also to exercise the rights of franchise.[2]

By the middle of the century it seemed to many people that the tide was turning in favour of this group. As a matter of fact after the year 1720, with the coming of Captain Charles Calvert as Governor, much of the persecuting spirit of the Protestants had vanished.[3]

"Your Committee conceive it their Duty to represent to your Honourable House," declared the committee of grievances of the House of Delegates of the Assembly on May 23, 1751, "that the Growth of Popery within this Province may (if not timely check'd by some additional Laws, or putting in Execution the Laws now in Being) become dangerous to his Majesty's Dominion and his Lordship's Government, as it now is manifestly prejudicial to the Protestant Interest, and a growing Grievance."[4]

As to the actual number of Catholics within the province in the middle of the eighteenth century, it is probably impossible to give accurate figures by reason of the fact that many Catholic sympathizers disguised their religious sentiments on account of the persecuting legislation.[5] Nevertheless, it seems to be true that there were comparatively few of this persuasion living in the region of the Eastern Shore [6] and that to the westward there were, it has been

---

[2] For the above legislation see Thomas Bacon: *Laws of Maryland* . . . (Annapolis, 1765) for the year 1704, Chap. 59; for the year 1715, Chap. 36; for 1716, Chap. 5; for 1717, Chap. 10.

[3] See M. P. Andrews: *History of Maryland* . . . (Garden City, N.Y., 1929), p. 226.

[4] *Archives of Maryland* (eds., W. H. Browne et al., 65 vols., Baltimore, 1883–1952), XLVI, 549. The Catholics were very numerous in St. Mary's County. See C. A. Barker: *op. cit.,* p. 43.

[5] In 1753 it was declared, for example, in a formal report drawn up by the clergy, that many Germans were coming into the province who were "concealed Papists." See Calvert Papers, No. 509, August 22, 1753, Maryland Historical Society, Baltimore. While the number of German Catholics in Maryland was small, two priests arrived in Maryland in 1741 to minister to them; one of them was Theodore Schneider and the other, Wilhelm Wappeler. Schneider had been both a professor at Heidelberg University and its president. See Dieter Cunz: *The Maryland Germans* (Princeton, 1948), pp. 87–90.

[6] Dr. Chandler to the Bishop of London, October 21, 1767, *Historical Collections relating to the American Colonial Church* (ed. W. S. Perry, 5 vols., Hartford, 1870–8), IV, 334. Cited subsequently as W. S. Perry: *Historical Collections.*

estimated, probably not more than four or five thousand at the most.[7] The alarm that had developed in Protestant circles regarding the growth in power of Roman Catholicism was, in other words, out of all proportion to the actual numerical strength of its adherents.

The Assembly was particularly concerned with the practice of Maryland Roman Catholics of sending their children "to foreign Popish Seminaries . . . where they imbibe Principles destructive to our Religious and Civil Rights."[8] It was charged in the committee report of 1751 that these children only too frequently returned as priests or Jesuits to propagate their doctrines with great industry; that, living in societies, they purchased many tracts of land and plantations, some of which extended into the back parts of the province where numbers of Germans, French, and other foreigners were settled who, as a result of these influences, bade fair to become a dangerous intestine enemy ready to join the French or Indians.[9]

It would appear that in the discussions that took place within the House of Delegates over the report of 1751 certain statements were made that were resented by the Catholic element. At least Charles Carroll, Esq., "a powerful and leading Roman Catholic," and father of the signer of the Declaration of Independence, felt constrained to fasten to the door of the House an advertisement said to contain "scandalous and malicious reflections on the Delegates," for which he was ordered into custody.[10]

In order to quiet the apprehensions of the people and in answer to the petition of the lower house, the Governor at this juncture agreed to appoint to places of trust and profit none but faithful Protestant subjects. That this petition had the support of Frederick, Lord Baltimore, is indicated by a letter he sent in 1755 to Horatio Sharpe,

---

[7] Edward Channing: *History of the United States* (6 vols., New York, 1905–25), II, 425.

[8] The following acts of Parliament contained clauses that related to the sending of children to foreign seminaries: 2 James I, c. 4, Par. 6; 3 James I, c. 5; 3 Chas. I, c. 2; 11 and 12 Wm. III, c. 4, Par. 6. It was considered that these British statutes held for Maryland as well. For the application of the English statutes to this province see the study by St. George L. Sioussat: *The English Statutes in Maryland* (Johns Hopkins University Studies, Baltimore, 1903).

[9] *Archives of Maryland*, XLVI, 549, 593–4. See also the Calvert Papers, No. 510, for a report of the resolutions passed by the Anglican clergy in October 1753. For the German settlements see L. P. Hennighausen: "Early German Settlements in Western Maryland," *Society for the History of Germans in Maryland, Annual Report*, 1891–1892.

[10] *Archives of Maryland*, XLVI, 572–3.

who had taken over the administration of the province from Samuel Ogle. A Protestant, as was his father, Charles, he declared that to prevent the growth of "Popery," and in light of the intimations coming to him that persons holding office in the province were violating the statutes against Roman Catholicism, it was his wish that such individuals should be prosecuted according to the laws.[11] Moreover, in 1746 and later in 1756 in the face of a war crisis, lawyers, judges, and other office-holders were called upon to sign a solemn declaration repudiating a belief in transubstantiation, and also to make declarations against the house of Stuart.[12]

In seeking the cause for the increased activities of the adherents of the Roman Catholic faith in the middle of the century, attention is attracted to the condition of the Established Church of Maryland.[13] In no part of North America was better provision made for the Anglican clergy. The benefices of the thirty parishes in 1741 averaged in value about £200 sterling a year.[14] These livings varied, according to a list prepared for the year 1767, from that of All Saints of Frederick County, which was estimated at £452.13, to that of St. Augustine, placed at £76.4.4.[15]

---

[11] Letter of October 27, 1755, Calvert Papers, No. 558. Horatio Sharpe became Governor of Maryland in 1752 and retained the office until 1769. For his public career in Maryland see P. H. Giddens: "Governor Horatio Sharpe and his Maryland Government," Maryland Historical Magazine, XXXII, 156–74. His official correspondence has been published in the Archives of Maryland, Vols. VI, IX, and XIV.

[12] The Declaration of the year 1746 contains sixty signatures. This with the Declaration of 1756 is to be found among the unprinted papers in the archives of the Court of Appeals at Annapolis, made available through the courtesy of Judge Bond. The Declarations are based on 25 Chas. II, c. 2; 13 Wm. III, c. 6; and 1 Geo. I, St. 2, c. 13.

[13] For a scholarly account of the Anglican Church in Maryland see N. W. Rightmyer: Maryland's Established Church (Baltimore, 1956); see also the excellent study by A. W. Werline: Problems of Church and State in Maryland during the Seventeenth and Eighteenth Centuries (South Lancaster, Mass., 1948).

[14] S. W. Perry: Historical Collections, IV, 323 and 339.

[15] Of the 44 parishes in existence in 1767, 18 were valued at over £200 and 14 between this amount and £150, while but 2 fell below the value of £100. Ibid., IV, 336–7. The Rev. Dr. Chandler, who visited the Eastern Shore in that year, reported that the parishes in which he travelled were very large and that the livings were generally worth £300 sterling and some £500, with very few as low as £200, which would seem to indicate that the figures given in the list just referred to were low. Ibid., IV, 334–5. For an estimate of the amounts of the annual income of the church livings in 1775 see ibid., IV, 343–5. William Douglass (A Summary, Historical and Political, of the . . . British Settlements in North-America . . . [2 vols., London reprint, 1760], II, 359) writes: "The clergymen of Maryland are upon the most profitable lay of all our plantation clergy; they are not confined to a fixed salary (in Virginia the parish ministers are fixed to 16,000 lb. wt. of tobacco per ann. salary) but in this growing country . . . are paid in

Handsome as was this provision for the clergy, all did not measure up to the highest standards of conduct. The Rev. Hugh Jones, rector of St. Stephen's Church, North Sassafras Parish, Cecil County, charged in 1741 that "the great remissness or mean capacity of some & the notorious immoralities of others of my Brethren here give great offence to many devout people, and occasion a contempt of the Clergy amongst many of the Laity. . . ." Dr. Thomas Chandler in 1767 was equally emphatic in declaring: "The general character of the Clergy, I am sorry to say, is most wretchedly bad. . . . It would really, my lord, make the ears of a sober heathen tingle to hear stories that were told me by many serious people, of several Clergy-men in the neighbourhood of the parish where I visited. . . ." In affirming that there were some of the clergy whose behaviour was "unexceptionable and exemplary," he was obliged to confess their number was indeed small, "they appearing like here & there lights shining in a dark place." [16] Under these circumstances it is not sur-prising that Anglicanism was declining in favour and that dissent-ing preachers were gathering in numbers of people. It was equally obvious, in view of the ineffective enforcement of the laws against them, that the Roman Catholics should take heart once again and begin to draw supporters to their side.

In attempting to explain the unhappy condition of the Anglican Establishment in Maryland one must take account of the unique power possessed by the Proprietor under the terms of the royal charter granted to Cecilius his ancestor. According to the charter, he was authorized to make presentations to all churches erected within the bounds of the province. Unfortunately, this authority was exercised in such fashion in the eighteenth century as to exclude the Bishop of London and his American commissaries [17] from any

---

proportion to the number of taxables, the more that colony increases in people, the larger is their income. . . ."

[16] The statements are contained in letters written by Jones and Chandler to the Bishop of London. See Perry: *op. cit.*, IV, 323 and 335. That many of the Maryland clergy were unfairly charged by those out of sympathy with their political views is indi-cated by a recent careful analysis of charges brought against them. See N. W. Right-myer: "The Character of the Anglican Clergy in Colonial Maryland," *Maryland Histori-cal Magazine*, XLIV, 229–50.

[17] The lay office of commissary in Maryland, it should be made clear, was the vehicle for the probating of wills and for granting letters of administration of estates and was considered a lucrative post. See Edith E. MacQueen: "The Commissary in Colonial Maryland," *ibid.*, XXV, 190–206, for a discussion of this office, which was not ecclesi-astical in nature.

participation in this function so vitally important to the spiritual welfare of the people of the province. The result was that many individuals without suitable qualifications for pastoral work were given
charges.[18]

The Governor was expected to see that the desires of the Proprietor were fulfilled, but apparently possessed little discretion in these
matters. For example, Baltimore sent instructions to Governor Sharpe
in 1754 enclosing at the same time commissions "with his scarf" for
Alexander Malcolm and Thomas Bacon to act as domestic chaplains
in Maryland. Sharpe, after delivering these commissions, was directed to give White Chapel, St. Mary's Parish in Dorchester County,
to Malcolm, also to give to the Rev. Mr. Mayer the living of St. Anne's
Parish, Ann Arundel County, and to turn over to the Rev. Mr. Copp,
a missionary in Georgia, a vacant benefice in Worcester County
valued at 30,000 pounds of tobacco. As to the remaining benefice
of 17,000 pounds of tobacco, he might dispose of it at his own
pleasure. Further, he was instructed to demand from the Rev. Ma-
thias Harris the certificate permitting him to act as a provincial
chaplain and to prevent him from enjoying any ecclesiastical prefer-
ment until he had cleared himself of the charge of forging a bill of
exchange. Finally, he was not to allow the clergy to assemble, "as
there was much warmth among them at their last meeting." [19]

The unhappy consequences resulting from the denial by the Proprietor of the right of the Bishop of London or his commissary to
interfere with the placing or displacing of the clergy or with their
discipline may here be further illustrated. For example, two clergymen compelled to leave Virginia under charges of immorality were
given Maryland benefices in 1730.[20] Further, James Cosgreve, a native of Ireland who had led a vagrant life for many years in America
and among other activities had kept a public house in Philadelphia,
although "an abandoned drunkard & when drunk an outrageous
Madman," secured from Baltimore, under the name of Colgrave, a
church living in the county of Prince George. Upon his arrival from

---

[18] The situation indicated above led to very serious differences between Charles,
Lord Baltimore, and the Bishop of London, who at the time was Dr. Gibson, over the
questions of ordination and licencing of the Maryland clergy. See W. S. Perry: op. cit.,
IV, 331, and Norman Sykes: Edmund Gibson, Bishop of London, 1669–1748 . . .
(Oxford, 1926), p. 354.

[19] Frederick, Lord Baltimore, to Horatio Sharpe, January 5, 1754, Calvert Papers,
No. 515.

[20] Norman Sykes: Edmund Gibson, p. 354.

England, officiating at divine services, he immediately "got drunk and behaved in the most outrageous manner, to the scandal and grief of the Friends of the Church of England, and to the triumph of its Enemies." [21] It may be added that Cosgreve (also going under the name of Congreve, Colgreve, and Congrave) was never inducted into his living and soon left the province.[22]

To protect themselves from such unworthy guides as the unspeakable Cosgreve, the parishioners were helpless except by remaining away from divine services — for they could neither dismiss nor discipline their clergy. "The inhabitants," declared Dr. Chandler, writing in 1767, "look upon themselves to be in a state of the cruelest oppression with regard to ecclesiastical matters. The Ch's are built & liberally endowed, entirely at their expense, yet the proprietor claims the sole right of patronage & causes induction to be made without any regard to the opinion of the parishioners; those who are inducted are frequently known to be bad men even at the very time, & others soon shew themselves to be so after induction. There is no remedy," he concluded, "as they cannot be removed, not even by the highest exertion of proprietary power." [23] It is, therefore, not surprising that many men of vicious lives who desired nothing more than be able to gratify themselves without danger of interference should seek to secure a Maryland benefice and that many succeeded. Nor it is surprising that the Rev. Thomas Bacon,[24] one of the most estimable and learned men within the province, should write in 1750 to the Society for the Promotion of Christian Knowledge: "Infidelity has indeed arrived to an amazing & shocking growth in these parts. . . . Religion among us seems to wear the face of the Country; part moderately cultivated, the greater part wild & savage.

---

[21] The Rev. Henry Addison to the Bishop of London, October 29, 1766, W. S. Perry: op. cit., IV, 333.

[22] See N. W. Rightmyer: "The Character of the Anglican Clergy . . . ," Maryland Historical Magazine, XLIV, 243–4.

[23] Chandler to the Bishop of London, October 21, 1767, W. S. Perry: op. cit., IV, 335; see also F. L. Hawks: Contributions to the Ecclesiastical History of the United States (2 vols., New York, 1836–9), II, 190, and A. L. Cross: The Anglican Episcopate and the American Colonies (New York, 1902), p. 6.

[24] Bacon published in London Two Sermons Preached to a Congregation of Black Slaves, 1749, and, in 1750, Four Sermons upon the Great and Indispensable Duty of all Christian Masters and Mistresses to bring up their Negro Slaves in the Knowledge and Fear of God; in 1765 came his best-known work, a compilation of the Laws of Maryland . . . (Annapolis, 1765).

Where diligent conscientious Pastors are seated, there improvement is to be seen, in proportion to their time & labours. Where others are fixed all things appear with a Desart aspect or over-running with an useless growth of Weeds and brush, sprung up since the decease of the last laborious husbandman." [25]

There were other results of the unhappy situation arising out of the unworthiness of many of the clergy. The Assembly was undoubtedly influenced unfavourably toward that body. This is indicated by the passage at this period of an act that changed the law of the year 1701 relating to the maintenance of the Establishment. Under the terms of the earlier act the incumbent of a church benefice was entitled to receive forty pounds of tobacco for all those within the parish who, whether free or slave, were counted for taxation purposes. The new measure deducted one fourth of this amount and also permitted the payment of the remainder in the paper currency of the province at the rate of twelve shillings and sixpence for each one hundred pounds of tobacco, which sum, according to the Rev. Alexander Adams, who wrote in 1751 in protest to the Bishop of London, was not by any means equal to the value of tobacco at that period. [26]

Except for the agitation against the growing power of the Catholics, the period between the Peace of Aix-la-Chapelle and the outbreak of hostilities in the last of the French and Indian wars is one of great tranquillity in the history of Maryland. It is true that, as the boundaries of the province had not been definitely established, there developed considerable friction with her northern neighbour in spite of the running of the temporary line of 1738, and that among other acts of violence accompanying this territorial dispute, a resident of Maryland was killed when an attempt was made on the part of Pennsylvania claimants to dislodge him from property patented to him by the Maryland government. [27] Yet, in most respects, there was quiet, in the midst of which population was rapidly increasing and so was the value of the colony's resources. The number of inhabitants in 1749 was computed at 136,000, of whom 36,000 were black, [28] which constitutes an increase of 100,000 from 1704, when the popula-

25 W. S. Perry, op. cit., IV, 324-5.
26 Ibid., IV, 326.
27 Archives of Maryland, XXVIII, 552, 556, 560, 572, 576, 579, 580.
28 "Answers to Queries," ibid., XXVIII, 469.

tion was estimated at 35,012, of whom 4,475 were black.[29] By 1756 the population was 154,188, of whom 46,225 were black.[30]

Many Germans, among other foreigners crowding into the back country, found the land very fertile and capable of producing everything in great abundance. That their presence was welcomed is indicated by Daniel Dulany, the elder, who declared in writing to Governor Ogle in 1745: "You would be surprised to see how much the country is improved beyond the mountains, especially by the Germans, who are the best people that can be to settle a wilderness; and the fertility of the soil makes them ample amends for their industry." [31] An interesting letter has survived among the Calvert Papers. Signed by thirty-five Germans in 1746, it stressed the religious as well as the material advantages of the province. "We here enjoy full Liberty of Conscience," they declared, in writing to others in Germany to join them, and continued:

". . . the Law of the Land is so constituted, that every man is secure in the Enjoyment of his Property, the Meanest person is out of reach of Oppression from the most Powerful, nor can anything be taken from him without his receiving Satisfaction for it." [32]

The great export staple of Maryland — as was the case with Virginia — was tobacco, which averaged about 30,000 hogsheads a year.[33] In 1749 some 200 vessels, totalling about 12,000 tons burden and navigated by 4,000 men, were employed to carry the crop to Great Britain. In 1756 but 180 vessels were required for the same work, totalling 10,000 tons, which would indicate something of a decrease in the quantity of this crop shipped abroad.[34] The province

---

[29] Shelburne Papers, 45:113–15, Clements Library.

[30] *Archives of Maryland*, XXXI, 145.

[31] See R. H. Spencer: "Hon. Daniel Dulany, 1685–1753," *Maryland Historical Magazine*, XIII, 204; see also A. C. Land: "A Land Speculator [Daniel Dulany (1685–1753)] in the Opening of Western Maryland," *Maryland Historical Magazine*, XLVIII, 191–203; and, by the same author, *The Dulanys of Maryland* . . . (Baltimore, 1955), Chap. 11. It is not surprising to note the above attitude on the part of Dulany toward the immigrant Germans if we bear in mind that Dulany himself had risen from an indentured servant to his eminence as a prominent lawyer. See *ibid.*, p. 3. For German settlements in Maryland see Dieter Cunz: *Maryland Germans*, previously cited.

[32] Calvert Papers, Orders and Instructions, No. 295½, Maryland Historical Society.

[33] See C. A. Barker: op. cit., pp. 105–6.

[34] *Archives of Maryland*, XXVIII, 469, XXXI, 145, and C. A. Barker: op. cit., pp. 104–5.

also produced for export certain quantities of grain, lumber, skins, and iron to the value of £16,000 sterling annually.[35]

As for iron, Maryland could boast of numerous mines, some of which were considered very valuable. The colony also possessed eight furnaces for making pig-iron and nine forges for producing bar-iron, with a plating-forge working with two tilt hammers. This gave Maryland a position of great importance among the colonies as perhaps the foremost producer of both pig-iron and bar-iron, with the notable exception of Pennsylvania.[36] Such men as George Rock, Richard Snowden, Edmund Jennings, Charles Carroll, and Nathaniel Chapman were among those who were most prominently identified with iron-production.[37] This industry, together with the favourable

---

[35] It is of interest that Maryland's commercial relations were apparently more intimate with Massachusetts Bay than with any other portion of the Empire outside of England. For example, according to the list of entries and clearances published in the *Maryland Gazette* for the year 1749, there were 23 vessels entering from that province and 17 clearing for it; 11 from and 11 to Virginia; 7 from and one to Rhode Island; 6 from and 2 to the West Indies; and 5 from the continent of Europe. Three ships came from Philadelphia and one departed hence; one from New York and one to it; one from New York and one to New Hampshire and 2 hence. The list is manifestly defective.

Maryland, even in the seventeenth century, considered that its commercial relations with Pennsylvania were such as to be highly disadvantageous. This was due to the fact that there was a tendency on the part of the traders of the latter province to drain off all the ready specie of whatever sort held by her people. To check this, discriminatory tariffs were levied against spirituous beverages such as rum, spirits, wine, and brandy brought from her northern neighbour. For the laws of 1704 and 1715 see *Maryland Archives*, XXVI, 281, and XXX, 327. In 1704 the difference amounted to 5 pence per gallon as against 9 pence per gallon imposed the following year.

[36] *Ibid.*, XXXI, 145, and C. A. Barker: *op. cit.*, pp. 106–9.

[37] George Rock was the owner of the plating-forge located at the head of North East River. See Archives of Maryland (Ms.) 26:485, State House, Annapolis. Snowden of Ann Arundel County was chief owner in the Patuxent Iron Works. These works were erected after 1736, when articles of agreement were drawn up between Snowden, Edmund Jennings, John Galloway, Joseph Cowman, and John Pichard for carrying on these works. In 1749 Snowden bought the shares possessed by Jennings and Cowman. See Land Office Records, Liber E. L. No. 9 B., 1749–56, p. 1. At the time of his death in 1763 he was completing a new forge on the north branch of the Patuxent River. That he made money from his enterprises is evidenced by his will, which was witnessed January 5, 1763. This made substantial provision for his wife, his three sons, and numerous grandchildren. See Maryland Wills, Vol. 31, folios 1011–16, State House, Annapolis. Descriptions of the business activities of Dr. Charles Carroll are contained in his accounts and letter books, extracts of which have appeared in the *Maryland Historical Magazine*, Vols. XXII and XXIV, covering the year 1750, many of which relate to the production of iron. For the beginnings and development of the Baltimore Ironworks from 1731 onwards, which were located on the Patapsco River and in which Carroll had a large interest, see Keath Johnson: "The Genesis of the Baltimore Ironworks," *Journal of Southern History*, XIX, 157–79.

location of the town of Baltimore for the development of a great overseas commerce in grain, was destined to produce a profound change in the economic life of Maryland in the course of the next century and would ultimately differentiate her from the more southern non-industrialized commonwealths.[38]

It was this fair province that Charles, Lord Baltimore, enjoyed as a proprietary from the year 1715 to the date of his death in 1751. Charles in the 1740's attached himself to the political fortunes of the Prince of Wales with the result that in 1747 he was created cofferer of the household, receiving one hundred marks annually in addition to the fees and profits of the office. At the same time he was also created the Prince's Surveyor-General of all "our Honours, Castles, Lordships, Manors, Messuages, Forests, Chases, Parks, Lands, etc.," for which he was to be rewarded, in addition to all fees and profits, the by no means extravagant sum of £66.13.4 annually. Subsequently he was advanced to the post of Lord of the Bed-Chamber to His Royal Highness, which, however, he resigned early in 1749, when it was announced that he was about to visit Maryland.[39] The extent of the revenue that he drew from the province is made clear through the survival of a schedule which shows that this proprietary yielded in 1751, after all deductions, the net sum of £9,582.2.10.[40] However, in dying, he left a personal estate valued at only £20,000.[41]

At his death Baltimore left as heir his son, Frederick, a minor. He

---

[38] See C. P. Gould: "Economic Causes of the Rise of Baltimore," in *Essays in Colonial History by Students of Charles McLean Andrews* (New Haven, 1931), pp. 238–40; see also Hamilton Owens: *Baltimore on the Chesapeake* (New York, 1941), a breezy book largely concerned with the city's characteristics and development after the eighteenth century.

[39] Calvert Papers, No. 96; also the *Maryland Gazette*, June 21, 1749.

[40] "A Schedule of Frederick, Lord Baltimore's Estate," Calvert Papers, No. 953. For the income received by the Proprietor from Maryland between 1731 and 1774 see C. A. Barker: *op. cit.*, pp. 380–1, and, by the same author, "Property Rights in the Provincial System of Maryland: Proprietary Revenues," *Journal of Southern History*, II, 211–32.

[41] On November 18, 1750, Baltimore made his will, which gave Maryland, entailed on his son, Frederick, and his two daughters, Louisa and Caroline, in trust to certain trustees. Further, his lands in Ireland were placed in trust for Mrs. Cecil Brenan and her two sons, Charles and Augustus, while his lands in Kent were placed in trust for Mrs. Jane Newton, together with those in Argyle Street, Hanover Square, Middlesex, with plate, china, etc. To the children of Jane Hyde, his sister, he willed £1,000; for Mrs. Jane Newton he provided an annuity of £100; for his daughters, mentioned above, he set aside £5,000 for each, in addition to the £5,000 secured to them by means of his marriage settlement. See Calvert Papers, No. 475.

therefore placed Maryland in trust of four friends: Thomas Bladen, who had acted as Lieutenant Governor from 1742 to 1747; John Sharpe, secretary to the Lords of the Committee of the Council; Samuel Ogle, then acting as Lieutenant Governor; and Samuel Farrant. The question arose immediately upon his death as to the nature of the power that these trustees had received. The opinion of Paul Jodrell, a distinguished jurist, was sought. He stated, in answer to certain questions, that the trustees had received the soil of the proprietary but not the government, which remained in Frederick. Therefore, they had no power to appoint a governor or to exercise any act involving political authority. Neither could they do so were Frederick to name them as his guardians in addition to their trusteeship, except by special authorization of the Crown, which must be made on the petition of Frederick himself.[42] This was done. The guardianship, however, was brief, for Frederick, born in 1731, soon reached his majority.[43]

By all accounts Frederick was not so serious-minded as some of his predecessors had been. He probably is best described as a man of fashion and a dilettante, who travelled, was given to horse-racing, and wrote some indifferent verse. About a year after taking over the responsibilities of his proprietary he made a serious effort to revive the family claims to the province of Avalon in Newfoundland, which effort, however, was abortive.[44] At this period he entered into a marriage contract with Diana Egerton, daughter of Scroop, late Duke of Bridgewater, which was not happy and which failed to provide an heir for Maryland. It appears that by 1756 a separation had taken place and that some time before the year 1761 Diana passed away.[45]

---

[42] Calvert Papers, No. 472.

[43] During the period of guardianship Cecelius Calvert, the uncle of Frederick, was offered the governorship of the province but declined it on account of the state of his health and his time of life. See his letter to Benjamin Tasker, July 9, 1752, Calvert Papers, No. 1147, 61.

[44] The above episode is considered in the chapter on "Bankers and Sackmen and the Province of Avalon," in Volume III of this series.

[45] A schedule of Baltimore's estate, including what he acquired by his marriage, was prepared at this time to aid arbitrators in fixing proper alimony. According to this, Frederick drew £9,582.10 from his estate in Maryland in one year from Michaelmas 1750 to Michaelmas 1751; his annual rentals in Surrey brought in £1,099.9.9; his personal estate amounted to £32,933.12.10, but out of this he was liable for certain payments to Lady Baltimore, Dowager, to his two sisters, and to his two cousins, the children of his aunt, Jane Hyde. Lady Diana brought as a marriage portion £10,000 and also one sixth of the personal estate of her father and her brother, amounting to £12,084.7.9. By the articles of marriage she was entitled to £500 yearly, payable quarterly during the lifetime of

Maryland therefore was conveyed in trust to Thomas Bennett and William Sharpe. They were to see that Frederick, during the remainder of his life, enjoyed it; then it was to go to his sons in priority of birth; thereafter to his uncle, Cecelius Calvert, and to the latter's sons in priority of birth, and finally to such successors as Frederick would direct by written instrument.[46] As a result of this conveyance of 1761 the province ultimately came into the possession of Henry Harford, a natural son of Baltimore, upon the latter's death.

Apparently Frederick was concerned almost entirely with the revenue possibilities of his proprietary during the period of his control. On one occasion at least he found that his eagerness to draw every penny that was possible from Maryland was defeating the end in view. In 1753 he had instructed Horatio Sharpe, whom he had appointed Governor,[47] to demand a quit-rent of ten shillings for each one hundred acres of land to be granted in the future. This had the effect, it appears, of keeping prospective purchasers away from the proprietary land office. As a result of the disappointing showing of his land commissioners he was obliged to write to Sharpe confessing that the rents had been set too high and very wisely authorizing him to fix the rate.[48]

In order to protect their great interest in America, it had been considered vitally necessary by the Proprietors, at every stage in the provincial history of Maryland, to see that the powers under the

---

Baltimore and as a survivor to £2,000 per annum. Her estate and portion were placed in trusteeship to guarantee to her this income, with the residue of the earnings of it going into the purse of Baltimore. Baltimore agreed to convey Maryland to the Duke of Devonshire, the Lord Bishop of Bangor, James Booth, and John Sharpe as trustees further to guarantee this settlement. At a later period two trustees were appointed to protect the interests of those having claims upon the estate. See Calvert Papers, No. 953.

[46] This conveyance in trust was signed January 31, 1761, Calvert Papers, No. 145.

[47] The relations of Baltimore with the Sharpe family were apparently very close. John Sharpe was appointed a trustee of Maryland at the time of Baltimore's marriage to Lady Diana; William Sharpe was made a trustee in the conveyance in trust in 1761, and the two acted as the securities of Horatio Sharpe at the time he was appointed Governor. See Frederick, Lord Baltimore, to Horatio Sharpe, March 9, 1753, Hist. Soc. of Penna. transcripts.

[48] Frederick, Lord Baltimore, to Horatio Sharpe, January 5, 1754, Calvert Papers, No. 515; see also C. P. Gould: The Land System in Maryland, 1720–1765 (Johns Hopkins University Studies, Baltimore, 1913), pp. 56–7; B. W. Bond, Jr.: The Quit-Rent System (New Haven, 1919), pp. 188–9; P. H. Giddens: "Land Policies and Administration in Colonial Maryland," Maryland Historical Magazine, XXVIII, 142–71; and Bernard Mason: "The Colonial Land System," The Eastern Shore of Maryland and Virginia (ed. C. B. Clark, New York, 1950), pp. 315–29.

charter granted to the second Lord Baltimore in 1632 remained as far as possible unimpaired. During the period of Crown control of this province that extended from the time of the Glorious Revolution to 1715 Charles, third Lord Baltimore, had to rest satisfied with such benefits as could be drawn from those non-political proprietorial rights that he had been allowed to retain. After the restoration of full authority to the family, when the fifth of the Baltimores, another Charles, embraced the established religion of England, its carefulness to prevent encroachments on its privileges, especially by the people of the colony, seems to have increased with the growing importance of this possession. In fairness to both Charles and his heir, Frederick, it may be said that — while they were determined not to be stripped of their valuable rights and certainly showed too much indifference to the just complaints of the inhabitants over the abuse of their power to grant ecclesiastical benefices — they undoubtedly sought to act with fairness in their general relations with the people of the province. Their attitude in general is well illustrated by an instruction that Charles sent to Lieutenant Governor Ogle in 1750. He declared:

> "It appearing that all undue Concessions serve only to lay a Foundation for further Incroachments & Endless Disputes, you must be very Carefull for ye future, not to part with or so lessen in ye least degree any of my just rights & to observe all my instructions with ye greatest exactness. . . ."

He then affirmed: "As I have never sent you any Instructions or ever shall but what are founded on Justice and Equity, I make no doubt but you will find all reasonable Men ready to support you." [49]

More specific consideration of the terms of the charter shows the nature of the powers it conferred upon the Proprietor. Of this instrument, James Abercromby (Abercrombie) in his "Examination" of the American colonies in the year 1752, declared that "this Charter contains the most Extensive Powers of any . . . in British America. But then it is to be consider'd, that such Charter was Granted in the 8th year of King Ch⁸. the first, many years before the Acts of Trade. . . ." Nevertheless, he went on to state, "the Latitude given by this Charter, to Trade with Foreign Countrys, in Friendship with this Kingdom is Restrained; The Powers of Government, and of

---

[49] Instructions of February 6, 1749/50, Calvert Papers, No. 295.

Transferring the Property of the Soil, are also Restrained, by the 7th and 8th of King William." [50]

By its terms, Cecilius and heirs were made absolute Proprietors, with the requirement that one fifth of the gold and silver ore mined within the province, together with two Indian arrows, should be given annually to the Crown, which should enjoy the allegiance and direct dominion of the territory. The Proprietor could appoint governors and, with the assent of the freemen of the province convened for that purpose, make laws not repugnant to the laws and customs of England; he could likewise constitute courts of judicature, appoint judges and justices, make war on all enemies of the colony, execute martial law on land or sea, and confer titles, provided the latter were not such as were conferred in England; he could erect ports of entry with liberties and privileges, impose reasonable duties on goods there loaded and unloaded, and in relation to the land of the proprietary, he could sell, convey, and alienate the same freely.[51] It is clear that he had in mind the creation of a semi-feudal system with the erection of manors the lords of which would be concentrated in an upper house of the Assembly. But this did not come to pass.[52] In practice, it had been necessary for the Proprietor to allow many of his powers to become public functions, which were carefully regulated in time by the laws of the province. This was especially true of the privilege of levying duties and the regulation of the proprietorial land office

---

[50] Shelburne Papers, 47:13, Clements Library, Ann Arbor, Michigan. A copy of Abercromby's "Examination" is also available in the Huntington Library, San Marino, California. The late Professor C. M. Andrews collated the two copies in an unpublished comparative study which is at the Yale University Library. For the text of the charter see Thomas Bacon: Laws of Maryland, for both the Latin original and the English version.

[51] The powers of the Proprietor were enumerated as follows in 1761, in the Conveyance in Trust executed by Baltimore at that time:

"Lord Baltimore, or any other coming into possession of Maryland, can always assent to legislative acts and acts of government . . . appoint all officers, civil and military, present all Benefices, Livings, etc. . . . agree to territorial divisions, arbitrate the Three Lower Counties and boundaries with the Proprietors of Pennsylvania . . . make grants in fee tail or fee simple and lease proprietary manors. Lord Baltimore can raise £20,000 on said lands for his daughters or younger sons, mortgaging them for term of 300 years, and so can Cecelius Calvert" (Calvert Papers, No. 1450).

[52] M. P. Andrews: The Founding of Maryland (Baltimore, 1933), pp. 43, 89–90. Many manors were established in Maryland, but by the eighteenth century they were manors in name only. For a list of manors in the early part of the eighteenth century see D. M. Owings: "Private Manors: An Edited List," Maryland Historical Magazine, XXXIII, 307–34.

as well as questions arising out of the operation of that office.[53] Moreover, in the struggle over the question of the extension of the English statutes to Maryland that took place in the first half of the eighteenth century after the restoration of the government to the Baltimore family in 1715, the Proprietor was compelled not only to recognize the right of the inhabitants "to such of the statutes as had been adopted in the practice of the province; but also to couch their recognition in such general terms, as to permit the future introduction of English Statutes." [54]

The government of Maryland therefore rested in the Proprietor or his deputy, serving with royal approval, an upper house of the twelve councillors, and a lower house consisting in 1750 of four delegates from each of the fourteen counties and two from the city of Annapolis.[55] The delegates were almost without exception large landowners and men of wealth. Much of their activity during the period under consideration was given over to the passing of what might be called special and permissive legislation for the counties and parishes and for the city of Annapolis. It is well-nigh amusing to follow the course of the Assembly, devoted so largely to matters of the merest local interest as it was. For example, Annapolis was obliged to petition the General Assembly to secure permission to erect a new market-house more advantageously located.[56] The justices of the county courts, in order to levy upon the inhabitants for such purposes as the restoration of church edifices within the parishes, were continually obliged to seek authorization of the Assembly, as were the vestrymen and churchwardens of the parishes who might desire to exchange a portion of the parish lands for other lands better suited for a glebe.[57]

---

[53] For the development of the Maryland land office see Elizabeth Hartsook and Gust Skordas: *Land Office and Prerogative Court Records of Colonial Maryland* (Annapolis, 1946).

[54] J. V. L. McMahon: *An Historical View of the Government of Maryland from its Colonization to the Present Day* (Baltimore, 1831), pp. 127–8. For a scholarly study of the question of the limitations of the authority of the Proprietor of Maryland see St. George L. Sioussat: *The English Statutes in Maryland*.

[55] Previous to 1748 there were seven counties to the east of the Chesapeake and six to the west. In June of that year Prince George County was divided and Frederick County thereupon erected. *Archives of Maryland*, XLVI, 142–4. See also Elihu S. Riley: *A History of the General Assembly of Maryland, 1635–1904* (Baltimore, 1905). This volume is made up largely of extracts from the proceedings of the two houses of the Assembly.

[56] *Archives of Maryland*, XLVI, 626.

[57] It is true that by an act of the year 1704 commissioners of the county courts were

Here and there among such acts were others of the gravest import to the province, such as the law passed in 1751 entitled "An Act for the more effectual Punishment of Negroes and other Slaves and for taking away the Benefit of Clergy from certain Offenders." [58] This statute provided punishment of death against any slave convicted of insurrection, of murdering or poisoning another, of ravishing a white woman, or of burning houses.

Of particular interest is the legislation passed by the Maryland Assembly down to the law of 1751 relating to the status and treatment in general of servants and slaves. While this body of law differs from the measures of other southern continental colonies in particular detail — especially in the case of South Carolina, as will be indicated later in this volume — it may be considered sufficiently typical for purposes of illustrating the trends of the period. [59]

For example, it was laid down in 1715 that all Negroes and other slaves and their issue should be slaves during their natural lives and that no Negro by receiving baptism secured any right to freedom. It was also enacted at the same time that any white woman suffering herself to be got with child by a Negro should, if free, become a servant for seven years, and, if a servant, should serve seven years after her present indenture would expire. Any white man begetting a child by a Negro woman should also serve for seven years, and the children of these inordinate unions should serve till thirty-one years of age. [60] While neither a Negro and mulatto slave nor a free Negro or mulatto born of a white woman could, during the time of his servitude, give evidence in any cause wherein any Christian white person

---

authorized to levy and raise tobacco to defray the necessary charges of their counties and parishes, which was explained and supplemented in 1745. This permitted the levy, without special authorization, of as much as 10,000 pounds of tobacco for the repair of a court house, 6,000 pounds for the repair of a prison, 8,000 pounds for repairing bridges, and 20,000 for building one. See Thomas Bacon: Laws of Maryland, 1748, Chap. 20.

[58] Ibid., 1751, Chap. 14. For a broad treatment of Maryland legislation designed to control Negro slaves see J. R. Brackett: The Negro in Maryland (Baltimore, 1889), Chap. 3, especially pp. 119–22 for laws passed in the eighteenth century.

It may be pointed out that the holding of slaves by Maryland Quakers was common in 1750 despite testimony against this practice by certain members of the Society of Friends. However, in 1768 the Yearly Meeting took a strong stand against the buying and selling of slaves and in 1777, at last, against the holding of slaves. See K. L. Carroll: "Maryland Quakers and Slavery," Maryland Historical Magazine, XLV, 215–25.

[59] For the legislation of Jamaica on the subject of slaves and slavery see Chapter VII of this volume, "The Caribbean Outpost of the Empire."

[60] Bacon: Laws of Maryland, 1715, Chap. 44, Pars. 23, 24, 26–8.

was concerned, yet such could, at the discretion of the court, give evidence against another Negro or mulatto — just so that it did not extend to life and limb.[61] Slaves charged with pilfering or stealing could be brought before a single magistrate, who was authorized to award punishment by whipping not to exceed forty lashes.[62] Any slave convicted before a single magistrate of striking any white person could be punished by having one of his ears cropped.[63] When any Negro had been convicted of a capital offence the county court was required to place a value on him or her so that a sum equivalent to three fourths the value might be paid to the owner.[64] Finally, a slave convicted of petit treason, murder, or the wilful burning of a dwelling-house should, after judgement, suffer the loss of his right hand, and should then be hung and quartered, and the head and quarters should be set up in the most public place of the county.[65]

The law of 1751 strengthened the law of 1717 by providing for a slave to give testimony even in the case of a death-offence felony and also for full compensation out of the treasury to the owner of a slave convicted of a capital offence.[66] These alterations in favour of the white master indicate that people in the province lived in a state of some apprehension of the Negroes.[67] There are, on the other hand, instances recorded of the warmth of feeling between the two races. John Gibbs's will and the issue that arose out of it may be cited as an example. This case throws light upon the prevailing social attitudes.

John Gibbs of Queen Anne County, a man of wealth, died in the

---

[61] *Ibid.*, 1717, Chap. 13, Pars. 2 and 3.

[62] *Ibid.*, 1717, Chap. 13, Par. 6.

[63] *Ibid.*, 1723, Chap. 15, Par. 4.

[64] *Ibid.*, 1717, Chap. 13, Par. 4.

[65] *Ibid.*, 1729, Chap. 4, Par. 1.

[66] With reference to the law of 1751, the following criticism put forth by Cecelius Calvert is of interest: "The Law concerning negroes and slaves is thought by the Guardians [of young Lord Baltimore, who were the Speaker and Mr. Sharpe] may be attended with much cruelty inasmuch as the Masters of such negroes and slaves upon accident of killing them, are not cognizable to Tryal, it being thought [by the guardians] reasonable that a person so killing should be accountable by law in some manner for such action [in order] to prove the occasion thereof" (Secretary Cecelius Calvert to Governor Ogle, March 30, 1752, Calvert Papers, No. 1147).

[67] "We hear that a Dead warrant is issued for the execution of a Negro fellow, condemned at last Calvert Court for a Rape. As also for a Negro fellow, condemned at . . . especial Court for burning his Master's Houses. They will both afterwards be hung in chains" (*Maryland Gazette*, December 13, 1749).

month of October 1747, leaving a will which he had made the preceding August. In it he bequeathed to his brother and the latter's son and a niece a shilling each and to a godson a riding-horse and other articles of value. But to his Negroes, eighteen in all, he gave not only freedom but the greater part of his personal estate and all his lands, consisting of extensive plantations, with buildings and appurtenances. This was the last of a number of wills he had made. His niece contested it. The case was tried before Daniel Dulany, the elder, Commissary-General and Judge of Probate of Wills, who decided that it was void on the grounds that the Negroes had exercised undue influence over the deceased, who was of unsound mind at the time. The case was appealed to the Governor by the executors of the will, and Ogle appointed a court of delegates for hearing the appeal. They, however, could not reach a decision. Thereupon another court of delegates was chosen, which finally handed down a unanimous verdict in favour of the Negroes.[68]

Another act passed in the year 1751 provided that in all criminal prosecutions against any convicts imported as such into the province, the testimony of other convicts should be received.[69] This statute calls attention to the great importance of the role played by the transported convict in the economic life of colonial Maryland.[70] In fact it would appear that between 1748 and 1775 well over 9,000 of these unfortunate people were sent to Maryland.[71]

The transportation of criminals to America, while by no means beginning in the eighteenth century,[72] secured a perfectly definite

---

[68] The parties to the issue were Jannett Cleland versus James Massey and John Hadley, executors of the will. The papers relating to this case are in the vaults of the Maryland State Court of Appeals. For the will see Maryland Wills, 25:148, State House, Annapolis.

[69] Thomas Bacon: *Laws of Maryland*, 1751, Chap. 11, Par. 2.

[70] See A. E. Smith: *Colonists in Bondage: White Servitude and Convict Labor in America, 1607–1776* (Chapel Hill, N.C., 1947); see also E. I. McCormac: *White Servitude on Maryland, 1634–1820* (Johns Hopkins University Studies, Baltimore, 1904). Another useful study on indentured white labour is by R. B. Morris: *Government and Labor in Early America* (New York, 1946), particularly Chap. 7, "The Nature of Bound Labor," Chap. 8, "The Sources of Bound Labor," and Chap. 9, "The Legal Status of Servitude."

[71] A. E. Smith: *op. cit.*, p. 119.

[72] See *ibid.*, Chap. 5, and, by the same author, "The Transportation of Convicts to the American Colonies in the Seventeenth Century," *American Historical Review*, XXXIX, 232–49; in this connection see also J. D. Butler: "British Convicts shipped to the American Colonies," *ibid.*, II, 12–33. Butler among other things stresses the presence in the eighteenth century of educated persons among the shiploads of convicts that

statutory basis in the passing of the law in the fourth year of the reign of George I entitled "An Act for the further preventing Robbery, Burglery, and other Felonies, and for the more effectual Transportation of Felons, and unlawful exporters of Wool." [73] According to this act, when any person should be convicted of an offence within the benefit of clergy (for which he was liable to be whipped, burnt on the hand, or ordered to the workhouse, which included cases of petty and even of grand larceny) it was lawful for the court to commute the sentence to labour in some one of His Majesty's plantations in America for a period of seven years [74] and to take the necessary steps to see to it that the criminal was transported and put to work for some master under an indenture. It was further recited by this act that where an individual stood attainted of any offence involving the penalty of death, with respect to whom His Majesty should be pleased to extend his mercy upon condition of transportation (which would so be signified by one of his principal secretaries of state), it would be lawful for any court having proper authority to allow such offenders the benefit of a pardon under the Great Seal and to direct the commutation of the sentence to labour in some one of the plantations for fourteen years.

The act of 1717 was supplemented by a statute passed by Parliament two years later which provided that the court of any county or riding where such offenders were convicted might appoint two or more justices of the peace, who should have authority to contract with anyone for the transportation of these felons.[75]

The first law that appears on the Maryland statute books in the eighteenth century relating specifically to transported convicts is apparently that of the year 1728,[76] which provided that every master of a ship importing convict servants should, under penalty of a fine of £5 for each instance of such neglect, bring an authentic testimonial of the offences whereof the person had been convicted and

----

were sent to North America. For example, one convict, "Henry Justin of the Middle Temple," was transported in 1736 (p. 26) for stealing books from Trinity College Library, Cambridge, among which was Field's Bible.

[73] 4 Geo. I, c. 11, Secs. 1–3 (1717).

[74] Persons convicted of receiving or buying stolen goods, knowing them to be such, however, were not to have their sentences thus commuted, but were to be transported for a period of fourteen years.

[75] 6 Geo. I, c. 23.

[76] Bacon: *Laws of Maryland*, 1728, Chap. 23, Par. 5. The legislation of the seventeenth century will be referred to later in this chapter.

the term of years that he or she was to serve. This was to be lodged with the clerk of the county in which the convict was to labour. Further, to protect the rights of individuals who might be kidnapped and brought to the colony under guise of being criminals, it was required by the same act that every person importing servants should take an oath before the naval officer whether to the best of his knowledge the person or persons he had brought in were under sentence of transportation. Those refusing the oath were to forefeit £100, while those falsely swearing or affirming were liable to be prosecuted for perjury.

The next law, that of the year 1751, which has been mentioned, now seemed to be necessary to enable the authorities to cope with the hundreds of convicts that were flooding the province each year.[77] That there were grave legal objections to the act may be understood by a letter that Cecelius Calvert sent to Governor Ogle the year following its passage. In this he declared that the rule established by it of allowing one convict to give evidence against another was questioned by both Mr. Onslow, Speaker of the House of the Commons, and William Sharpe, the other guardian of young Lord Baltimore, on the ground that it was repugnant to the laws of England. "However, as this Law is so necessary for the Preservation of the Lives of the people of Maryland," wrote Calvert, "it is thought and hoped it will pass the opinion of the Attorney-General, the necessity thereof being so urgent." [78]

That the planters of Maryland, as a group, now welcomed the appearance of these convicts, but with mixed feelings, cannot be seriously questioned. In the previous century an adverse attitude was clearly indicated by laws passed in 1676 and 1692 without avail, forbidding the bringing of criminals to the province.[79] The basis of the popularity of the use of convict transports in eighteenth-century Maryland lay in the fact that it became possible for the poorer planters to acquire labour for their small tobacco plantations on terms far

---

[77] In 1767 it was estimated that during the previous thirty years the number of convicts imported averaged about 600 per annum. See J. T. Scharf: *History of Maryland* (3 vols., Baltimore, 1879), I, 371–2. For a list of convicts brought to Maryland in 1740 by Captain Anthony Bacon in the ship *York*, see F. F. White, Jr.'s article in the *Maryland Historical Magazine*, XLIII, 55–60.

[78] Cecelius Calvert to Governor Ogle, March 30, 1752, Calvert Papers, No. 1647.

[79] *Archives of Maryland*, II, 540–1, XIII, 539–40. See E. I. McCormac: *op. cit.*, p. 97.

more advantageous than those involved in the purchase of slaves.[80] It must be remembered that they thus were able to secure the services of an acceptable white man for a period of at least seven years — the period of the economic life of a slave in the West Indies — by paying, as a rule, not much more than the costs of his transportation, together with other necessary incidental charges.[81] Indeed, William Eddis, writing from Annapolis, asserted that the Marylanders preferred convict labour even to that of the so-called indentured free-willer,[82] and that Negroes, a property for life, were "almost in every instance, under more comfortable circumstances than the miserable European, over whom the rigid planter exercises an inflexible severity."[83]

It was this exploitation of the labour of these transported convicts as well as of those brought over under indenture that permitted the small planters of both Maryland and Virginia to produce and market their crops successfully in competition with the large tobacco plantations operated by slave labour both in Maryland and to the south of the Potomac.[84] They doubtless found that white convicts were more efficient than Negro slaves in growing the Oronoko, a variety in which they specialized, that was inferior only to the Sweet-Scented tobacco grown in Virginia and which required intelligent handling for the best results.[85] In practice, it was also doubtless found

---

[80] In the period from 1749 to 1760 the holdings of the various counties averaged from 255 to 477 acres for the smaller land-holders, although the lands of the great land-holding families such as the Dulanys, the Carrolls, the Dorseys, the Bennetts, the Lloyds, etc., ran into the thousands. See C. P. Gould: *The Land System* . . . , pp. 65–8, 70–80.

[81] It appears that in the eighteenth century the cost to the planter of an indentured white was between £15 and £20 sterling. See M. S. Morriss: *Colonial Trade of Maryland, 1689–1715* (Baltimore, 1914), p. 77; see also J. C. Ballagh: *White Servitude in the Colony of Virginia* . . . (Baltimore, 1895), pp. 41 and 92.

[82] Eddis makes the following comment: "From this persuasion, they rather consider the convict as the more profitable servant, his term being for seven, the latter only for five years; and, I am sorry to observe, that there are but few instances wherein they experience different treatment" (*Letters from America, historical and descriptive* . . . *from 1769 to 1777* . . . [London, 1792], pp. 63–75, 109–10).

[83] *Ibid.*

[84] While E. I. McCormac took the position in his *White Servitude in Maryland* (p. 107) that during the twenty years before the revolt of the American colonies Maryland received most of these convicts, A. E. Smith in his *Colonists in Bondage* makes clear (p. 117) that Virginia, between 1729 and 1770, received 47 shiploads of convicts as against 53 received by Maryland.

[85] For a brief discussion of the above point see *A Letter from a Merchant of the City of London* (London, undated, but internal evidence shows that it was written

that most of the seven-year convicts, perhaps the overwhelming majority of them all, were, according to the court certificates which the shipmaster brought, if not mere petty offenders, yet not really desperate criminals.[86] They were, as a rule, amenable to good as well as bad influences and on the small farms operated without overseers, where the family was at all times thrown into intimate contact with the field hands, were more desirable in general than Negroes, especially jungle blacks. This was not the case, of course, on those great plantations of the Chesapeake Tidewater where a rigid type of supervision of the workers was maintained by the overseers and where the family in the great house, outside of the master, was compelled to see little of the slaves other than the carefully selected and trained household group.

At the same time that very practical considerations were operating to make Maryland the dumping-ground of the English jails, a view based on other sentiments found forcible expression from time to time in sweeping protests, such as the heated denial in 1767 "that the general sense of the people is in favour of this wide importation." The writer had been stung to the quick, it seems, by "that false and bitter reproach, so commonly thrown upon us, *that we are the descendants of convicts.*"[87]

An illustration of the methods employed in the introduction of criminal labour into Maryland may add insight into the nature of these operations. For example, on January 17, 1749, James Walker, clerk of the peace for the county of Middlesex, certified that at the general session of the delivery of the King's goal of Newgate held for the county of Middlesex forty-nine persons convicted of diverse felonies, of whom ten were women, were directed by the court to be transported to some of His Majesty's colonies and plantations in

---

about the middle of the eighteenth century). A copy is in the Public Archives of Canada.

[86] See A. E. Smith: "Transportation of Convicts . . . ," *American Historical Review*, XXXIX, 248. One convict, David Benfield, of Oxford, who had picked up a knowledge of physic and surgery, according to his letter written in 1772 to his former Oxford gaoler, very much enjoyed his life in Maryland, where he lived like a gentleman and carried on his professional work from "My Lady's Manor" in Baltimore County. See P. B. Gove: "An Oxford Convict in Maryland," *Maryland Historical Magazine*, XXXVII, 193–8. That he was no university man is indicated by his letter.

[87] The above statement is quoted from *Green's Gazette* of August 20, 1767, by Professor McCormac. For a discussion of this point see his *White Servitude in Maryland*, Chap. 8, in which he inclines to the generally accepted view as to the attitude of the people of Maryland toward convict labour.

America for the term of seven years, while one was ordered to be transported for fourteen years. These felons were thereupon transferred to Andrew Reid and James Armour of London, merchants, to be carried to America.[88] On the same day the clerk of the city of London signed an order for the transfer of thirty-three more felons, of whom seven were women, to the same merchants for transportation, all for seven years. That both of these groups were brought to Maryland and there sold for the periods of their sentences respectively is indicated by a statement in the records of the Provincial Council.[89] To these merchants, likewise, groups from Middlesex County at large as well as from the city were consigned on March 10 of the same year, and in this instance two convicts were transported for life by the county in question while four were given the same sentence by the city.[90]

The number of these convicts ordinarily brought to the province on one ship may be ascertained by announcement of their arrival printed in the *Maryland Gazette*. On June 14, 1749, there appeared the following brief item:

> "Annapolis. Last week arrived here the Ship *Prince Frederick*, Captain Crowley, from London with 46 Convicts."

Sometimes additional information is supplied by the *Gazette*, as in its issue of December 6, 1749, when it announced:

[88] Andrew Reid was the chief contractor for transporting convicts between the years 1739 and 1757. His contract was taken over by John Stewart, who continued to carry out the agreement until his death in 1772. See A. E. Smith: *Colonists in Bondage*, p. 114.

[89] See "Records of the Provincial Council, 1749–1756," pp. 64–6, State House, Annapolis.

[90] *Ibid.* The calendar of the Middlesex County Court for the period under consideration is full of details of people sentenced to transportation. See, for example, Session Book 1072, Public Record Office, London. The Treasury Papers also shed light on the transport of criminals. For example, John Stewart, a London shipowner and merchant, had a contract running for a period of twenty-one years, which was due to expire in April 1763. On December 30, 1762, he applied for a renewal of it. This contract extended to the city of London, Middlesex, and Buckinghamshire, as well as to the "five counties of the Home Circuit." It provided that "after every second session at the Old Bailey, of which there are eight in the year," and that after every assize in Buckinghamshire and the home circuit, he was to take away the prisoners sentenced to transportation and put them on shipboard. In his application he affirmed that while "almost every species of complaint" was made against the person who formerly had the contract for the past sixteen years — that is, Andrew Reid — he himself had never incurred the least censure in executing "this part of Public Justice" in a task few people were fitted for or wished to undertake since it was "so perilous a business" (P.R.O., Treas. 1. 416, f. 32).

"Last Wednesday arrived here, after a passage of seven weeks, Captain James Dobbins on the Ship *Thomas Frigate* belonging to Messrs Reed and Stuart, in London, with about 120 convicts."

That all the convicts destined for Maryland did not come from London at this period is also made clear by the statement in the same paper of January 24, 1750:

"On Wednesday last arrived here the Ship *Britannia*, Captain Lancey, in about eight weeks from Bristol with 85 transports."

Between the year 1745 and October 1775 there were sent from Bristol alone to Maryland, according to returns from the naval-office shipping-lists, 3,279 convicts and 3,707 indentured servants; from the various ports of Great Britain and Ireland during these same years there were sent, "mainly to the port of Annapolis," 9,360 convicts and 10,560 servants.[91]

By 1754 the convicts imported had apparently mounted to such a figure that a strong sentiment manifested itself in favour either of placing some restriction upon this movement or at least deriving some general profit from it.[92] In that year an act was passed that provided a duty of twenty shillings upon each convict transported to the province;[93] it was stated that this was for the purpose of assisting in the raising of £6,000 required for defence of the western frontier. The opposition to the law was naturally centred in the home government, in the importers of this labour, and in those desirous of exploiting it to their advantage. William Murray, who was the British Attorney-General, in sending his opinion of this statute to the Proprietor the year following its enactment, pointed out that the measure, if allowed to stand, would lead to one of two consequences: either the English courts must no longer order the felons to be transported to Maryland or the additional expense must be paid by the treasurer of the county from which the criminals were transported. In his judgement no colony could make such a law, as to him it

---

[91] See W. E. Minchinton: *The Trade of Bristol in the Eighteenth Century* (Bristol, 1950), p. 34, and A. E. Smith: *op. cit.*, p. 325, who also sets (p. 119) the number of convicts transported between 1748 and 1775 at 9,332, as previously cited.

[92] Professor Barker indicates that in 1755 unfree whites in Maryland numbered 8,851, or about six per cent of the population, and that one in four or five was a convict. The total population in that year, according to the census, was 153,505. See C. A. Barker: *op. cit.*, p. 3.

[93] Thomas Bacon: *Laws of Maryland*, 1754, Chap. 9.

seemed in direct opposition to the authority of Parliament.[94] Doubtless Maryland was not prepared to see her supply of cheap labour suddenly cut off, and in 1756 the law was repealed.[95]

In the application of the system of convict labour it was only natural that the results should vary according to the degree of adaptability of the person who had been indentured as well as with the capacity of the master to use wisely the great authority placed in his hands. For practical purposes the status of the servant was not far removed from that of the slave during the period of his commitment. Nevertheless, Eddis asserted that in many instances these convicts were better treated than were the German redemptioners.[96] Undoubtedly conditions frequently became intolerable for the indentured and, possibly less frequently, for the master or mistress. There probably was a tendency toward harshness on the one hand and sullen reluctance on the other. Although it would appear that as a rule a *modus vivendi* was attained of such a nature as to make existence bearable for both parties, yet the papers were full of notices of runaway convicts. Dr. Charles Carroll of Annapolis was obliged to advertise in 1749 for information as to the whereabouts of Mary Rider, "an English convict woman of a mulatto complexion, much given to Drunkeness and taking Snuff," who talked plausibly and used excellent English.[97] From Somerset County later in the same year notification was made of the disappearance of an Irish servant man with broad face, red hair, wearing blue pea-jacket, who spoke but indifferent English. Some convicts, it appears, assumed airs and showed evidence of past adventures. George Gold, who left Annapolis without leave, also that year, had "a large scar on his right cheek, under his eye and several about his Head" and carried himself with "a proud strutty walk although his knees stand somewhat in." He had when he went away "a short wig, a darkish camblet coat, a cloth waistcoat without sleeves and . . . a pair of Fustan breeches with brass buttons, and grey stockings." [98]

As to the social effects of the transportation of thousands of convicts to the shore of the fair province of Maryland, it seems to be generally agreed that they were not pronounced. Eddis, apparently

---

[94] For this opinion dated May 6, 1755, see Calvert Papers, No. 554.
[95] *Archives of Maryland*, VI, 295, 328, 330.
[96] William Eddis: *Letters from America* (1769–1777), p. 75.
[97] *Maryland Gazette*, April 19, 1749.
[98] *Ibid.*, August 30, 1749.

a careful observer, declared in a letter from Maryland that those who survived the term of servitude seldom established a residence in the region of their labours. His explanation of this was that "the stamp of infamy is too strong upon them to be easily erased: they either return to Europe, and renew their former practices; or, if they have fortunately imbibed habits of honesty and industry, they remove to a distant situation, where they may hope to remain unknown, and be enabled to pursue with credit every possible method of becoming useful members of society." [99] Nevertheless, it appears that some of them — having turned their backs on "former Follies" — settled down in both Maryland and Virginia and became successful planters. Edward Kimber, who went through the two colonies, wrote in 1746: "Several of the best Planters or their Ancestors, have in the two Colonies been originally of the Convict-Class, and therefore are much to be esteemed for forsaking their old Courses." [100] At the same time it is to be feared that the influence of this convict group upon these and neighbouring colonies was far from favourable.[101] This is given forcible expression in 1751 by a writer in the *Virginia Gazette* who declared: "When we see our papers filled continually with accounts of the most audacious Robberies, the most cruel Murders, and infinite other Villainies perpetrated by Convicts transported from Europe, what melancholy and what terrible Reflections must it occasion. . . . These are some of the Favours [of] Britain. Thou art called Mother Country; but what good Mother ever sent thieves and villains to accompany her children; to corrupt with their infectious vices and to murder the rest?" [102]

While the above considerations throw light on the political and social aspects of Maryland in the middle of the eighteenth century, the economy of the province — closely allied as it was with that of Virginia both in the staple product, tobacco, and the geographical area of its production, the Chesapeake Bay — bears further examination.

---

[99] *Letters from America* (1769–1777), p. 64.

[100] For Kimber's "Itinerant Observations" see the *Maryland Historical Magazine*, LI, 315–36.

[101] As to the probable adverse effect upon Pennsylvania of these transports see the author's "Crime and its Punishment in Provincial Pennsylvania," *Pennsylvania History*, II, 3–16.

[102] This statement is quoted by M. W. Jernegan in his *Laboring and Dependent Classes in Colonial America, 1607–1783 . . .* (Chicago, 1931), p. 224.

CHAPTER III

The Chesapeake Bay Staple

Iɴ the tobacco of Virginia and Maryland, Great Britain possessed a treasure greater by far than all the mines of Mexico and Peru. By the year 1750 the two colonies were sending some 72,000,000 pounds packed in 80,000 hogsheads to the British Isles.[1] It was stated in 1764 that the British government realized almost £300,000 sterling annually out of duties on tobacco and that the British merchants secured a like sum in its sale abroad.[2]

For over two hundred and fifty years tobacco had been coming from the New World to the Old without serious interruption. First raised and introduced into Europe by the Spaniards and later by the Portuguese, its cultivation was promoted in Virginia by the activities of such men as John Rolfe, with the result that it soon became the staple product of the Old Dominion and, after some years, that of Maryland.

By the middle of the eighteenth century tobacco was also grown rather widely to the north and south of the Chesapeake Bay region,

---

[1] For the most recent study of the growth and sale of tobacco see A. P. Middleton: *Tobacco Coast: A Maritime History of Chesapeake Bay in the Colonial Era* (Newport News, Va., 1953), Chap. 4; see also L. C. Gray: *History of Agriculture in the Southern United States to 1860* (2 vols., Washington, 1933), Chaps. 10 and 11.

[2] D. Fenning and J. Collyer: *A New System of Geography* (2 vols., London, 1765), II, 660. The writer of *A Letter from a Merchant of the City of London* (London, undated, but internal evidence shows it was published during the French and Indian War, copy available in the Public Archives of Canada) estimated that the value of tobacco consumed at home would average £500,000 sterling, while the value of re-exported tobacco he placed at £440,000. See also William Douglass: *A Summary, Historical and Political, of the British Settlements in North America* (2 vols., London, 1760 edn.), II, 372. William Tatham in his *Essay on the Culture and Commerce of Tobacco* (London, 1800) shows that in 1750 Virginia and Maryland sent commodities valued at £508,939 (table of imports to Great Britain, p. 285).

although not yet as an important export staple except in parts of North Carolina and in the Lower Counties on the Delaware.[3]

The demand in Europe by 1750 for the Indian weed was enormous and its manufacture for the consumer into smoking-tobacco of quality, snuff, and tobacco for chewing entailed very considerable technical skill, giving employment to hundreds of thousands of people in Great Britain and on the European continent.[4]

The tobacco of the Chesapeake had been obliged to compete with the product of the Spanish colonies for the markets of Great Britain. This it was able to do successfully owing to the fact that the foreign-produced article paid higher duties.[5] Nevertheless, small quantities of the Spanish production continued to be imported by merchants as the result, doubtless, of a demand for this type of tobacco.[6] As to the continental markets, it was asserted by a contemporary that by the middle of the century the Chesapeake Bay staple had rather generally supplanted other tobacco not only in western and northern Europe but elsewhere outside of the Iberian peninsula and Russia.[7]

---

[3] For example, around 1750 the Albemarle region of North Carolina exported some 2,000 hogsheads, or roughly 1,600,000 pounds. As early as November 1702, the Assembly of the Lower Counties had declared that ten vessels were sent to England that year freighted with tobacco. See L. C. Gray: op. cit., I, 215; C. P. Nettels: The Money Supply of the American Colonies before 1720 (Madison, 1934), p. 121.

[4] There was little effort to manufacture tobacco products in the British colonies during the period under consideration, although snuff of inferior quality was produced. See J. M. Price: "The Beginnings of Tobacco Manufacture in Virginia," Virginia Magazine of History and Biography, LXIV, 3–29, and J. C. Robert: The Tobacco Kingdom: Plantation, Market, and Factory in Virginia and North Carolina, 1800–1860 (Durham, N.C., 1938), as well as his later volume The Story of Tobacco in America (New York, 1949).

[5] Under the law of 1660 Spanish and Brazilian tobacco was burdened with a duty of sixpence on the pound, while plantation tobacco entered at the rate of a penny a pound. See 12 Chas. II, c. 4, "Rates of Merchandise." C. M. MacInnes, in his The Early English Tobacco Trade (London, 1926, pp. 130–52), deals with this point.

The average price of Spanish tobacco in England in the seventeenth century, according to J. E. T. Rogers, was 9s. 3½d. a pound, that of the colonies 2s. 2½d. The colonial tobacco rapidly displaced the Spanish. See Rogers: A History of Agriculture and Prices in England (7 vols., Oxford, 1866–1902), V, 467–8, 782.

[6] In the late 1730's and early 1740's it appears that about 100,000 pounds of foreign-grown tobacco was brought into England. See Alfred Rive: "The Consumption of Tobacco since 1600," Economic History, I, 62.

[7] "Observations on Tobacco and Sugar in the American British Colonies," Wilmington Papers, 1735–1765, Library of Congress; see also G. L. Beer: Old Colonial System, 1660–1754 (2 vols., New York, 1912), I, 136. It would appear that tobacco grown in the Levant was largely consumed in southern Europe. See Joshua Gee: Trade and Navigation of Great Britain Considered (3rd edn., London, 1731), p. 51. Small amounts of Spanish-American tobacco were also sold in northern Europe. See R. D. Hussey: The Caracas Company, 1728–1784 (Oxford, 1934), p. 181.

According to the writer of *A Letter from a Merchant of the City of London*, the Sweet-Scented variety of tobacco was then largely grown in the sandy soil of Virginia and was consumed especially by the peoples of Great Britain and France; while Oronoko (Oronoco, Orinoco) tobacco, in which the planter of Maryland, using his bottom lands, specialized at that period, was ultimately marketed largely in Holland, Germany, and the Baltic.[8] It is true that on account of the high price of tobacco, especially during the war periods in the first half of the eighteenth century, farmers in Holland and Flanders and also in parts of Germany and France turned to its cultivation. This might have had the most serious consequences for the two tobacco colonies had not Parliament come to the assistance of the British exporters, enabling them by remission of heavy duties to sell at a price that discouraged competition, especially in northern Europe.[9]

The system of tobacco-culture prevailing in colonial America demanded a continuous supply of labour and virgin woodland. Tobacco-planters, as a group, were therefore speculators in labour, land, and their products, by necessity. Slave-breeding had established itself as a feature of the plantation economy, modified by whatever humane and Christian sentiments motivated the masters. The Englishman Edward Kimber, in his "Itinerant Observations on America" (which appeared in the *London Magazine* in 1745 and 1746), on the subject of slave-breeding, deplored some of the practices: "Such as the giving them [that is, the male slaves] a Number of Wives, or in short setting them up for Stallions to a whole Neighbourhood. . . ."[10] There is evidence that Virginia planters by the middle of the eighteenth century had been so successful in this field

---

[8] The Oronoko tobacco had a larger, heavier leaf than the Sweet-Scented. According to Bruce, it was sometimes more advantageous to grow the Oronoko than the other, and vice versa. See P. A. Bruce: *Economic History of Virginia . . .* (2 vols., New York, 1935), I, 436–8. For the best treatment of the varieties of tobacco grown in the Chesapeake area see A. P. Middleton: *Tobacco Coast*, pp. 97–9. Middleton points out that Sweet-Scented tobacco lost its place to Oronoko before the end of the eighteenth century and disappeared as a distinct variety. However, Captain J. F. D. Smyth, in his *A Tour of the United States of America . . .* (2 vols., London, 1784), II, 129, listed the following varieties of tobacco: "Hudson, Frederick Thick joint, Shoe-string, Thickset, Sweet-scented, and Oronoko." For an account of the varieties of native tobacco in the New World see W. A. Setchell: "Aboriginal Tobacco," *American Anthropologist*, new ser., XXIII, 397–8.

[9] "Observations on Tobacco," Wilmington Papers, Library of Congress; see also T. J. Wertenbaker: *The Planters of Colonial Virginia* (Princeton, 1922), pp. 148–50.

[10] For Kimber's "Observations," see *Maryland Historical Magazine*, LI, 315–36.

of activity that the natural multiplication of the stocks of slaves was almost sufficient to take care of their labour needs. Leading planters consequently became increasingly reluctant to face the very real problems involved in introducing the wild blacks from the Guinea coast into the midst of great numbers of domesticated American-born Negroes, especially in light of the fact that the price of the latter was thereby adversely affected.[11] Importation of slaves, however, continued and was encouraged by many influential Virginians.[12]

During the first half of the eighteenth century there was a rapid increase in the number of blacks in Virginia. The exact figures are apparently unattainable. In 1700 it was estimated that the total number was but 6,000; [13] in 1708, the number was placed at 12,000; [14] in 1715 there were supposed to be 23,000; [15] in 1756, somewhat more than 120,000,[16] with something over 170,000 whites.[17]

The growth of the slave population is in itself strong evidence of the profitable nature of tobacco-cultivation that fostered the great importations of blacks from the African jungles. It also indicates how favourable were the conditions for survival and increase by propagation of the Negro living in the region of the Chesapeake. This last factor gave the tobacco-planter an enormous advantage over the sugar-producer of the West Indies, since he was not obliged to lay out his capital continuously for the purchase of new increments of labour, as was the sugar-planter.

In addition to employing slaves in tobacco-culture, considerable

---

[11] The increasing hostility of Virginians to the foreign slave trade is stressed by J. C. Ballagh: A History of Slavery in Virginia (Baltimore, 1902), pp. 11–19.

[12] Colonel Lee to the Board of Trade, September 29, 1750, Shelburne Papers, 45:84–90, Clements Library. Between the years 1751 and 1763 15,000 slaves were brought to the Chesapeake Bay colonies, over 10,000 of whom were landed in Virginia. See A. P. Middleton: op. cit., pp. 136–7.

[13] Bruce: Economic History of Virginia, II, 108; see also the article "Virginia," The Encyclopaedia Britannica (11th edn.), giving the number as 20,000.

[14] Colonial Records of North Carolina (Raleigh, N.C., 1886–90), I, 692.

[15] George Chalmers: An Introduction to the History of the Revolt of the American Colonies (2 vols., London, 1782), II, 7.

[16] J. C. Ballagh: History of Slavery in Virginia, p. 12, accepts 120,156 as the number of blacks in the middle of the century; G. W. Williams: History of the Negro Race in America . . . (2 vols., New York, 1883, I, 133) places the number at over 100,000 in 1758; John Fiske: Old Virginia and Her Neighbors (2 vols., Boston, 1900, II, 272 and note) gives the figure of 250,000 in 1750, manifestly an exaggeration. Nevertheless, A. P. Middleton: op. cit., p. 136, indicates that by 1790, according to the first census, Virginia and Maryland had 395,663 Negroes.

[17] E. B. Greene and V. D. Harrington: American Population before . . . 1790 (New York, 1932), pp. 140–1.

white indentured-labour supply was still available in 1750. This was true especially of the less prosperous planters who could not afford to purchase slaves, but who found that whites indentured for long periods, as was the case of those transported for crime, were profitable.[18] The labour of whites, in fact, had been the chief resource of all tobacco-growers in Virginia in the seventeenth century, but was gradually displaced in favour of that of slaves by the greater planters, among other reasons because of the ease with which the supply of the latter could be maintained.[19]

As to the second factor, land, every successful planter felt that it was a matter of vital importance to have at hand, whenever possible a considerable acreage of virgin woodland, portions of which could be in process of clearing during the slack season between harvest and planting.[20]

Tobacco is well known for its soil-exhausting qualities.[21] The art of the application of fertilizers, while somewhat understood by English agriculturists at that period, was not widely practised even in England, except by the process of crop-rotation and the use of marl and manure, if available. In Virginia there had been no scientific study of soil-preservation and, according to the unknown author of *American Husbandry* published in 1775, the general practice was the most unscientific imaginable.[22]

---

[18] While non-convict white indentured labour was the characteristic type of seventeenth-century Virginia, after 1717 the convict element assumed some importance in that colony. See J. C. Ballagh: *White Servitude in the Colony of Virginia . . .* (Baltimore, 1895).

[19] See L. C. Gray: "Economic Efficiency and Competitive Advantages of Slavery under the Plantation System," *Agricultural History*, IV, 31–47, for the displacement of indentured servitude by slavery; see also J. C. Ballagh: *op cit.*, for the rise and decline of indentured labour. It is of interest that Colonel William Byrd of "Westover" was strongly opposed to Negro slavery. In 1739 he wrote to the Earl of Egmont of the bad effect of having 10,000 slaves in their midst and feared a "Servile War" that would "tinge our Rivers as wide as they are with blood." See the *American Historical Review*, "Documents," I, 88–9. But Byrd continued to hold slaves, as did many Quakers, as indicated in Chap. 1 of this volume.

[20] A. O. Craven in his *Soil Exhaustion as a Factor in the Agricultural History of Virginia and Maryland, 1606–1680* (Urbana, 1926, p. 69) gives the estimate of forty or fifty acres to each slave as a desirable proportion of land to labour. With the slave capable of caring for five acres it was possible to rotate land and thus allow worn-out lands to go back into woodland for some twenty years before again being brought under cultivation.

[21] *Ibid.*, p. 32.

[22] See *American Husbandry* (London, 1775), pp. 229–36. A newer edition of this valuable work, edited by H. J. Carman, was published in New York, 1939; see pp. 186–

Tobacco grew to perfection in the humus soils of bottom lands made available by turning into arable land the forest where the decomposition of vegetation had gone on for centuries. But the humus was extraordinarily difficult to preserve. The moment that the fields were cleared of trees and brush and the ground turned up by spade, hoe, and plough,[23] unless great precautions were taken, the torrential rains would wash the precious topsoil into creeks and rivers. The result was that after a time all that was left was the sandy clay of the subsoil. This tendency toward erosion was greatly accentuated on lands with even a moderate slope. On most tidewater plantations three or four years was considered the profitable life of tobacco-planting and then came the necessity of turning to new land.[24] The use of fertilizers and scientific contouring to prevent erosion would have created a different situation. Unfortunately, the colonial planters had neither the knowledge nor the skill for these agricultural methods. Nor was there a sufficiently large margin of profit to guarantee this protection to old lands so long as new woodlands were available at low prices.[25]

---

91 of it for the above reference to soil-exhaustion. It is true that the "penning" of cattle on tobacco lands was practised by some planters, which aided in the maintenance of the fertility of the soil. For example, Richard Corbin, the owner of several Virginia tobacco plantations, stressed, in writing to his agent, the great importance of penning. See his letter to James Semple, January 1, 1759, Documentary History of American Industrial Society: Plantation and Frontier, 1649–1863 (ed. U. B. Phillips, 2 vols., Cleveland, 1910), I, 110.

[23] The plough, while not unknown in colonial Virginia, was little used in tobacco-culture owing to the presence on the land that had been freshly cleared of numerous trees with the stumps left standing. See P. A. Bruce: Economic History of Virginia, I, 298.

[24] See A. O. Craven: op. cit., pp. 28–32. Of interest in this connection is the comparable use of the lands by the Indians at the coming of the whites. They, also, were limited to three years of profitable planting on cleared lands, not only because of soil-exhaustion but also because their rude agricultural economy could not conquer the inroads of volunteer grass.

[25] The existence in 1748 of large bodies of fresh lands in the tidewater counties of Virginia is indicated by the establishment of new tobacco warehouses which sprang up at distant points from existing ones. Two new warehouses were in that year ordered erected for Henrico County, two each for Nansemond and Northumberland, with an additional warehouse for King William, New Kent, and Westmoreland counties respectively. See W. W. Hening: The Statutes at Large . . . of Virginia (13 vols., Richmond, 1809–23), VI, 174–5. Further, many tobacco-planters, having exhausted the soil on their estates, sold them to new settlers as corn lands and thereupon moved "backwards with their negroes, cattle and tools, to take up fresh land . . . ; this is common and will continue so long as good land is to be had upon navigable rivers" (American Husbandry [1939 edn.], pp. 164–5).

There was, moreover, another inducement to impel the planters to engage in the clearing of new lands. Perhaps hundreds of hands would otherwise remain idle for weeks unless put to some such winter labour as the clearing of portions of the plantation woodlands. Indeed, the preservation of morale on the plantation demanded this type outlet for slave activity during the slack season.[26]

The price of land in Virginia naturally varied according to its quality and location. For example, in Northumberland County in the Tidewater, fifty acres of land brought 10,000 pounds of lawful tobacco and £2.3 currency money of the province in the 1740's; at the same time as high as £25 of current money was also paid for the same amount of land and £50 current money for 128 acres and improvements.[27] As for the Piedmont, Burnaby in 1759 found that the higher one went from the river bottoms up toward the mountains the greater was the value of the land, "for it grows more strong, and of a deeper clay."[28]

While the centre of tobacco-cultivation was still in the Tidewater, by 1750 the planters had made more than a beginning in the exploitation of the Piedmont, where hundreds of them had acquired lands and were engaged in tobacco-production. The Piedmont, however, was to remain for some time to come, as emphasized in the chapter on Virginia, a region settled predominantly by white families of the pioneer type comparable to those living in the back country of Pennsylvania, Maryland, and the Carolinas. Thousands of them were making a comfortable living producing general farm crops for the market. The extreme western limit of the commercial production of tobacco in 1750 may be gauged with a fair degree of accuracy by the distribution of public warehouses for the inspection and storage of the crop before sale. A list of these warehouses in the journal of the Virginia Council for that year indicates that the following counties from north to south were the western limits of tobacco culture as the principal staple: Fairfax, Prince William, Stafford, Spotsylvania, Hanover, Henrico, Chesterfield, Prince George, Surry, the Isle of

---

[26] For model instructions for the care of slaves and their constant employment see those of Richard Corbin to his agent, James Semple, dated January 1, 1759, *Documentary History of American Industrial Society*, I, 109–12.

[27] Northumberland County Record Book, 1743–1749, under date of March 4, 1744/5, Virginia State Library.

[28] Andrew Burnaby: *Travels through the Middle Settlements in North America in the Years 1759 and 1760* (London, 1775), pp. 6–7.

Wight, and Nansemond.[29] It would, however, be a mistake to think that tobacco was not produced for sale, at least in small quantities, in the more western counties. For example, to the Falmouth warehouses in Stafford County was brought the crop grown in Culpeper County and even in distant Frederick in the Valley of Virginia.[30]

In certain respects tobacco-cultivation differed widely from that of sugar. To produce the latter commodity successfully at this period required the preliminary expenditure of a considerable fortune in the purchase of the proper units of land, labour, and plantation animals, and in the erection of a mill, a distillery, and other costly buildings. The Virginia tobacco plantation, on the other hand, varied from an inexpensively furnished farm of a few acres on which the owner lived and worked, perhaps quite alone or with the assistance of a black or two, or the same number of indentured whites, to the lordly estates of such families as the Fairfaxes, the Lees, the Masons, the Washingtons, the Nelsons, and the Custises, where scores of blacks, and even hundreds, as in the case of the plantation of John Mason, were living and labouring under the systematic direction of the master and his overseers.[31] For example, the record books of a typical tidewater county, Northumberland, for the year 1745 lists the inventories of twenty-six freemen, only six of whom were owners of slaves; of the six, one possessed twenty-seven, another had twenty-two, two owned seven each, one had two, and finally one individual was credited with one slave and two indentured whites, the latter with one and two years still to serve respectively.[32] The typical tide-

---

29 See the *Executive Journals of the Council of Colonial Virginia* (ed. H. R. McIlwaine and W. L. Hall, 5 vols., Richmond, Va., 1925–45), V, 327–31. Immediately to the west of these counties were already Culpeper, Orange, Louisa, Albemarle, Goochland, Amelia, Lunenburg, Brunswick, Sussex, and Southampton counties. See *Journal of the House of Burgesses of Virginia, 1752–1758,* pp. vii–viii, for counties in existence in 1752. In Maryland all the tobacco warehouses designated in 1747 were in the tidewater area. See *Archives of Maryland,* XLIV, 608–9.

30 *Journal of the House of Burgesses, 1752–1758,* p. 11. See "Henry's Map of Virginia," *William and Mary Quarterly,* 1st ser., XIV, 8566, for the region of tobacco-culture.

31 "Gunston Hall," the Mason mansion on the Potomac, was built in the late 1750's; for a description of it see the chapter on "The Empire of the Old Dominion" in this volume.

32 See Northumberland Record Book, 1743–1749, Virginia State Library. In a list of twenty-three estates given for the year 1746, only eleven were credited with slaves. Of these there was one with thirty-four, another with eleven, two with eight each, two with six each, one with five, another with four, one with three, and two with but one each.

water plantation of the better sort, such as "Mount Vernon," seems to have comprehended a rather considerable body of land, from 1,000 to 6,000 acres; it was almost sure to enjoy a water frontage, and, whenever practical, the great house of the master and his family would be built on an elevation sloping down to the shore and in view of the private wharf. To the rear of the mansion were the Negro quarters and the barns and drying-sheds, and beyond these the open fields skirted by the wilderness of the woodlands. Moreover, for production purposes these great plantations frequently were subdivided into farm units, on some of which were tenants.[33]

An impression of the vast extent of hand labour required in tobacco-culture may be gained by examining the processes involved in it in the middle of the eighteenth century — processes which, in the main, survived in Virginia until the Civil War.

Then, as now, the plant, although produced by a small seed, if allowed to grow in rich bottom lands without interruption would reach a height of over five feet, having clammy, hairy stalks and bearing leaves of a yellowish-green colour of greatest size at the bottom of the stalk. This plant, indigenous to America, was found growing wild by the early settlers. But wild tobacco, while consumed by the natives, was not fit for the market and South American seed was imported. Gradually a system of cultivation and curing was evolved that, having met the test of experience, was enforced by law to maintain quality production in its most important features.

The tobacco seed of carefully selected plants was sown in beds, where it sprouted. After growing for a month these sprouts were removed during the first rainy weather and transplanted to the fields, where the earth was mounded about them. Within the space of another month they would grow to the height of nearly a foot, after which they were topped and deprived of their lower leaves. As a rule, only seven or eight leaves were then allowed to remain on the stalk that they might be the better fed and become perfect specimens.[34] Within six weeks following this process the plants received

Ibid. For landowners in Hanover County in the 1730's see R. D. Meade: Patrick Henry, Patriot in the Making (Philadelphia & New York, 1957), p. 43.

[33] For accounts of various of Washington's tenant farmers see the Diaries of Washington, 1748–1799 (ed. J. C. Fitzpatrick, 4 vols., New York, 1925), I, 163–9.

[34] In 1632 it was provided by law in Virginia that no more than nine leaves should be picked from any plant. Indeed, so vitally interested was the government in this question of producing only the best grades of tobacco that the constables of each parish were required to view the fields to see that the requirements of the law were met, especially

their full growth, and during the interval it was necessary to keep the ground about them free of weeds and to remove the suckers and the hornworms each week. The leaves would, after this, begin to turn a brownish colour, to spot, and to thicken — all signs of ripening. As fast as this occurred the plants were cut down and piled into heaps and allowed to lie overnight for sweating; they were then carried to the curing-sheds. There every plant was hung up with some space between it and the next, remaining thus for a period of three to six weeks. The next step was to take the plants down during a period of wet weather and pile them into heaps upon sticks in the tobacco house, where they remained covered up for a week or fortnight in order to sweat. After this the bulk was opened on a wet day and the stalks stripped of leaves. The latter were then sorted, the top leaves being the choicest and the bottom the least desirable. The sorted piles were now ready to be packed in hogsheads, the leaves lying flat — a process also requiring rainy weather.[35] In the middle of the eighteenth century the hogsheads contained between 800 and 1,000 pounds of tobacco, the exact weight of each hogshead varying somewhat from time to time according to weather conditions and shrinkage.[36]

The step following the curing and packing was the transportation of the tobacco to the most conveniently located warehouse. This was

those concerning restrictions on second-growth tobacco from suckers. In 1742 when the representatives from the county of Accomac [Accomack] proposed to repeal the laws for the inspection of the fields, the Burgesses voted against it. See *Journal of the House of Burgesses of Virginia, 1742–1749*, p. 19.

[35] See Fenning and Collyer: *A New System of Geography* (1765), II, 660, for an account of these processes in Virginia; see also *American Husbandry* (ed. H. J. Carman), pp. 159–61; J. F. D. Smyth: *A Tour of the United States of America* (1784), II, 134–6; L. C. Gray: *History of Agriculture in the Southern United States to 1860*, I, 215–17; and A. P. Middleton: *Tobacco Coast*, pp. 99–101.

[36] For example, according to the collector of the customs of Penryn in Cornwall, England, a hogshead of tobacco received from Virginia in 1752 contained "according to answer" 881 pounds, according to certificate and oath 872 pounds, and according to inspection 868 pounds. See "Copy of Several Representations made by the Register-General of Tobacco, 1751–1760," Lansdowne Papers, 661:49–150, British Museum. For the regulations regarding hogsheads see L. C. Gray: *op. cit.*, I, 220–30.

The size of the hogshead was regulated by act of Parliament earlier in the century (10 and 11 Wm. III, c. 21), and, after 1751, by an act (24 Geo. II, c. 41) for the more effectual securing of tobacco duties. This the Governors of the tobacco colonies were instructed to enforce. See *Acts of the Privy Council, Col. Ser., 1745–1766*, 200. The Maryland law of 1747 provided that the length of the barrel stave should be forty-eight inches and the diameter of the hogshead at the bulge should not be more than seventy inches. See *Archives of Maryland*, XLIV, 602.

required by both Virginia and Maryland law.[37] One hundred and four Virginia warehouses and seventy-four in Maryland were scattered throughout the tobacco staple area in the middle of the eighteenth century. Usually some twelve or fourteen miles apart,[38] they were invariably in locations accessible by water — either by direct approach or close to the branch of a river.[39] The planter therefore experienced little difficulty in delivering his tobacco to the warehouse. If by water, the process involved transportation by means of barges; if by land, the rolling of the hogsheads by a slave gang, or by carting, or by a single horse drawing a cask through the centre of which passed a pole projecting at either end.[40] There were generally at hand at the warehouse two inspectors to examine and weigh the hogsheads. They were expected to refuse the contents if below minimum lawful standard of quality and, if above, to so stamp the casks.[41]

Unfortunately, the inspector's stamp was not always a guarantee of the quality of the tobacco. For example, in 1753 Governor Dinwiddie in his address to the Virginia Assembly declared: "I am

[37] Hening: Laws of Virginia, IV, 32–6, V, 125. Before 1747 Maryland did not have an effective inspection law to guarantee the quality of tobacco exports. See V. J. Wyckoff: Tobacco Regulations in Maryland (Baltimore, 1936), Chap. 6. However, in the above year a detailed act was passed based largely upon the Virginia law of 1730. It was still in force in 1750. For the Maryland law of 1747 see Archives of Maryland, XLIV, 595–638.

[38] See Hening: op. cit., VI, 172–5; see also a list of Virginia tobacco warehouses in Executive Journals of the Council (V, 327–33) for the year 1750. For a list of warehouses established in Maryland by the law of 1747 see Archives of Maryland, XLIV, 608–9.

[39] The counties may be rated as to their relative importance as tobacco-producers in 1748, on the basis of the number of warehouses established by law, making allowances, however, for the fact that crops were always taken to the nearest warehouse whether or not it was within the county. In Virginia, Henrico comes first with seven; King William, Richmond, and Essex follow with six each; Accomac, Lancaster, Fairfax, and Westmorland, with five each; Gloucester, King and Queen, King George, Northumberland, and York, with four each; Hanover, Isle of Wight, Norfolk, New Kent, Prince George, and Stafford, with three each; Caroline, Charles City, Middlesex, Northampton, Surry, and Spotsylvania, with two each; Elizabeth City, Prince William, Warwick, and James City, with one each, See Hening: Laws of Virginia, VI, 172–5.

[40] See Hugh Jones: The Present State of Virginia (ed. R. L. Morton, Chapel Hill, N.C., 1956), p. 88. It appears that the practice of rolling the tobacco casks had fallen into disrepute in Virginia by the middle of the century, although the Maryland planters still utilized it. See the Maryland Gazette, May 5, 1747, and C. P. Gould: Money and Transportation in Maryland, 1720–1765 (Johns Hopkins University Studies, Baltimore, 1915), pp. 142–4.

[41] Rejected tobacco had to be burned in the owner's presence. For a list of Virginia tobacco-inspectors appointed in 1750 "in Consequence of the last Tobacco Law," see Executive Journals of the Council, V, 327–31.

heartily sorry, for the bad Accounts we have of the Price of Tobacco at Home, and of its bad Quality; which I conceive must be greatly owing to the Neglect and Dishonesty of the Inspectors." [42] He thereupon suggested a reduction in the number of warehouses and the appointment of an inspector general for each river, who would examine the books of the inspectors. The latter were expected to maintain exact accounts of all tobacco received and a history of all tobacco transactions, and were, moreover, empowered to issue, to those who had deposited their hogsheads at the warehouse, tobacco notes, called either "crop notes" or "transfer notes," which were regarded as provincial legal tender and with which the planter might settle his obligations. [43]

The rapid growth in the population, white and black, and the equally rapid exploitation of new lands led to an increase in the volume of tobacco exported from Virginia in the 1740's and the early 1750's. This increase amounted to over 7,000,000 pounds between the years 1745 and 1754, with a total export in the latter year of 45,722,000 pounds. [44] And it took place in spite of the fact that hundreds of thousands of acres in the Tidewater that had at one time produced large crops of tobacco were now little better than waste

---

[42] *Journal of the House of Burgesses, 1752–1758*, p. 103. In 1747 John Baxter, inspector at Quantico warehouse in the county of Prince William, was found guilty of "many base Crimes in the execution of his Office" (*Executive Journals of the Council*, V, 247).

[43] Transfer notes were employed in both Virginia and Maryland to authorize the warehouse inspector to transfer to the bearer either the amount of "lawful" tobacco designated on its face, without reference to its origin, or its equivalent in money. After October 1 of each year the inspector was required to sell all transfer tobacco in his possession at public auction at the door of the court house to satisfy holders of the notes. Taxes and other obligations of this nature were usually paid with transfer notes. Although it had passed inspection, the tobacco covered by these notes was apt to be of an inferior quality.

Crop notes, on the other hand, called for the surrender of particular hogsheads of tobacco left at the warehouse. The crop-note tobacco was, it goes without saying, the choice tobacco.

For regulations on the disposal of Virginia tobacco see Hening: *Laws of Virginia*, V, 125, 133–8; VI, 155, 163, 168, 190, 252, 474–5. For treatment of this subject see L. C. Gray: *History of Agriculture* . . . , I, 228.

[44] However, in 1702 Virginia exported 36,747,192 pounds. Thereupon a decrease took place in the amount exported. In 1714 it was 28,100,265 pounds. See R. A. Brock: "A Succinct Account of Tobacco in Virginia," *Tenth Census of the United States*, III, 242, and A. O. Craven: *Soil Exhaustion* . . . , p. 66. In 1748 calculations of the total tobacco imported into Great Britain ranged from 72,000,000 pounds down to 55,800,000 pounds. See [Adam Anderson]: *An Historical and Chronological Deduction of the Origin of Commerce* (rev. edn. by W. Combe, 4 vols., London, 1787–9), III, 546.

lands.[45] This volume poured upon the market tended to keep the price of tobacco at a low level. In the 1750's it was selling within the province for fifteen shillings Virginia currency, or nine shillings sterling the hundredweight, or somewhat over a penny sterling a pound.[46] Its price in England in 1749 ranged from twopence to twopence-halfpenny sterling a pound, if for re-exportation, and from eightpence to eightpence-halfpenny, if for home consumption.[47] It is therefore not surprising that the price aroused little enthusiasm on the part of the planters, many of whom began turning their attention to securing a desirable substitute crop for their acres.[48]

The growing of indigo at this period seemed to hold out great inducements to some Virginians because of the special encouragement offered by Parliament for its production and importation into Great Britain.[49] By 1757 a considerable quantity was being grown in the James River area. William Allason, acting in Virginia for the Glasgow tobacco firm of Alexander Walker and Company, wrote to his employer in the latter part of 1757 predicting a great decrease

---

[45] The results of soil-exhaustion and the consequent shifting to new tobacco fields is well illustrated by the following clause from "An Act for Amending the Staple of Tobacco . . ." passed in 1748: "And that from and after the ninth day of November, the warehouses at Coan shall be discontinued; and new warehouses erected at Ferry-Neck, on the upper side of Coan River, on the land of Rodham Kenner, dec'd, and on the land of Major Waughop, on the other side of Coan River; to be under the same inspection" (Hening: *Laws of Virginia*, VI, 175). Coan is in Northumberland County.

[46] See, for example, the agreement between Anselm Bailey and William Allason of June 30, 1757, Allason Papers, Virginia State Library; see also L. C. Gray: "The Market Surplus Problem of Colonial Tobacco," *William and Mary Quarterly*, 2nd ser., VII, 232–5.
The problem of the oversupply of tobacco is illustrated by a report of the Board of Trade to the House of Lords of June 5, 1714, to the effect that several ships had lain in the Thames for twenty months with some 7,000 hogsheads on board because of the high duties. See C. P. Nettels: *Money Supply of the American Colonies before 1720*, p. 63, n.

[47] Extract of a letter from London of November 19, 1749, printed in the *Maryland Gazette*, April 4, 1750. For charges against the British merchants of price-fixing and of other means of depriving the planters of their profits, see A. O. Craven: *Soil Exhaustion . . .* , pp. 49–50.

[48] By reason of the numerous charges that faced the planter in disposing of his crop abroad it was estimated in 1730 that his net gain on a hogshead of tobacco sold abroad for £27 was but 15s., certainly a discouragingly low return. See P. R. Kelbaugh: "The Tobacco Trade in Maryland, 1700–1725," *Maryland Historical Magazine*, XXVI, 1–33, for this and other information regarding the discouragements under which the grower of Maryland tobacco laboured in the early part of the century.

[49] By 21 Geo. II, c. 30, a premium of sixpence a pound was paid on all indigo grown in the British plantations that was imported into the Kingdom. This was continued by subsequent legislation.

in the number of hogsheads of tobacco. "The planters who have gone upon the Indigo this year," he declared, "will profit 3, 4, & some 5 times as much as had they continued in Tob.°, nothing else is talked of here but Indigo." [50] Somewhat later in that year he informed another correspondent that the following year very little tobacco would be grown near the James River, "every one gone upon the Indigo scheme." [51] Indigo production, however, never assumed great importance in the economic life of Virginia.

One factor involved in the low returns on the sale of tobacco in the eighteenth century was the many incidental charges involved in selling tobacco on commission [52] through the merchants of London, Bristol, Liverpool, Whitehaven, Bideford, and Plymouth respectively. [53] Another factor — at least as so charged by the planter group — was the existence of secret understandings among the British tobacco-importers whereby prices were fixed and kept at a low level.

While there is doubtless a measure of truth in the planter point of view, it seems quite unlikely that any arrangements regarding prices to be paid could have been maintained effectively for any length of time, especially in face of the very keen competition that undoubtedly existed at certain periods between various mercantile houses for the annual crop. [54] For example, in spite of the fact that the amount of tobacco exported by Maryland and Virginia did not increase but rather decreased during the first forty years of the eight-

[50] William Allason to Alexander Walker and Co., September 1757, Allason Papers, Virginia State Library. On December 1, 1756, Allason signed an agreement with James Baird, Jr., and Alexander Walker to act as their agent. The terms of this agreement are to be found in the above-mentioned papers.

[51] William Allason to Robert Young, September 12, 1757, ibid. Early in the century there was a tendency for Virginians to turn from tobacco to the planting of cotton and flax; this was regarded as adverse to England's interest, and Lieutenant Governor Edward Nott was instructed by the Board of Trade to discourage it. See Board of Trade to Governor Nott, March 1, 1706, C.O. 5:1362, p. 7; see also C. P. Nettels: The Money Supply . . . , p. 138.

[52] For a discussion of the above point see A. O. Craven: Soil Exhaustion . . . , pp. 49–50.

[53] The following figures illustrate the distribution of the tobacco importations into England for the year 1732: London received 28,860,300 pounds, Bristol 4,508,206 pounds, Liverpool 2,430,562 pounds, Whitehaven 1,472,069 pounds, Bideford 1,408,886 pounds, and Plymouth 548,265 pounds, with a total of 41,683,833 pounds received by all British ports. See P.R.O., Treas. 64. 273.

[54] "Besides you are all Rivals in the Trade & are as jealous of one another as you would be for a mistress," wrote William Byrd, 2nd., in 1733, referring to the interest of the British in the Virginia tobacco trade. See "Letters of William Byrd, 2d, of Westover, Va.," Virginia Magazine of History and Biography, IX, 115.

eenth century,[55] Whitehaven almost succeeded in trebling the amount that it received between the years 1712 and 1739/40, with a total of 4,419,218 pounds for the latter year.[56] It is improbable that the Whitehaven merchants were able to achieve this happy result without offering inducements which brought the tobacco in increasing volume to their warehouses at the expense of the merchants of other towns. Further, with the union of the kingdoms of England and Scotland, the Scots of Glasgow plunged fully into the tobacco trade, with which they had long been dabbling surreptitiously, and apparently offered such inducements that a large proportion of this commerce was diverted from the English ports in favour of their own. Even Whitehaven in the 1740's and 1750's had to witness the decay of a business that had been so successfully developed.[57] In fact, as early as 1721 the English merchants were led to make a public issue of what they felt were the unfair and even lawless practices of the Scots in drawing this trade to themselves.[58] As a result the customs service was reorganized and new regulations were passed for securing tobacco duties and for putting an end to frauds in tobacco exports.[59]

"A most terrible confederacy," declared John Gibson, an eighteenth-century Glasgow merchant, "was entered into by almost all the tobacco-merchants in South-Britain against the trade of Glasgow." [60] The growth of the tobacco trade of that city is indicated by the value of the bonds that importers gave to customs officers at the time of the arrival of the tobacco ships. From May 1707 to September 1708 the value of the bonds amounted to £10,746.19.6; for the fiscal year 1724–5 from September to September, to £65,144.18.11½; for that of 1749–50, to £253,405.5.4½; for that of 1774–5 to £598,-065.18.[61] Before the outbreak of the American Revolution, out of a

---

[55] See R. A. Brock: "A Succinct Account of Tobacco in Virginia," *Tenth Census of the United States*, III, 212.

[56] P. Ford: "Tobacco and Coal; a Note on the Economic History of Whitehaven," *Economica*, IX, 192–6.

[57] *Ibid.*

[58] See *Journals of the House of Commons* (1721), XIX, 674; (1722), XX, 63–4, 104, 107–8; see also Alfred Rive: "The Consumption of Tobacco since 1600," *Economic History*, I, 67–9.

[59] See 9 Geo. I, c. 22, passed in 1722.

[60] John Gibson: *History of Glasgow* . . . (Glasgow, 1777), p. 207.

[61] See "The Account of the Revenue in Scotland under the Management of the Commissioners of the Customs which arose from that Branch thereof commonly called

total of 90,000 hogsheads which Great Britain secured from America, 49,000, or over one half, were received by this Scottish city alone.[62] Thus, in 1771 some 47,000,000 pounds of tobacco were carried to the Clyde.[63]

The story of this remarkable achievement of the Glasgow merchants has never been fully told. Eighteenth-century Scottish writers emphasized the frugality of the Glasgow merchants and their agents, while English rivals stressed their dishonest methods. Behind all other explanations rests the fact that they, by means of their thrifty, if sometimes questionable, methods, were able to outbargain the English merchants in offering goods in return for tobacco.[64] That they could do this is not surprising in view of the fact that Glasgow had an advantage over London of some two or three weeks in making the voyage to the Chesapeake by reason of its more favourable situation — a voyage not only quicker but safer in time of war.[65] Significant is the further fact that the Scots did not wait for tobacco through the slow channels of establishing business connections with the Chesapeake Bay planters by correspondence. Agents were sent to set up stores and private warehouses at commercially strategic points. There they not only handled tobacco on commission but most frequently paid whatever was necessary to purchase the quantity desired for waiting Scottish ships. In other words, there can be little doubt that the appearance of the Scots in Virginia was highly advantageous to tobacco-growers, as it intensified the competition for the yearly crop and helped to guarantee the businesslike planter the limit of value for his crop.[66]

the Impost on Tobacco for the year 1707-8 . . . 1774-1775," Register Office, Edinburgh.

[62] See George Eyre-Todd: *The Story of Glasgow* (Glasgow, 1911), pp. 85-90, and James Pagan: *Sketches of the History of Glasgow* (Glasgow, 1847).

[63] See J. M. Price: "The Rise of Glasgow in the Chesapeake Tobacco Trade, 1707-1775," *William and Mary Quarterly*, 3rd ser., XI, 180.

[64] Alexander Walter of the Glasgow firm of Walker and Baird throws light upon the advantages that accrued to the planter who consigned his tobacco to Scottish rather than English merchants. Writing in 1759 to the firm's Virginia agent, he said: "You can easily show them the gr^{te} difference of the charges here; by what it is in England & that they'll save a good deal by that, neither freight or insurance to Clyde is near so high nor so many plagued charges wch runs away wth the whole almost" (Alexander Walker to William Allason, March 1, 1759, Allason Papers, Virginia State Library).

[65] See again J. M. Price in the *William and Mary Quarterly*, 3rd ser., XI, 187-8.

[66] "Because Glasgow agents were frequently more interested in buying [tobacco] in a hurry than in watching the price, they often drove up the price — to the great annoyance of the solicitors of consignments and native buyers," writes J. M. Price in his

In seeking to account for the problem that confronted the planter of the Chesapeake Bay in his endeavour to maintain profitable tobacco-production, we find that the chief source of difficulty lay perhaps not so much in the regulations of the mother country or in the unfair practices of the British merchants, but rather in the continuous opening up of new lands that came into competition with the older plantation areas. The importance of this did not escape Thomas Jefferson, who found that those who were growing tobacco on the fresh and fertile soils of the West were able to sell at so low a price that it could not be produced advantageously on the depleted soils of the lower Tidewater.[67]

The tidewater tobacco-planter of Virginia in 1750 was, therefore, differently circumstanced than, for example, the rice-planter of tidewater South Carolina, who had nothing to fear from the back-country development beyond the region of the fresh-water cypress swamps. In fact, that development rather added to his prosperity, since it afforded him needed plantation food supplies at less financial outlay than had been the case when earlier he had been obliged to procure his flour and meat from the colonies to the northward. Nevertheless, while the Virginia tobacco-grower suffered in comparison with the rice-planter, it may be asserted that he was far more favourably situated than the owner of a sugar plantation in the British West Indies — so frequently thought of as being in the more enviable position. Although the problems of the sugar-planter are considered in a later chapter of this volume, it may be emphasized here that he was faced with continuous high costs in replacing his labour supply because of the relatively brief span of profitable working years of

article on the Chesapeake tobacco trade previously mentioned. But all writers do not agree that the Scots helped the tobacco-planters; see William and Mary Quarterly, 3rd ser., XI, 190. J. H. Soltow ("The Role of Williamsburg in Virginia Economy, 1750–1775," William and Mary Quarterly, 3rd ser., XV, 466–82) stresses the point that planters and tobacco merchants were accustomed to meet in Williamsburg, where they agreed on the prices to be paid for tobacco. Thereupon purchases would be made wherever it was offered for sale in the province. Prices actually paid would of course depend upon its quality as well as upon other factors.

[67] For Jefferson's views see Notes on the State of Virginia, by Thomas Jefferson (ed. William Peden, Chapel Hill, N.C., 1955), p. 166; see also L. C. Gray: History of Agriculture in the Southern United States to 1860, I, 233.

A situation analogous to this in some ways existed in the United States during the decade subsequent to the First World War in the wheat trade. Although the older wheat-raising areas suffered huge losses in attempting to sell wheat in an already glutted market, the farmers of western Kansas in putting their prairie lands under cultivation for the first time were able to prosper with wheat as low as fifty cents a bushel.

the Negro in the West Indies. Further, because of the hurricanes that swept the islands every fall,[68] he had to anticipate occasional very heavy losses from damage to valuable buildings the replacement of which involved importing lumber and other construction materials. Moreover, he laboured under the necessity of importing much of his food supplies — at best an expensive method of providing for his workers. Finally, he was forced to meet a destructive type of competition from his rivals in the French sugar islands, who were heavily subsidized by their own government and thereby were able not only to undersell him in the open market but to drive him from many of those areas of trade supposed to be closed to the French — such, for example, as the markets of the continental British colonies — and to threaten him even in the British Isles by the illegal introduction of their products through British traders.

In contrast, the tobacco-planter had the advantage of being able, as a rule, to maintain his labour population without buying new slaves periodically. The upkeep of the buildings on the tobacco plantation was but slight as compared with that on a sugar plantation, with excellent building-materials frequently growing on the estate of the Virginia planter or, at the worst, not far removed from it. The cost of food for the slaves was also moderate, as most of it was generally produced on the plantation.[69] In addition, the markets for the Chesapeake tobacco were secure.

In the seventeenth century the English Parliament had sternly forbidden the production of tobacco within both England and Ireland.[70] This had led to the destruction of many tobacco plantations established in the Bristol area by wealthy merchants as well as others in Warwickshire, Oxfordshire, and the southwestern counties of Gloucestershire, Worcestershire, Monmouthshire, and Herefordshire.[71] Consequently it would appear that but little tobacco was

---

[68] See [Charles Leslie]: A New History of Jamaica . . . (London, 1740), p. 40.

[69] Robert Carter of "Nomini Hall," a great planter (1728–1804) who owned 70,000 acres of land, gave great attention to crops other than tobacco on his various plantations, which were operated with business efficiency. As a result of sound planning he avoided going heavily into debt to British agents. See Louis Morton: Robert Carter of Nomini Hall: A Virginia Tobacco Planter of the Eighteenth Century (Williamsburg, 1941).

[70] See 12 Chas. II, c. 34; 15 Chas. II, c. 7, Par. 18; and 22 and 23 Chas. II, c. 26. For the continuation in the eighteenth century of the prohibition on growing tobacco see 5 Geo. I, c. 11, Par. 19. The restriction was finally extended to Scotland, but not until after the period under consideration.

[71] See, for example, The Case of Dorothy Gray . . . Late of the City of Bristol

raised in the British Isles in the eighteenth century. It follows that, British plantation tobacco monopolized not only these markets but also those of most of the northern European countries. Therefore, if prices were unreasonably low at times, the overproduction of the American planters was largely responsible for this self-made situation.

Although many planters were committed to maintain business relations with particular British mercantile houses by obligations, some of which were inherited, nevertheless, the impression gained from studying the history of Virginia in the 1740's and 1750's is that many tobacco-growers were free to dispose of their crops as they saw fit and were doing so with shrewd business acumen.[72] Writing from Brandon on the James River in 1757, William Allason, who was in charge of a store established at that place for the Scottish firm of Alexander Walker and Company, complained of the independent attitude of the planters: "Those who had ready Tob° would not part with it but on such terms as I am sure the purchaser must be a considerable Sufferer." He further declared that there were "more new stores [in this region] than ever was known before; its a mystery to many where they are to be Supply'd with from, every one seeming to be fonder of purchasing than another, which must considerably raise

---

(1703). Her husband, John Gray, had petitioned in 1694 for payment of his services in destroying tobacco-growing about Bristol. This is printed as a broadside, a copy of which is in the Brackinridge Collection, Bristol Reference Library. The history of this struggle against English tobacco-planting is set forth in various acts of the Privy Council. For orders in council relative to this, covering the period from the year 1626 to 1689 see *Acts of the Privy Council, Col. Ser., 1613–1680*, pp. 107–8, passim; 1680–1720, pp. 7, passim. For orders to send troops into Gloucestershire, Worcestershire, Warwickshire, and Herefordshire in 1689 to assist in destroying tobacco crops see *ibid.*, p. 135; see also L. C. Gray: "The Market Surplus Problem," *William and Mary Quarterly*, 2nd ser., VII, 238, and Alfred Rive: "The Consumption of Tobacco since 1600," *Economic History*, I, 60.

72 Much of the tobacco was sent to Great Britain to be sold on commission and frequently the British broker would handle the consignments of a large number of planters who had forwarded their hogsheads in the same ship. For example, in 1755 forty-three consignees sent 164 hogsheads on board the *Clio* to John Burns of Bristol. The total value of these was £6,292.10.7, of which Burns received £188.14.10 handling commission. See "The Account of John Burns," August 1755, Virginia Historical Society, File 3. Washington shipped much of his tobacco to the London firm of Robert Cary & Co. See the *Diaries of Washington*, I, 168–9. For the relations of tobacco-planters to London merchants at an earlier period see J. S. Bassett: "The Relation between the Virginia Planter and the London Merchant," *American Historical Association Report*, 1901, I, 553–75.

the price of Tob° here tho' possibly not at home." [73] Before being able to dispose of most of his goods on terms satisfactory to himself he was obliged to travel 1,200 miles. He could not interest the planters either on the Potomac or the Rappahannock, although he finally succeeded in disposing of all but £1,000 worth of his stock for spring tobacco.

The customary mark-up of these Scottish tobacco merchants was from seventy to seventy-five per cent over the price which they themselves paid for the goods at home clear of incidental charges, with a discount of ten per cent for immediate payment in tobacco. However, Allason, a shrewd Scottish trader, succeeded in raising his profits twelve and one half per cent above that margin. [74] In comparing this profit with the margin of 300 per cent increase secured by the Cales Trading Company of Spain, enjoying a monopoly of trade with certain of the Spanish colonies, it does not seem excessive.

To transport the annual tobacco crop to Great Britain and take care of the other commercial needs of the province required the services of over 200 ships, about one fourth of which were owned by Virginians, according to a report made in 1743 by Dinwiddie, then acting as Surveyor General of the customs for the Southern District in North America. [75] The typical tobacco ship carried a burden of from 200 to 300 tons and was capable of transporting from 300 to 500 hogsheads of tobacco. These hogsheads, weighing between 800 and 1,000 pounds, would total some 375,000 pounds of tobacco. [76] Upon this cargo duties were collected after the arrival of the ship in Great Britain.

For over a century tobacco had been enumerated under the law. [77]

---

[73] William Allason to Alexander Walker, July 25, 1757, Allason Papers, Virginia State Library.

[74] Allason to Walker, August 26, 1757, ibid.

[75] P. S. Flippin: The Royal Government in Virginia, 1624–1775 (Richmond, 1931), p. 51; see also A. P. Middleton: Tobacco Coast . . . , pp. 239–43.

[76] For example, the ship President left Virginia in 1748 with 469 hogsheads. See Executive Journals of the Council, V, 280. The ship Jenny of 240 tons burden, according to a charter-party drawn up January 24, 1770, could be loaded to the extent of 400 hogsheads. See Broadside, Virginia Historical Society. Planters sought to get as much tobacco as possible into a hogshead in view of the fact that the freight rate for a ton from both Virginia and Maryland was based upon 4 hogsheads, irrespective of the weight. As a result, while in the seventeenth century a hogshead would average less than 500 pounds, in the middle of the eighteenth century it was close to 1,000 pounds. See J. M. Hemphill, Jr.: "Freight Rates in the Maryland Tobacco Trade, 1701–1762," Maryland Historical Magazine, LIV, 40.

[77] As early as 1621 a royal order in council was issued restricting the exportation of

The navigation act of 1660 provided that it could not legally be carried to foreign countries for sale without first being landed in England, where it was subject to duties and had to be warehoused, examined, and weighed. The duties in 1750 amounted to seven and a third pence on the pound weight of tobacco, which was many times greater, as has been pointed out, than the price of the tobacco itself before importation. That which was called the "old subsidy," first levied under Charles II,[78] provided for a tax of a penny a pound, which in reality amounted to three farthings, owing to the twenty-five per cent which was remitted in place of the older allowances granted to compensate for the loss of weight and spoiling in transit. This duty had to be paid immediately upon entering the cargo at the customs. As to the other duties, these were the "additional penny," levied by the same act providing for the "old subsidy"; "the impost," laid at the beginning of the reign of James II,[79] amounting to threepence; "the New Subsidy" of William III, amounting to a penny;[80] "the one-third" grant provided by Parliament under Anne;[81] and, lastly, the levy in the general subsidy granted to George II in 1747.[82] As the law stood, it was provided that the importer could

---

Virginia tobacco to England. For this order see *Acts of the Privy Council, Col. Ser.,* 1613–1680, pp. 48–9; see also C. M. Andrews: *The Colonial Period of American History* (4 vols., New Haven, 1934–8), IV, 15–17. The purpose of the restriction lay in the desire of the mother country not only for an adequate supply of this valuable commodity but also, in the words of Professor Nettels, "that the colonial trade should be in the hands of English merchants — that tobacco should be sold to England that it might be paid for with English goods; and, if it were shipped in English vessels, English shipowners would earn freights and English merchants, the middleman's profit." The added importance of other items of profit that would come to Englishmen by these regulations, such as those derived from insurance, commissions, and interest on invested capital, are also to be stressed. See C. P. Nettels: *op. cit.,* pp. 131–2.

[78] See 25 Chas. II, c. 7, Par. 2; see also 12 Chas. II, c. 4, under "Rates Inward," for the levy that became the perpetual "old subsidy." As early as 1619 tobacco had paid a duty. See H. Saxby: *British Customs* (London, 1757), for a treatment of tobacco duties; see also G. L. Beer: *Commercial Policy of England toward the American Colonies* (New York, 1893), pp. 47–51.

[79] 1 Jas. II, c. 4, Par. 1.

[80] 9 and 10 Wm. III, c. 23, Par. 5. For regulations on the importation of tobacco from the plantations see 10 and 11 Wm. III, c. 21, Par. 29.

[81] 2 and 3 Anne, c. 9, Par. 1.

[82] 21 Geo. II, c. 2, Par. 2. This was "An Act, for granting to his Majesty a Subsidy of Poundage upon all Goods and Merchandize, to be imported into this Kingdom." By this, an additional duty of twelve per cent ad valorem was laid upon all goods mentioned and expressed in the book of rates, entitled "The Rates of Merchandise," which amounted to one penny per pound upon all tobacco imported and consumed in Great Britain. To be freed from this on April 17, 1749, the Burgesses appointed a committee

give bonds [83] signed by one or more responsible people for the payment of this additional six and one-third pence on the pound starting within a period of eighteen months.[84] However, should he be prepared to make immediate payment, he was entitled to the same discount as in the case of the old subsidy — that is, a discount of twenty-five per cent. Otherwise he might secure a fifteen-per-cent discount if, before the termination of the eighteen months, the bonds were cancelled.[85] Again, in case it was found upon inspection at the time of importation that a portion of the tobacco was spoiled, the merchant could separate it from that which was not and thereupon the customs officers burned it.[86] Not only were no duties paid upon this tobacco, but the importer received an allowance of a halfpenny a pound weight up to the amount of thirty shillings per hogshead to indemnify him for the loss he had suffered.[87] Finally, should he re-export his tobacco within a period of three years from the time of importation, he received an entire remission of duties.[88]

The history of a typical consignment of tobacco shipped by a Virginia planter to a broker in England throws light upon the entire process of duties, subsidies, and marketing in the middle of the eighteenth century. That the document utilized is dated January 1,

---

"to prepare a humble address to His Majesty and a petition to Parliament, against the retention of this duty" (*Journals of the House of Burgesses, 1742–1749*, p. 366). This Sir William Gooch carried to England and presented to the ministry without avail. Pelham informed him that it would not be received by Parliament, nor would any other that affected the duties, since the latter were mortgaged to pay the nation's debts. Tobacco at this period, however, did not carry an excise tax, although it was feared by the British tobacco merchants that this would soon come. See an extract of a letter from London to Virginia written November 19, 1749, and printed in the *Maryland Gazette*, April 4, 1750.

[83] See 7 and 8 Wm. III, c. 10, Par. 5, and 9 Anne, c. 21, Par. 2.

[84] In this connection see [G. M. Butel-Dumont]: *Histoire et Commerce des Antilles Angloises* ([Paris] 1758), pp. 199–206.

The collection of tobacco duties in the eighteenth century down to 1750 was regulated by the following laws: 1 Anne, Stat. 1, c. 13; 5 Anne, c. 8 (the Act of Union, Art. VI); 5 Anne, c. 27, Par. 5; 6 Anne, c. 19; and 8 Anne, c. 13, Par. 2.

[85] Henry Saxby in his *British Customs* (London, 1757, p. 326) shows, for example, that on 4,800 pounds of British plantation tobacco the importer would pay £110 if the duties were paid down and £122.15 if the duties were simply secured by bonds. On Spanish tobacco the duties on 1,200 pounds would be £111.11, which shows the advantage that colonial planters enjoyed with respect to the customs.

[86] 12 Geo. I, c. 28, Par. 11.

[87] 9 Geo. I, c. 21, Pars. 4 and 13.

[88] 9 Geo. I, c. 21, Par. 6, and 21 Geo. II, c. 2, Pars. 5 and 6. See also Butel-Dumont's treatise *Histoire et Commerce des Antilles Angloises* for a rather full treatment of the above topic.

1765, focuses attention on the slight difference which would have existed from any similar brokerage account in the middle of the century, owing to the imposition of the additional penny in 1760, making the import duty eight and one-third pence instead of seven and one-third.[89] The tobacco in question was shipped by the Hon. Robert Carter of "Nomini Hall" on board the *Dove* to James Buchanan & Co., of London. There were ten hogsheads, each of which averaged 1,088 pounds at the time of arrival at the port of London. The old subsidy on these at one penny a pound less twenty-five per cent amounted to £35.–.4, which had to be paid at the time of entering; the other duties of seven and one-third pence per pound less fifteen per cent equalled £282.14.2; the freight at £8 sterling per ton was £20; the impost and cocket came to £1.1; the primage and other petty charges, at two shillings, sevenpence, and two farthings per hogshead, to £1.6.3; for entering inward the fees, including land-waiter fees and fees for bonds at one shilling and sixpence per hogshead, were fifteen shillings; those for entering outward, including the charges for the cocket and for searching at one shilling and sixpence per hogshead, were fifteen shillings; for cooperage at the time of entering inward and outward, at two shillings a hogshead, £1.7 was demanded; for porterage, wharfage, and lighterage, at one shilling per hogshead, ten shillings; warehouse rent and cartage, at four shillings per hogshead, came to £2; brokerage, at two shillings per hogshead, to £1; the fee for watching outward was five shillings; that for culling two hogsheads which were found defective was four shillings; and the commission and insurance on the debt was three per cent on £391.14.10 or £11.15. From one of the defective hogsheads, fifty-one pounds of tobacco were removed; from another, fifty-six pounds. Out of the original 10,885 pounds sent over, 10,041 pounds were available for sale, owing to shrinkage and other unassigned causes.[90]

As to the sale of this tobacco, two hogsheads were disposed of by the broker May 2, 1764; other sales were made in June, July, and August, and on November 22 the last hogshead was sold. The first of

---

[89] For the additional tax of a penny see 32 Geo. II, c. 10, Par. 1.

[90] See L. C. Gray: *History of Agriculture in the Southern United States to 1860* (I, 223–5) for a study of costs of transport and marketing of tobacco. The freight rates on Maryland tobacco between 1705 and 1762 varied from £4 per ton to £18, with the norm in 1749 at £7 per ton. See J. M. Hemphill, Jr.: "Freight Rates in the Maryland Tobacco Trade, 1705–1762," *Maryland Historical Magazine*, LIV, 36–58, 152–87.

the sales brought the highest price, at twopence a pound, or £15.16.6 for two hogsheads containing in all 1,899 pounds; the lowest price was a penny two farthings a pound. The total value of the sales was £74.8.5, which made an average of £7.9 sterling per hogshead. It may be added that a drawback was secured on £316.14.6 for duties since the tobacco was purchased for re-export, and that for the 107 pounds of spoiled tobacco destroyed at the wharf an allowance of two farthings per pound was given by the government. As can be seen, there was a very modest profit upon this consignment, amounting in all to £34.9.1 that was credited to Carter's account current.[91]

Most of the tobacco imported into Great Britain was not destined to remain there. Out of 40,000 hogsheads received by the merchants of Glasgow in 1754 only 1,342 were sold "inland," while almost 11,000 went to Holland, over 10,000 to France, and lesser numbers to Germany, Scandinavia, and Ireland.[92] In 1731 out of 41,683,833 pounds of tobacco arriving in English ports, 28,932,297 were re-exported.[93]

No merchant of moderate means could engage successfully in the tobacco trade at this period. The old subsidy, which had to be paid upon the arrival of the ship, amounted frequently to £1,500 sterling, and the total duties might run well over £10,000 if the tobacco were sold for domestic consumption.[94] Moreover, it was necessary to be content with a narrow margin of profit in light of the strong competition among tobacco merchants.[95] Should the market fall ever so little it might force such a merchant into bankruptcy. George Whitehead of Bristol, merchant, testified at this period that he had been a

---

[91] The document cited above is in the Virginia Historical Society. In 1730, a hogshead of tobacco netted £21 upon sale in England. See M. S. Morriss: *Colonial Trade of Maryland, 1689–1715* (Baltimore, 1914), p. 37.

[92] James Pagan: *Sketches of the History of Glasgow* (Glasgow, 1847), pp. 80–2. In 1771 this port received 46,255,139 pounds, of which 21,280,000 were re-exported to France, 14,780,000 to Holland, and smaller amounts to Germany, Scandinavia, Italy, and Ireland. See John Gibson: *History of Glasgow*, pp. 213–39.

[93] See David Macpherson: *Annals of Commerce* . . . (4 vols., London, 1805), III, 583.

[94] For example, Jonathan Forward of London, merchant, gave a bond November 7, 1745, for the payment of £7,555.10 in sixteen months, to cover the duties on a cargo of tobacco imported by him from Virginia in the *Prince of Denmark*. See P.R.O., Treas. 11. 23, p. 440.

[95] It was calculated in 1748 that the average price secured for re-exported tobacco was sixpence a pound, according to statements then made by merchants. [Adam Anderson]: . . . *Origin of Commerce* (rev. edn. by Combe, 4 vols., London, 1787–9), III, 546. The total value of the sales abroad was £1,000,000 in that year.

considerable trader in tobacco and had paid large sums to the Crown, but that as a result of great losses he had sustained in the trade he was ruined. At this time he had seven bonds outstanding against him for which he and his sons were securities.[96]

The tobacco trade, precarious as it was at this period, was further liable to be adversely affected in Great Britain by the wholesale operations of smugglers. They, by eluding the duty of seven and one-third pence on the pound, were able to sell at a great profit far below the margin upon which the lawful trader was compelled to operate and thus could cause fluctuations in the market price.[97] How much tobacco was annually smuggled into Great Britain cannot be determined, but the quantity must have been very large. In 1722 it was charged that the Scots in three years supplied England with almost 4,000,000 pounds of tobacco upon which duties had not been paid.[98] For a period of somewhat over seventeen years preceding Michaelmas in 1750 a total of over 1,250,000 pounds of tobacco was seized along the English coast, and it may be assumed that this constituted but a small portion of the quantity that was run during this period.[99] Parliament, in an endeavour to grapple with this evil, passed an act in 1750 for more effectively securing the duties on this commodity.[100] The difficulty seemed to lie not only in an inadequate number of customs officers but also in the tendency of those in the service to act in collusion with the smuggler. As a result there was a great shaking up of the service the following year. Many dismissals took place. Posts such as that of tidesman or waiter, which had for years been vacant, were now filled, and other posts, occupied by people too elderly to be effective in the discharge of their duties, were declared vacant.[101]

The region of the most widespread violation of the customs laws on tobacco was undoubtedly the shoreline of Scotland. It was as-

---

[96] P.R.O., Treas. 11. 24, p. 151.

[97] Testimony was given in 1722 before a parliamentary committee that tobacco brought from Scotland was being sold for as low as fivepence a pound, which was below even the duty charges and did not cover the many heavy charges involved in transportation from Chesapeake Bay. See *Journals of the House of Commons* (1722), XX, 104; see also Alfred Rive: "The Consumption of Tobacco since 1600," *Economic History*, I, 68–9.

[98] *Journals of the House of Commons*, XX, 107–8.

[99] Lansdowne Papers, 661:1–48, British Museum.

[100] 24 Geo. II, c. 41.

[101] P.R.O., Treas. 11. 24, pp. 72–6.

serted by the Lord President of the Sessions in 1754, in referring to the situation in the northern kingdom, that "the shameless Smuggling in this Country is Chiefly owing to the Officers of the Customs. They are named by the Treasury upon the Recommendation of members of Parliament and of other great men of this country. And when they fail in their duty, in favour of the friends of their Patron, or Against the enemies, the Commissioners are afraid to interpose and thereby tryals that are brought go against the Crown." [102] However, in that same year the High Court of Justiciary in Edinburgh ordered the transportation of three of the most notorious smugglers to America with the warning that they were never to return to Scotland.[103]

This brief analysis of tobacco-production and marketing in the middle of the eighteenth century cannot be concluded without examining the question of who paid the tobacco duties. Was it the producer or the consumer? It has been argued that certain circumstances in the tobacco trade would lead one to question whether it can be assumed that the burden was shifted to the consumer. The force of a restricted market, it is suggested, was operating in a direction opposed to higher prices for the consumer and, further,

> ". . . in a glutted market the added duties were not liable to greatly affect the selling price of the commodity or to allow a duty to be shifted to the consumer. . . . Under these circumstances the price of tobacco did not rise with the duties, and it seems reasonable to conclude that the burdens of the government fell largely upon the planters in the colonies who continued to pour their crops into an already saturated market." [104]

It is certain that the Virginia House of Burgesses in 1749 appointed a committee to prepare a humble address to His Majesty and a petition to Parliament that the penny added in 1747 to the duties earlier laid on tobacco be dropped. Manifestly they felt that this duty adversely affected them.[105] It is incontestable that in so far as tobacco was burdened with high duty charges its sale, under ordinary cir-

---

[102] See Lansdowne Papers, 661:49–150, Brit. Mus., for an account of tobacco frauds. For a brief account of tobacco-smuggling see Alfred Rive: "A Short History of Tobacco Smuggling," Economic History, I, 554–69; also, by the same author, "A Brief History of the Regulation and Taxation of Tobacco in England," William and Mary Quarterly, 2nd ser., IX, 81–6.

[103] C. M. Andrews: Colonial Period of American History (4 vols., New Haven, 1934–8), I, 63, note.

[104] See A. O. Craven: op. cit., pp. 45–6.

[105] Journals of the House of Burgesses, 1742–1749, p. 366.

cumstances, would be necessarily restricted in some proportion to the weight of these charges.[106] This may have been what was in the minds of the Virginia planters in desiring a lowering of duties. On the other hand, it can hardly be maintained that the government or the merchant was able by any device to shift the burden of the duties to the backs of the producer except under most unusual circumstances for brief periods wherein the planter would indubitably be faced with heavy losses in his business operations. The history of tobacco-smuggling shows that the smugglers sought to bring the tobacco to the English manufacturer of the finished product under such advantageous terms as would induce the latter to assume the risks of accepting goods that had been run. The manufacturer well knew that otherwise he must ask of the local distributor who sold to the ultimate consumer a price that would amply cover not only the first cost of the tobacco with brokerage and other charges but also the duty of seven and one-third pence on the pound.[107] In saying this, it is not to be denied that the market was subject to glut by the vast exportation of this tobacco commodity from both Virginia and Maryland. Under such circumstances the tobacco brokers would buy advantageously and the planters would consequently suffer. Even so, the practice of "feeding the market" had by this period been so well established by the middlemen that it is not clear how the consumer in Great Britain gathered much relief from the distress of the planters.[108]

---

[106] It appears that there was a considerable decrease in the consumption of pipe tobacco among the upper ranks of society in the eighteenth century. See Alfred Rive: "The Consumption of Tobacco since 1600," *Economic History*, I, 63–4. This, however, was not because of the price of tobacco but rather because its use, except in the form of snuff, was no longer fashionable.

[107] How narrow was the margin of profit received by the consignee of tobacco in England is indicated by the following item that appeared in the *Maryland Gazette*, April 4, 1750, in an extract of a letter from London dated November 19, 1749: "Tobacco sells here, and at Bristol, from two pence to two pence half penny for export, and from eight pence to eight pence half penny for home consumption. There is no hope of getting the one penny per pound duty off, it being already mortgaged for payment of national debts."

[108] For careful statements regarding the above question see L. C. Gray: *History of Agriculture in the Southern United States to 1860*, I, 257–8, 275–6.

CHAPTER IV

The Region of the Southern Pine Barrens

O F the older southern North American colonies, none diverged more widely from the characteristic plantation system in 1750 than did North Carolina, whose outstanding economic activity was not field crops but the production of naval stores; in no other was the proportion of white to black inhabitants so great; and nowhere else were so many people living what may be called a marginal existence in contrast to those enjoying a state of affluence. In no other southern colony did there exist barriers so formidable to the development of a profitable foreign trade; nowhere else did the problem of private land monopoly cause more concern or the public financial system become more chaotic; and, finally, in no other was the conflict between the executive and the legislative so bitter. Such, then, is the focus required in looking at the history of North Carolina in the middle of the eighteenth century.

The Chowan River region had been colonized almost a century before by the settlers coming from Virginia, and in the course of the last half of the seventeenth century and the early part of the eighteenth, home-seekers had penetrated well into the back portions of the coastal plan, especially along the courses of the Chowan, the Roanoke, the Tar, and the Neuse rivers. Yet even as late as 1724, when he became Governor under the Proprietors, George Burrington stated that North Carolina was little known or mentioned and the inhabitants few and poor.[1] However, Burrington assisted in the estab-

---

[1] Captain Burrington's "Representation of the State of North Carolina," January 1, 1732/3, Shelburne Papers, 45:191–6, Clements Library. Burrington was appointed royal Governor in 1730.

lishment of a permanent settlement on the Cape Fear River and it appears that in the course of his administration people began flocking into the colony in increasing numbers, not only westward by way of the rivers but also southward through the Virginia back country. In 1733 the population was computed at 30,000 whites and 6,000 blacks,[2] which appears to be too low.[3] There is evidence that many who had settled within the province, especially those living inland in the region of the northern border, were enjoying a considerable degree of prosperity.[4]

By the middle of the eighteenth century the colony was attracting large numbers of people from the northern plantations into the back country, creating a type of settlement that appeared characteristic of a pioneer movement. They came primarily from Virginia, Maryland,[5] and Pennsylvania, where, according to a leading North Carolinian, Matthew Rowan, writing in 1751,[6] they considered the price of land high, while in North Carolina they were able to secure a hundred acres for £5 Virginia currency. As a result, these land-hungry people — only too frequently after a long, tiresome journey — were happy to be able to secure grants in the province and thereupon settled down "with great contentment." "The grants lately made to newcomers from the Northern Province are very considerable," declared Rowan, "and I believe now there is little vacant land good in 250 miles westward from the seacoast." As to colonization further inland, he added: "I am credibly informed that the westernmost Branches of Pedee are better seated than other navigable Rivers in these Lower Parts. . . ."[7] Another writer of this same period stated that the "Lands in Black River & heads of Cape Fear are now in great esteem as they abound with swampy, reedy places and are exceeding

---

[2] *Ibid.*

[3] In 1734 the population was estimated to be 50,000, according to W. L. Saunders, editor of the *Colonial Records of North Carolina* (10 vols., Raleigh, N.C., 1886–90), IV, xx. This reference will be cited hereafter as *North Carolina Colonial Records.*

[4] Colonel William Byrd mentions this prosperity in his *History of the Dividing Line* (ed. W. K. Boyd, Raleigh, 1929).

[5] According to Governor John Seymour of Maryland, as early as the first decade of the century it was customary for planters who feared imprisonment because of financial involvement to desert their lands in Maryland and flee to North Carolina. For his letter of December 1705 see C. P. Nettels: *Money Supply of the American Colonies before 1720* (Madison, 1934), p. 58.

[6] [Matthew] Rowan to S[amuel] S[mith], September 19, 1751, Dobbs Papers, Public Record Office of Northern Ireland, Belfast.

[7] *Ibid.*

good ranges for cattle. Our people drive 200 miles to these places."[8] The Moravian Bishop Spangenberg declared in his diary in 1752 that he and his party had traversed the counties of Chowan, Bertie, Northampton, Edgecombe, and Granville to a point 153 miles from Edenton and that, although the land they had seen was not particularly good, they were informed that it had all been taken up. Toward the west, nearer the mountains, he found families moving in from parts as distant as New England. "In this year alone," he further recorded in his diary, "more than four hundred families have come with horse and wagon and cattle."[9]

Many of the newcomers in the province, it was asserted by a contemporary, made no attempt to purchase land but would "sit down on any place they fancy, [and] plant away," fully expecting the rightful owner to claim it, whereupon they intended to purchase.[10] The movement therefore resulted in undeniable confusion in titles and all land matters.[11] The Palatines, who had come earlier under Baron de Graffenried, were the victims of this state of affairs. As in the case of the Palatines who came to New York during the administration of Governor Hunter,[12] these people settled on lands that they understood had been granted to them by Queen Anne, and, just as the former were driven from the Schoharie, so the latter in turn found themselves dispossessed by Colonel Thomas Pollock, who had taken over Graffenried's interest. Finally they petitioned His Majesty in the late 1740's for restoration of their claims, but instead were settled upon other lands.[13] Still the people came — Scottish Highlanders, French Protestants, Ulster Scots, and others — lured on by the hope of finding here at last a happy place of rest. By 1760 the white population had reached a total of 80,000, at least according to Governor Dobbs's estimates.[14] This gave the province a white population prob-

---

[8] John Campbell to —— without date, but manifestly referring to the same period as the previous letter. The Dobbs Papers.

[9] For the Spangenberg "Diary" see Records of the Moravians in North Carolina (ed. Adelaide L. Fries, 5 vols., Raleigh, 1922–41), I, 39, 41.

[10] John Campbell to —— without date, Dobbs Papers.

[11] Records of the Moravians in North Carolina, I, 32.

[12] For further treatment of the Palatines in New York and later in Pennsylvania see Volume III of this series, Chaps. 5 and 7.

[13] Board of Trade Journal, 1741–1749, p. 249; Acts of the Privy Council, Col. Ser., 1745–1766, pp. 45–7.

[14] See North Carolina Colonial Records, VI, 223. In 1761 Dobbs gave the Negro population as 12,000, ibid., VI, 613–14.

ably over twice that of South Carolina, where, however, the blacks were vastly more numerous by comparison.[15]

From 1663 to 1729 the region lying between Virginia and Florida called Carolina had, under letters patent issued in 1663 and 1665, been governed by eight Proprietors. In 1729 an act of Parliament laid down the terms of agreement whereby the Proprietors might be induced to surrender their claims to and within the two now distinct provinces of North Carolina and South Carolina.[16] Seven of the eight proprietarial families thereupon accepted these terms; Lord Carteret, refusing to sell his one-eighth interest in the two colonies, was in 1744, nevertheless, prevailed upon to give up all pretensions to the exercise of political power in the Carolinas in exchange for a definite assignment of land in the northern part of North Carolina. As a result all the land from the northern boundary of the province (36° 30′) southward to 35° 34′ became the property of John Carteret, Earl Granville, to dispose of as he saw fit. To him were to be paid the quit-rents on lands already settled or to be settled within these limits.[17] He also possessed the rights to escheated and forfeited lands therein and could make grants under conditions that he himself might lay down.[18]

The creation of this Carteret reserve, known as the Granville Grant, was held to be highly prejudicial to the interests of the inhabitants of the province. This is not surprising in light of the fact that it included that portion of North Carolina where were located both the lands considered to be among the best as well as the older settlements. Thus the people living within the Carteret proprietary doubtless apprehended that effective steps would inevitably be taken to collect the quit-rents — about which there had been great remissness — and also to secure whatever additional advantages apper-

---

[15] According to Governor Glen in 1749, South Carolina had 25,000 whites and at least 39,000 blacks. See his report to the Board of Trade, September 13, 1749, Shelburne Papers, 45:60–83, Clements Library. In 1763 the white population of South Carolina was estimated at between 30,000 and 40,000 people as against 70,000 Negroes, according to Dr. George Milligan-Johnston. See his A Short Description of the Province of South-Carolina (London, 1770), pp. 24–5.

[16] See 2 Geo. II, c. 34, which ratified the agreement entered into by six of the Carolina Proprietors with the Privy Council on March 22, 1728. For this agreement see Acts of the Privy Council, Col. Ser., 1720–1745, pp. 174–7.

[17] For the agreement entered into by the Privy Council with John Lord Carteret on May 9, 1744, see ibid., pp. 267–9.

[18] F. X. Martin: History of North Carolina (2 vols., New Orleans, 1929), II, 111–14.

tained to the Carteret rights. Although the Proprietor could exercise no political authority and the province still remained a governmental unit, there was little consolation to be drawn from this fact. The land revenues had previously been largely employed in the payment of the provincial officials,[19] and now that the greater part of them — at least two thirds — would be lost to public purposes, it was felt that all within the colony would be liable to greater charges for the administration of government.

Prospective settlers were now manifesting considerable reluctance, and rather naturally, to purchase land within the Granville Grant. Nevertheless, the Moravians entered into an agreement in London with the Earl to take over 100,000 acres, to which he held them. At the same time immigrants from the northward continued to squat upon his lands, whereas others hesitated to accept the opportunities offered to purchasers through his land office established at Edenton. For example, in 1747 Arthur Dobbs — who was occupied with the work of laying out patents for 400,000 acres that he and Colonel George Selwyn had purchased, and was later to come to North Carolina as Governor — instructed his agent, Captain Rowan, to take care that in locating the land none of it should fall within Lord Granville's division.[20] Henry McCulloh, who in 1737 had received a grant of 1,200,000 acres under condition that he would bring 6,000 foreign Protestants into the province and who had had a survey made in 1745 of this immense tract, part of which he had turned over to Dobbs, was dismayed to find that 475,000 acres of the total lay within this grant.[21] At the same time it may be added that a good many Virginians of substance, attracted by the rich lands, acquired holdings within it, with the result that in 1746 Granville County was erected to meet their needs, and Orange County to the west of it followed in 1752.[22]

---

[19] Coralie Parker: *The History of Taxation in North Carolina . . . 1663–1776* (New York, 1928), p. 63.

[20] Dobbs to Rowan [May 1747?], Dobbs Papers. For a study of the Granville Grant see E. M. Coulter: "The Granville District," *James Sprunt Historical Publications*, XIII, No. 1, 35–56.

[21] *Ibid.*, p. 49; see also *North Carolina Historical Review*, II, 475–9. For an account of McCulloh's various land deals and the opposition to them by South Carolinians see C. G. Sellers: "Private Profits and British Colonial Policy: The Speculations of Henry McCulloh," *William and Mary Quarterly*, 3rd ser., VIII, 535–51. For McCulloh's identity see John Cannon: "Henry McCulloh and Henry McCulloh," *ibid.*, XV, 71–3.

[22] Nannie M. Tilley: "The Settlement of Granville County," *North Carolina Historical Review*, XI, 1–19.

The existence of the Granville Grant was, likewise, indirectly a cause of intense dissatisfaction when in 1730 the Crown fixed the quit-rents in the region to the southward of it at four shillings proclamation or three shillings sterling for each 100 acres — double the amount, it was asserted, paid in Virginia. This led also to a sharp decrease in the payment of these dues, which dropped from £1,182 sterling, collected in 1735, to £323 proclamation in 1745; but £146 proclamation was collected in 1748 and only £161.8 in 1750.[23] So intense, in fact, was the opposition to this separation of the Carteret claims from the main body of the provincial lands that it doubtless was a leading cause of the later uprising in the early 1770's known as the Regulator Movement.[24]

Despite its great increase in population, the province was by no means prosperous. Little progress had been made by 1750 in establishing even the simplest of the handicrafts. One of the most important towns, Edenton, which had long enjoyed the distinction of being the provincial capital (before it was established at New Bern in 1746),[25] was a low-lying, fever-stricken community in 1752, "hardly one quarter so large as Germantown," a suburb of the city of Philadelphia. The Moravian Spangenberg found but one smith, one cobbler, and one tailor at work in Edenton. He declared: "Of handecrafts I have seen practically nothing in the 150 miles we have travelled across this Province. Almost nobody has a trade." [26]

While the soil was generally of good quality and frequently composed of rich loam in the Piedmont, that of the eastern part of the province in the region of the coastal plain, extending inland to the fall line some 80 to 150 miles, was held to be not well adapted to agricultural processes. Governor George Burrington, writing to the Board of Trade in 1730, stated "that North Carolina has vast tracts of Land not improveable by the Power of man some part thereof being Pine barren Land which can never redound to the least ad-

---

[23] B. W. Bond, Jr.: The Quit-Rent System in the American Colonies (New Haven, 1919), p. 300, n.; see also Coralie Parker: The History of Taxation in North Carolina . . . 1663–1776, p. 63 and W. Neil Franklin: "Agriculture in Colonial North Carolina," North Carolina Historical Review, III, 539–74, and especially p. 542."

[24] See Archibald Henderson: "The Origin of the Regulation in North Carolina," American Historical Review, XXI, 320–32.

[25] Walter Clark, ed.: Laws, 1715–1776, State Records of North Carolina, XXIII, 252–67. The State Records begin where the Colonial Records end; however, the volumes continue the numbering with the State Records beginning with Volume XI.

[26] Records of the Moravians in North Carolina, I, 39.

vantage of the Owners (except once in 20. or 30. years) when they . . . make pitch and tarr, and many vast tracts there are very low and exceeding wett, in soe much that noe place thereon can be found to raise the least structure to dwell in. . . ." [27] Outside of these swampy places the soil was mostly composed of sand, mixed here and there with marl, while to the south of the Neuse River it was largely loose sand. "In Chowan and Bertie Counties," declared Spangenberg, "one can ride for three hours without seeing anything except Pine Barrens, that is, white sand grown up in pine trees, which will hardly produce anything else." He further stated: "In 140 miles I saw not one wagon or plough nor any sign of one." [28] However, here and there were considerable bodies of lands upon which were growing oak and other trees that indicated the presence of better soil. When those spots were cleared, small farms as a rule were laid out which were worked by the owner and his family with the aid perhaps of a few slaves [29] who raised corn and hogs or tobacco.

While most of the settlers in the interior lived apart, the town of Bethabara was established in 1753 on a branch of the Gadkin. This was within the area of the land purchase of the Moravian Brethren that took the name Wachovia. Here at least was to be found a nucleus of cultivated and highly resourceful people living in the wilderness, who proceeded to establish a number of local industries and who also made their settlement a religious and educational centre. [30]

In addition to these small farmers, many of whom were impoverished, a considerable number of families of wealth were to be found living either in the Cape Fear region or to the northward around New Bern [31] and Edenton. These families owned large bodies of land and operated numerous farm units. Some of them had built homes that compared not unfavourably with those of the Virginia planters.

---

[27] North Carolina Colonial Records, III, 78.

[28] Records of the Moravians in North Carolina, I, 34.

[29] Before 1754, as has previously been suggested, about one sixth of the population of North Carolina was black; in 1767 there were some 39,500 slaves in North Carolina, the number having more than doubled since 1754. See J. S. Bassett: Slavery and Servitude in North Carolina (Baltimore, 1896) for an account of slavery during this period.

[30] See Adelaide L. Fries: "The Moravian Contribution to Colonial North Carolina," North Carolina Historical Review, VII, 1–14; E. H. Holder: "Social Life of the Early Moravians in North Carolina," ibid., XI, 167–84; and, especially, The Records of the Moravians in North Carolina, already cited.

[31] For an account of New Bern in the middle of the eighteenth century see A. T. Dill, Jr.: "Eighteenth Century New Bern, A History of the Town and Craven County, 1700–1800," North Carolina Historical Review, XXII, 460–89, XXIII, 47–78.

They therefore lived the life of cultured, prosperous country gentry, dressing in a fashionable manner and enjoying the possession of household slaves, valuable plate for their tables, and excellent libraries.[32]

North Carolina, in addition to its farms, had many cattle ranches. "It is not an uncommon thing," declared the author of *American Husbandry*, published in London in 1775, "to see one man the master of from 300 to 1200 and even to 2000 cows, bulls, oxen, and young cattle; hogs also in prodigious numbers." [33] Within the region of the pine barrens, which fringed the cattle ranches, vast quantities of tar, pitch, and turpentine were made from the longleaf pine (*pinus palustris*) whenever it was possible to bring these barrelled heavy stores to some river down which they could be carried on flat-bottomed boats or "perriaugers" equipped with sails and oars.[34] Further, some rice was produced in the vicinity of Cape Fear.[35] But the agricultural economy was of the crudest sort as a rule.

During the winter the cattle and horses were generally turned out to care for themselves, and consequently at this season there was neither milk nor butter for household use, nor was there manure for the fields. By the coming of spring the livestock was frequently so reduced by privation that the animals hardly recovered before fall and were consequently stunted in growth. The horses were described as of the size of English colts and the cattle no larger than yearling calves.[36]

One of the major problems in the economic life of the province was the isolation of its settlements, separated as they were by swamps, rivers, and sand barrens. The seriousness of this handicap may be judged by the fact that in 1732 Arthur Dobbs was seeking to introduce camels to aid in transporting commodities across these wastes. In his behalf the British government had inquired of the Governor of Gibraltar the price of African camels and upon what

---

[32] See Julia C. Spruill: "Virginia and Carolina Homes before the Revolution," *ibid.*, XII, 332–5; see also James Sprunt: *Chronicles of the Cape Fear River, 1660–1916* (Raleigh, 1916), pp. 40–5, 55–7.

[33] See *American Husbandry* (ed. H. Carman, New York, 1939), p. 24. The writer adds: "Such herds of cattle and swine are to be found in no other colonies."

[34] *Ibid.*, p. 244; see also F. W. Clonts: "Travel and Transportation in Colonial North Carolina," *North Carolina Historical Review*, III, 19.

[35] James Abercromby's "Examination," May 22, 1752, Shelburne Papers, 47:36.

[36] *Records of the Moravians in North Carolina*, I, 39; see also *American Husbandry*, p. 250.

terms they could be possessed at Gibraltar in case the Moors would allow them to be transported to America.[37] The province was likewise isolated by its shores. Dangerous shoals lying in the vicinity of Capes Hatteras, Lookout, and Fear, the shallow waters of the sounds, especially at Ocracoke (Oracoke) Inlet, and the sand bars at the mouth of the rivers warned away the larger ships, with the result that what commerce existed between North Carolina and the outside world was limited largely to small sloops, brigantines, schooners, and snows engaged in coastwise trade.[38] Although an attempt was made to improve the situation by the establishment of the town of Portsmouth on the Core Banks, a Mr. Townshend, who had commercial dealings with the province, informed the Board of Trade in 1749 that he was obliged to carry on his correspondence through Boston or South Carolina, "there being no direct trade thither." [39] At this same meeting of the Board the poverty and what was considered to be the financial irresponsibility of the people of the colony were stressed. It was asserted that the debts of the British merchants in North Carolina "were generally desperate and no redress could be obtained," [40] although at this period there was an annual demand for British goods

---

[37] Arthur Dobbs to C. R. Dobbs, December 16, 1732, Dobbs Papers, P.R.O., Northern Ireland. Although Dobbs was still a resident of Ireland at this period, he had already become interested in North Carolina. For inland travel and transportation see F. W. Clonts: "Travel and Transportation in North Carolina," *North Carolina Historical Review*, III, 16–35; C. C. Crittenden: "Overland Travel and Transportation in North Carolina, 1763–1789," *ibid.*, VIII, 239–57; and, by the same author, "Inland Navigation in North Carolina, 1763–1789," *ibid.*, VIII, 145–54, and "Means of Communication in North Carolina, 1763–1789," *ibid.*, VIII, 373–83.

[38] See C. C. Crittenden: "The Sea Coast in North Carolina, 1763–1789," *ibid.*, VII, 433–42, and, by the same author, "Ships and Shipping in North Carolina, 1763–1789," *ibid.*, VIII, 1–13; see also David Stick: *Graveyard of the Atlantic: Shipwrecks of the North Carolina Coast* (Chapel Hill, N.C., 1952), and "A Description of Occacock Inlet . . . , 1795," *North Carolina Historical Review*, III, 624–33.

[39] Board of Trade Journal, 1741–1749, p. 374. The port of Brunswick at the mouth of the Cape Fear River, it is true, had a good deal of ocean-borne commerce in the 1760's because deep water gave anchorage to cargo vessels. Heavy naval stores were carried to it from Wilmington on rafts to be loaded on ships for England. See E. L. Lee: "Old Brunswick, the Story of a Colonial Town," *North Carolina Historical Review*, XXIX, 230–45. The decline of this port was due to its exposed situation in time of war.

The importance of the commercial relations between North Carolina and Boston in the second decade of the eighteenth century is indicated by the fact that in 1715 twenty-nine vessels arrived in the colony from the New England metropolis, while in 1717 only three vessels brought food exported from South Carolina. For these figures see C. P. Nettels: *The Money Supply of the American Colonies before 1720*, p. 113.

[40] Board of Trade Journal, 1741–1749, p. 374.

amounting to £50,000 sterling.[41] In 1746 William Borden, in his *An Address to the Inhabitants of North Carolina*, gave forcible expression to the difficulties confronting the people in connection with their commercial relations:

> "How are the Inhabitants puzzled and put to their Shifts, in regard to Trade and Commerce? And how grievously are the Commonalty streightned, in buying them Necessaries of Life, for want of a proper *Medium*? And how helpless is the Province in respect to Navigation? Are not the Inhabitants (for want of a proper Navigation in the Government) obliged to purchase all their foreign Necessaries at the very last and dearest Hand? When, perhaps, a Parcel of Goods or Merchandize have passed . . . through the Hands of many Merchants or Traders, and they have all had their Profits on them, and Livings from them, then, perhaps, poor *North Carolina* Planters have the Honour of eating, drinking, and wearing some of the riff-raff Remains, at a dear Rate: . . ."[42]

The indebtedness of the inhabitants to the British merchants and the merchants' feelings of the insecurity of these obligations were in great part the result of laws passed in 1748 and 1754 which were approved and carried into effect.[43] These acts provided for the substitution of local currency for payment of debts contracted in sterling. By them bills of credit were given lawful-tender character in all payments whatsoever to be made either in sterling or proclamation money. The bills were to pass at the rate of four shillings for three shillings sterling.

The implications involved in these acts apparently were not sensed by the Board of Trade at the time, as was the case with the debtor act passed by Virginia in 1749. However, by the year 1759 the British creditors, facing the loss of a large part of their advances to the settlers, presented their case to the Lords Commissioners. At this date instead of £133.6.8 in bills of credit having an actual value of £100

[41] James Abercromby's "Examination," May 22, 1752, Shelburne Papers, 47:37.

[42] See William K. Boyd: "Some North Carolina Tracts of the Eighteenth Century," *North Carolina Historical Review*, II, 204, and "William Borden's Addresses to the People and the Burgesses (1746)," *Some Eighteenth Century Tracts Concerning North Carolina* (ed. W. K. Boyd, Raleigh, 1927), pp. 55–100.

[43] For the laws of 1748 and 1754 making the currency of the colony a "lawful Tender, in all Payments whatsoever" see *Laws, 1715–1776, North Carolina State Records*, XXIII, 294 and 392.

sterling, they were not then worth more than £70 sterling.[44] As a result the Lords Commissioners hastened to prepare a representation to the Lords of the Committee of the Council that the Governor of the province be instructed to call upon the Assembly to pass an amending act which by revising the obnoxious laws would protect the rights of creditors.

The Board of Trade in its representation pointed out that this legal-tender legislation was "a Notorious Breach of public Faith," the effect of which would be "the Total Destruction of the Trade and Credit of the province since no Man can trust any property in a Country where such laws are subsisting." [45] As a consequence, the Privy Council issued an instruction to the Governor to procure the passing of a law that would declare that all debts "between British subjects and the inhabitants of N. Carolina are to be payable in the said Bills of Credit (if the Creditor be willing to accept the sum and not otherwise) not according to their nominal Value . . . but according to the real difference in Value between such Paper Bills and Sterling Money at the time of discharging such debts." Further, he was not to assent to any subsequent act providing that current money should be made a legal tender.[46]

But the issue was not over. In 1764 merchants of Great Britain trading to America presented memorials against colonial tender acts which particularly stressed the losses they had sustained from the introduction of this "fraudulent system into the colonies of Virginia and North Carolina." [47] As a result the Board of Trade was again impelled to represent to His Majesty in Council that "It is this Circumstance of declaring these Bills to be a legal Tender, which we humbly conceive Constitutes all the fraud and abuse Attendant upon this practice, and that if this was not allowed, the Colonies whenever they should find it necessary to make use of their Public Credit would be constrained to do it in a just and equitable manner." It also recommended that Parliament should act to declare that all colonial legal-tender acts to be passed in the future should be null and void,

---

[44] In 1741 the North Carolina bills of credit were the most highly depreciated of any in the colonies. It took £1,400 in these bills to equate to £100 sterling, as compared with £800 for South Carolina bills, £525 for New England bills, £200 for Maryland bills, £170 for Pennsylvania bills, and £160 for New Jersey and New York bills. See Boston Evening Post, January 12, 1741.

[45] Acts of the Privy Council, Col. Ser., 1745–1766, pp. 414–15.

[46] Ibid.

[47] Ibid., p. 624.

as well as all acts by which the period fixed for the redemption of bills of credit was extended.[48] Parliament, however, limited itself to striking at all colonial *legal-tender* acts and all acts that would prolong the period of circulation of *legal-tender* bills of credit already issued.[49]

One of the difficulties that faced the debt-burdened North Carolina farmer was to find a ready and profitable market for his produce. The tobacco, amounting to some two thousand hogsheads,[50] was mostly taken to Suffolk or Norfolk in Virginia, where it was disposed of to the tobacco merchants, who set the price. The cattle and hogs were also frequently driven into Virginia, where the cattle at least were sold on the hoof, frequently at a loss, for the buyer paid only for the meat, by weight, after butchering had taken place, with no allowance for hides or tallow.[51] The total value of the produce of the province was estimated in 1752 at £100,000 sterling, while that of little Barbados was put at £450,000.[52]

Despite all hindrances to the development of its economic life, North Carolina easily held first place within the Empire in 1750 in one field of activity: that of the production of tar, pitch, resin, and turpentine. By 1775 the export of these naval stores to Great Britain had reached the total of 130,000 barrels, a quantity far in excess of all such stores shipped by the rest of the colonies.[53]

Before the eighteenth century, England had been quite dependent upon Scandinavia for the supply of some naval stores, especially pitch and tar. The serious disadvantage and even danger to naval supremacy involved in this dependence became increasingly evident with the outbreak of the prolonged struggle with Louis XIV of France.[54] Therefore, in seeking a solution of this specific problem

---

[48] *Ibid.*, pp. 630–1, 646. As a recent writer has pointed out, among the colonies to the south of New England, North Carolina was the chief offender in the field of legal-tender legislation. See E. J. Ferguson: "Currency Finance: An Interpretation of Colonial Monetary Practices," *William and Mary Quarterly*, 3rd ser., X, 162.

[49] "An Act to Prevent Paper Bills of Credit, hereafter to be issued in any of His Majesty's Colonies in America, from being declared a legal Tender . . . ," 4 Geo. III, c. 34. The subject of colonial finance, 1750–75, will be emphasized in Volume X of this series.

[50] James Abercromby's "Examination," May 22, 1752, Shelburne Papers, 47:35.

[51] *Records of the Moravians in North Carolina*, I, 39.

[52] James Abercromby's "Examination," *op cit.*, 47:35.

[53] See Justin Williams: "English Mercantilism and Carolina Naval Stores," *Journal of Southern History*, I, 169–85.

[54] The experts in the employ of the Navy Board were far from enthusiastic over the

and to help realize the ideal of a self-sufficing empire, Parliament passed an act providing encouragement in the way of bounties for the production of naval-stores commodities in the plantations upon shipment to England.[55] The response to this measure was such that by 1717 the total value of these imports from the plantations was £47,072 and by 1719 England was able to re-export one half of the total supply.[56] Under George II the government reaffirmed its policy of guaranteeing to the British shipping interests a supply of American-produced naval stores.[57] The bounties, however, were substantially reduced by comparison with the amounts granted in the days of Queen Anne; for tar it was £2.4 in place of £4 a ton, for pitch £1 in place of £4 a ton, and for turpentine from £1.8 to £1.10 in place of £3 a ton.[58] While most of the American colonies seem to have produced certain amounts of these stores, the chief sources of supply were the Carolinas, with North Carolina, as already indicated, well in the lead.[59] In 1753 the exports from the province included over 60,000 barrels of tar, 12,000 barrels of pitch, and 10,000 barrels of turpentine.[60] In addition, 750,000 staves and 60,000 bushels of corn, together with considerable amounts of other commodities such as deerskins, were marketed abroad.[61]

---

prospect of depending upon the inferior products of the colonies. In fact, in 1700 Governor Bellomont of New York suggested that naval officials were really in league with merchants of the Eastland Company to maintain the established trade. Bellomont to the Board of Trade, October 17, 1700, *Calendar of State Papers, America and the West Indies,* I, 1700, p. 579.

In passing the Naval Stores Act of 1705 the English government had in mind not only securing these stores from the colonies and thus freeing England from its dependence upon Sweden for pitch and tar, but also providing America with additional exports with which to settle accounts with the merchants of the mother country. It was, moreover, felt that this new industry would divert the people in the northern colonies, especially in New England, from the manufacture of cloth, which was becoming a threat to the balance of trade. C. P. Nettels: *The Money Supply* . . . , pp. 146–55.

[55] The importer, as the agent of the North Carolina exporter, would apply for and receive the bounty of £4 a ton for both tar and pitch and £3 a ton for both resin and turpentine. See 3 and 4 Anne, c. 10.

[56] See G. L. Beer: *The Commercial Policy of England toward the American Colonies* (New York, 1893), p. 102.

[57] 2 Geo. II, c. 35, Par. 3, 9; 13 Geo. II, c. 28; 24 Geo. II, c. 52.

[58] See 2 Geo. II, c. 35.

[59] See G. L. Beer: *op. cit.,* pp. 101–2.

[60] F. X. Martin: *History of North Carolina,* II, 59–60. Most of these naval stores were earlier exported out of Charleston. This was not true by 1750, owing to adverse legislation.

[61] For example, in 1753 North Carolina appears to have exported some 30,000 deerskins. Witt Bowden: *Industrial History of the United States* (New York, [1930]), p. 62.

Among the political problems facing North Carolina, undoubtedly that of paramount importance in 1750 was the maintenance of even the semblance of an orderly government over those heterogeneous elements which were entering its borders. From its beginning, almost a century earlier, the colony had been the scene of turbulence and frequent uprisings. In 1721 the complaint was made that it had "become a place of refuge for all the vagabonds whom either debt or Breach of the Laws, have driven from the other Colonies of the continent and Pirates have too frequently found entertainment amongst them." [62] In 1731 Colonel William Byrd of Virginia had perhaps unnecessarily warned George Burrington — who in 1723 had acted as Deputy Governor and in 1730 had received a commission as Governor — that "people accustomed to live without law or gospel will, with great Reluctance, Submit to either," while at the same time wishing him success "in bringing the chaos into form and reducing that Anarchy into a regular Government. . . ." [63]

That the task of securing respect for law and order in North Carolina was still unfulfilled by the middle of the century is indicated by the fact that in 1755 Governor Dobbs, in addressing the Assembly, declared:

> "The Desertion from your Companys is become so excessive from the base Principals in the lowest class of men for want of education that they carry off their Arms and Livery and steal Horses to carry them away, and appear publickly in this Province without being secured by any Magistrate, and the Jayls are so weak without any Jaylor or Person to guard them, that no Criminal can be secured."

He further confessed that it had become too much the practice for those who were entrusted with the collection or the expenditure of public money to keep it in their own hands, "laying it out for their benefit," and that many either died or left the province without being brought to account, by which actions the public was defrauded.[64] Writing from North Carolina in the fall of 1751, Matthew

---

[62] *North Carolina Colonial Records*, II, 419–20.

[63] *Ibid.*, III, 194–5. In 1732 Captain Burrington recounted his efforts "in resettling the Authorities of the Judicatures, and restraining profligate lawless men from unruly actions." See the "Representation of the Governor on the Present State and Conditions of North Carolina," January 1, 1732/3, Shelburne Papers, 45:192–6.

[64] Governor Dobbs to the Assembly, September 25, 1755, Dobbs Papers, P.R.O., Belfast Ireland, and *North Carolina Colonial Records*, V, 497.

Rowan lamented: ". . . certainly this poor province is entirely forgot and neglected by our Min—y or the full well grounded proved complaints of an injured people would have been redressed long before now and not left at the mercy of a nefarious crew who have trampled on all our laws, justice and regularity that no man may say he knows . . . how to Act." [65]

In 1750 Gabriel Johnston, a Scot, was presiding over the destinies of the tumultuous colony as the second of the royal governors. A graduate of St. Andrews, a student of languages and of medicine, and later a London political pamphleteer, it would seem that he had possessed considerable temerity to seek an office from which Burrington, broken in health and in fortune, had been relieved at his own request in 1734.[66] However, for fifteen years now Johnston had been serving the Crown under his royal commission.[67] As might be anticipated from the foregoing, his office was no easy one. He was, in fact, at this juncture engaged in a great struggle with his Assembly, or a portion of it, over an act of that body passed in the year 1746 for ascertaining the number of deputies to be chosen to it.[68]

The members of the Assembly from the older-established part of the province, especially the region about Albemarle Sound, were bitterly opposed to the above law, which they insisted took away the privileges their counties had enjoyed for fifty years. For the statute

---

[65] [Matthew] Rowan to S[amuel] S[mith], September 19, 1751, Dobbs Papers.

[66] "Having lived in this Province some years without receiving any money from the King, or the Country, was constrained to sell not only my household goods, but even linnen, plate and Books, and mortgage my Lands, and stocks . . . I humbly desire my Lord Duke will be pleased to obtain his Majesty's leave for my return to England" (Burrington to the Duke of Newcastle, June 1, 1734, North Carolina Colonial Records, III, 625).

[67] For Governor Johnston's commission see C.O. 5:323, pp. 128–218. According to Henry McCulloh's memorial to the Board of Trade of the year 1751, he himself almost entirely supported Gabriel Johnston with funds between the years 1726 and 1734 to the amount of £2,900 sterling, having not only paid the fees involved in Johnston's commission as Governor under the Great Seal and at his own expense freighted a ship to carry the Governor and his retinue to North Carolina but also having bought plate and furniture for his house and given him a credit for £250. See North Carolina Colonial Records, IV, 1149, and C. G. Sellers: "Private Profits and British Colonial Policy: The Speculations of Henry McCulloh," William and Mary Quarterly, 3rd ser., VIII, 535–51.

[68] For the Assembly act of 1746 reapportioning representation see "Laws of North Carolina, 1746," c. 1, State Records of North Carolina, XXIII, 251–2. It may be noted in the above connection that the northern counties had as a special London agent, in their struggle against the act of 1746, Henry McCulloh, who laid their case before the Board of Trade. See Ella Lonn: The Colonial Agents of the Southern Colonies (Chapel Hill, 1945), p. 136.

had equalized the power in the Assembly of the older and the newer counties by depriving the older one of three of the five representatives that each had possessed. The Albemarle people, indeed, refused to recognize its validity and in the election following its passage chose the usual number of deputies. However, this election was invalidated by the reorganized legislature. Thereafter, for eight years, in the course of the struggle over this issue, the northern counties were not represented and refused to recognize the validity of the colonial government or to support it by taxes.[69] The situation had become impossible, and finally the issue came before the Board of Trade in March 1751.

The petitioners against the law of 1746 went back to 1696, when John Archdale, holding a Palatine Court, directed the election of five members from each of the four precincts of Albemarle County, which gave the Assembly its original form.[70] When other counties and precincts were erected, some were permitted to send five deputies, some three, and some but two.[71] Until the year 1736 each of the old precincts had received writs to elect five members, and after that date, although the form of the writ had been changed and had since directed only in general terms that representatives be chosen, the number had remained the same until the act under consideration had been passed. The petition of the resisters denounced the methods employed by the Governor to secure the law, declaring that he had transferred the meeting of the Assembly to the distant town of Wilmington along the southern coast and that it was called at a time of the year when some of the rivers were seven miles in breadth, the

---

[69] See L. F. London: "The Representation Controversy in Colonial North Carolina," *North Carolina Historical Review*, XI, 255–70.

[70] See the Board of Trade *Journal*, 1749–1753, p. 176; *North Carolina Colonial Records*, VI, 85; and also J. S. Bassett: *The Constitutional Beginnings of North Carolina*, 1663–1729 (Baltimore, 1894), pp. 56–7.

[71] Out of the original four precincts of Albemarle County of Chowan, Perquimans, Pasquotank, and Currituck, two others were made: Bertie and Tyrrell. These received five members each, but when Northampton was taken from Bertie and Edgecombe from Tyrrell the newer counties were each given two deputies and the former two were reduced to three apiece. Bath County, which was erected in 1696, at that time received an allotment of two deputies also; it was subsequently divided into districts, each of which received two each. See *North Carolina Colonial Records*, IV, 1231. In 1746, besides the districts (excluding Northampton) listed above, there were Granville, Orange, Bladen, New Hanover, Onslow, Beaufort, Carteret, Craven, Hyde, and Johnston. See *ibid.*, IV, 1171, V, xxxix. For a map of the counties in North Carolina in 1750 see Paul M. McCain: *The County Court in North Carolina before 1750* (Durham, N.C., 1954), frontispiece.

weather inclement, and the people engaged in butchering their cattle and pigs. Further, it was contended that the act had been passed "by management and surprise," with only a few members of the Assembly present, and that it was of such a nature that the Governor should not have assented to it. That these charges were correct was affirmed by both His Majesty's Attorney and Solicitor-General.[72]

The supporters of the law, however, insisted at this hearing before the Board that there was no surprise and that their opponents were the ones guilty of management. The time and place of the Assembly, they argued, had been fixed four months in advance of the meeting held in November; that less than four months' notification was considered sufficient even for the Parliament of Great Britain; and that it was not necessary to give special notice of any act intended to be passed. If it were objected that only fifteen members of the Assembly were present at Wilmington and that consequently the Governor should have waited for more, the answer was that the Governor had no reason to expect a greater number of deputies since there was a conspiracy to stay away, which, if tolerated, would be a dangerous precedent for all American assemblies. As to the charges of precipitation in the passing of the law, it was stated in defence that the bill had never been read twice in one day in either house but was brought in November 21 and was not finally passed until the 25th. The true motive of the opponents of the law, it was finally asserted, was to vest themselves with independence and to attain a power within the province superior to that of the Crown. This would be accomplished, were the views accepted of these men who, previously constituting a majority of the members in the Assembly and coming from the remote northern part of the colony, insisted that a majority must be present for the transaction of business.[73]

It was not until the year 1754 that the Board of Trade was prepared to make representation to the King on the proper course to pursue concerning the issues that had thus been presented by the warring factions within the province. Neither side was able to draw full satisfaction from this report. On the one hand, in harmony with the opinion of the Attorney and Solicitor-General, the position was taken that the law passed under the peculiar circumstance was void; on the other hand, the contentions of the opponents of Johnston to

---

[72] *North Carolina Colonial Records*, IV, 1232.
[73] Board of Trade *Journal*, 1749–1753, p. 179.

the effect that a majority of the representatives were obliged to be present to constitute a quorum was characterized as "very extraordinary and liable to great inconvenience." [74]

Two other circumstances may here be mentioned that added to the hopeless confusion in the public affairs of the colony: first, the uncertainty regarding the location of the public records; second, their neglect. "The Public Records," complained Johnston in 1748, "lye in a miserable condition, one part of them at Edenton near the Virginia Line, in a place without Lock or Key; a great part of them in the Secretary's House at Cape Fear, above Two Hundred Miles Distant from the other, Some few of 'em at the Clerk of the Council's House at Newbern, so that in whatever part of the Colony a man happens to be, if he wants to consult any paper or record, he must send some Hundred Miles before he can come at it." [75]

It is noteworthy that during the contest over the law of 1746 strenuous efforts were made by the Albemarle opposition to remove Governor Johnston. This group not only fought his legislative programs in the Assembly but also lodged three charges against him with the home government. First, he was accused of contempt and disobedience of the orders of the Crown, particularly in his neglect to correspond with the home government; secondly, it was asserted that he violated his instructions in signing an act for the issue of bills of credit without a suspending clause; thirdly, his loyalty to the Hanoverians was called into question on the charge that he appointed suspected people to office. He was accused, under the first head, of never transmitting accounts of the affairs of his government, neither the acts passed by the Assembly nor other public papers, and especially of failure to forward a statement of the depredations made along the coast during the last war. Under the second head, he was made responsible for the destruction of the credit of the colony, to the prejudice of the merchants, by allowing the passage of an act for issuing paper money without insisting upon the required suspending clause. Under the third head, he was accused of appointing a former Scottish rebel to office while the recent rebellion of the Highlands was in progress, a person, one McGregor, who had shown great sympathy for the rebels in 1715. [76] He was further charged with giv-

---

[74] Representation of the Board of Trade to the King, March 14, 1754, *North Carolina Colonial Records*, V, 81–108.

[75] Governor Johnston to the Board of Trade, December 28, 1748, *ibid.*, IV, 1165.

[76] *Board of Trade Journal*, 1741–1749, p. 371.

ing out contracts to build and repair forts to persons under his influence who, although receiving the money appropriated for these
defences, contented themselves with employing a few Negroes to
throw up a little dirt as an excuse for a fort. Lastly, he was accused
of neglecting public business, of living one hundred miles distant
from the seat of government, of allowing other public officers to live
at a great distance from the capital, and of failure to hold courts
of chancery with his council. In fact, poor North Carolina was described by his enemies as a place of "great distress and confusion
and scarce better than an asylum for fugitives." [77]

In the face of these accusations, Johnston did not escape a severe
rebuke from the home government, but no steps were taken for his
removal before the news reached London of his death in 1752.[78] Appointed to fill the vacancy was Arthur Dobbs — whose interest had
been shifted from a contest with the Hudson's Bay Company and
the lure of a Northwest Passage (to be described in the next volume
of this series) to the exploitation of lands he held in North Carolina.

Dobbs, an enlightened native of Ireland,[79] was sent to the faction-
ridden colony in 1754 with instructions to quiet disturbances.[80] The
manner of electing members of the Assembly, the number composing
it, and the necessary quorum for the conduct of its business, placed
at fifteen, were specified in his instructions. Provision was also made
for the erection of towns and counties in the southern portion of the
colony, and the Governor was directed to confirm by charters of in-
corporation the rights of the several towns, precincts, or counties.
Finally, he was forbidden to assent to any law that would limit the

---

[77] See *ibid.*, p. 374. It is of interest that Arthur Dobbs, who was to succeed Johnston as Governor, was one of the group who drew up the above charges. See *North Carolina Colonial Records*, IV, 925–6.

[78] At the time of Johnston's death on July 17, 1752, the arrears of his salary
amounted to £13,402.19.2. See *Acts of the Privy Council, Col. Ser., 1745–1766*,
pp. 238–9.

[79] For a sympathetic account of Dobbs's rise from member of Parliament to Surveyor-General of Ireland, the writing of his forward-looking *Essay on the Trade and Improvement of Ireland* that advocated a fundamental reform in Irish land tenure, and his
careful scheme for the colonization of North America that resulted in his being designated as Governor of North Carolina, see Desmond Clarke: *Arthur Dobbs, Esquire,
1689–1765, Surveyor-General of Ireland, Prospector, and Governor of North Carolina*
(Chapel Hill, N.C., 1957).

[80] For Dobbs's commission as Governor, sealed on February 23, 1753, see P.R.O.,
C.O. 5:200, pp. 729–46; for his instructions, dated June 24, 1754, see C.O. 5:200,
pp. 1050–1149.

duration of the Assembly or regulate it in any manner contrary to His Majesty's rights and prerogative.[81]

While the new Governor was destined to have to struggle with the Assembly to carry out his royal instructions and also in other respects to protect the royal prerogative in the face of the forces of self-determination directed against its use,[82] he was at least relieved of one embarrassment that dogged his predecessor: the Assembly's failure over a period of many years to vote funds for Johnston's salary. Realizing that the province was poor, and that the income of the quit-rents was scanty and at times almost non-existent — unlike the situation in Virginia, where there was an accumulation of funds from this source — he sought and secured an agreement from the Treasury whereby his salary would be paid from the Exchequer in England.[83] This fact, it should be pointed out — especially in view of the attitude American colonials later displayed toward the idea of the payment of a governor's salary by the Crown — was apparently not resented by the people but, to the contrary, was a relief welcomed by them.[84]

That the people of North Carolina, despite everything that may be said to the contrary, had a feeling of great dependence on the laws and institutions of the mother country in 1750 is indicated by the fact that in the preceding year the Assembly passed "An Act to put into Force in this Province, the several Statutes of the Kingdom of England, or South Britain, therein particularly mentioned," [85] whereby a great body of statutory law, extending from Magna Charta to the eleventh year of the reign of George II, was given force.[86] Furthermore, it was enacted by the same Assembly that "all and every Part of the Common Law of England, where the same is not altered by the above enumerated Acts, or inconsistent with the particular Constitutions, Customs, and Laws of this Province," should

---

[81] *Acts of the Privy Council, Col. Ser.,* 1745–1766, pp. 187–90. The Dobbs instructions of 1754 follow very closely those prepared for George Thomas the preceding year when he was appointed Governor of the Leeward Islands.

[82] See Desmond Clarke: *op. cit.,* pp. 137–72.

[83] *Ibid.,* p. 103.

[84] Writing to the Board of Trade on March 29, 1764, at a period when his administration was drawing to its close, Dobbs affirmed that "the Assembly refuses to settle any Salary upon the Governor as directed by His Majestys Instructions or even pay the rent for the residence of Governors . . ." (*North Carolina Colonial Records,* VI, 1038–9).

[85] *Laws,* 1715–1776, *State Records of North Carolina,* XXIII, 317.

[86] *Ibid.,* XXIII, 317–26.

be made a part of the law of the colony.[87] Again, the mercantile policies of Great Britain received strong support in the middle of the eighteenth century from many of the inhabitants of the province who had benefited greatly from the navigation and trade acts of Parliament, particularly those providing a bounty on naval stores produced in the American colonies.[88]

Legally, the Church of England was the Established Church of North Carolina. While liberty of conscience was provided by the charters of 1663 and 1665, these at the same time specified that all churches erected should be dedicated according to English ecclesiastical law. In 1701 five parishes were erected and vestries set up with power to levy upon the inhabitants for the building of churches, the purchase of glebes, and the payment of the clergy.[89] This was followed in 1715 by "An Act for Establishing the Church & Appointing Select Vestrys," [90] which specified that the Church of England was "appointed by the Charter . . . to be the only Established Church to have Public encouragement" in the colony. In specifying nine parishes, the names of the twelve vestrymen for each of them were also specified, with the added provision that vacancies in any vestry were to be filled by the active members of it.

This close vestry system, comparable to that of Virginia, was altered in 1741, when the settled part of the province was divided into fifteen parishes and provision made for the election of the vestrymen every two years by the freeholders in each parish. However, to guard against the control of the vestries by those hostile to the Church of England, it was provided that each vestryman should subscribe to a declaration that he would not oppose "the Liturgy of the Church of England, as it is by law established. . . ." [91] Although under terms of this act known dissenters who were elected to the vestry were not subject to fine for refusal to make the declaration as were others, their exemption from penalties was eliminated in 1764 by the Vestry Act of that Year.[92] Not only were vestrymen now fined for refusal to

---

[87] Ibid., XXIII, 327.

[88] See C. R. Haywood: "The Mind of the North Carolina Advocates of Mercantilism," North Carolina Historical Review, XXXIII, 139–65.

[89] North Carolina Colonial Records, I, 601. The act was disallowed in view of the fact that but £30 was specified as the annual stipend of the minister.

[90] Laws, 1715–1776, State Records of North Carolina, XXIII, 6–10.

[91] Ibid., XXIII, 187–91.

[92] Ibid., XXIII, 601–7; see also Paul Conkin: "The Church Establishment in North Carolina, 1765–1776," North Carolina Historical Review, XXXII, 1–30.

qualify in order to serve, but freeholders were also subject to an amercement for refusal to vote in vestry elections. In 1754 this fine was raised to twenty shillings.

But these laws and others passed to strengthen the Established Church in North Carolina did not lead to the erection of many churches. Apparently only four clergymen of the Anglican communion actually had churches in 1764, and but six were in the province, although it had twenty-nine parishes.[93] In 1765 Lieutenant Governor Tryon listed only three churches capable of holding services: that at New Bern, in good repair, and one each at Bath and Edenton in bad condition. The church of Brunswick in that year had the outer walls and a roof, while that at Wilmington had only the walls. In fact, when Governor Dobbs passed away that year at his Brunswick home there was no clergyman living within a hundred miles, with the result that a justice of the peace had to perform the funeral rites.[94] The five churches were the only Anglican churches in existence in 1775 and were, it may be noted, all in the Tidewater, although it is true that here and there were chapels of ease served either by clergymen or by lay readers.[95] While every one of the parishes had its vestry, it is also evident that most of the vestries neglected their prescribed duties; their members were either indifferent to religion or were of another religious persuasion, or they failed to secure the necessary resources by parish levies to support a minister. Yet they held with utmost tenacity to the right of choosing the person who would fill the post.

If the Established Church did not appeal to people of the frontier, those of other religious denominations did. The Rev. James Reed,

---

[93] Governor Dobbs to the Board of Trade, March 29, 1764, North Carolina Colonial Records, VI, 1036.

[94] Tryon to the Society for the Propagation of the Gospel in Foreign Parts, July 31, 1765, ibid., VII, 102–3. That the Establishment had some consecrated ministers in North Carolina in the middle of the eighteenth century is clear by a letter written by the Rev. Clement Hall in the spring of 1750: "In Easter-week I set off and journeyed about 427 miles through my south mission, and in about thirty days preached nineteen sermons, baptised about 495 white and 47 black children, three white and eleven black adults . . . administered . . . sacrament of the Lord's Supper to about 235" (see E. L. Pennington: "Some Observations Regarding the Colonial Clergy," Historical Magazine of the Protestant Episcopal Church, X, 47).

[95] See Sarah M. Lemmon: "The Genesis of the Protestant Episcopal Diocese of North Carolina, 1701–1825," North Carolina Historical Review, XXVIII, 439; Paul Conkin: "The Church Establishment in North Carolina," ibid., XXXII, 5; and Elizabeth H. Davidson: The Establishment of the English Church in the Continental American Colonies (Durham, N.C., 1936), pp. 47–57.

writing from New Bern to the Society for the Propagation of the Gospel in Foreign Parts in 1760, complained that in Craven County "dissenters of all denominations [had] come & settled amongst us . . . Particularly Anabaptists, Methodist, Quakers and Presbyterians. . . ." He did not have a very high opinion of these dissenters, outside the Presbyterians, for he affirmed that the "Anabaptists are obstinate, illiterate & grossly ignorant, the Methodist, ignorant, censorious & uncharitable, the Quakers, Rigid, but the Presbyterians are pretty moderate except here & there a bigot or rigid Calvinist. As for papists, I cannot learn there are above 9 or 10 in the whole County." [96]

Nor was the public support of education much in evidence in North Carolina in 1750. It is true that in 1745 a bill was presented to the Assembly authorizing the commissioners of Edenton, among other things, "to build a school House in the said Town," which was passed into law. But as the law was later reaffirmed and was still before the Assembly of 1767, it is not clear when the school was constructed and when it started to operate. [97] Another bill for a free school, passed in 1749, met with similar delaying action. Further, although Governor Dobbs in January 1755 approved an appropriation of £6,000 for the erection of a public school, he appears to have fostered the current concept of mixing church and school, which did not result in the building of the necessary schools in a period when the appropriations for defence were eating up the funds of the province. [98] Meanwhile, the children of North Carolina were taught under church auspices (as among the Moravians in Wachovia), as part of

[96] North Carolina Colonial Records, VI, 265. For a brief but scholarly treatment of the dissenter groups in North Carolina in the latter part of the eighteenth century see H. T. Lefler and A. R. Newsome: North Carolina . . . (Raleigh, 1954), pp. 125–32.

[97] On December 29, 1767, a bill was passed by the Lower House to establish a school house in Edenton; this was amended by the Council so as to provide that no one should be made a master of the school who was not of the Established Church and who had not been licenced by the Governor. This amendment was rejected by the Lower House early the following year. Yet it appears that a school house was built in 1768, as on December 3 the Governor vetoed a bill to vest "the school house in Edenton" in a board of trustees. A similar bill was presented to him on January 21, 1771. See North Carolina Colonial Records, IV, 783, VII, 98, 561, 588, 632–3, 921–2, VIII, 299 and 477.

[98] North Carolina Colonial Records, IV, 993–4, 1321–2; V, xxv, 314–15. It was not until 1765 that a school, later named the New Bern Academy, was constructed in New Bern. See C. L. Raper: The Church and Private Schools in North Carolina . . . (Greensboro, N.C., 1898), p. 25.

the civic duties of the clergy and the vestries, a function that was generally performed by a local minister or lay reader.[99] The Presbyterians, a much stronger group numerically in the colony than the Moravians, were also deeply concerned with education.[100]

Closely related to education, the printed word is always indicative of progress. The growing maturity of North Carolina may be dated from the setting up of a press in New Bern in 1749 by James Davis as the result of strong encouragement given by the Assembly. Davis then began printing its journal and in 1751 started publishing the *North Carolina Gazette* that appeared somewhat irregularly until 1759. He also issued a collection of the laws of the province and a book of Christian devotion and daily prayer.[101] It is therefore not surprising that, despite handicaps, North Carolina was not without some young men prepared to meet the challenge offered by advanced legal studies in such places as the Inns of Court in London. At least ten of them were admitted to one or another of the Inns between 1731 and 1774.[102] Yet it must be confessed that this was not an impressive showing in view of the fact that during the same period

---

[99] *North Carolina Historical Review*, XXVIII, 441, and XXXII, 20–1. For the part played by Anglican missionaries in education of the youth of North Carolina see D. D. Oliver: *The Society for the Propagation of the Gospel in the Province of North Carolina* (Chapel Hill, N.C., 1910); for education in general in colonial North Carolina see H. T. Lefler and A. R. Newsome: *op cit.*, pp. 132–5. That public education had to await the period after the War for American Independence is indicated by C. L. Coon in his *The Beginnings of Public Education in North Carolina: A Documentary History, 1790–1840* (2 vols., Raleigh, 1908).

[100] The Presbyterians secured a law to establish Queen's College in Mecklenburg County in 1770, which, unhappily, failed to meet the approval of the Privy Council in England. See *North Carolina Colonial Records*, VIII, 448, 525–7; see also R. D. W. Connor: "The Genesis of Higher Education in North Carolina," *North Carolina Historical Review*, XXVIII, 1–7, and M. de L. Haywood: "Story of Queen's College or Liberty Hall," *North Carolina Booklet* ([Raleigh], 1912), XI, 169–75.

[101] For a facsimile of Davis's and North Carolina's first imprint see *Journal of the House of Burgesses, of the Province of North Carolina, 1749* (Introd. by W. S. Powell, Raleigh, N.C., 1949); see also D. C. McMurtrie: "The First Twelve Years of Printing in North Carolina," *No. Car. Hist. Rev.*, X, 214–34, and *Eighteenth Century North Carolina Imprints* (Chapel Hill, N.C., 1938). In the latter part of the seventeenth century the Rev. Thomas Bray and his associates had begun sending collections of books to the colonies. By 1699 thirty libraries had been established, and in 1700 Bath, North Carolina, received one of them which numbered about 1,000 volumes. In 1715 a library-keeper was appointed by the local Board of Commissioners. See B. C. Steiner: "Rev. Thomas Bray and His American Libraries," *American Historical Review*, II, 72–3.

[102] J. G. de Roulhac Hamilton: "The Southern Members of the Inns of Court," *North Carolina Historical Review*, X, 273–86.

forty-eight were admitted from South Carolina, and thirty-seven from Virginia.[103] In fact, this only adds further emphasis to the point that North Carolina, in comparison with its two neighbours, was not only economically but also culturally a backward colony in the middle of the eighteenth century.

---

[103] *Ibid.* With respect to the two great English universities, Oxford and Cambridge, no North Carolina students matriculated in them in the eighteenth century. During the same period Virginia sent 10 to Oxford and 19 to Cambridge, South Carolina sent 10 to Oxford and 11 to Cambridge, and Maryland sent 5 to Oxford and 6 to Cambridge. See W. Connely: "Colonial Americans in Oxford and Cambridge," *The American Oxonian,* XXIX, 1–17, 75–7; see also W. L. Sachse: *The Colonial American in Britain* (Madison, 1956), Chap. 5.

CHAPTER V

Aristocrats of the Rice Swamps

IN spirit and in fundamental agricultural processes the Cape Fear region of North Carolina was part of the same economy that prevailed in tidewater or "low country" South Carolina. Similarly, in a sense North Carolina had overflowed its southern boundary to people the northwestern portion of South Carolina. The settlement of boundaries and the development of the frontier lands were among the problems facing this provincial government in the middle of the eighteenth century. Within the colony most of the people were busily engaged in the profitable production of rice, indigo, naval stores, and cattle as well as in trade with the southern Indians for deerskins. To their great advantage, they possessed the seat of the metropolis of the south, Charleston, from which, as an important seaport, the export of the staples proceeded and where was centred the government and most of its agencies.

"Here," declared Governor James Glen, in referring to South Carolina in 1749, "is a large Tract of Territory hitherto but thinly inhabited, numbers of Navigable rivers which make carriage easy and afford safe ports, a fertile soil and a pretty healthful climate, liberty of conscience, equal laws, easy taxes, and I hope I may add with truth, a Mild Administration of the Government." [1] While its boundaries were not clearly settled either to the north or the west, or even to the south, the stand was taken by its officials, upon the basis of the charter of 1665, that the province comprehended all of that region to the south of North Carolina and to the north of Florida not

---

[1] Governor James Glen to the Board of Trade, July 19, 1749, "Answers to Queries," Shelburne Papers, 45:60–83, Clements Library; see also Board of Trade Journal, 1741–1749, p. 453.

otherwise expressly conveyed by the Crown to the Trustees of the Colony of Georgia — which meant that its claim, overleaping Georgia, extended to the south of the Altamaha River "as far as the Bay of Mexico," and from sea to sea.[2] The population of South Carolina, which embraced in 1749 some 25,000 white people composed of English, Huguenots, Germans, Swiss, and Ulster Scots, and at least 39,000 Negroes,[3] was successfully engaged in the raising of rice and indigo, pork and beef; in lumbering; in producing pitch and tar; and in trading profitably with the Indians for deerskins. From the viewpoint of its economy the colony might have been divided roughly into some four zones: [4] first, there was the region of the fresh-water cypress swamps, which, when cleared of trees and undergrowth, was ideally adapted to the raising of rice; secondly, frequently in juxtaposition with these swamps, there were the better-drained lands given over to indigo, to Indian corn, and to general farming; thirdly, on the edges of this zone, there were those regions where lumbering was carried on with the purpose of clearing the lands and where also took place the extracting of pitch and other naval stores. Here also, beyond the more thickly settled parts, were to be found the cattle pens. Fourthly, beyond the country of the pens and off through the wilderness lay the villages of the Catawbas to the northward, and those of the Creeks and Cherokees to the westward, where

[2] Regarding the northern boundary Glen stated that "a little before my Arrival here a Line was run, or said to be run by Persons who, I am afraid, did not rightly understand, or at least did not rightly understand or duly do His Majesty's Instructions, wherefore if the Governor of North Carolina were de novo instructed upon that head agreeable to His Majesty's pleasure express'd in the 36 Article by My Instructions, I make no Question but His Majesty's Gracious Intentions might yet be fulfilled" (Glen's "Answers to Queries," loc. cit.); see also Journal of the Commons House of Assembly of South Carolina, 1754 (ms.), 29:317–18, South Carolina Archives. (Publication of these journals as the first series of the Colonial Records of South Carolina is now proceeding under the able editorship of Dr. J. H. Easterby and his assistant, Ruth S. Green. In view of this fact, unpublished volumes are cited as manuscript (ms.), giving the manuscript volume number and page, whereas the published volumes are cited by year and page.)

For the issue of the North Carolina–South Carolina boundary see M. L. Skaggs: North Carolina Boundary Disputes Involving her Southern Line (Chapel Hill, N.C., 1941).

[3] Glen to the Board of Trade, July 19, 1749, Shelburne Papers, 45:60–83; see also E. B. Greene and V. D. Harrington: American Population before . . . 1790 (New York, 1932), pp. 174–5.

[4] For a statement regarding the geographical divisions of the province see E. L. Whitney: The Government of the Colony of South Carolina (Baltimore, 1895), pp. 56–8; see also L. C. Gray: History of Agriculture in the Southern United States to 1860 (2 vols., Washington, 1933), I, 279–80, for a discussion of the rice lands.

centred one of the most profitable activities of the province, the Indian trade.[5]

Naturally, there was a concentration of slaves in the region of the fresh-water cypress swamps, where their labour was held to be absolutely essential. Nevertheless, the plantation system here developed required no such large investments of capital in labour or equipment as was the case in the British sugar islands, where it was considered desirable to have as a working unit not less than 250 slaves. In contrast to this but 30 slaves and one overseer to a rice plantation were regarded as the proper unit. Each slave was expected under ordinary conditions to produce in a season between four and five barrels of rice, each weighing 500 pounds, and in addition a considerable quantity of provisions during those periods when the rice did not require attention. This labour was considered profitable when utilized in this manner with rice selling at a price of from 45 to 55 shillings per hundredweight, South Carolina currency.[6] Therefore, instead of possessing great estates, enterprising South Carolina planters might have a number of plantations or settlements of moderate size, as described above, either in juxtaposition or scattered about in the various parishes of the low country.

The operations in rice-production [7] were happily all quite simple and could be carried through by slave labour. In this respect it differed widely from sugar-production, which demanded a rather high order of skill in the handling of the products of the cane after the first process at the mill. "The best Land for Rice," wrote Governor Glen in his *Description of South Carolina*, published in 1761, "is a wet, deep, miry soil; such as is generally to be found in Cypress

---

[5] During the fiscal year from November 1747 to November 1748, the value of deerskins exported was £36,000 sterling, which was almost equal to the total value of all other exports combined — exclusive of rice, the value of which was £88,600 sterling — which totalled £36,761. See "Exports from Charles Town from Nov. 1747 to Nov. 1748," *American Husbandry* (original edition in 1775, edited by H. J. Carman and reissued New York, 1939), pp. 308–10. The value of the Indian trade in 1749 was £252,000 South Carolina currency; see Glen's "Answers to Queries," Shelburne Papers, 45:60–83. For an excellent account of the Indian trade up to the middle of the eighteenth century see V. W. Crane: *The Southern Frontier, 1670–1732* (Durham, N.C., 1928; reissued without bibliography, Ann Arbor, Mich., 1956). Indian relations and trade are given full consideration in later volumes of this series.

[6] Gov. Glen to the Board of Trade, "Answers to Queries," Shelburne Papers, 45:60–83.

[7] For the beginnings of rice-planting in South Carolina see A. S. Salley, Jr.: *The Introduction of Rice Culture into South Carolina* (Columbia, 1919); see also L. C. Gray: *History of Agriculture in the Southern United States to 1860*, I, 277–9.

Swamps; or a black greasy mould with a Clay Foundation. . . ." [8] Planted in the spring in shallow furrows far enough apart for cultivation, the rice was weeded and flooded at intervals and by September was ready for cutting; this was done by sickle. Whereupon it was stacked in great heaps or placed in sheds or barns and then threshed with the old-fashioned flail. After this, the chaff was separated by winnowing with a windfan, which by 1750 was supplanting the more tedious and primitive process of hand fanning — a "prodigious improvement." It was then ready for grinding in the handmill to remove the outer husk, was winnowed once more, then placed in a wooden mortar and, by use of a pestle, freed of its thick skin, a most laborious part of the work. After sifting, it was at last packed in barrels for the market. Such was the simple process involved in the production of rice, with land and common slave labour the principal items of capital investment.[9]

Three other advantages, in addition to the two previously mentioned, were possessed by the South Carolina rice-planter over the West India sugar-planter. His markets were fairly secure from competition. Again, he could realize on his investment within the first year. Finally, his capital in slave labour was less in need of renewal from year to year. Governor Glen declared in 1749 [10] that the number of slaves was not decreasing on the South Carolina plantations, although there had been no fresh supply for almost nine years, which would indicate that the birth rate was holding its own against the death rate — something that was not true in the British sugar islands.[11] The number of active workers employed in growing rice was

[8] *Colonial South Carolina: Two Contemporary Descriptions by Governor James Glen and Doctor George Milligen-Johnston* (ed. C. J. Milling, Columbia, S.C., 1951), p. 14.

[9] *Ibid.*, pp. 15–16. The unknown author of *American Husbandry* (1939 edn., p. 277), written before the beginning of the War for American Independence, must have observed closely in South Carolina the processes of rice-culture. He gives us a picture of Negroes working ankle or mid-leg deep "in a furnace of stinking putrid effluvia" while engaged in the process of cultivating rice in the swamp land.

[10] Glen's "Answer to Queries," 1749, Shelburne Papers, 45:60–83. While these answers in 1749 form the basis of Glen's description of South Carolina in 1761, some of the figures given in the latter are different.

[11] Governor Glen's "Answers to Queries," 1749, Shelburne Papers, 45:60–83. Elizabeth Donnan, in her *Documents Illustrative of the History of the Slave Trade to America* (4 vols., Washington, 1930–5, IV, 301–2 and 310–12), shows that some Negroes were imported into South Carolina in 1749, beginning with the arrival of the *Hector* in June from the Windward Coast of Africa; two other ships arrived later in the year with slaves, but the number brought was small. However, by 1755 Henry Laurens and his business

probably little less than 12,000. In 1748 they produced for exportation 55,000 barrels of this cereal valued at £618,750 South Carolina currency, or £88,600 sterling. In 1761 Glen estimated the quantity to be exported at above 90,000 barrels.[12]

One of the problems confronting the rice-planters in connection with the maintenance of the supply of slave labour created widespread anxiety at this time. It grew out of the tendency for considerable numbers of their blacks to desert and flee southward along the coast through the swamps to the Spanish settlements in Florida. The existence of scout boats employed for the purpose of putting an end to this had by no means fulfilled the general expectations, although manned by persons well acquainted with the passages across the inlets. Indeed, so serious had this problem become by 1749 that Governor Glen in his speech to the Assembly declared: "Unless a stop be put to this Practice it may . . . prove . . . destructive to the Province." [13]

In addition to the use of the patrol boats, there was a highly organized system of land patrols in South Carolina from the year 1704 to the end of slavery. After a slave insurrection at Stono in 1739 the province was divided into districts, each of which was covered by patrol riders at least once a month. These riders were selected by the captain of the local militia company and served for two months.

---

partner, Austin, were handling annually on commission some 700 imported slaves. See, by the same author, "The Slave Trade into South Carolina before the Revolution," *The American Historical Review*, XXXIII, 811.

[12] Glen's "Answers to Queries," 1749, *loc. cit.*, and his account of South Carolina in 1761 in *Colonial South Carolina: Two Contemporary Descriptions* . . . , *op. cit.*, p. 47. Although the quantity of rice exported in 1748 was some 25,000 barrels short of the amount exported in 1740, yet it required some 160 ships of 100 tons burden to move this commodity to the overseas market. According to the author of *American Husbandry* (1939 edn., p. 311), in 1754 South Carolina exported 104,682 barrels of rice against Glen's estimate of over 90,000 barrels. For further contemporary comment on the production and sale of rice see Alexander Hewat's . . . *Rise and Progress of the Colonies of South Carolina and Georgia* (2 vols., London, 1779), II, 90.

[13] Governor Glen's speech of November 23, 1749, *Journal of the Commons House of Assembly, 1749–1750, Colonial Records of South Carolina* (J. H. Easterby and Ruth S. Green, eds., Columbia, [1959]), p. 286. (Pre-publication pagination for this volume has been provided through the great kindness of the editors.)

Among others, Colonel Pinckney and Colonel Austin especially suffered by the disappearance of their Negroes. Many slaves at this period, it was charged, also attempted to poison their masters. Fortunately for the latter, a slave by the name of Caesar, a famous herb doctor, cured many of these cases. For this, and for information he gave which effected the cure of other ailments, he was given his liberty and a pension for life. See *ibid.*, 1749–1750, pp. 293–4, 302–4, 326, 338–9, 478–80.

They were expected to examine every plantation within their district, to whip slaves found away from home without leave, to search for concealed weapons in Negro houses, and in case of resistance to kill all resisting slaves.

In examining the position of the South Carolina Negro in the middle of the eighteenth century one finds that his circumstance might be one of comfort and not unkindly direction and even distinction, or otherwise — depending, as a rule, on his master or overseer and his own attitude. Before 1739 there was apparently so little fear of the slaves that in that year, in face of the menace of the Spaniards garrisoned at St. Augustine, the Assembly authorized the Governor to permit the militia captains to enlist Negroes who were recommended for their good conduct, and to promise them freedom for acts of bravery while under arms and other suitable rewards. But before the act could be implemented, the Assembly was led to reverse itself and draw back from a position that was now considered to be a dangerous one in view of a small-scale slave uprising that occurred at Storo in the latter part of 1739.[14] Perhaps the account of South Carolina in 1763 that Dr. George Milligen-Johnston, long a resident of the province, has left us will indicate with a fair degree of accuracy the position of the Negro in 1750. In his *A Short Description of the Province of South Carolina*, published in London in 1770, he has the following to say respecting the slaves:

> "They are in this Climate necessary, but very dangerous Domestics, their Number so much exceeding the Whites; a natural Dislike and Antipathy, that subsists between them and our *Indian* neighbours, is a very lucky Circumstance, and for this Reason: In our Quarrels with the Indians, however proper and necessary it may be to give them Correction, it can never be our Interest to extirpate them, or to force them from their Lands; their Ground would be soon taken by runaway *Negroes* from our Settlements, whose Numbers would daily increase, and quickly become more formidable Enemies than *Indians* can ever be, as they speak our Language, and would never be at a Loss for Intelligence."[15]

---

[14] See Benjamin Quarles: "The Colonial Militia and Negro Manpower," *Mississippi Valley Historical Review*, XLV, 649–50.

[15] The Milligen-Johnston *Short Description* is reprinted on pp. 111–206 of *Colonial South Carolina: Two Contemporary Descriptions* (ed. C. J. Milling, Columbia, S.C., 1951); for the above quotation see p. 136.

The very comprehensive "Act for the better Ordering and Governing Negroes and other Slaves in this Province," passed May 10, 1740, sets out with great fullness the legal restrictions it seemed necessary to place upon them.[16] Its fifty-seven clauses constitute a slave code — a code in force in 1750. Among its provisions was one stating that any slave found outside his master's property must carry a letter or ticket. Failure to do so would involve twenty lashes on the bare back. Should a wandering slave refuse to be examined, any white man could kill him upon such refusal. However, if he were beaten or maimed without cause by a white person, that individual upon conviction should forfeit forty shillings to the poor and if the slave were thereby disabled he should forfeit fifteen shillings a day to the owner for each day of lost time.

The trial of a slave accused of a capital offence had to be held before two justices of the peace and at least three and not more than five freeholders. If he were accused of an offence not capital he was to be tried by one justice of the peace and two freeholders, and the decision of the justice of the peace supported by one of the freeholders was sufficient for conviction. There were to be witnesses at such trials. Those that were white were to be sworn; free Indians and slaves gave their testimony without oath. A free Negro, accused of a crime, was to be proceeded against as in the case of a slave.

To guide those presiding at trials involving slaves, it was specified that all crimes committed by them that by the laws of England and of the province were felonies without benefit of clergy should carry the death penalty. Further, this penalty should be inflicted should a Negro strike any white person and thereby grievously wound or maim him. On the other hand, if any white person should wilfully murder a slave, he should pay a fine of £700 current money and thereafter be incapable of holding any office within the province; if he were unable to pay the fine, he was either to be sent to serve seven years in one of the frontier garrisons or committed to the Charleston workhouse at hard labour for the same period of time. Should a white man, however, in sudden passion or by undue correction kill a slave, he was to forfeit £350 current money, and £100 should he cut out the tongue, put out the eye, castrate, or cruelly scald, burn, or mutilate a slave.

---

[16] For the above statute see *Public Laws of the State of South-Carolina* (ed. J. F. Grimké, Philadelphia, 1790), pp. 163–73.

Moreover, the statute took notice of the fact that many Negroes wore clothes "much above the condition of slaves," for the securing of which they used "sinister and evil methods." To put an end to such ostentation and keep them in their places, it was enacted that, under penalty, no owner of slaves (except those slaves who were "livery-men and boys") should permit them to wear apparel "finer, other, or of greater value than negro cloth," in which category were placed such cheap fabrics as duffels, kerseys, oznabrigs, and blue linen. Finally, to guard against the tendency for slaves to seek to elevate themselves above their status, it was stated that "as the teaching of slaves to write may be accompanied by many inconveniences," any person so doing should forfeit £100 current money.[17]

In 1750 many thousands of slaves were engaged in the production of indigo as well as rice, which went hand in hand in the Tidewater, although indigo demanded better drainage and a different kind of soil — "a rich light soil, unmixed with Clay or Sand," in the words of a South Carolina indigo-planter.[18] For that reason it was more inti-mately related to the type of lands where Indian corn was then grown and later cotton. It therefore was to be found in the economic zone of diversified farming, in contrast to that of the reclaimed cy-press-swamp region with its specialized production. Its cultivation, on a commercial scale at least, was of recent date in South Carolina. Apparently not until 1745 was the discovery made of the native indigo plant. Interest in its production was further stimulated by successful experiments taking place in the French West Indies and by the decline in the price of rice.[19] As a result 134,118 pounds of

---

[17] See D. D. Wallace: *The Life of Henry Laurens* . . . (New York, 1915), pp. 72–8. For this topic see also Marguerite B. Hamer: "A Century before Manumission: Side-lights on Slavery in Mid-Eighteenth Century South Carolina," *North Carolina Historical Review*, XVII, 232–6; F. J. Klingberg: *An Appraisal of the Negro in Colonial South Carolina: A Study in Americanization* (Washington, D.C., 1941), in which the author sets forth the efforts to Christianize and educate the Negro by missionaries supported by the Society for the Propagation of the Gospel in Foreign Parts, even after the passing of the statute of 1740; C. E. Pierre: "The Work of the Society for the Propagation of the Gospel in Foreign Parts among the Negroes in the Colonies," *Journal of Negro History*, I, 352; and M. W. Jernegan: "Slavery and Conversion in the Colonies," *American His-torical Review* (XXI, 523–4), for the testimony in 1759 by the Rev. Mr. Harrison of St. James Parish, Goose Creek, that in his church he had 31 whites and 26 Negroes as communicants with a congregation of 150 whites and 50 to 60 Negroes.

[18] See *American Husbandry* (1939 edn.), pp. 281–90; see also *Colonial South Caro-lina: Two Contemporary Descriptions*, p. 203.

[19] [Sir Edward Leigh]: *Further Observations Intended for Improving the Culture and Curing of Indigo* . . . *in South Carolina* (London, 1747), p. 5. For the experi-

indigo, valued at £117,353 South Carolina currency, was exported in 1748.[20]

Three kinds of indigo were produced at this period and were sharply differentiated by experts: copper indigo, with a copperish color, the most desirable in the dying of woollens and commanding the highest price in the English market; purple indigo, utilized especially by the linen-makers and the makers of bluing; and blue indigo, sought by the silk-manufacturers. While there was a steady demand for each of these, more of the first variety was used than of the other two combined. In 1747 the question of a bounty on indigo-production was urged in Parliament, where it was pointed out that Great Britain was consuming annually over 600,000 pounds of French indigo,[21] paying at the rate of five shillings a pound or a total of £150,000 sterling — all of which, it was urged, might be saved to the Empire. Merchants trading to the Carolinas, English clothiers, and the dyers joined with the planters and Charleston (Charles Town, as it was then called) merchants in petitions which culminated in the Act of 1748, providing a bounty of sixpence a pound on all indigo manufactured in the British American plantations and sent directly to Great Britain.[22] In anticipation of this legislation, the quantity produced in South Carolina in 1748 was 124,118 pounds, which was not quite one fourth of the total required in British manufacturing. Unfortunately, the quality did not compare with that of the French West Indies article,[23] and its price on the market was but two shillings and sixpence. Nevertheless, it was a paying crop with the bounty included, for "planters doubled their capital every three or

---

ments of Eliza Lucas before 1745 see H. H. Ravenel: *Eliza Pinckney* (New York, 1896), pp. 79, 103–6; and for a recent view of the support of the mercantilistic policy of the mother country by South Carolinians as it related particularly to the effort to make indigo a second great staple for export, see C. R. Haywood: "Mercantilism and South Carolina Agriculture, 1700–1763," *South Carolina Historical Magazine*, LX, 15–27. For a picture of a 600-acre plantation growing both rice and indigo, as well as other diversified crops for subsistence, see T. O. Lawton, Jr.: "Captain William Lawton: 18th Century Planter of Edisto," *South Carolina Historical Magazine*, LX, 86–93.

[20] Governor Glen's "Answers to Queries," 1749, Shelburne Papers, 45:60–83.

[21] Between 1734 and 1745 an average of 681,806 pounds of indigo was imported annually into England. See *Further Observations Intended for Improving the Culture and Curing of Indigo . . .* , p. 1.

[22] 21 Geo. II, c. 30.

[23] In 1749 Governor Glen suggested the desirability of giving suitable encouragement to some skilful persons from either the French or Spanish settlements to remove to South Carolina. See the Governor's message of November 23, 1749, *Journal of the Commons House of Assembly, 1749–1750*, p. 286.

four years." By 1750 several thousand acres of land were devoted to the growing of this plant, and by 1754 the colony was exporting 200,000 pounds.[24]

The seed used in the middle of the eighteenth century was not that of the native indigo plant, as a rule, but was so-called "true Guatimala," only surpassed by the "French, or Hispaniola" variety.[25] The black seed planted in shallow trenches in April soon sprouted and for four months the plant was cultivated. When in full bloom, it was cut down and was ready for processing. It appears that during the summer a good slave would not only care for two acres of indigo, which might yield as much as 160 pounds of dye, but would find time to provide himself with much of his food, while in the winter months he would give considerable effort to sawing lumber and to other gainful activities.[26] The land in South Carolina yielded two crops each season, but this contrasted unfavourably with the three and four crops secured in the French islands as the result of their longer growing-period.[27]

The process of production of indigo was not so simple as that of rice. As in the case of sugar, the phases beyond the growth of the plant required competent supervision. According to the description left by Dr. Milligen-Johnston, the plants were placed in a vat called a "steeper," where they were allowed to ferment under pressure for some twelve to fifteen hours. Thereupon the liquid was drained off

[24] See Witt Bowden: *The Industrial History of the United States* (New York, 1930), p. 67.

[25] *Colonial South Carolina: Two Descriptions*, p. 203. The author of *American Husbandry* (1775, 1939 edn., p. 281) states: "There are three sorts of indigo cultivated in South Carolina — the Hispaniola, the Bahama, which is a false Guatemala, and the native; the first two are most valuable, but the last is much better adapted to the climate."

[26] Governor Glen to the Board of Trade, July 19, 1749, "Answers to Queries," Shelburne Papers, 45:60–83.

[27] In contrasting the production of indigo in St. Domingue and South Carolina, Dr. John Mitchell makes the following observation: "This is planted by the French on the fresh woodlands . . . which is too rich and moist even for sugar. . . . They likewise cut it every six weeks, or eight times a year, and for two years together; whereas in Carolina it is cut but thrice; and . . . the third cutting is but of little value, as even the second is in Virginia. Neither does the soil or climate seem fit to yield the rich juice which makes this dye in any plenty or perfection. The French and Spaniards make great quantities with eight and ten shillings a pound, when the little we make in Carolina is not upon an average worth above two shillings, and a great deal has been sold for a shilling and less" (*The Present State of Great Britain and North America with regard to Agriculture, Population, Trade, and Manufactures* [London, 1767], pp. 148–9).

into another vat, called a "battery," and was agitated violently for a few minutes with paddles or some other device. It was then curdled by the application of lime water while being stirred continuously until it reached a deep purple colour. The indigo granules were now allowed to settle at the bottom of the vat, and after some eight or ten hours the water was drained off. The next step was the straining of the indigo in horse-hair sieves to clean it of foreign substances. This was followed by a second drainage in cloth bags to remove the remaining moisture. With this done, the indigo paste, now stiff, was removed from the bags, spread on planks, and cut into small squares. The final steps were its removal to a drying-house where it would be protected from the sun and where the squares were turned over at intervals. When properly cured it was placed in barrels.[28] These processes required extraordinary care and expert knowledge and were by no means mastered by all the South Carolina producers.

The chief defect of much of the Carolina indigo was that it became too hard on the surface and not fully cured in the centre. Importers also noticed that in many of the casks there was nothing but a black spongy substance producing a muddy effect, as if the indigo were mixed with soil. In others the dye was so very light in colour as to convey the suspicion that flour or starch had been added; while in still others different grades of indigo were mixed. Further, great carelessness was shown by planters in providing proper containers for this valuable commodity. Old rice barrels were frequently used, with the result that there were serious losses by reason of leakage and exposure.[29] All this contrasted unfavourably with the high quality of the French product made in convenient, uniform sizes for the use of the trade and carefully shipped in iron-bound pipes each weighing between 700 and 800 pounds.[30] As a result the Assembly sought by

---

[28] See *Colonial South Carolina: Two Descriptions,* pp. 204–6. For a detailed account of the growing and manufacturing of indigo in South Carolina see the article by "C.W." in the *Gentleman's Magazine,* 1755, XXV, 201–3, 256–8. C. E. Jones, in his article "Charles Woodmason as a Poet," *South Carolina Historical Magazine,* LIX, 189–91, presents evidence that "C.W." was none other than the Rev. Charles Woodmason, whose journal and other writings relating to South Carolina, edited by R. J. Hooker under the title *The Carolina Backcountry on the Eve of the Revolution,* is cited later in this chapter.

[29] *Further Observations Intended for Improving the Culture and Curing of Indigo* . . . , pp. 3–5.

[30] *Ibid.,* p. 5.

means of legislation to do away with various abuses practised by planters and exporters.[31]

It was considered desirable to raise both rice and indigo on the same plantation where the varied nature of the soil would permit, or on a nearby plantation, so that the owner could derive the greatest returns from his slave labour by alternating from rice to indigo. Nevertheless, indigo was really a product of the diversified-farming region, as has been previously pointed out.

By the middle of the eighteenth century, settlers were pushing their way far beyond the low country up the north bank of the Savannah, along its tributary, Stevens Creek, off toward Ninety-six; they were about to penetrate beyond Orangeburg on the Edisto, also along the branches of the Santee and its tributary, the Saluda, up the Great Pedee toward North Carolina almost as far as the Cheraws, and on the Wateree toward Wateree Creek and the Catawba Indian Nation. Beyond were the vast wilderness stretches.[32] In this great back country many thousands of people were living, and their farms yielded substantial quantities of grain, pork, and many other articles to meet the demand of the low-country population, which previously had been supplied with these commodities almost wholly from New York and Philadelphia. The province was so self-sufficient, in the main, that in 1749 Governor Glen declared that beer was the only article that could not be supplied locally and therefore was being imported from the northern colonies.[33] Nevertheless, it is clear that in 1753, by act of the provincial government, £2,513.14 in the hands of the Powder Receiver at the port of Charleston was set aside to allow the importation of 50,000 bushels of Indian corn because of the scarcity of that article.[34]

The people of the South Carolina back country, according to Governor Glen, were living in sad neglect. Not a single minister was there to inspire them to better things, not a schoolmaster to relieve their ignorance and illiteracy. Even the courts of justice were far removed from all the newer settlements.[35] In a petition from the peo-

---

[31] See *South Carolina Statutes at Large* (5 vols., ed. T. Cooper, Columbia, S.C., 1863-9), III, 718.

[32] Report of the Committee to search out lands for poor Protestants, December 1, 1752, Journal of the Commons House (ms.), 28:64-5.

[33] Governor Glen to the Board of Trade, July 19, 1749, "Answers to Queries," Shelburne Papers, 45:60-83.

[34] *South Carolina Statutes at Large*, IV, 1-3.

[35] "The people in Amelia, Saxe-Gotha and New Windsor, tho' they are old settled

ple of Granville County, located in the extreme southeastern part of the province, it was declared in 1750 that they were subject to an attendance in Charleston at "the several courts of Common Pleas and Courts of Sessions" and for other legal purposes, which involved them not only in many inconveniences but hardships as well. They therefore prayed that courts might be held at Beaufort and that commissioners might be appointed for taking probate of wills and granting letters of administration of estates and marriage licences.[36]

An effort had been made by the Assembly to remedy some of the inconveniences of the judicial system by means of an act passed in 1747 empowering two local justices of the peace and three freeholders, or a majority of them, to determine all actions for debt involving between £20 and £75 current South Carolina money — that is, between £4 and £15 proclamation money — to the exclusion of any other court of judicature. Since most of the cases fell within the above limits, this obviously would have been a serious blow to the Court of Common Pleas, wherein all actions involving amounts above £20 current money had heretofore been determined by juries; it would also have been a blow to the office of the Provost Marshal; for the local constables were empowered by it to execute all processes that fell to the newly established courts. But it failed

---

Townships yet have never had any Minister or School Master amongst them and there are several thousands of Settlers near them on the Wateree, Saludy and Broad Rivers and Stephens's Creek in the same situation. This is truly a great Evil but admits of a Cure. It will be perhaps more difficult to relieve them from another[,] that the Courts of Judicature are too far from them" (Governor Glen to the Assembly, January 16, 1754, Journal of the Commons House [ms.], 29:20–1). In 1754 the Commons voted to make provision for two ministers of the Established Church to serve in the more thickly settled parts of the back settlements, who should "preach in the English tongue" and also instruct the youth in the English language. See ibid., 29:52–3.

Dr. Easterby, South Carolina Archivist, is of the opinion that religion and education were not as much neglected in the back country as Governor Glen indicated to be the case. His view is reinforced by Dr. R. L. Meriwether in his Expansion of South Carolina (Kingsport, Tenn., 1940), pp. 47–8, passim, when he points out that from 1739 onward Christian Theus of the German Reformed Church was preaching in the German language in Saxe Gotha, that the Presbyterian John Giessendanner, later to become an Anglican, was active in Amelia and Orangeburg and also visited the Congarees occasionally, and further that the Welsh immigrants from 1738 on "constituted a religious group as compact and vigorous as that which settled Williamsburg," as did the close-knit community in the Waxhaws. For Dr. Meriwether's estimate of all the social conditions in the back country by 1759 see ibid., pp. 178–80. See also G. P. Voight: "Religious Conditions among German-Speaking Settlers in South Carolina, 1732–1774," South Carolina Historical Magazine, LVI, 59–66.

[36] Journal of the Commons House of Assembly, 1749–1750, March 8, 1749/50, pp. 438–9.

of approval by the Privy Council. Further, in 1752, to meet the needs of the back country for courts of justice, an elaborate plan was drawn up for the establishment of three circuit courts: one at Georgetown, whose precincts should extend to the north side of the Santee River; one at Beaufort, bounded by the Ashepoo; and the last at Congaree, bounded on the southeast by Amelia and Orangeburg townships. Serious objections also were found to this plan, much to the discontent of the back regions.[37]

The measure was reasonable and it was clearly in line with the desires of the people of the province to make the courts more accessible — especially to those living in isolated parts — and more democratic. However, in signing the bill Glen directly violated his instructions. When the act came before His Majesty in council, serious exception was taken to the bill itself as its many defects came to light under scrutiny. It was, therefore, not only disallowed, but orders were given to signify to the Governor His Majesty's high displeasure at this violation of his trust.[38] Thus the expansion of the judicial system of South Carolina had to await the development of the crisis which was to come in the 1760's, known as the Regulation (which is considered in a later volume of this series).

All this lack of cultural facilities in the newer settlements was in striking contrast to conditions in the low country. Here several substantial church edifices had been erected and supplied with ministers; here the children of the wealthy planters, after spending some years under tutors or at the free schools, were frequently sent away to England to finish their education; [39] here also, with legal remedies always at hand, was abundant opportunity to influence the shaping

---

[37] The act of 1747 was passed January 13, 1747 — see *Public Laws of South-Carolina* (Grimké), No. 780; see also *Acts of the Privy Council, Col. Ser., 1745–1766*, pp. 59–60. For the bill of 1752 and its fate see *Journal of the Commons House* (ms.), 29:137–40; see also the proceedings of the Commons House of Assembly on March 5, 1752, *ibid.*, 29:186–9. Conditions bordering on anarchical in the back country, as set forth by the Rev. Charles Woodmason and other contemporaries during the late 1760's and early 1770's, will be dealt with in a later volume of this series.

[38] *Ibid.*

[39] It appears, however, that the provincial government was lacking in proper facilities even in the low country. Governor Glen, in his speech to the Assembly in 1750, referred to the "inconvenient places" in which both the Council and Commons met, and to the fact "that the Courts are kept in Taverns, and the Prisons in private Houses" (*Journal of the Commons House* [ms.], 26:13–14; *Journal of the Commons House of Assembly, 1749–1750*, p. 287). In fact, in 1751 the Assembly met in the house of Colonel Robert Brewton. See *Journal of the Commons House* (ms.), 26:432.

of the law.[40] Here, too, beginning with the year 1732, was published the *South-Carolina Gazette* giving news of world events. How different were conditions along the frontier!

Under the circumstances it is not surprising that it was extremely difficult to bring certain of the frontiersmen under proper control, especially the Ulster Scots who had moved southward from North Carolina. Many of them, although living well to the south of the line agreed upon by the two colonies in 1732, refused to pay quit-rents on the grounds that they were North Carolinians, and in general they ignored the authority of the government of the province. After all, what did the government centred in Charleston mean to them?

The peopling of great stretches of this back country with desirable settlers from abroad was certainly a leading objective of the Glen regime. Additional lands were purchased of the Cherokee in the region called Long Canes, which was to the north of the Savannah and 250 miles from Charleston. Thereupon, agents were offered a premium of one shilling sterling on each settler brought in and were given encouragement to go to Germany and Switzerland for the purpose of securing Protestant immigrants, who in turn were promised the sum of £6 proclamation money if between the ages of twelve and fifty, and £3 if under twelve and over two years. The recipients of this bounty were expected to settle along some part of the southern frontier lying between the Ponpon and the Savannah rivers or in the central parts of the colony between the Santee and the Ponpon. To promote a permanent type of settlement it was agreed, moreover, that an additional bonus of £4 should be given to those between twelve and fifty years of age who were still occupying their land allotments three years after settlement, and £2 to those between twelve and two years of age. As a further inducement it was provided that for ten years these settlers should be tax exempt. By an act of the year 1751 it was also agreed that one fifth of the tax imposed on the first purchases of Negroes and other slaves imported — which amounted to £11,168 — should be devoted to the defraying of the expense of surveying lands and passing grants in favour of poor Prot-

---

[40] It is of interest that a greater number of young South Carolinians studied at the Inns of Court in London in the eighteenth century than students of any other American colony. See J. G. de R. Hamilton: "Southern Members of the Inns of Court," *North Carolina Historical Review*, X, 273–86. For the most extended account of the education of Americans in England see W. L. Sachse: *The Colonial American in Britain* (Madison, 1956), especially p. 64.

estants. Finally, in 1753 the sum of £6,000 was borrowed to make advances to the poorer people so that they might finance the first year's planting.[41]

Among those who were active in bringing foreign settlers into the province were the Swiss Jacob Reminsperger (Remeirspergher, Rümersperger), Frederic Grienzweig (Grienzweick), and Andrew Seyer. In 1748 the first named of these agents succeeded in interesting over 3,000 Germans, who, even before preparations were completed for their sea voyage, sold their possessions and came down the Rhine to Rotterdam. There, to the infinite chagrin of Reminsperger, a majority of them were gathered together by an elert Mr. Headman of that city, acting in the interests of Pennsylvania, and speedily shipped to that province. Others were persuaded to go to Georgia. So that, finally, when the necessary arrangements were made, a little over 600 were salvaged for South Carolina.[42]

In addition to the activities of these special immigration agents, attempts were made to organize certain large land companies for settling South Carolina. The first of these schemes originated with William Livingston and his associates, who had purposes similar to those of the promoters of the Ohio Company of Virginia. Through an order secured from the Privy Council, the provincial government was called upon to survey and grant to them 200,000 acres under condition that they would settle 1,000 Protestants upon these lands within a period of ten years. The order first given in 1742 was renewed in 1749 [43] and came before the provincial government in June 1751.[44] Another, promoted by James Peyn (Payn), a London merchant, and associates, sought in 1746 a grant of 500,000 acres "lying waste and uncultivated," with the idea in mind of settling poor Jews of Europe on these lands, as well as foreign Protestants.[45] Finally, a South Carolinian, John Hamilton, who had discovered improved methods of producing pitch and tar as well as an essential oil, sought in 1748/9, in partnership with a group of wealthy mer-

---

[41] Journal of His Majesty's Council for South Carolina, 18, Part 2:570–2; see also Journal of the Commons House (ms.), 26:60 and 28:305.

[42] See the petition of John Jacob Reminsperger, December 1, 1749, Journal of the Commons House of Assembly, 1749–1750, pp. 313–14, 322–3, and ibid. (ms.), 27:128–9, 262–3; see also P.R.O., C.O. 5:402, pp. 195–206, and further Acts of the Privy Council, Col. Ser., 1745–1766, p. 81.

[43] Board of Trade Journal, 1741–1749, pp. 39 and 455.

[44] Journal of His Majesty's Council, 18, Part 1:139–42, 157–8.

[45] Board of Trade Journal, 1741–1749, pp. 263–5.

chants, to secure orders in council to survey 200,000 acres of land advantageously situated both for the manufacturing and shipping of these commodities and for settling 1,000 Protestants.[46]

While the last three proposals for colonization were abortive ones, the general results of the provincial government's encouragement to immigration was a flow of population into the province in such proportions as at last to overwhelm the authorities and to lead the government to instruct the London agent, James Crockatt, to try to prevent more than 1,000 foreign Protestants arriving in any one year.[47] Thus, when Governor Glen notified the Commons House of Assembly in September 1752 that 800 foreign Protestants had arrived in the Charleston harbour and that two more shiploads were expected hourly, the legislature in alarm appointed a committee to revise the law so as to limit strictly the number of foreigners entitled to settle annually within the colony.[48] The following year, as previously indicated, it was necessary to appropriate a certain sum for the aid of those who had landed.[49] In this colonization movement the authorities strongly favoured the steady-going German and Swiss Protestants and made no attempt to encourage certain types of immigrants such as the Ulster Scots. These, they had already been made to realize, they could neither keep from coming nor easily control after their arrival within the province. In other words, they sought a well-disciplined, industrious group of agriculturists to engage in diversified farming or cattle-raising on frontier lands. For there were regions on the outskirts of the zone of diversified farming and even interspersed within it which were well adapted to livestock.

"Our Country abounds in Cattle and lies commodiously to the Sugar Colonies and foreign Settlements for a market," affirmed Governor Glen in addressing the Commons House of Assembly on November 23, 1749.[50] Despite his statement, in the preceding year the value of beef exported was less than one tenth that of indigo and even less than the value of tanned leather.[51] The explanation for this

---

[46] C.O. 5:402, pp. 181–4; see also Acts of the Privy Council, Col. Ser., 1745–1766, pp. 60–1, and Council Journal, 18, Part 1:139–42. Hamilton's original application was made in 1742.

[47] Journal of the Commons House of Assembly, 1749–1750, February 7, 1750, p. 395.

[48] Ibid. (ms.), 27:582–8.

[49] Ibid. (ms.), 28:304–5.

[50] Ibid., 1749–1750, p. 285.

[51] Glen's "Answers to Queries," Shelburne Papers, 45:60–83.

lies less in the fact that the quantity offered for export was comparatively small than in the fact that the beef was inferior in quality to that of the northern plantations. For South Carolina was denied the privilege that New England enjoyed of importing salt from any part of the world and was therefore obliged, according to Glen, to rely on American salt, which, he asserted, was "of so corrosive a Nature that it wastes what it should preserve." [52]

The only town in the province worthy of the name was Charleston, the capital and chief seaport, which was called Charles Town at that period, as has been mentioned. Jean Pierre Purry, the founder of Purrysburgh, left the following very flattering description, as of the year 1731:

> "There are between 5 and 600 Houses in *Charles Town*, the most of which are very costly; besides 5 handsome Churches, *viz.* one for those of the Church of *England*, one for the Presbyterians, one for the Anabaptists, one for the Quakers, and one for the *French*. If you travel into the Country, you will see stately Buildings, noble Castles, and an infinite Number of all sorts of Cattle." [53]

The heart of the city, thus pictured by Purry, was gutted by a great fire in 1740. From its ashes, as the result of generous gifts — with Parliament appropriating £20,000 — it was soon rebuilt in such a fashion as to be described later as "the most perfect Georgian city in the world." Pleasantly situated at the confluence of the Ashley and Cooper rivers, Charleston enjoyed refreshing ocean breezes which relieved the intensity of heat and humidity afflicting the neighbouring lowland regions in summer. The streets were broad and straight, running from river to river, and intersecting so as to produce a series of city blocks with residences facing the streets on all sides and with the offices and gardens enclosed in the rear. These homes, to the number of some seven hundred in 1750, were, as a group, spacious,

---

[52] *Journal of the Commons House of Assembly*, 1749–1750, p. 285.

[53] *Gentleman's Magazine*, II (1732), 896. With respect to the Charleston churches, it may be noted that St. Philip's was called in 1765 "the most elegant religious edifice in British America" by the Rev. Charles Woodmason. See *The Carolina Backcountry on the Eve of the Revolution* (ed. R. J. Hooker, Chapel Hill, N.C., 1953), p. 70. In 1751 the parish of St. Michaels was created in Charleston and by 1763 another splendid Anglican church structure adorned the city. See G. W. Williams: *St. Michaels, Charleston, 1751–1951* (Columbus, S.C., 1951). For a general description of Charleston in the eighteenth century see Harriette K. Leiding: *Charleston, Historic and Romantic* (Philadelphia, 1931), pp. 84–128.

built solidly of brick, and were generally three storeys in height, embellished with balconies and piazzas. In them lived the principal low-country planters, merchants, professional men, and public officials of the colony. It was to Charleston, the metropolis of the South, that people of wealth and ambition tended to gravitate, whether they came from rural South Carolina or even from Georgia. The city was the centre of a most hospitable social life that featured innumerable clubs, assemblies, balls, concerts, and plays.[54] Its prosperity is indicated by the fact that the swarming of coaches, chariots, and chaises about the churches at the time of divine services was so great as to require regulation in 1750.[55] On such occasions there was ostentation and display of fashion, with men and women in the latest European creations and household slaves in livery. In fact, the people of the province were accused of importing too many things, and especially those goods "too fine and ill-calculated for the circumstances of an infant colony," such as expensive laces from Flanders, the finest Dutch linens, French cambrics, chintzes, East India goods, and gold and silver fabrics. The extent of importation of luxuries into South Carolina can be judged by the fact that in 1747, besides bills of exchange, there was remitted to England 200,000 Spanish silver dollars to balance accounts.[56] Indeed, Charleston was famed for the shops of its merchant princes and was the most important commercial centre along the Atlantic seaboard south of Philadelphia. In the language of a committee of the Commons House in 1752, the city "for the num-

---

[54] The student is referred to the very informative book by H. Cohen: *The South Carolina Gazette, 1732–1775* (Columbia, S.C., 1953), which classifies aspects of the cultural life of Charleston as set forth in the columns of the *Gazette*; see also [Alexander Hewat]: *Rise and Progress of the Colonies of South Carolina and Georgia* (2 vols., London, 1779), II, 289–90; D. D. Wallace: *South Carolina . . .* (Chapel Hill, 1951), pp. 194–203; Carl Bridenbaugh: *Myths and Realities: Societies of the Colonial South* (Baton Rouge, La., 1952), Chap. 2, and *Cities in the Wilderness* (New York, 1955), pp. 440–1; L. B. Wright: *The Atlantic Frontier: Colonial American Civilization, 1607–1763* (New York, 1951), pp. 287–9; and Eola Willis: *The Charleston Stage in the Eighteenth Century* (Columbia, S.C., 1924), p. 1–56. On the important part played during the latter part of the eighteenth century in the life of Charleston by mechanics — shipwrights, coopers, coachmakers, cabinetmakers, house builders, and those of other trades — see the recent interesting study by Richard Walsh: "The Charleston Mechanics: A Brief Study, 1760–1776," *South Carolina Historical Magazine*, LX, 123–44. Despite the wealth that many of these mechanics accumulated, as Mr. Walsh points out (p. 140), none of them ever had a seat in the Commons House of Assembly.

[55] *Journal of the Commons House of Assembly, 1749–1750*, p. 383.

[56] Governor Glen to the Board of Trade, July 19, 1749, "Answers to Queries," Shelburne Papers, 45:60–83.

ber of its inhabitants carrys on as great, if not a greater trade than any Town in America or perhaps in the King's Dominions." [57]

Of the 200 vessels that left the harbour of Charleston from January 1748 to January 1749, 68 sailed to Europe, 87 to the West Indies, and 38 for the northern colonies, with 7 to other ports. The total value of the exports for that year was £1,129,559.13.2 South Carolina currency.[58] This had the happy effect of providing the province with an abundant supply of gold and silver as a medium of exchange, something that few of the other English colonies could boast.[59] Practically all of this commerce, it seems, was carried in ships coming from Great Britain with supplies, or in those built in New England on commission for British merchants — the latter frequently being sent to England on their maiden voyage by way of Charleston to pick up freight there.[60] It is of interest to note that of the rice exported from Charleston in these ships, hardly one fifteenth of it went to consumers living within the British Empire. From 1729 to 1739, out of a total of 499,525 barrels sent from this port, 83,379 went to Portugal, 3,570 to Spain, 9,500 to France, 30,000 to Great Britain, Ireland, and the British plantations, and 372,119 to Holland, Germany, and Scandinavia.[61] To open up markets in the region of the

---

[57] Journal of the Commons House (ms.), 28, Part 1:115. The prosperity of Charleston was also indicated by the abundance of bills of exchange. Henry Laurens in writing to business correspondents in 1755 declared: "We have for 4 or 5 Years past had so great a Plenty of Bills that we have been at little loss at any time to Gratify our Friends with a Remittance" (Elizabeth Donnan: "The Slave Trade into South Carolina before the Revolution," American Historical Review, XXXIII, 815). For the abundant supply of silver and gold in Charleston in 1752 see also the Journal of the Commons House (ms.), 28, Part 1:40.

[58] Glen's "Answers to Queries," Shelburne Papers, 45:60–83.

[59] James Crokatt, London agent, to the Committee of the Commons House, August 5, 1752, Journal of the Commons House (ms.), 28, Part 1:39–40.

[60] "I must acquaint your lordship," wrote Governor Glen to the Board of Trade in 1749, in his "Answers to Queries," "that we have few or no ships of our own." However, that year he expressed the hope to see Carolina soon engaged in shipbuilding. "It is well known that our Live Oak and Yellow Pine are as good as any in the world. We have plenty of masts and the convenience of water carriage make these materials come cheap," he declared to the Assembly. See Journal of the Commons House of Assembly, 1749–1750, p. 286. In line with this, a fund was set up for the encouragement of shipbuilding which, however, was later partly appropriated as a bounty for poor Protestants who would settle within the province. See ibid. (ms.), 29:297–300.

[61] From 1730 to 1737, 32,523,871 pounds of rice were shipped from South Carolina to ports southward of Cape Finisterre. See Custom House Report, March 1738/9, P.R.O., Treas. 64. 273; see also [Alexander Hewat]: op. cit., II, 90, and G. L. Beer: Commercial Policy of England Toward the American Colonies (New York, 1893), pp. 52–5.

Mediterranean, the Charleston merchants in 1729 had secured a relaxation by Parliament of the requirements laid upon rice as one of the enumerated commodities, with the result that they were permitted to ship it directly to Europe to all those points southward of Cape Finisterre.[62] This concession placed them safely in control of the market of Portugal, but did not relieve them from the competition within the region of the Mediterranean of the more cheaply produced if inferior Turkish rice, grown largely in Egypt and in Lombardy.

In considering matters of a public nature in South Carolina, it is hardly possible to overstress the influence exercised on the affairs of the province by the planter-merchant-lawyer group in and about Charleston. This coterie was led by such men as Charles Pinckney, John Cleland, James Kinloch, William Middleton, William Bull, and James Græme, all of whom were members of the Governor's Council at this period, together with others who were not, such as Andrew Rutledge, Jordan Roche, George Austin, William Boone, Benjamin Smith, and Thomas Lloyd. In fact, they and their predecessors of the low country had taken steps to see that the provincial government was run in complete accordance with their own interests and they jealously guarded against any challenge to their authority on the part of those who had settled in the more distant parts of South Carolina. This was possible through the control that they exercised in the Commons House of Assembly. In 1749 it consisted of some forty-five members who were elected every third year by the freeholders [63] of the sixteen different parishes [64] from among those who

---

[62] 3 Geo. II, c. 28.

[63] According to the law of 1745, only those professing the Christian religion who had a freehold estate in a settled plantation, or 300 acres unsettled, upon which taxes had been paid the previous year, were entitled to the franchise. Previously only a 50-acre freehold was required. See *South Carolina Statutes at Large*, I, 135–40, and III, 656–8; see also E. L. Whitney: *The Government of the Colony of South Carolina*, pp. 49–50. In practice, according to Governor Glen, a law passed in 1721 was still followed, whereby "every free White Man who is Taxed twenty shillings Currency is capable of electing a Representative to serve in the Assembly whether he be a free-holder or not" (Glen to the Board of Trade, April 1753, L. W. Labaree: *Royal Instructions to British Colonial Governors, 1670–1776* [2 vols., New York, 1935], II, 881).

[64] According to testimony presented before the Board of Trade in 1748, South Carolina some years previous had changed from triennial to annual election of members of the Commons House. This, however, was not a successful experiment. At the election in the year 1747 but four out of the sixteen parishes made returns by the parish officers. In fact, there was no election in the rest of the parishes by reason of the disinclination of people to go to the polls and vote. Moreover, it was stated that the Governor had been

enjoyed the possession of 500 acres of land and twenty slaves. But this representation was by no means equal, for the parishes were classified. In 1745 one (St. Philips, in Charleston) chose five members, two chose four members, six chose three members, and, finally, six others chose two members.[65] So jealous was the low-country area of losing power that Governor Glen declared: "Some Towns [that] by the King's Instructions have a right to be created into Parishes and to send two Members are allowed to send none." [66]

This influence of the Charleston group was strengthened by the presence of the Governor, who nominated to the Provincial Council men largely from the city or its neighbourhood. Indeed, a variety of influences was directed to keep even the Crown's chief representative in subjection, under ordinary circumstances, to the will of the ruling low-country aristocracy. Although commissioned Captain General and Governor in Chief in and over the Province, Chancellor, Vice Admiral, and Ordinary of the same, Glen was obliged to lament: "Alas! these high sounding titles convey very little Power, and I have often wish'd that Governors had more. . . ." [67]

The most powerful organ of government in South Carolina in 1750, in truth, was the Commons House of Assembly controlled by the Charleston group. The degree of influence exercised by this body is indicated by its claim put forward and sustained respecting the control of all money bills [68] and of all expenditures of money, and

---

obliged more than once to issue new writs for want of sufficient members of the Commons House to make a quorum, which was nineteen, on account of the tendency of the people of property not to attend after being elected. See the testimony of Colonel Vanderdussen, May 25, 1748, Board of Trade Journal, 1741–1749, pp. 288–9. Under terms of the law, plural voting was permitted by those who met freeholder requirements in more than one parish.

[65] For the election returns in 1745 see Journal of the Commons House of Assembly, 1745–1746, pp. 2–5. In 1745 there were but fifteen parishes; two years later St. Peter in the extreme southeast part of the province in the Purrysburgh region was created and given two representatives, which made a total of forty-five members in the House. See D. D. Wallace: op. cit., pp. 228–9, and E. L. Whitney: Government of the Colony of South Carolina, pp. 39–40.

[66] Glen's "Answers to Queries," July 19, 1749, Shelburne Papers, 45:60–83.

[67] Ibid. See also E. L. Whitney: op. cit., pp. 39–40. For Glen's commission as Governor of South Carolina, dated June 15, 1739, see P.R.O., C.O. 5:198, pp. 77–96; it is to be found in print in L. W. Labaree: Royal Instructions to British Colonial Governors, II, 816–25. For Glen's instructions, dated September 7, 1739, see C.O. 5:198, pp. 101–58; for the Governor's extended observations on these instructions see his letter to the Board of Trade, April 1753, in Labaree: op. cit., II, 880–905.

[68] Journal of the Commons House of Assembly, 1749–1750, pp. 470–2, and ibid. (ms.), 25:547–9.

by its maintenance and supervision of the London agent, a Mr. James Crockatt, who was not allowed to slip from under its control despite the efforts in 1754 of the Governor and the Council.[69] Glen, however, happily knew how to work with these masterful men. When in 1751 he ventured upon very good grounds to veto an omnibus bill, it was voted on May 10 that a humble petition and representation be prepared to His Majesty with articles of complaint against him.[70] Yet he showed his ability to ride out the crisis, so that on June 14 the desired legislation, freed of objectionable features, received his assent.

Glen was not only a popular Governor but also a man of excellent ability who deserved the encomium addressed to him in 1749 by the Commons when they declared: "We acknowledge with gratitude your Excellency's great Care for our Happiness, and your extraordinary Knowledge in our provincial Affairs which so conspicuously appear in the several Matters recommended to us." [71] The secret of his power lay in his enthusiasm and industry in promoting the best interests of the colony as well as in his humaneness and his approachability by men of all ranks.[72]

It may be stated fairly that the lot of most of the people of South Carolina — especially those of the low country — was far from unhappy in spite of the disadvantages of the climate, the presence of endemic diseases,[73] and a manner of life that, according to one who spent some years in the colony, made men and women out of children and the sight of an elderly person a curiosity.[74] Further, despite the influence of the presence of thousands of slaves steeped in the superstitions and degradations of the African jungles, and the lamentable lack of provision for the development of the higher life among the inland settlements, as well as the presence along the frontier of powerful Indian tribes which might at any moment become tools in the hands of Spanish and French rivals, probably in

---

[69] *Ibid.* (ms.), 29:60–1, 73–4, 77–8, 122–5, 128–9.

[70] *Ibid.* (ms.), 26:463; also, 420–4, 458.

[71] Address of the Commons House, November 25, 1749, *Journal of the Commons House of Assembly, 1749–1750*, p. 296.

[72] See the address to Gov. Glen framed by a committee of the Commons, May 11, 1754, on the occasion of the notification of his departure from the province. *Ibid.* (ms.), 29:421–4.

[73] See John Duffy: "Eighteenth Century Carolina Health Conditions," *Journal of Southern History*, XVIII, 289–302.

[74] [Alexander Hewat]: *op. cit.*, II, 294.

few parts of the British possessions did there exist a more generally prosperous condition. Writing in 1765, the Rev. Charles Woodmason, an Anglican, declared that "there is not a Beggar in the Province." [75] "It has been remarked," declared the Rev. Alexander Hewat, pastor for a decade of the Charleston Presbyterian Church, "that there are more persons possessed of between four and ten thousand pounds sterling in the province, than are to be found anywhere among the same number of people." [76]

In other respects, too, the situation of the inhabitants of South Carolina was favourable. "Peace and Plenty are great Blessings, but they are not the only Ones we possess," said Governor Glen in 1751. "We enjoy all our religious and civil Rights, and there is not the least attempt to invade any of them. We live in the full fruition of those Laws and Liberties that are the Birth-right of British Subjects." [77] Regrettably, this felicitous state of affairs was built upon the institution of slavery, nor did it reach the back country, as has been noted. The implications of this inequality will, however, be dealt with in a later volume of the series.

One final comment may be made. To no other southern colony, outside of the infant province of Georgia, was such generosity shown by the government of Great Britain as to South Carolina. Not only did the Governor receive from the royal exchequer in the way of annual salary £800 sterling — taken out of the 4½-per-cent fund

---

[75] *The Carolina Backcountry on the Eve of the Revolution*, by Charles Woodmason (ed. R. J. Hooker, Chapel Hill, N.C., 1953), p. 72.

[76] [Hewat]: op. cit., II, 294. In accounting for the wealth and general prosperity of the planter group in South Carolina the author of *American Husbandry* has the following to say (1939 edn., pp. 301–3): "Now it must be apparent . . . that no husbandry in Europe can equal this of Carolina; we have no agriculture in England — where larger fortunes are made by it than in any other country — that will pay any thing like this, owing to several circumstances which deserve attention. First, land is so plentiful in America that the purchase of a very large estate costs but a trifle, and all the annual taxes paid afterwards for ten thousand acres, do not amount to what the window duty in England comes to on a moderate house; no land-tax, no poor's rate, no tythe." The cost of the services of two Negroes in Carolina as against the cost of one English labourer he found to be £10.6 a year as against from £20 to £25. The chief staple product of this slave labour, he pointed out, was of "a constant high value" and the support of it in food supplies largely raised on the plantation stood the owner little. These favourable factors, he concluded, "explain the causes of a Carolina planter having such vastly superior opportunities of making a fortune than a British farmer can possibly enjoy."

[77] Governor Glen to the Assembly, June 15, 1751, Journal of the Commons House (ms.), 26:12–13.

supplied by the Leeward Islands and Barbados on all dead exports [78] — but the so-called Independent Companies that ranged along the back country as a protection to the settlements were really British regulars controlled and supported by the government of the mother country; further, funds from time to time were also appropriated by Parliament for the purchase of Indian presents, which in 1748 and years thereafter amounted to £3,000 sterling.[79] Surely the people of South Carolina could be counted upon, with such treatment, to remain steadfast in their loyalty to the Crown of Great Britain — whatever might be the attitude of other American colonials!

---

[78] For the allocation of the 4½-per-cent fund in 1750 see P.R.O., Treas. 30. 11.

[79] For a treatment of the topic of Indian presents see Volume IV of this series, Chap. 3.

CHAPTER VI

An American Arcadia

In the founding of the English colonies in the New World the chief motives of the colonists were desire for economic opportunity and desire for unrestricted religious expression unhampered by the laws of the mother country. But in the case of Georgia, humanitarianism, combined with the idea of creating a defensive northern barrier to the Spaniards, was uppermost in the minds of those who took leading parts in bringing the colony into existence. Although it alone of all the American colonies was a Trusteeship in 1750, even so it was clear by that date that this experiment in idealistic government had failed. To determine the causes for this failure it is necessary to analyse the unique polity of the colony and the nature of the problems arising from its implementation under the conditions existing in the middle of the eighteenth century.

Beyond the broad Savannah River, which marked the southern limits of the actual settled area of the province of South Carolina if not then its designated southern boundary, lay the trusteeship of Georgia. The colony had come into existence in the fifth year of the reign of George II as the result of an upwelling of humane sentiments on the part of influential Englishmen.[1] These sentiments were

---

[1] See R. A. Roberts: "The Birth of an American State: Georgia: An Effort of Philanthropy and Protestant Propaganda," *Royal Historical Society Transactions*, 4th ser., VI, 22–49.

For the connection between the society called "The Associates of the late Rev. Dr. Bray" and the Georgia Trustees see V. W. Crane: "The Philanthropists and the Genesis of Georgia," *American Historical Review*, XXVII, 63–9. A. B. Saye (see his "The Genesis of Georgia: Merchants as well as Ministers," *Georgia Historical Quarterly*, XXIV, 191–206, and his *New Viewpoints in Georgia History* [Athens, Ga., 1943]) questions the above connection between the purposes of Bray Associates and those of the Georgia

blended with a desire to support the long-established program of English colonization in North America by blocking Spanish claims to all territory extending from Florida up to and beyond Charleston, and an equally strong desire to hold in check the powerful Creek and other Indian tribes to the southwest of the settled part of South Carolina through settlement of this region, which had been the scene of the bloody Yamasee Wars some fifteen years preceding the founding of the colony.[2]

The two outstanding figures in this overseas enterprise were the Irishman John, Viscount Percival, who became the first Earl of Egmont, and who was designated in the Georgia charter itself as the first president of the corporation,[3] and James Edward Oglethorpe, a member of Parliament, former soldier of fortune and Jacobite, who was to lead the colonization of this province in person during the first decade of its history.[4] Both of these men had served on the parliamentary committee, the appointment of which Oglethorpe had brought about, for investigating the conditions of the debtor prisons in England and the treatment there accorded debtors. Both were aghast at what they had uncovered and most generously dedicated themselves to remedying this blot on civilization.[5] The law of 1729 passed by Parliament, one of the fruits of this investigation, brought about the release of a swarm of debtors.[6] To rescue some of them, as

---

Trustees. For Professor Crane's reply see the William and Mary Quarterly, 3rd ser., I, 410–13, and also the Georgia Historical Quarterly, XXVI, 311–13.

[2] For earlier plans for the settlement of the region to the north of the Spanish settlements in Florida see V. W. Crane: "Projects for Colonization in the South, 1685–1732," Mississippi Valley Historical Review, XII, 23–35; see also his "Origins of Georgia," Georgia Historical Quarterly, XIV, 93–110.

[3] The activities of Percival are set forth at great length in Manuscripts of the Earl of Egmont: Diary of Viscount Percival . . . (1730–1747), Historical Manuscripts Commission (ed. R. A. Roberts, 3 vols., London, 1920–3), hereinafter referred to as "Percival's Diary," and in the Journal of the Earl of Egmont, . . . (1738–1744), which constitutes Volume V of The Colonial Records of the State of Georgia (ed. A. D. Candler, 26 vols., Atlanta, 1904–16), hereinafter referred to as Colonial Records of Georgia.

[4] For a scholarly life of Oglethorpe see A. A. Ettinger: James Edward Oglethorpe, Imperial Idealist (Oxford, 1936); see also L. F. Church: Oglethorpe: A Study of Philanthropy in England and Georgia (London, 1932), a work especially valuable for the light it throws upon the developments of the period.

[5] For the work of the Select Committee of the House of Commons in 1729 see S. Gordon and T. G. B. Cocks: A People's Conscience . . . (London, 1952), Chap. 2, "The Case of the Naked Men." For the condition of prisons at this period see S. and Beatrice Webb: English Prisons under Local Government (London, 1922); for the movement for prison reform see especially L. F. Church: op. cit., Chap. 3.

[6] 2 Geo. II, c. 20.

well as other hapless British people in and out of prison,[7] to substitute a promise of usefulness for the futility of bankruptcy, and to offer a refuge for the persecuted Protestants of Europe, provided that they were of good character, while allowing them at the same time to serve a very important public interest — that of defending the southern boundary of British North America — these formed ultimately the great objectives of those who secured the charter of the year 1732.[8]

This charter created out of that part of South Carolina between the Savannah and Altamaha rivers, stretching from sea to sea, a separate and independent province to be governed for a period of twenty-one years by a body of Trustees, who at the end of that period were to surrender their authority as a governing body into the hands of the King.

The type of government to be set up under the Georgia charter was a reversion, as it were, to that plan established for Virginia under the charter of 1609 and maintained until the year 1618, when the first Virginia Assembly was called. By this instrument all legislative power was in the hands of a corporation sitting in London which also had supreme regulatory jurisdiction under the Crown. Local self-government, in other words, was not contemplated in the case of either, but nevertheless under each corporation made its appearance before the respective charters were withdrawn. While the two enterprises had this in common, it must be kept in mind that in the case of the Virginia corporation profits to the members was the chief objective; in the case of Georgia, on the other hand, the charter itself forbad members of the corporation to derive pecuniary benefits either by office-holding or by land-appropriation. In other words, the mission of the Georgia Trustees was to labour exclusively for the benefit of others. The first twenty Trustees were named in the charter itself. Four of them were clergymen active in philanthropy as members of the "Associates of the late Rev. Dr. Bray" charitable or-

---

[7] It would appear that when the Trustees finally approached the problem of the colonization of Georgia very few of those imprisoned for debt were chosen to go to the colony. See A. B. Saye: "Was Georgia a Debtor Colony?" *Georgia Historical Quarterly,* XXIV, 323–41.

[8] *The Georgia Charter of 1732* (ed. A. B. Saye, Athens, Ga., 1942) presents it in facsimile from the patent-roll copy with an account by the editor of the steps leading to its granting by the King; see also *Colonial Records of Georgia,* I, 11–26.

ganization. Other Trustees were elected from time to time.[9] The Trustees, as a body, were expected to meet whenever necessary to consider larger questions of policy and the problems of the Trust. Fifteen of them were designated in the charter itself as members of the Common Council of the corporation charged with caring for routine details, such as the making and regulation of specific land grants and the auditing of accounts. In the course of time the number of members of the Common Council increased to twenty-four.[10]

Those who were most active among the Trustees during the earlier period of the Trusteeship were the Hon. James Vernon, Thomas Tower, Esq., George Heathcote, Esq., the Rev. Samuel Smith, Captain Thomas Coram, James Oglethorpe, Esq., the Rev. Stephen Hales, Robert Hucks, Esq., and Viscount Percival.[11] At the meeting on January 9, 1735, when the important acts relating to the prohibition of the importation and use of slaves and rum were enacted, there were present William Sloper, who acted as president, Oglethorpe, Hon. William Talbot, Rev. Dr. Thomas Rundle, Hon. James Vernon, Captain Francis Eyles, Robert More, Rev. Mr. Smith, and Captain Thomas Coram.

The meetings of the Common Council as well as those of the Trustees were held in London and for eighteen years all regulations sprang from those two bodies.[12] In light of the fact that it was proposed to settle the colony largely by poor people, most of whom had enjoyed little or no participation in government in England and would therefore hardly be especially competent in the exercise of political responsibilities, it is not surprising that the Trustees deemed it wise to withhold the powers of local government, particularly since the colony was to be a semi-military establishment. The purest type of idealism, moreover, was combined with certain practical

---

[9] *Ibid.*, I, 27–30.

[10] *Ibid.*

[11] Other Trustees were not so active. Out of 26 meetings up to January 1733, William Belitha attended 8, Lord Carpenter 7, Adam Anderson and Roger Holland 6, John Laroch 5, the Rev. Arthur Bedford 4, Edward Digby 3, Francis Eyles 2, and Robert More, the Rev. Richard Bundy, and the Rev. John Burton but one. See "Journal of the Trustees," *ibid.*, I, 65–94. For the attendance record at the meetings of the Georgia Trustees 1732–52 and of the Common Council covering these same years see J. R. McCain: *Georgia as a Proprietary Province* . . . (Boston, 1917), pp. 31–7. McCain also has sketched out the careers of some of the active Trustees. *Ibid.*, pp. 41–56.

[12] That is, beyond the parliamentary regulations.

considerations in the bitterly criticized laws that were passed regarding various restrictions on landholding and the prohibition against the importation and use of both rum and slaves.[13]

This history of the Georgia trusteeship — in spite of its disappointments, its failures, and its mistakes in public policy, in spite also of the indifference of some toward the work of this benevolent corporation — is one of the brightest pages in all eighteenth-century English history. The journals of the corporation, extending over a period from the first meeting held at the Palace Court, Old Palace Yard, Westminster, on July 20, 1732, to its final meetings in the vestry room of St. Margaret's Church, June 23, 1752, testify to the wealth of human sympathy and Christian piety existent in an age notorious for its coarseness, corruption, and cynicism.

Many people who rallied to the support of the Trustees in the founding of Georgia, one of the last of the English colonies established before the American Revolution in North America,[14] may well have seen in it a consummation of the desire of the ages. They may have dreamed that out of the experiences of the Old World, with its sordidness, its harshness, its degradation, would appear somewhere in the New a social order which, avoiding the errors of earlier schemes of colonization, would be a true Arcadia — a place far removed from the slums of cities and centres of human depravity — where all men would walk in bucolic simplicity, soberness, and self-respect before God; where there would be no great social cleavages; where all would engage in manly labour while ever ready to defend their little homes and plantings. That it was truly the type of undertaking to appeal to men of goodwill appears to be borne out by the fact that in answer to appeals for assistance, there was for years a flood of benevolence in the form of money — chiefly in relatively small amounts ranging from 10s. 6d. to £500 — and various articles of value, among which were books. Parenthetically it is pleasing to record that many of the gifts came from anonymous donors.[15] In the

---

13 It should be noted that Oglethorpe was a Director and Deputy Governor of the Royal African Company. See A. A. Ettinger: op. cit., p. 150. At the same time his humanitarianism was shown by the part he played in rescuing from slavery the educated Negro Job Jalla, who had been seized in Gambia and carried as a slave to Maryland. See ibid., p. 148.

14 The English colonization of Nova Scotia in the middle of the century and the partial success in peopling East Florida and West Florida after 1763 represent the last British colonizing efforts before 1775 in North America.

15 See Accounts, Monies and Effects, 1732–1751, Colonial Records of Georgia, III.

words of another writer: "The Georgia philanthropy was in fact a part of a vast organized benevolent movement in early eighteenth-century Britain, which developed a body of ideas, a theory of social action, and a network of interlocking enterprises." [16]

In launching this enterprise the Trustees realized the value of publicity and made liberal use of the newspapers. Oglethorpe was given the responsibilty of seeing that nothing disadvantageous to the plans should be published.[17] The results, as has been suggested, were all that could perhaps have been desired under the circumstances, for a legion of supporters appeared, rich and poor, each one ready to do something to promote the good work. Commissions were granted to the ministers and churchwardens of various parishes to be the recipients of gifts. As an indication of the response, and to cite but one example, over 160 parishioners of St. George's, Hanover Square, London, united in contributing.[18]

However, colonization on such a scale as the promters of the Georgia plans had in mind was an expensive operation. Private benefactions alone would not suffice. Government support had to be sought.

Little as Robert Walpole, then in power, might have sympathized with some of the more idealistic aspirations of the leaders of the Georgia movement, he was nevertheless led to endorse the project for motives that were based upon important political and economic considerations. His approval induced Parliament in 1733 to make the grant necessary for the plan to become actuality.[19] By this very fact of having parliamentary assistance, the province of Georgia was at one time placed in a category by itself among all the other Eng-

---

In 1733 an unknown person, for example, sent to the Trust 200 copies of each of the following books: Dr. Thomas Gouge's Christian Directions, Shewing How to Walk with God all the Day Long, William Burkitt's An Help and Guide to Christian Families, Bishop Edmund Gibson's Family Devotions, The Book of Common Prayer, and Friendly Admonitions to the Drinkers of Gin, Brandy and other Spirituous Liquors, together with 100 copies of Lewis's Catechisms. See Colonial Records of Georgia, I, 121.

[16] M. S. Heath: Constructive Liberalism: The Role of the State in Economic Development in Georgia to 1860 (Cambridge, Mass., 1954), p. 15.

[17] In 1732 the Secretary of the Georgia Trust, Benjamin Martyn [Martin], with the approval of the members of the Common Council, prepared his Reasons for Establishing the Colony of Georgia with Regard to the Trade of Great Britain, which appeared the following year. See Percival's Diary, I, 289. This stressed the employment that would be given to the poor of Great Britain and to foreign Protestants.

[18] Colonial Records of Georgia, III, 40–4.

[19] By 6 Geo. II, 25, Par. 7, a grant of £10,000 was made out of the fund arising from the sale of lands in the island of St. Christopher.

lish overseas establishments in the New World. It continued to be the exception, moreover, until the settlement of Halifax in Nova Scotia — a province also designed as a semi-military buffer. From 1733 to 1752, during the period of the trusteeship, a total of £ 136,- 608 was appropriated by the British government to promote the Georgia colony — surely not an excessive amount.[20]

The providing of funds was but one element in the success of the enterprise. The right sort of colonizers among the unfortunate classes had to be found; for only those who were really worthy of the great opportunity to start life anew were to be considered. As a result, clergymen sought out in their respective parishes respectable people who had fallen on evil days and who appeared to have the moral and physical fitness required for the work of settlement. These in turn presented themselves before the cautious Common Council of the Trustees, who finally voted that out of the applicants not over thirty-five men and their families should be carried to Georgia on the first trip.[21] Those accepted were to be transported to America without charge, supplied with provisions for three months after their arrival, also with coats and other necessaries, such as arms and ammunition for defence, and furnished with limited quantities of land.

It seemed wise, before the actual work of colonization began, to make very definite provision for the local government under the Trust. Oglethorpe had previously signified his willingness to assume the responsibilities of leadership, although it appears he was unwilling to receive a formal appointment as Governor. This was owing to the fact that he would have been compelled thereby to resign both from his trusteeship of the province under the restrictions of the charter and from his seat in Parliament by reason of the so-called placemen's bill passed under William III. However, he was empowered to exercise a wide range of authority which transcended

[20] For an account of the steps taken to secure the various parliamentary grants see Percival's Diary, I, 273, 364, passim, and III, 1, passim. For records of the Trust relative to sums actually received see Accounts, Monies and Effects, 1732–51, Colonial Records of Georgia, III, 31, 102, 136, 162, 186, 206–7, 224, 238, 266, 303–4, 339–40, 352–3, 364. For the part played by those Georgia Trustees who were also members of Parliament in securing these grants see R. S. Dunn: "The Trustees of Georgia and the House of Commons, 1732–1752," William and Mary Quarterly, 3rd ser., XI, 551–65; see also the article by H. B. Fant: "Financing the Colonization of Georgia," Georgia Historical Quarterly, XX, 1–29.

[21] Minutes of the Common Council, October 3, 1732, Colonial Records of Georgia, II, 6.

that of others who accompanied him to Georgia. Further, to watch over the welfare of the town of Savannah — to be created — three bailiffs were named at this time, as were a recorder, two tithing-men, and two constables. The Trust also erected a court of judicature for both civil and criminal cases to be known as the Town Court.[22]

By the middle of November the people — 114 in number, according to the figures kept by the Trust — were placed on board the *Ann*.[23] After a two months' voyage and with the loss of only two lives, both infants, they arrived at Charleston harbour, where they were hospitably received by Governor Robert Johnson and the planters and merchants of the city. Here they rested for a period. Then, upon securing fresh supplies at Beaufort, they sailed southward to the Savannah and up its waters to the site of their new homes.

On the south bank of this splendid river Oglethorpe found an Indian trader by the name of Musgrove, living there with his Indian wife, Cousaponakeesa, who had taken the Christian name of Mary and who played a great role in early Georgia history under the various names of Musgrove, Matthews, and Bosomworth.[24] It might almost be said that during the first twenty-five years of the life of the colony she held its fate almost literally in the hollow of her hand by reason of the commanding influence that she exerted over the great Creek nation, of which she was a member. This powerful, warlike tribe, made up of the Upper and the Lower Creeks, numbered in all about 25,000. Indeed, some of the gravest problems confronting the settlers grew out of the presence in their midst of this Indian woman. However, her potential value to the colony was not overlooked by Oglethorpe, who showered her with presents.[25] She thereupon undertook to bring to a general meeting the leaders of the Creeks and their allies. The most useful of these finally to enlist in the support of the white settlement was Tomochichi [Tomachichi], chieftain of the Yamacraws, a detached group of Creeks living on the lower Savannah. At a great council a treaty of friendship, commerce, and land cession was consummated. Among other things it

---

[22] See the Secretary's (Benjamin Martyn) report, *An Account Shewing the Progress of the Colony of Georgia in America from its First Establishment* (London, 1741), printed in *Colonial Records of Georgia*, III, 379.

[23] *Ibid.*

[24] See E. M. Coulter: "Mary Musgrove, 'Queen of the Creeks': A Chapter of Early Georgia Troubles," *Georgia Historical Quarterly*, XI, 1–30.

[25] *Colonial Records of Georgia*, VI, 272.

was agreed that, in consideration of presents distributed among the Indians, the lower coastal lands south of the Savannah that were not inhabited by the Indians should be ceded to Oglethorpe; further, that licenced traders might resort to the Indian country; and, finally, that the Creeks would resist the attempts of the French and Spanish to penetrate into the region of the English settlements by way of their hunting-grounds.[26] Under these conditions, the colony of Georgia and the town of Savannah came into existence — the town rising on the sandy Yamacraw bluff, a slight elevation some forty feet in height above the low-lying malarial region and about fifteen miles distant from the sea.

There has survived a description of the beginnings of Savannah in the *South Carolina Gazette* of March 22, 1732/3, by an unknown writer. The settlement had been in existence about two months when the following picture of it was penned:

> "Mr. Oglethorpe is indefatigable, takes a vast deal of Pains. . . . He is extremely well beloved by all his People; the general Title they give him is Father. If any of them is sick, he immediately visits them, and takes a great deal of Care of them. If any Difference arises, he is the Person that decides it. . . . He keeps a strict Discipline; I never saw one of his People drunk, or heard one swear, all the Time I was there: He does not allow them Rum, but in lieu gives them English Beer. It is surprising how chearfully the Men go to work, considering they have not been bred to it: There are no Idlers there; even the Boys and Girls do their Parts. There are Four Houses already up. . . . He has plowed up some Land, part of which he has sowed with Wheat. . . . He has Two or Three Gardens. . . . He was palisading the Town round, including some Part of the Commons. . . . In short, he has done a vast deal of Work for the Time, and I think his Name justly deserves to be immortalized."

The anxiety of the Trust to provide the infant colony with proper religious guidance in the person of a devoted and properly equipped Anglican clergyman was at all times very great. It was also one of the most baffling problems.[27]

The first minister, a distinguished divine, the Rev. Dr. Henry Herbert, who went out with the first group, returned home a few

---

[26] For the Creek treaty see C. C. Jones: A History of Georgia (Boston, 1883), p. 140; see also J. P. Corry: Indian Affairs in Georgia, 1732–1756 (Philadelphia, 1936), and E. M. Coulter: "Mary Musgrove . . . ," op. cit.

[27] For a broad treatment of the above topic see Reba C. Strickland: Religion and the State in Georgia in the Eighteenth Century (New York, 1939), pp. 11–99.

months later to die. Samuel Quincy, his successor, a native of Boston and kinsman of the Massachusetts Bay Quincys, became discouraged after two years and in 1735 deserted his post to go to South Carolina, where he acted as a minister in three parish churches before moving to Boston.[28] Then followed zealous young John Wesley, accompanied by his brother Charles. Wesley had hoped to be able to convert the Indians, but circumstances did not favour him. In Savannah he set up a very High Church service [29] which displeased many. There he became involved in a love affair, yet decided not to marry; but when the young lady married another, for reasons that seemed best to him he refused to admit her to the communion. Other people were disciplined from time to time in a similar fashion by the serious young minister, and in diverse ways he offended many of his parishioners. These rather autocratic actions finally led to his being presented to the grand jury of the colony, which in turn brought about his sudden departure from the province.[30] Although it seems that Wesley was able to explain things to the entire satisfaction of the Trustees, they now appointed George Whitefield, the great evangelist, to the post at Savannah. Whitefield's chief energies while in the province were directed to establishing an orphanage.[31] Also sent out — to Frederica, a settlement on the Altamaha which came into existence after Savannah — was a William Norris, who led an idle life, was recalled, and finally sued the Trust in the Court of Kings' Bench.[32] In 1743 came the appointment of Thomas Bosomworth, a man who had been in the colony previously and who had returned to the mother country to take holy orders. Commissioned to take charge of the Savannah church, Bosomworth was attracted

---

[28] The Rev. W. B. Stevens: *History of Georgia* . . . (2 vols., New York, 1847), I, 321–2.

[29] Not until 1750 was Christ Church completed for the holding of divine services. Wesley and others used the court house. See Reba C. Strickland: "Building a Colonial Church," *Georgia Historical Quarterly*, XVII, 276–85.

[30] For the most understanding account of Wesley in Georgia see L. E. Church: *Oglethorpe*, pp. 194–211; see also *The Journal of John Wesley* (ed. N. Curnocky, 8 vols., London, 1910–16), I, 328–426, especially pp. 388–9 for the charges against him, together with the *Journal of the Earl of Egmont, Colonial Records of Georgia*, V, 60–1, 76; E. M. Coulter: "When John Wesley Preached in Georgia," *Georgia Historical Quarterly*, IX, 317–51; J. R. McCain: *op. cit.*, pp. 311–15; and W. B. Stevens: *History of Georgia*, I, 330–8.

[31] E. C. Surrency: "Whitefield, Habersham, and the Bethesda Orphanage," *Georgia Historical Quarterly*, XXXIV, 87–105.

[32] *The Journal of John Wesley*, I, 420; see also W. B. Stevens: *op. cit.*, I, 355–7; and J. A. McCain: *op. cit.*, pp. 320–2.

to Frederica, where he busied himself in secular activities, marrying at this time the famous Indian woman Mary, who had lost her second husband, Matthews. The neglect of his ecclesiastical duties brought from the Trustees a crisply written letter acquainting him with the fact that they expected him to go to Savannah to reside. Although he returned to that town in 1745, he suddenly slipped into Carolina in a clandestine manner, so it was charged, in order to proceed to England. Nor did he make any provision for the performance of divine services during his absence.[33] Arriving in England, he wrote to the Trustees that he had no intention of returning to Georgia soon and that he was planning to join the army that was proceeding against the forces of the Young Pretender in northern England at the time. The Trustees grasped at the opportunity that seemed to present itself of freeing the colony of this gentleman's presence, holding that his letter constituted a resignation of his commission, and thereupon so wrote to him. As his successor they appointed a well-educated Swiss of St. Gall, by the name of Bartholomew Zouberbuhler.[34] The latter displayed much commendable activity in behalf of the Church until his death in Georgia in 1766.[35] But little did the Trustees realize how difficult it would be for Georgia to rid itself of Bosomworth and his Indian wife; nor did they anticipate the infinite embarrassments that the continued presence of this man upon his return would bring to the government of the colony!

The Trustees had early conceived the idea that the great and beneficent purposes of the Trust would be best served by the establishment of a land system particularly applicable to those occupying the double role of planter and soldier.[36] The land granted to individuals was therefore considered in the light of a military fief, for which the possessor was to appear in arms and take the field when called upon for the public defence. In harmony with this idea, the owner could not alienate the land without special leave of the Trust; it was, moreover, granted in what was called tail-male. Under this limita-

[33] *Proceedings of the President and Assistants*, June 14 and 15, 1745, *Colonial Records of Georgia*, VI, 135–6.

[34] "Journal of the Trustees," October 28, 1745, *ibid.*, I, 476, 478.

[35] That Zouberbuhler was, in spite of his zeal for the Church, a very good business man is indicated by the fact that he gathered a small private fortune, of from 5,000 to 6,000 guineas, by the making of brick. E. L. Pennington: "The Reverend Bartholomew Zouberbuhler," *Georgia Historical Quarterly*, XVIII, 362.

[36] See *An Account Shewing the Progress of the Colony of Georgia* . . . (London, 1741), *Colonial Records of Georgia*, III, 373–5.

tion, through failure of a male heir, the land would revert to the Trust to be regranted,[37] with this saving feature, that the Trustees agreed to pay due regard to the claims of daughters of those who had made improvements, especially when no other provision had been made for them.[38] Widows of such persons were also entitled to a life interest in one half of the improved portions of the land and in the mansion house.

There was still another requirement in connection with all grants, one that dealt with the actual utilization of the land. By it, if any part of an allotment should not be cultivated, cleared, and enclosed with a worm fence six feet high within eighteen years from the date of the grant, such portion was to revert to the Trust.[39] Further, every person receiving land was expected to plant mulberry trees — a hundred trees to every ten acres of land — to help start silk production.[40] As to the size of the grants, it was decided that those who were sent out at the expense of the corporation were to be given a maximum of 50 acres; those, on the other hand, who would go at their own expense and would carry from four to ten white menservants with them were entitled to as much as 500 acres.[41] To servants, after the period of their indenture had expired, would be allotted either 20 or 25 acres.[42] All of these grants at first were upon the basis of a payment of an annual quit-rent of ten shillings sterling for each 100 acres, after the expiration of ten years.[43]

In defence of this land policy, the Trustees pointed out that the typical grant of 50 acres to the poor planter and his family was agreed upon because it was considered quite sufficient for their maintenance and because no more could be farmed advantageously by one man without the help of servants. What they had in mind was

---

[37] Special concessions were made to those who sailed on the *Ann*.

[38] See "Conditions for the Granting of Lands," *Colonial Records of Georgia*, III, 412–13. With respect to the amount of land granted in small tracts as against the larger grants between 1732 and 1741, see J. E. Callaway: *The Early Settlement of Georgia* (Athens, Georgia, 1948), p. 19; for the number of large and small grants between 1741 and 1752 see *ibid*., p. 39. The table shows that only beginning with 1747 was there any great desire or pressure for the larger tracts of land.

[39] For the larger allotments the requirement was the cultivation of 200 out of 500 acres granted.

[40] *Colonial Records of Georgia*, III, 375. Later the number of trees to be planted was changed. For the act of 1750 see *ibid*., I, 56–62, and II, 498–500.

[41] *Ibid*., II, 14; III, 375, 412–13.

[42] *Minutes of the Common Council*, March 21, 1732/3, *ibid*., II, 23–4.

[43] *Minutes*, December 7, 1732, *ibid*., II, 14–15.

the peopling of the province with those who would become small farmers — the re-creation, as it were, of a yeoman class in Georgia which unhappily was fast disappearing in England largely on account of the effects of increased taxation in connection with the enclosure movement. In harmony with this ideal they sought to prevent accumulations of land in the hands of a few men by the restriction against alienation. Were this to be allowed they felt it would weaken the military defences of the colony, as would the right of women to inherit land. They feared also that without these restrictions land might get into the hands of those hostile to the religious and political constitution of the mother country and consequently work to the advantage of the neighbouring Spaniards and French to the south and west of Georgia. As to the quit-rents, which were set at a high figure, after satisfying the claim of the Crown for four shillings on every one hundred acres as reimbursement of the grant by Parliament, they hoped to garner the excess amount to be used as a fund for the continual promotion of the colonization of the province.[44]

From the very beginning the Trustees were convinced that the welfare of Georgia would demand hardier types of colonizers than "the poor indigent People" gathered in from the various parishes of England. They felt that what was needed were men who could do aggressive pioneering and who would be fitted to bear the brunt of threatened attack from the Spaniards, the French, or hostile Indians. To seek such settlers and encourage them to emigrate, invitations to join the settlement were spread among the Protestants of nearby countries. By the latter part of July 1732 a proposal was drawn up by the Trustees for transporting to Georgia a number of the Protestant Salzburg exiles who were being aided by the Society for the Promotion of Christian Knowledge in their distress as they fled from persecution.[45] As a result, a group of these people, under their able leader and spiritual guide, Martin Bolzius, was sent by this Society to the province and settled some distance above Savannah on the river at a place which in gratitude they called Ebenezer. But the location was poor and a new site was soon afterward secured.[46] Scottish High-

---

[44] See [Benjamin Martyn, Secretary]: An Account Shewing the Progress of the Colony of Georgia (London, 1741), ibid., III, 368–432.

[45] "Journal of the Trustees" for July 27, 1732, ibid., I, 67–77.

[46] For an account of these people see J. M. Hofer: "The Georgia Salzburgers," Georgia Historical Quarterly, XVIII, 99–117; see also Milton Rubincam: "Historical Background of the Salzburger Emigration to Georgia," ibid., XXXV, 99–115; R. L.

landers were also invited. A group of 130 from Inverness agreed to go. They proceeded to establish the town of New Inverness on the Altamaha along the southern border, facing the Spaniards.[47] Further, Moravian Brethren sought a place of refuge here under August Gottlieb Spangenberg, after David Nitschmann had prepared the way. Before sailing they gave bonds to the Trustees for the amount of £260.10 required to cover the expense of their transportation and other necessary charges, and this money was punctually repaid, according to figures kept by Egmont.[48] Between 1733 and 1744, at the expense of the Trust, a total of some 2,500 people had been carried to Georgia, most of them on the *Charity* chartered for that purpose.[49] This of course does not take into account those who went to Georgia at their own expense, some of whom took with them white indentured servants.

In spite of this influx of settlers the colony did not flourish. It had been hoped to make Georgia not only a wine-producing plantation but also the centre of the silk-raising industry of the Empire, which

Brantley: "The Salzburgers in Georgia," *ibid.*, XIV, 214–25; P. A. Strobel: *The Salzburgers and their Descendants* (Baltimore, 1855); Hester W. Newton: "The Agricultural Activities of the Salzburgers in Colonial Georgia," *Georgia Historical Quarterly*, XVIII, 248–63, and, by the same author, "Industrial and Social Influences of the Salzburgers in Colonial Georgia," *ibid.*, XVIII, 335–43. For a history of Old and New Ebenezer see C. C. Jones: *Dead Towns in Georgia* (Savannah, 1878), pp. 11–44.

[47] Early in 1736 the Highlanders settled at Darien. For a period after 1739 the town was called New Inverness. However, the name Darien was restored. Darien, of course, referred not only to the Scottish attempt to penetrate the Spanish Main in 1698 by establishing the colony on the Isthmus of Panama, but also to continued defiance of the Spaniards by settling the lands on the Altamaha which they still claimed. See Bessie M. Lewis: "Darien a Symbol of Defiance and Achievement," *Georgia Historical Quarterly*, XX, 185–98; G. A. Gordon: "The Arrival of the Scottish Highlanders at Darien," *ibid.*, XX, 199–209; and A. R. MacDonell: "The Settlement of the Scotch Highlanders at Darien," *ibid.*, XX, 250–62.

[48] For the Moravian settlement see Adelaide L. Fries: *The Moravians in Georgia* (Raleigh, N.C., 1905).

[49] Up to June 9, 1733, 152 people were sent, 11 of whom were foreign Protestants; the following year to June 1734, 341 were sent, of whom 104 were foreigners; the next year to June 1735, 81 were sent, 58 of whom were foreigners; the fourth year to June 1736, 341 were sent, of whom 129 were foreigners; the fifth year, 32 were sent, all of whom were British; the sixth year 298 were sent, 163 of whom were foreigners; the seventh year 9 were sent, 7 of whom were foreigners; the eighth year, 138 were sent, 134 of whom were foreigners; the ninth year, 6 were sent, 3 of whom were foreigners; the tenth year, 320 were sent, 230 of whom were foreigners. Up to 1744, 1,133 men and 741 women were sent out. See the *Journal of the Earl of Egmont*, March 15, 1744, *Colonial Records of Georgia*, V, 721. It should be noted that all foreigners were Protestants. Roman Catholics, called "papists" in the charter, were not desired, nor were they given freedom of conscience. See *ibid.*, I, 21.

would in the end supply the demands of the English silk-weavers for materials. However, these industries were very slow in getting under way and never proved to be profitable.[50] This was so in spite of the presence of a Piedmont family brought into the province for the express purpose of teaching the art of silk-production and the making of various varieties of grape wines. Indeed, the most discouraging aspect was the fact that men made little headway in the clearing of their lands, and until this was done there could be no other progress.[51] It is true that the Scots, the Salzburgers, and the Moravians set a splendid example of energy — the latter being designated "the most Laborious, cheapest workers and best subjects in Georgia" — but most of the settlers hung back. Perhaps they made the inevitable contrast between the unfavourable conditions in Georgia and the absence of onerous restrictions in South Carolina to the immediate north of them.

First of all, while the Georgians were obliged to labour with their own hands — or at best assisted by a few white servants — to clear the lands of trees and level and cultivate the soil, the South Carolinians across the Savannah could stand by at comparative ease while watching their slaves engage in this vastly laborious undertaking. Again, while the settlers in Georgia were limited to small allotments, they could by going to South Carolina secure extensive land-holdings without the restrictions of male-tail and be liable for a quit-rent amounting at most to one half, and to as little as one fifth in some cases, of that which they had agreed to pay in Georgia after the expiration of the first ten years. Further, while they were favourably situated for developing a West India trade, they could not take molasses, a commodity which the sugar islands were anxious to offer in exchange for Georgia lumber and other products, by reason of the law prohibiting the importation, manufacture, and use of rum.

---

[50] The production of wine never made any real headway. Silk seemed to be more promising, especially as it was subsidized by Parliament up to 1768 by a yearly grant of £1,000. In 1755 438 pounds were produced, and in 1762 1,047 pounds. When the government ceased supporting the silk-production by withdrawing even the modest £100 appropriation it had been providing yearly since 1768, the Georgia silk filatures were finally closed in 1771. See P. S. Flippin: "The Royal Government in Georgia," *Georgia Historical Quarterly*, IX, 237–45, and especially Marguerite B. Hamer: "The Foundation and Failure of the Silk Industry in Provincial Georgia," *North Carolina Historical Review*, XII, 125–48, and Mary T. McKinstry: "Silk Culture in Colonial Georgia," *Georgia Historical Quarterly*, XIV, 225–35.

[51] Stephens' *Journal*, December 30, 1737, *Colonial Records of Georgia*, IV, 59.

Thus the West India trade passed to the north of Savannah, while
Georgian lumber rotted. Lastly, those who remained in Georgia
came to realize that not only were they excluded from all participation in government, but that in case of hostilities they were in the
front line of danger.

When war broke out between Great Britain and Spain in the late
1730's, these were among the reasons that contributed to a decided
drift of settlers away from the province. Many of the more enterprising planters, discouraged at the outlook, moved over into South
Carolina. The Moravians, opposed to military duty even in the defence of the province, dispersed,[52] some to find their way to Pennsylvania and others to North Carolina. The colony, in fact, was held
in great contempt by its neighbours,[53] and the model upon which it
was founded became the object of derision.[54]

In July 1742, Oglethorpe — with the aid of a regiment of British
regulars, troops from the Independent Companies of South Carolina,
and the support of local military units — succeeded in saving the
province from Spanish conquest after his failure to capture St. Augustine.[55] The crisis at last over, but in the face now of the most
bitter opposition to his policies, he left for England in July 1743 to
face a court-martial. Although he was vindicated,[56] Oglethorpe was
destined never to return to the region where he had spent over ten
years in labouring to realize the ideals of the Trust. In fact, previous
to his departure the actual control of the administration of civil
affairs had gradually been slipping from his hands during his periodic absences in England and when he was commanding the troops
in the campaign against Florida and later at Frederica along
the southern border.[57] By 1741 the colony had been divided into
two counties. In the northern, which contained Savannah and
most of the settlements, William Stephens, a capable man, acted
as president of the governing board.[58] In October, following Oglethorpe's departure, this board took over the administration of the

---

[52] *Journal of the Earl of Egmont, ibid.,* V, 165, 374, and 452.

[53] *Ibid.,* V, 139.

[54] *Ibid.,* V, 140.

[55] A. A. Ettinger: *James Edward Oglethorpe,* pp. 234–5, 243–4.

[56] *Ibid.,* pp. 251–3.

[57] *Journal of the Earl of Egmont, Colonial Records of Georgia,* V, 221, 349, 406, 409.

[58] For a brief account of the activities of William Stephens in Georgia see Natalie F. Bocock: "William Stephens," *Georgia Historical Quarterly,* XVII, 243–58.

entire province. With these changes came others that were funda-mental.

As early as 1738, while Oglethorpe was in command of the regi-ment in southern Georgia, the opposition to the land policy came to a head. The people of Savannah had been complaining bitterly, and at last the Trust took notice when a strong representation drawn up by the popular leader Robert Williams was sent to them.[59]

At a session of the Common Council it was resolved to introduce a modification in the system of land tenure so as to provide that in case of no issue, male or female, a proprietor of Georgia lands would be able to appoint any other person "not professing the Errors of the Church of Rome" as his successor, and that lands should not revert to the Trust on failure of male issue.[60]

This relaxation of the restrictions on devising property was an entering wedge. Other changes followed rapidly. In June 1740 it was agreed that freeholders should be allowed to rent their lands to tenants for a period up to seven years under condition that the renter would reside upon and improve them.[61] Early the following month the maximum of 500 acres that could be inherited in Georgia was set aside in favour of a maximum of 2,000 acres, all of which might be inherited by a daughter as well as by a son.[62] Later in the same month it was agreed that those who had received or would re-ceive a grant of 500 acres of land need only put 60 acres of "wood ground" under cultivation within the first ten years, as against the previous requirement of 200. As for the stipulation regarding the planting of mulberry trees, this was also modified to provide that only 1,000 need be set out during the first ten years, in place of 2,000.[63]

All this opened the way for the resolutions of the Council in March 1741, as a special concession to a group of distressed Ger-mans, by which tenure of lands by tail-male was discarded in favour of tenure by tail general with the right, therefore, of disposal of the land by will. At the same time it was agreed that an annual quit-rent of but four shillings for every 100 acres of land was to be paid.[64]

[59] Stephens' Journal, December 9, 1738, Colonial Records of Georgia, IV, 242–3; "Journal of the Trustees," June 20, 1739, ibid., I, 351.

[60] Minutes of the Common Council, May 2 and August 8, 1739, ibid., II, 271, 300.

[61] Minutes, June 6, 1740, ibid., II, 336.

[62] Minutes, July 7, 1740, ibid., II, 338.

[63] Minutes, July 21, 1740, ibid., II, 340; also ibid., II, 412.

[64] Minutes, March 9, 1741, ibid., II, 358–9.

Other changes were to follow. In the general law passed in March 1742, while the Trustees reaffirmed the principle of tenure in male-tail,[65] it amounted to nothing, for in July of that same year they came to the decision, in the face of a parliamentary investigation, to recommend to the Common Council of the corporation that land be granted no longer in male-tail but in fee simple to those who would carry white servants over to Georgia at their own expense.[66] A subsequent qualification provided that those securing such grants should not have the power of alienating their lands until the expiration of ten years, within which time they would be expected to cultivate one eighth of them.[67] This, with the decision to request His Majesty to reduce the quit-rents from four to two shillings proclamation money for every 100 acres,[68] marks out the general lines in the evolution of the land policy under the Trust. The way was thus gradually opened for the accumulation of land-holdings of considerable size and the building up of a landed aristocracy — in that one region within the old British Empire originally dedicated to the rehabilitation of the poor and distressed.

In enacting the law of January 9, 1734/5, against both the importation of rum and brandies into Georgia and their use within the colony, the Trustees stated that it was found by "Experience that the use of Liquors called Rum and Brandys in the Province of Georgia, are more particularly hurtfull and pernicious to Man's Body and have been attended with dangerous Maladies and fatal distempers. . . ." [69] This measure, which was approved by the Privy Council, came about as the result of a dispatch from Oglethorpe in which there was an account of the death of several of the settlers, which he imputed to the drinking of rum.[70] The devastations wrought in the West Indies by the drinking, especially among new-comers, of a fiery potation known as rum-punch was well known in England, where self-examination had also painted a vivid picture of the harm to morals, industry, and order resulting from the con-

---

65 *Minutes*, March 8, 1742, *ibid.*, II, 401.

66 "Journal of the Trustees," July 12, 1742, *ibid.*, I, 398.

67 "Journal," August 7, 1742, *ibid.*, I, 405.

68 "Journal," August 7, 1742, *ibid.*, I, 407 and 409.

69 For the law see *ibid.*, I, 44–8.

70 See *Minutes*, August 11, 1733, *Historical Collections of Georgia* (ed. G. White, New York, 1854), p. 16. Oglethorpe was present when the law of 1735 respecting the use of rum was ordered enforced. See *Percival's Diary*, II, 194; see also *Acts of the Privy Council, Col. Ser., 1720–1745*, p. 842.

sumption of Holland gin by the lower classes. Oglethorpe, with his strong humanitarian sentiments, was, in fact, ardently opposed to the use of these strong drinks and was largely responsible for the act by the Trust. It must not be understood that there was a prohibition against the importation and consumption of all spirituous beverages. The production of wines was encouraged, as has been noticed, and on one occasion the Common Council of the corporation sent over fifteen tons of strong beer to be sold with the understanding that the profits thereof should be applied to the clothing and maintenance of the indentured servants employed in the cultivation of lands for religious uses.[71] But wine or beer, even strong beer, was a weak substitute for men who in England had been accustomed to drink liquor with an alcoholic content of forty per cent. As a result, violation of law was rife and enforcement broke down.

William Stephens, who was Secretary of the province, refers in his *Journal* in January 1738 to the great mischief which he apprehended would ensue from the unlimited number of houses in the province that sold liquors surreptitiously. As he remarked, however, "it was pretty well known who divers of them were" that were responsible for these resorts. He asserted that they were selling the worst of spirits from New England or elsewhere, which they got at a low price, and thereby were able to lure many of the working-people. The latter, drawn to the places, spent what little money they had; or, if they had none, were readily given credit, for which they ultimately dearly paid by their labour. Stephens even accused the police officials — the constables and the tything-men, as they were called — of helping the owners of these public houses to secure the liquor, incidentally profiting thereby themselves; "for such Things," he recorded, "had been whispered to me as greatly suspected." [72] The following year he lamented "how fatal this Excess of Rum-drinking is likely to prove among the common People; and how ineffectual all Means have hitherto been found, for suppressing the Sale of it by unlicens'd Persons in all the bye Corners of the Town!" [73]

---

[71] *Minutes of the Common Council*, January 31, 1738, *Colonial Records of Georgia*, II, 262.

[72] *Stephens' Journal, 1737–1740, ibid.*, IV, 62.

[73] *Ibid.*, IV, 389. Colonel William Byrd of Virginia, writing to the Earl of Egmont on July 12, 1736, while warmly approving the exclusion of rum and Negroes from Georgia, warned: ". . . tho' with Respect to Rum, the Saints of New England I fear will find out some trick to evade your Act of Parliament [that is, the Molasses Act of

For ten years the Trustees struggled to maintain the act prohibiting rum, but they finally had to admit utter defeat in the face of the attitude of those violating the law. Early in January 1742 they arrived at the decision to write to Colonel Stephens, now not only Secretary of the Colony but President of the Board of Assistants of Savannah County, "to wink at the Importation of Rum and to discourage seizures thereof. . . ." This resolution of the Trust proceeded from the information that the law was totally disregarded when it came to the drinking of smuggled liquor.[74]

Later in the year the whole question of the policy of the Trustees came before the government in the form of a humble petition to His Majesty from the people of Georgia. This petition had been brought over from the colony by Thomas Stephens, the son of President Stephens, who had broken violently with his father. It represented the deplorable condition of the colony occasioned by the extraordinary laws and the administration thereof and was, in fact, a bitter attack on the chief policies of the Trustees as they related to land, rum, and slaves. The petition was referred by the Lords of the Committee of the Privy Council to the Trustees.[75] At the May meeting the Trustees drew up an answer to it, which was ordered to be laid before the Lords Commissioners.[76] The question then engaged the attention of the House of Commons, which on the 14th of the month resolved itself into a committee of the whole house. Evidence against the Trustees was heard from Thomas Stephens, Robert Williams, and Andrew Grant, all Georgia settlers, who appeared in person. It seems that Stephens's testimony made an especially deep impression, and the Earl of Egmont, one of the Trustees, recorded that his son, who was present, perceived that there was a disposition to take the colony out of the Trustees' hands: "The evidence bespatter'd Col. Oglethorpe much. . . ." Williams declared that he had lost £2,400 "by cultivation," while Andrew Grant testified that he had lost as much and that he knew that at one time there had been 4,000 persons in the colony but now there were but 500.[77] The opposition of

---

1733]. They have a great dexterity in palliating a perjury . . . nor can any people like them slip through a penal statute. . . . A watchful Eye must be kept on these foul Traders or all the precautions of the Trustees will be in vain" (from the Byrd letter-books at Brandon, Virginia, *American Historical Review*, I, 88).

[74] *Journal of the Earl of Egmont*, January 17, 1742, op. cit., ibid., V, 583.

[75] "Journal of the Trustees," April 19, 1742, ibid., I, 396.

[76] Ibid., I, 397.

[77] *Journal of the Earl of Egmont*, May 14, 1742, ibid., V, 619.

settlers to the idealitic policies of the Trustees did not stop there. Three landholders, Patrick Tailfer, Hugh Anderson, and David Douglas, assailed them in their pamphlet, *A True and Historical Narrative of the Colony of Georgia . . .* , published in South Carolina in 1741 and sent to London. Further, Thomas Stephens, after circulating it in manuscript form, published in London in 1743 his *A Brief Account of the Causes that have Retarded the Progress of the Colony of Georgia; Attested upon Oath* — another bitter arraignment of the Trustees.

Doubtless as a result of this well-planned attack, the Trustees in July 1742 not only recommended to the Common Council the discontinuance of land grants in male-tail in favour of fee-simple grants, as has been previously noticed, but resolved to repeal so much of the act against the importation and use of rum and brandy in Georgia as prevented the importation of strong liquors into the province from other British colonies.[78] The amendment to the act, which was now prepared and approved, declared that since the passage of the prohibitory law of 1735 the province had been further settled and improved, and that there was now good reason to believe the importation of rum to be used as barter for Georgia lumber and other commodities would be of advantage and would promote the trade of the inhabitants. It would therefore be lawful hereafter to import rum into the province, but only from some other English colony in order to make payment for exports, which for this purpose were limited to the products of the colony.[79] That this concession was made with the most extreme reluctance and only as a result of great external pressure is evident. Indeed, the true attitude of the Trustees was revealed in a measure which they passed in January 1743 designed to regulate public houses and retailers of rum in Georgia and also, to quote the language of the act, to suppress "the odious and loathsome Sin of Drunkenness." [80] This provided, among other things, that any who sold rum without licence must give security to the amount of £10 not to offend again in the like manner.

The two laws, as was true of all acts passed by the Trustees for the colony, had to be submitted to the King's Council for approval or rejection; they were in turn referred by that body to the Board of

---

[78] "Journal of the Trustees," July 12 and 14, 1742, *ibid.*, I, 398–9.

[79] For this act, repealing the act of 1735 prohibiting the importation and sale of rum, see *ibid.*, I, 54–6.

[80] "Journal of the Trustees," January 11, 1742/3, *ibid.*, I, 411.

Trade to be studied and reported back. In April 1744 the Secretary for the Trustees, Benjamin Martyn, was requested to appear before the Lords Commissioners to discuss certain matters relating to them. At this meeting objections were raised to some of the provisions of the act for allowing the importation of rum. Among these provisions, exception was taken to the restriction of importing rum to barter for Georgia commodities, also to the proviso limiting the commerce in rum to other British colonies, thus forbidding this trade to the distillers of Great Britain, and, finally, to the severity of the penalties imposed on selling rum without a proper licence. When these objections came before the Trustees they made a resolution to the effect that they could not consent to any alteration in either of the two acts and instructed their Secretary to desire the Board of Trade to return the law in particular question to them in the event that body could not approve its provisions.[81]

In the objections to the law against slavery — "An Act for rendering the Colony of Georgia more Defensible by Prohibiting the Importation and use of Black Slaves or Negroes," passed in 1735 — the Trustees found themselves confronted with a third major problem. The prohibition of slavery ranked with the controversial land and liquor policies as problems to which solutions were essential for the realization of Georgia's arcadian program.

The most heartening support of the institutions of freedom and human equality came from the Scottish Highlanders at Darien along the southern border and especially from the Salzburgers at New Ebenezer. Nevertheless, the influence of the precedents in South Carolina was powerful. In the movement of population, slave-owners from that colony crossed the Savannah and entered Georgia from time to time, settling with their slaves in the more isolated sections, thus being fairly safe from interference by the magistrates at Savannah — some of whom, in point of fact, were by no means heartily in favour of the Trustees' policy. In December 1738 a representation was drawn up setting forth the discouragements that people laboured under in cultivating land with white servants only. Its promoter was the same Robert Williams who testified later before a parliamentary committee regarding conditions in Georgia.[82]

---

[81] "Journal of the Trustees," May 5, 1744, ibid., I, 453–4; Acts of the Privy Council, Col. Ser., Unbound Papers, p. 254.

[82] Stephens' Journal, December 9, 1738, Colonial Records of Georgia, IV, 242–3; and Journal of the Earl of Egmont, ibid., V, 93–4.

However, the most powerful advocate of slavery in Georgia was the Thomas Stephens whose petition addressed to the King in Council had led to an investigation of the state of the province by the House of Commons in 1742 and a threat to the Trustees that they would be relieved of their responsibilities unless they established a form of government better suited to the needs of the people.[83] It was out of the discussions of Stephens's representations that had arisen the concessions mentioned above regarding land tenure and rum, and that those on slavery ultimately would come. But the only indications at that time of an inclination to yield on the question of slavery were the drafting of another letter by the Trustees to President Stephens at Savannah, requesting him to make an inquiry among the people "whether it is their Opinion in general That it is proper to admit the Use and Introduction of Negroes," and the appointment of a committee to consider how far it might be proper to allow their introduction.[84]

As for the colony itself, it was torn by factions over the slavery issue. John Dobell, the Savannah schoolmaster, writing in 1746 declared: "The grand Article of Th. Stephens's Scheme is; Nothing but Negroes will do (to make, I Suppose, this Colonie like Carolina)"; Dobell further asserted that the President of the governing board in the province, "Col. Stephens, and his Assistants superciliously affirm the same Thing and Take every artfull Measure to Work the Trustees to tire and weary the Trustees in that Opinion," [85] and he even accused the local board of treachery to the Trustees' scheme of making the colony a happy settlement for poor Protestants.[86]

Dobell was ardently supported in his anti-slavery views by John Martin Bolzius, the able, consecrated, and indefatigable minister

---

[83] *Journals of the House of Commons*, XXIV, 192, 216, 221, 288, 376.

[84] "Journal of the Trustees," July 14, 1742, *Colonial Records of Georgia*, I, 400–1.

[85] *Original Papers, Correspondence, Trustees* . . . , 1745–1750, ibid., XXV, 73–9.

[86] In December of 1746 President Stephens wrote to the Secretary of the Trustees, Mr. Martyn, defending himself against the charge of being favourable to slavery. "I cannot imagine what Information the Trustees have had of such an Expectance being raised among us, as you write, of their Intention to allow the Use of Negroes in a short time: That divers have entertain'd such Wishes, cannot be denied, nor can it that many yet do: but I assure you 'tis never with any Encouragement from Me. . . . 'tis well known that I have often declared my natural Aversion to 'em" (ibid., XXV, 143–4). That he was not aggressively opposed to slavery is, however, quite manifest. For his preoccupations with his office see *The Journal of William Stephens, 1741–1743* (ed. E. M. Coulter, Athens, Ga., 1958), the first of a projected two-volume edition carrying the journals to 1745.

and magistrate of the Salzburgers at New Ebenezer, who eloquently declared, in words worthy of William Lloyd Garrison or Wendell Phillips a century later:

"I am in Christ's Name resolved rather to suffer hardships, heinous reflectings, revilings, reproaches and I don't know what else than lend the least finger to promote the Introduction of Black Slaves to the apparent destruction of our Well Situated and fertile Province as an intended Asylum for many poor labouring Protestants who I know Sigh and groan under the Yoke of Spiritual and Temporal Slavery in Germany and would be very thankful to God and his Instruments to find under the Government of our most Gracious King a corner to live by the fruit of their own labour. . . . If I have in this Colony only one single person in Authority and power that would agree with me in the wise scheme of their Honors it would give me Comfort and encouragement, but I find that all from the highest to the lowest Vote for Negroes and look upon me as a Stone in their way toward which they direct all their Spite and they will, I suppose, not rest until they have removed it one way or other. I commit my Cause to the Almighty who will not leave nor forsake me, tho' my life should be forced from me." [87]

This ideal that Dobell and Bolzius were fighting to maintain in Georgia was still vivid in the minds of the Trustees.

It appears that in 1746 the Trustees continued to be optimistic about their ability to hold the province for freedom, in spite of all grumblings. They were therefore surprised and not a little indignant when at their December meeting, in perusing the journal of the governing board at Savannah, they noticed a statement to the effect that a former minister within the province, the Rev. Mr. Thomas Bosomworth, had that year brazenly sent to South Carolina for six Negroes to be employed on his plantation at the forks on the Altamaha River, and also a casual comment that Negroes had been "creeping into the Colony at Augusta and other remote Places." [88]

---

[87] Rev. John Martin Bolzius to John Dobell, Ebenezer, May 20, 1748, *Colonial Records of Georgia*, XXV, 282–6.

Outside of the idealistic aspects involved in the issue, the Salzburgers were strongly opposed to slavery not only because the introduction of this labour would, they felt, lower the price of farm produce, but because their fields and gardens would be robbed and white persons put in danger of life. See Hester W. Newton: "The Industrial and Social Influences of the Salzburgers in Colonial Georgia," *Georgia Historical Quarterly*, XVIII, 348–9.

[88] "Journal of the Trustees," December 29, 1746, *Colonial Records of Georgia*, I, 495.

Thereupon the Secretary was ordered to write to President Stephens to acquaint him that the Trustees were surprised that he, as President, and the Assistants had neither taken any steps to punish and put a stop to such violation of the law against the use of Negroes nor proposed any means whereby the corporation itself might do so, and that further, in the face of these violations, they had contented themselves with simply complaining of them.[89]

In reply to the rebuke the Georgia board at Savannah addressed a letter to the Trustees in October 1747 affirming that it had acted earnestly in discouraging the use of Negroes, but admitting that some planters from the Carolinas had come into the province and had settled on the Little Ogeechee, where, until discovered, they employed a few Negroes. The board went on to state that these newest settlers had now withdrawn out of the colony and that others were on the eve of withdrawing, particularly the whole body of inhabitants of Augusta who for many years had had Negroes among them but were now preparing to cross over to the Carolina side of the Savannah.[90]

The truth is that the local governing group in Georgia was weak and quite unable, had it so desired, to enforce the law in the face of the determination and power of those violating it. The people living about the lower Altamaha in the neighbourhood of Frederica, as well as those settled in the region of Augusta on the upper Savannah, were especially guilty of smuggling in Negroes. Nevertheless, in 1748 the Savannah board went on record regarding the granting of lands to those bringing in slaves when three South Carolinians, Joshua Morgan, Middleton Evans, and Edward Ellis, applied for allotments to be located near the mouth of the Altamaha. These planters had set forth that they were able to cultivate the lands in question, since one of them had thirteen servants, another twelve, and the third five. Their petitions were refused upon the grounds that it was reputed that those they called "servants" were none other than black slaves. At the same time, the board resolved to reject like petitions from all inhabitants of South Carolina, "being fully convinced that their general Design is to introduce and use their Negroes notwithstanding their many Promises and Protestations to the Contrary." The members further pledged themselves "to use their

---

[89] Ibid.
[90] President and Assistants to Mr. Martyn, Savannah, October 2, 1747, ibid., XXV, 225–37.

utmost Endeavours to seize or drive out all Negroes that are or shall be found within the Colony." [91]

One of the things that most galled the board was that Colonel Alexander Heron, in charge of the garrison at Frederica, "who assumes to himself the Government of the Southern part of this Colony," had possessed himself of a tract of land near Saint Catherine's Sound which was supposed to contain upwards of 2,000 acres and, according to report, had settled several Negroes upon it. Heron was accused both of declaring that he would protect his slaves in opposition to all, and of asserting on divers occasions that any person should have liberty to introduce Negroes into that part of the province where he was in military command.[92]

When the news of this situation reached the Trustees they gathered in the vestry room of St. Margaret's Church and resolved:

"That, after so many Declarations that the Introduction and Use of Negroes in the Colony is not only inconsistent with the Intention of his Majesty's Charter, but also directly contrary to an Express Act approv'd of by his Majesty in Council in the Year 1735 . . . for prohibiting the Importation and Use of Negroes . . . ; The Trustees are surpris'd any Expectations of them can yet remain at Savanah, and in other Parts of the Colony; And therefore it must be, and is, upon that foundation, a Resolution of the Trustees never to permit the Introduction of Negroes within the Colony of Georgia, as the Danger which must arise from them in a Frontier Town is so evident; And as the People, Who continue to clamour for Negroes declare that the Colony can never succeed without the use of them, it is evident they don't intend by their own Industry to contribute to its Success, and must therefore rather hinder than promote it; The Trustees therefore require it may be signified to all the Inhabitants of the Colony, that if any of them persist in declaring they cannot succeed without Negroes, it would be of service to the Colony, as well as themselves, for them to retire into any other Province, where they will be freely allow'd the Use of Negroes." [93]

It was an idle gesture. Sentiment in Georgia had turned overwhelmingly in favour of slavery. Even the great Whitefield was numbered among the supporters of the institution. President

---

[91] *Proceedings of the President and Assistants*, for January 30, 1747/8, *ibid.*, VI, 207–8.

[92] *Ibid.*

[93] Resolutions of March 17, 1747/8, *ibid.*, I, 506–7.

Stephens and the four other members of the governing board in Georgia on May 8, 1748, directed a letter to the Trustees setting forth that "Abundance of People had applied to them for Grants of Land in Georgia and Numbers of Negro's had been introduc'd into the Province . . ." and added that they had taken methods to drive the said Negroes out of the province, but "ineffectually." They went on to declare that they were convinced that any further attempts to put the act against the use of Negroes into execution would depopulate the colony, and expressed the hope that the Trustees might permit slaves in the province under restrictions.[94]

This letter was followed early in the following year by a memorial dated January 10, 1748/9, signed by the President and Assistants in Georgia and a great number of the inhabitants, setting forth several restrictions and regulations under which they prayed that Negroes might be introduced into the colony.[95] At the meeting of the Trustees the following May, with only four members present, after considering the letters and the representation, they finally acknowledged defeat and the repudiation of the last of the great ideals for which they had stood. In line with this they resolved that a petition be presented to His Majesty in Council that the Act of 1735 prohibiting Negro slaves be repealed.[96]

On August 8, 1750, the common seal of the Trust was therefore affixed to an act repealing the anti-slavery law of 1735.[97] It carried with it, true enough, a series of restrictions upon slaveholding. Among these were the requirement that for every four male slaves a plantation-owner must have living on the plantation where they were employed one white manservant of military age; further, it was specified that no artificer within the province should take any Negro as an apprentice, the coopers or barrel-makers excepted; that any owner of a slave who should inflict corporal punishment endangering the life of a Negro was to pay £5 sterling and if he killed

---

[94] "Journal of the Trustees," May 16, 1749, ibid., I, 530–1.

[95] Ibid.

[96] Ibid. "The fate of the original Negro Act is not clear. According to the Repeal Act, which was dated 8 August 1750, slavery as a legal institution in Georgia was recognized to exist from and after 1 January 1750. Whether or not the limitations imposed by the Trustees and included in the Repeal Act gained the sanction of the Board of Trade or of the Privy Council does not appear in the records of the Trust" (H. B. Fant: "The Labor Policy of the Trustees for Establishing the Colony of Georgia in America," Georgia Historical Quarterly, XVI, 14).

[97] Colonial Records of Georgia, I, 550–1.

the Negro he was to be tried according to the laws of Great Britain.

Under the terms of the law an office was to be set up for the annual registration of all Negroes to be brought into the province or who were already there, and it was further laid down that ships bringing slaves were to be inspected by a health officer before landing their cargoes. The law also contained other interesting provisions. For example, an owner not obliging his Negroes to attend divine service on the Lord's Day, whenever held contiguous to their abodes, should forfeit £10 sterling; any intermarrying between white and black was forbidden and illicit intercourse between them was to be punished by fine or whipping as the judge might direct. Moreover, to encourage the silk industry, the law decreed that for every five male Negroes one female should be kept who should be taught the winding of silk from the cocoons, and also that every planter should have 500 mulberry trees for each 500 acres of land. The final clause of the act put the seal of high sanctity on this great moral concession in declaring that for the maintenance of ministers of the gospel and officers of the government and for building and keeping in repair churches and other necessary buildings, a duty of fifteen shillings was to be paid on all blacks twelve years old or more who should be brought in subsequently, and a duty of one shilling annually on all Negroes inhabiting the province.[98]

Thus one after another of those cherished ideals which had animated the Trust and its supporters in envisaging a commonwealth along arcadian lines faded away in the face of opposition on the part of those who were expected to give effect to them in the New World.[99]

Already, at a meeting of the Common Council on March 19, 1749/50, it had been voted to create an Assembly in Georgia with power to propose, debate, and represent to the Trustees — still vested with the legislative power — what should appear to be for the general benefit of the province. In this connection it was provided that deputies to the Assembly must have 50 acres of cleared

---

[98] For the act of the Trustees of August 8, 1750, permitting slavery see *ibid.*, I, 56–62; also *Minutes of the Common Council*, April 11, 1750, *ibid.*, II, 504. It would appear that the Privy Council took no action on the new law, doubtless in view of the fact that the Trust was about to petition the Crown to be dissolved.

[99] In the above connection see the article by D. M. Potter, Jr.: "The Rise of the Plantation System in Georgia" (*Georgia Historical Quarterly*, XVI, 114–35), which stresses the opposition of the settlers to the idealism of the Trustees.

land containing 100 mulberry trees, and that after 1753 no one should be a deputy who had not conformed to the new regulations respecting the holding of slaves.[100] On May 6, 1751, at a meeting attended by but five Trustees, the seal of the corporation was attached to a memorial directed to His Majesty indicating that they were no longer able to support the civil government of the colony and the encouragement of the silk industry.[101] This was followed on December 14 of that year by an offer to the Privy Council to surrender the charter to the Crown with the proviso, among other conditions, that "the Colony of Georgia be confirmed a separate and independent Province, as . . . declared in his Majesty's Charter." [102] Then, on June 23, 1752, the seal was affixed to "the Deed of Surrender and Grant of the Trust. . . . After Which the Seal was defaced." [103]

The transition, however, was slow. Not until August 16, 1754, was John Reynolds, a naval officer, given his commission as first royal Governor of Georgia, into which duties he entered in the month of October at Savannah.[104]

So it was that by 1754 Georgia had become just another British royal province with no distinguishing marks except perhaps an intense hostility to the very type of people it had been founded to aid. It is no wonder that, with defeat facing them, many of the Trustees even before this time had lost interest in the enterprise — some undoubtedly sick at heart, as was Oglethorpe. The days of the great vision of twenty years before had run their course, and with their passing that fervour and elevation of spirit which come to men who rally to any great and good cause, who dare to look above the repelling realities of their present surroundings into some land of promise. But to most of the inhabitants of Georgia, faced by the realities of wresting a livelihood from the soil under prevailing conditions, the dissolution of the Trust, and with it the end of experiments of colonization by meddlesome idealists, was greeted with joy.[105]

---

[100] *Colonial Records of Georgia*, II, 498–500.

[101] *Ibid.*, I, 557.

[102] *Ibid.*, I, 569–70.

[103] *Ibid.*, I, 578.

[104] For the career of Governor Reynolds see W. W. Abbot: *The Royal Governors of Georgia* (Chapel Hill, 1959).

[105] For a severe indictment of the Georgia colonizing enterprise see D. J. Boorstin: *The Americans. The Colonial Experience* (New York, 1958), pp. 71–96.

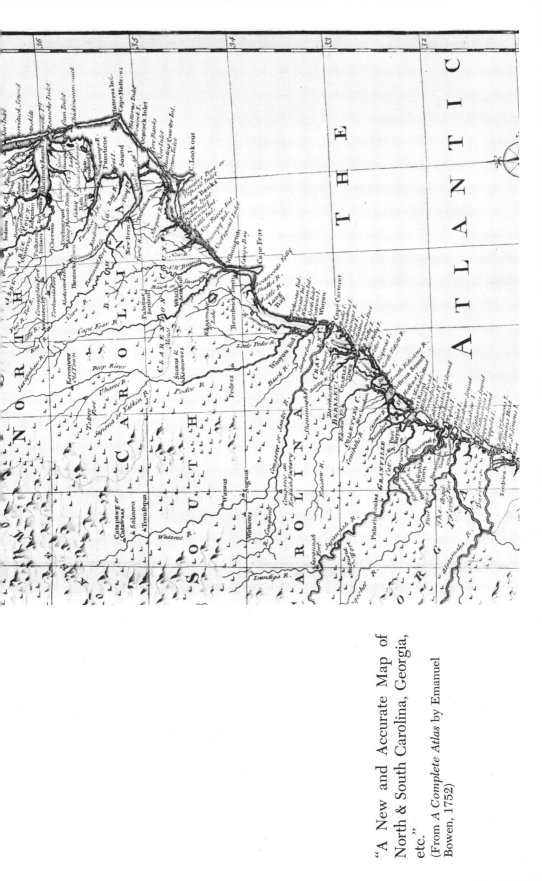

"A New and Accurate Map of North & South Carolina, Georgia, etc."

(From *A Complete Atlas* by Emanuel Bowen, 1752)

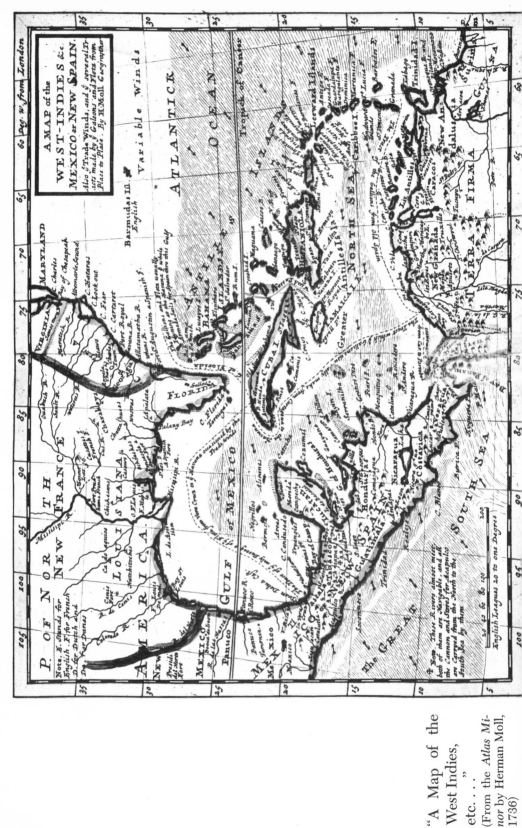

"A Map of the West Indies, etc...."
(From the *Atlas Minor* by Herman Moll, 1736)

CHAPTER VII

The Caribbean Outpost of the Empire

IT is difficult today to appreciate the fact that the island of Jamaica was perhaps the most prized of Great Britain's overseas possessions in 1750. Its singular characteristics as a colony can best be shown by an analysis of the chief problems that faced its government: the absenteeism of the great planters, the need for additional settlers, the maintenance of economic vitality, and the proper control of the Negro slaves. In addition, the history of Jamaica in the middle of the eighteenth century is incomplete without some account of its mainland political dependencies — the logwood region of the area now called British Honduras and that of the neighbouring Mosquito Coast.

After Newfoundland and Ireland, Jamaica was the largest island possession of Great Britain at this period. The most important British Caribbean outpost, it enjoyed a strategic location — lying in the midst of the Spanish possessions, only 170 leagues to the northward of Porto Bello and Cartagena, 20 leagues south of Cuba, and 24 leagues to the west of the French possession of St. Domingue. In the words of the Governor, Edward Trelawny,[1] in 1749, it was "a Frontier Province surrounded on all sides wth Powerful Neighbours

---

[1] For Edward Trelawny see Frank Cundall: *The Governors of Jamaica in the First Half of the Eighteenth Century* (London, 1937), pp. 171–207. This does not contain a biography of Trelawny but rather excerpts of documents relating to his administration in Jamaica. It may be pointed out that while Cundall spells the name uniformly Trelawney, the Governor spelled it Trelawny. See, for example, the letter addressed to the Earl of Wilmington, April 22, 1739, which is in the manuscript files of the Institute of Jamaica.

that do not wish us well." [2] In view of these circumstances it is not surprising that a regiment of foot soldiers and three regiments of horse, together with thirteen of foot militia — making 5,000 troops in all — were constantly maintained for defence and that the ports of the island were protected by forts. These had been built wholly at the expense of the people, the most important being Fort Charles at Port Royal, which was provided with over 200 cannon.[3] However, this and other defences had been allowed to fall into a state of decay after the late conclusion of the War of Jenkins's Ear.

The government of Jamaica, a typical royal colony, rested in the Governor — the best paid imperial post, outside of the governorship of Ireland, in the gift of the Crown, and also one of the most important [4] — a Council of twelve members, and the House of Assembly. At this period the island was divided into nineteen parishes, each of which sent to the Assembly two members elected by the freeholders.[5] Located in the midst of hostile Spanish and French possessions, with a white population of but some 12,000 living

---

[2] Governor Trelawny to the Board of Trade, June 8, 1749, P.R.O., C.O. 137:25, pp. 89–92.

[3] "State of Jamaica, 1752," C.O. 137:25, pp. 243–5.

[4] [Charles Leslie]: A New History of Jamaica . . . in Thirteen Letters from a Gentleman to his Friend (London, 1740), p. 301.

According to Bryan Edwards (A History, Civil and Commercial, of the British Colonies in the West Indies [3 vols., London, 1793–1801], I, 223) the Governor received from all sources — that is, from the perpetual revenue, from special legislative grant, and from perquisites of office — an income equal to £5,000 Jamaica currency. William Burke (An Account of the European Settlements in America [2 vols., London, 1757], II, 80) put it at some £10,000.

For a careful appraisement of the historical works of Leslie, Edwards, and Burke just cited and also of the writings of Edward Long concerned with Jamaica or with the West Indies in general, see Elsa V. Goveia: A Study on the Historiography of the British West Indies (Mexico, 1956), pp. 47–62, 69–72, and 81–9.

For Governor Trelawny's commission, issued in 1737, see P.R.O., C.O. 5:196, pp. 351–70; for his general instructions see C.O. 138:18, pp. 135–216.

[5] In order to vote in 1750 one had to be a freeholder having real estate of the annual value of £10, or a plantation, five acres of which were under cultivation, or be the owner of a cattle pen and of at least six head of cattle. In order to have a seat in the House of Assembly one had to have lands, Negroes, or other hereditaments of an annual value of £300 or £3,000 in gross. See "An Act to Secure Freedom of Elections," passed in 1732, Acts of Assembly passed in the Island of Jamaica, from 1681, to 1754, inclusive (London, 1756), pp. 179–81, cited hereafter as Acts of Assembly (1756).

Jamaica had a number of wealthy Jews, and in 1740 an effort was made by one of them as a land-holder and freeman to vote. This right was, however, refused by the Assembly. See Frank Cundall: op. cit., pp. 197–8. That some Jews had actually exercised the right of franchise was asserted in a private letter from Kingston. See Aris's Birmingham Gazette, February 4, 1751.

among 130,000 Negroes — most of them slaves, according to an estimate made in 1754 — the island might well have presented a much more extreme form of centralized power concentrated in the hands of the Governor than was the case. The House of Assembly could be and was at times very articulate in opposing and thwarting the Governor while insisting on its rights, especially under some of Governor Trelawny's predecessors and successors.[6] Nevertheless, the Governor could generally depend upon the support of the Council. He also had at hand in administering affairs of a local nature the support of the powerful *custodes rotulorum,* whom he appointed and who were described as his "eyes and ears."

The *custos,* who was sure to be a great landowner and a man of wealth, in fact dominated the government of his precinct, which might, as was the case of the western part of the island, be but a single parish or, in the case of the eastern part, be made up of two parishes, or even consist of four parishes, as in the area about the capital, Spanish Town.[7] He was not only the chairman of the vestry or vestries, performing many important parish functions, but also presided at the court of quarter sessions, made up of the justices of the peace. In addition, he was frequently the chief judge of the district court of common pleas, as well as the chief militia officer within his precinct. Responsible for the supervision of his district, his power over all appointments relating to it was very real.[8] During the mid-eighteenth century Philip Pinnock of St. Andrew Parish, the owner of almost 4,000 acres of land, held this office, as did John Scott in Clarendon Parish with 5,800 acres, and William Lewis, possessed of 2,700 acres.[9] Indeed it may be affirmed that in no other British colony was a royal governor kept so closely in touch with local affairs, and also in no other colony was his influence in local affairs more potent.

That the influence of the Governor in such matters as the tenure of judges and the elections of members to the House of Assembly

---

[6] Governor Charles Knowles to the Board of Trade, December 31, 1754, C.O. 137:28, Y 55. In the above connection see Agnes M. Whitson: *The Constitutional Development of Jamaica, 1660–1729* (Manchester, 1929), p. 44, 47–8, *passim,* and also Mary P. Clarke: *Parliamentary Privilege in the American Colonies* (New Haven, 1943), pp. 80–1, *passim.*

[7] See H. P. Jacobs: "Roger Hope Elletson's Letter Book," *Jamaican Historical Review,* II, 67–73.

[8] *Ibid.*

[9] *Ibid.*

was felt to be too great, despite Trelawny's complacency and popularity, is indicated by the passing of two acts in 1751 which he reluctantly signed without a suspending clause. One of them provided that judges of the Superior Court of Judicature should hold office *quam diu se bene gesserint* — that is, during good behaviour.[10] The other provided that members of the Assembly should be elected by ballot.[11] These laws, however, failed to win approval in England.[12]

The political relationship between Jamaica and the mother country had begun in 1655 with the capture of the island from the Spaniards by Penn and Venables. This connection had thereupon become a source of great wealth to the English people.[13] According to a report sent by Governor Trelawny to the Board of Trade in 1741, the value of the commodities exported annually was £1,500,000 Jamaica currency.[14] The products involved were sugar, molasses, rum, cotton, ginger, cocoa, coffee, pimento, spices, fustic, ebony, lignum-vitae, and mahogany. It was stated that about £700,000 currency was annually paid in England for duty and excise alone on these imports, and upwards of £300,000 for freight, commissions, storage, etc.[15] But with all of its productiveness Jamaica lacked most of the necessities of life. From North America came bread and flour, cod and

---

[10] *Acts of Assembly* (1756), p. 25.

[11] *Ibid.*

[12] The position of the law officers of the Crown and of Sir Matthew Lamb, the Board of Trade's legal adviser, was that the positions of the judges of the Supreme Court of Judicature were already sufficiently protected from unwarranted interference on the part of the Governor by Article 44 of his general instructions and that since the act seriously affected the royal prerogative and also since there was no claim that the Governor had abused his power of removal, it should be repealed. With respect to the act for electing to the Assembly by ballot, these same jurists pointed out that, by the Governor's commission, assemblies of freeholders and planters were to be called and that this was to be done "according to the usage of the said Island," by which persons elected by the major part of the freeholders of the respective parishes and places, having duly qualified themselves, were to be deemed the Assembly of Jamaica. It was further pointed out that the method hitherto employed was that used in England for electing members of Parliament and in all the other colonies but South Carolina, where voting by ballot was instituted when that province was still under the government of the Proprietors. See *Acts of the Privy Council, Col., Ser.,* 1745–1766, pp. 215–18.

[13] The commerce between Jamaica and Great Britain at the period under review employed some 207 ships annually, according to the Commissioners of the Customs. See the Board of Trade to the House of Commons, February 22, 1753, Library of Congress accessions, No. 2413.

[14] See Trelawny's "State of Jamaica," November 21, 1741, Shelburne Papers, 45:24–37, Clements Library; see also P.R.O., C.O. 137:25, pp. 243–5.

[15] *Ibid.*

other fish, Indian corn, rice, horses and other livestock, and wood products of various kinds, especially for barrels and house-construction. From Ireland came barrelled beef and pork, firkins of butter and herring; from South America, mules for the sugar plantations; and from England a bewildering volume of supplies, especially manufactures, valued at not less than £350,000 sterling in 1752.[16]

The island was important not only for its natural products and fertility, but because of its advantageous location for trade. It had greatly benefited under the Asiento (Assiento) Treaty enjoyed by the South Sea Company before the Spanish War that began in 1739. According to estimates, the annual value of this trade to the local merchants before 1739 had amounted to over £60,000 sterling.[17] Nor does this calculation take into account the immense smuggling activities of Spanish-American merchants who, especially between the years 1722 and the outbreak of the war, resorted in their own small ships to Jamaica from the mainland "to escape the exorbitant charges of the Spanish Cales Company which maintained its exclusive right of exporting all goods that came from Spain to her colonies and asked upwards of 300 per cent beyond what the inhabitants had been accustomed to pay when the trade was open." [18]

Although the outbreak of the War of Jenkins's Ear had put a legal termination to all British commerce with Spanish America, at least traffic in dry goods with the enemy had continued, accord-

---

16 North America, among other things, sent yearly 18,000 tierces and barrels of bread and flour, 4,000 barrels of beef and pork, 3,000 hogsheads of cod, and 4,000 barrels of wet salted fish such as mackerel, alewives, and shad. Ireland sent 15,000 barrels of beef and pork, 13,000 firkins of butter, and 4,000 barrels of herring. See "State of Jamaica," 1752, *ibid.* For two studies relating to North American trade with the West Indies see Richard Pares: *Yankees and Creoles: The Trade between North America and the West Indies before the American Revolution* (London, 1956), and H. C. Bell: "West Indies Trade before the American Revolution," *American Historical Review,* XXII, 272–87.

17 See [G. M. Butel-Dumont]: *Histoire et Commerce des Antilles Angloises* (Paris, 1758), Chap. 3, which states that the above sterling amount was equal to 1,500,500 livres tournois (the livre tournois having been equal to 1/23 the value of the pound sterling as a rule).

For an excellent account of the relations of the planters of Jamaica both with the Royal Africa Company and with the asientists in the early part of the eighteenth century see C. P. Nettels: "England and the Spanish-American Trade, 1680–1715," *Journal of Modern History,* III, 1–32. This article brings out clearly the sharp divergence of interest between groups interested in slave-trading and in slave supply. See also G. H. Nelson: "Contraband Trade under the Asiento," *American Historical Review,* LI, 55–67.

18 [James Wallace]: *A General and Descriptive History of the Antient and Present State of the Town of Liverpool . . .* (Liverpool, 1795), pp. 206–8.

ing to Trelawny's report. It is also certain that a clandestine trade with Spaniards living about Porto Bello and Cartagena survived the outbreak of hostilities by using the harbours of outlying towns as "bases of rendezvous." To these points many Negroes were carried and were eagerly purchased by Spanish planters.[19] With the restoration of peace between Great Britain and Spain the slave trade was again legalized, but not by restoration of the asiento privileges to the South Sea Company.[20] Under the new system established by Spain, certain contractors were awarded *cedules,* as the licences were called, which permitted them to supply the demand for blacks made by those living on the Spanish Main and in Cuba. During the middle of the eighteenth century Jamaica was sending out some 2,500 Negroes annually under these *cedules.*[21]

Despite the commercial advantages set forth above, the island was apparently not in a flourishing condition at this period. "I am sorry to tell you," wrote Henry Livingston in 1749, then residing at Kingston, to William Alexander of New York, "this Island is almost ruin'd for want of trade. Everything is at a stand & no money, wch is worst of all, stiring among us." The writer blamed the loss of the asiento for the business stagnation and described the return to Jamaica of the "South Sea fleet" from the Spanish Main without being permitted to trade. This would explain, he made clear to his correspondent, why, "as we have no export, all your produce must be Sold this summer." [22]

In 1752 the Jamaica Assembly emphasized the disastrous results to the island of the withdrawal of the asiento. "This fruitful Spring of Trade is now gone and we are confined in our Commerce with the Spaniards solely to the vending of Negroes (a merchandise they cannot do without)," it complained in addressing the King. The memorial then went on to affirm "that not more than a Fourth part of the money hath been annually brought into this Island since the late war as usually was before and not a Twentieth part of what was brought in during the same [war], so that we have little other trade at present but of exporting of commodities of the growth and prod-

---

[19] See [G. M. Butel-Dumont]: *op. cit.*

[20] For the South Sea Company and the surrender of the asiento privileges, see L. H. Gipson: "British Diplomacy in the Light of Anglo-Spanish New World Issues, 1750–1757," *American Historical Review,* LI, 627–48.

[21] See "State of Jamaica," 1752, C.O. 137:25, pp. 243–5.

[22] Henry Livingston to William Alexander of New York, May 28, 1749, Sterling Papers, New York Historical Society Library.

uce of this Island to Great Britain." [23] Indeed, the value of the exports, which was placed at £1,500,000 currency in 1741, had fallen to £700,000 by 1752, according to Trelawny.[24]

It was largely due to this sharp drop in the value of their trade that the people of the island were becoming restless under the weight of public financial obligations.[25] In April 1749 the Council and the Assembly had united in a petition to the Crown in which they stressed "those burdens which disturb the happiness of your People and threaten the ruin and destruction to a Colony of such importance to your Majesty's Government." In this they referred also to the loyal support they had given during the late war "with a warmth and cheerfulness disproportioned to our Abilities, and as we apprehend, in a much greater degree than the rest of your Subjects." They went on to say:

> "These were our efforts; whilst we were labouring under an additional duty on molasses [and] spirits, which though unavoidable from the exigency of the times, does in a most grievous manner affect the inhabitants in general, but more particularly the poorer sort and prevents the cultivation of unsettled lands, it being evident that sugar, produced from new lands, abound with a greater proportion of syrup than that raised from old plantations. And, whilst we are under the pressure of that duty, we [have] had the mortification to find ourselves subjected to the further tax of one shilling and six pence per hundred imposed the last session of Parliament upon all sugar produced from your Majesty's colonies, which we fear, if continued, must in the end transfer that valuable commodity to our great rivals in trade, the natural enemies of your Majesty's crown and government." [26]

It is not surprising that under such adverse conditions there was expressed a determination to continue to saddle with additional

---

23 Address of the Jamaica Assembly to the King, November 20, 1752, C.O. 137:25.

24 *Ibid.* The figures of the Board of Trade are £692,164.13.6. The sugar was valued at £537,153.14.4½; the rum, at £46,626.5.10. See the address of the Board of Trade to the House of Commons, February 22, 1753, Library of Congress accessions, No. 2413.

25 According to a letter written by Governor Trelawny on November 14, 1747, to the Board of Trade, under terms of a law passed in that year quit-rents, which before then had been very irregularly paid, brought in a revenue of £58,981.18 Jamaica currency "of which not one farthing would have been gott in under the former Laws" (*ibid.*); see also B. W. Bond, Jr.: *Quit-Rent System in the American Colonies* (New Haven, 1919), pp. 362–5. These levies, under the circumstances, must have proved burdensome.

26 The date of this address is April 29, 1749; it is printed in the *Maryland Gazette*, August 30, 1749.

taxes those great planters or merchant princes in possession of large bodies of land who resided in the mother country while confining their interests in Jamaica largely to the exploitation of their plantations by factors, agents, and overseers.[27] For thirty years, from 1718 to 1747, these absentees had been taxed in greater proportion than residents, and no exception had been taken to it by the British government. This was doubtless because of an appreciation of the fact that the location of the island made it imperative to bring every resource to bear for its defence and that the money thus raised had been applied to the support of a body of troops. However, in the early 1740's the islands of Antigua and St. Christopher had turned to the same practice without the same justification, with the result that in 1745 the Board of Trade declared against their measures and recommended that the Governor of the Leeward Islands be instructed not to sign any such act in the future without a suspending clause. This was so ordered.[28] Thereupon the Jamaica absentees applied for similar relief.[29]

A bill, commonly called the Deficiency Law, passed by the Jamaica Assembly in 1747, was immediately referred to the King in Council by the Governor in view of the new instruction. It provided that absentees should pay half again as much taxes as residents, which, however, they might escape by sending the required number of white servants to their plantations.[30] The Privy Council, after hearing the arguments pro and con, decided that the taxing of the absentees was not only inequitable but unjust.

Thus, the Crown at last took a serious view of this practice of discrimination against the expatriated planters, with the result that Governor Trelawny received instructions not to pass any act for taxing absentees in a greater proportion than residents without a suspending clause.[31] The matter was not allowed to drop there. On November 28, 1748, the Governor, Council, and Assembly memorialized the Crown to alter this instruction to the Governor so as to permit him to assent to some sort of deficiency bill in which the

---

[27] See L. J. Ragatz: "Absentee Landlordism in the British Caribbean, 1750–1833," *Agricultural History*, V, 7–24.

[28] See "Copy of an Order of Council, dated 23rd of July, 1746, forbidding the Governor of the Leeward Islands to pass any Act whereby absentees shall be taxed more than residents in any of the said Islands," *Board of Trade Journal, 1741–1749*, p. 238.

[29] *Board of Trade Journal, 1749–1753*, under date May 5, 1752, pp. 310–13.

[30] *Acts of Assembly* (1756), p. 21.

[31] *Acts of the Privy Council, Col. Ser., 1745–1766*, pp. 39–40.

absentees were rated in greater proportion than residents.[32] Moreover, the Jamaica London agent, John Sharpe, was called upon to
exert himself in this connection, and in the spring of 1750 he appeared before the Board of Trade together with Ferdinand Paris,
the solicitor for the absentees, and there the two exchanged arguments.[33] In 1752 the issue again came before the Board, which
unanimously recommended the continuance of the royal instruction.[34]

At this period — during the governorship of Admiral Sir Charles
Knowles,[35] who received his appointment in the spring of 1752, thus
replacing the popular Trelawny — there came to the front the question of the removal of the capital of the island from Spanish Town
or St. Iago de la Vega, as it was still called, to Kingston, the chief
port of entry, and a bill to that effect was passed and signed by the
Governor in 1755.[36] This issue thereupon divided the island into factions, with the Council strongly favouring the move and the Assembly reversing itself and opposing it. Each side drew up memorials
to the home government; each collected elaborate depositions regarding the relative merit of the two places. The change was en-
thusiastically supported by British shipping interests, which found
it a matter of considerable inconvenience and no little expense to be
obliged upon arrival to carry the ship papers overland to the Governor's office.[37] Not until 1872, however, did Kingston permanently
become the capital of Jamaica.

---

[32] For the address see P.R.O., C.O. 137:25, pp. 101–2.

[33] Board of Trade *Journal*, 1749–1753, p. 51.

[34] *Ibid.*, pp. 310–13; see also *Acts of the Privy Council, Col. Ser.*, 1745–1766, pp. 160–1.

[35] For Knowles's commission, dated March 28, 1752, see C.O. 138:19, pp. 173–93; for his instructions of the same date see C.O. 138:19, pp. 202–92.

[36] See W. J. Gardner: *A History of Jamaica* . . . (London, 1909), pp. 125–9.

[37] For the remonstrance of the Bristol Merchants of September 2, 1754, against having the records of Jamaica kept at Spanish Town rather than at Kingston by reason of the delays and expense involved in resorting to the former in the hill country, see "The Merchants Hall, Book of Charters of the Society of Merchant Venturers of Bristol," for the year 1749, pp. 310–11; see also the Newcastle Papers, B.M., Add. Mss. 33029, folios 182–97. For three years Kingston was the capital, but in 1758 the act pro- viding for the removal was disallowed. See *Acts of the Privy Council, Col. Ser.*, 1745– 1766, pp. 248–55. With the return of the seat of government to Spanish Town, there began the construction of "an immense pile of spacious apartments" to provide suitable accommodations for the House of Assembly, the Supreme Court, and the various offices of the Crown, which took thirty years to complete. See Thomas Southey: *Chronological History of the West Indies* (3 vols., London, 1827), II, 320–1.

The island, in spite of its economic importance, was not densely populated. It was estimated in 1741 that not one third of the total of over 3,750,000 acres was under cultivation, and of this only about 250,000 acres were in cane and 100,000 in cotton. Against this arable region, 650,000 acres were devoted to grazing,[38] an industry not very profitable in Jamaica since the cattle remained lean and did not multiply as did the black cattle on Santo Domingo. It would appear that those who had patents for large bodies of land frequently culti- vated perhaps only one tenth of the land or even left the whole un- cultivated. In a report prepared by the Board of Trade, it was stated that while two thirds of the land paid quit-rents — which was a half- penny an acre — one half was uncultivated.[39] In 1751 Governor Trelawny sought to remedy the situation, which he described as a great evil due to the engrossment of vast tracts by private parties. He recommended imposing a special tax on uncultivated land.[40]

It appears, nevertheless, that large tracts that had once been culti- vated were now in a wild state owing to the fact that some parts of the island which previously had produced hundreds of hogsheads of sugar were now fit only for grazing, by reason, so it was affirmed, of the lack of moisture which the cutting down of the neighbouring woods had brought about. This was particularly true of Liguanea on the south side of the island. The parish of St. Catherine, which had been one of the choicest and richest spots for sugar-production, was, according to Charles Leslie, given over largely to cattle by 1740, and it was stated that for almost nine months in the year it was dry. On the other hand, along the north side of the island the wet and dry seasons were quite regular, and there the cane was planted from August to January, during which period the rain fell in abundance.[41]

The population of Jamaica, although almost a century had passed

---

[38] "State of Jamaica," November 21, 1741, Shelburne Papers, 45:24–37. In 1752 it was estimated that the island contained 3,840,000 acres, of which four tenths were in- accessible mountains and barren lands, leaving 2,133,336 acres of good land, of which some 500,000 acres were occupied and 1,633,336 were available to be placed under culti- vation. See "State of Jamaica," 1752, C.O. 137:25, pp. 243–5. In 1752 the amount of land patented was given as 1,500,000 acres. See T. Southey: op. cit., II, 314. There were 429 sugar plantations in 1739 and after some twenty years the number had in- creased to but 640. See W. J. Gardner: op. cit., p. 156.

[39] C.O. 137:25, pp. 243–5; see also H. A. Wyndham: The Atlantic and Slavery (London, 1935), p. 273.

[40] Trelawny to the Board of Trade, September 16, 1751, C.O. 137:25, p. 215.

[41] [Charles Leslie]: A New History of Jamaica . . . , p. 22.

since the conquest of the island, was still concentrated largely about its rim, especially in the southern portion around Kingston, the trading-centre, and Spanish Town, the capital.[42] This tendency to hold to the region of the coast was doubtless because of the richness of the lowlands, the poor quality of the roads, the precipitous course of the rivers — most of them mere mountain streams — and the presence in the interior of former Spanish slaves. These free Negroes, later known as the Maroons, had reached an agreement with the English by 1750 and were no longer held in great dread.[43]

The comparative weakness of the white population was a matter that caused no little concern to those responsible for the government of the island. "We have been for many years, increasing in wealth & diminishing in strength," complained Governor Trelawny in 1749. He then asserted that "the Negroes who were some years ago above ten to one white men, are continually advancing in their superiority of numbers, & I am sorry to say the white men almost as much decreasing, so that we are at once growing more easy to be made a prey, & a more tempting one every day." [44] The truth of this is apparent in light of the statement furnished the Board of Trade in 1752 to the effect that since 1734 the white inhabitants had increased but 1,500 while the blacks were more numerous than at the

---

[42] In order to encourage the settlement of the interior a series of laws was passed between the years 1733 and 1738 providing for the cutting of roads and the building of barracks some twenty to thirty miles apart; further, lands in the central area, reverting to the Crown for non-cultivation, were offered to newcomers. The measures brought very favourable results in the Parish of St. Mary, "making that place a Flourishing part of the Country which before was only a Receptacle for Wild and Runaway Negroes" (Address of the Board of Trade to the House of Commons, February 22, 1753, Library of Congress accessions, No. 2413).

[43] At the time of the conquest of Jamaica in 1655 slaves who had been held by the Spaniards escaped into the mountainous interior. There they remained and multiplied, particularly during the 1740's while the war with Spain was in progress. The extension of the white influence into the region of the Negro towns is manifested during this period by the passing of an act in the Jamaica Assembly for raising companies in several of these towns for defence against the enemy; the same act also held out encouragement to the Maroons to capture rebellious and runaway slaves. Another act provided for the better order and government of the inhabitants of the several Negro towns and for preventing them from purchasing slaves. See *Acts of Assembly* (1756), for the year 1741, p. 17, and for the year 1744, p. 19; see also the Board of Trade Journal, 1749–1753, p. 189. For the treaty of 1738 with the Maroons see W. J. Gardner: *A History of Jamaica*, p. 119. For details of their activities see R. C. Dallas: *History of the Maroons . . .* (2 vols., London, 1803).

[44] Governor Trelawny to Board of Trade, June 8, 1749, C.O. 137:25, pp. 89–92.

earlier date by 35,000.[45] Under these circumstances there was danger not only of foreign invasion but of slave insurrection. In order to guard against these possible events, laws had been passed obliging owners of plantations to maintain one white man or woman for every 30 slaves, old and young, and also one for every 150 horses, mares, mules, asses, and neat cattle, under penalty of a heavy quarterly payment for each deficiency, which amounted to £30.5.[46]

To encourage the immigration of white people into the island, land grants had been made in 1736 upon a headright system of 50 acres to a single man, 50 in addition for a wife, 20 for each child, 15 for each servant, and 10 for each slave, with a maximum of 300 acres.[47] Moreover, the passage of the newcomer with that of his family and up to 20 slaves had been paid, together with subsistence for a year — to be settled for at the end of seven years — with tax exemptions for five years.[48] As a result of these inducements about 100 settlers, after the pacification of the Maroons in 1739, had come from the Windward Islands and had taken up 30,000 acres. Nevertheless, it was a matter of general agreement that the island had little to offer the poorer sort of people unless, as Governor Trelawny stated in his report of the year 1741, they could be colonized in some particular place and maintained by the government for a longer period than those coming in with slaves. This was not done. Poor whites, eager to emigrate, were attracted rather to the continental colonies. However, in 1749, to induce artisans and their families to come to Jamaica, an act of the Assembly supplementing the earlier law provided that the passage of each family would be paid, that they would receive not only twenty acres of land, four of which would await them already planted with the provisions of the island, but also a house worth £50, a Negro slave worth £35, plus £20 in money.[49] Because of these new inducements, a movement of whites to Jamaica was again proceeding, although slowly.[50] By 1753 it was

[45] "State of Jamaica," 1752, C.O. 137:25, pp. 243–5.

[46] "Address of the Governor, Council and Assembly of Jamaica to His Majesty," November 28, 1749, P.R.O., C.O. 137:25, pp. 101–2; see also H. A. Wyndham (op. cit., pp. 270–1) for the acts of 1681 and 1730 relative to the above requirement, which provided a quarterly payment of but £6.10 for each deficiency.

[47] For the law of 1736 vesting in the Crown 30,000 acres for the use of newcomers, see C.O. 137:25, pp. 243–5.

[48] Ibid.

[49] Acts of Assembly (1756), pp. 296–300.

[50] See the act for total remission of debts due to the public from divers new settlers, affirmed by the King in Council in 1751, C.O. 137:25, pp. 180–2.

asserted that in St. James's Parish there were thirty-six sugar works as against but six in 1740 and that the population had mounted to upwards of 2,000 white people, the greater part of whom were small planters of pimento, coffee, cotton, and ginger.[51]

With all of its enticing features, Jamaica, however, was not a place that encouraged the home-seeker. The yellow fever not infrequently visited the land; other fevers were always present. Further, many of its principal landowners, people of wealth and culture, were, as has been made clear, absentees. Social conditions were generally unfavourable to the progress of education, morality, and religion. The planter group, frankly despotic and really constituting an oligarchy, bore the reputation of manifesting a disposition of great haughtiness, not only toward those who were white servants but also those who had previously been indentured. Consistent with this, the planters required of their dependents utter submission to their will.[52] This attitude was doubtless encouraged by reason of the fact that there were few "middling Freeholders" on the island — most of the white men being either gentlemen or indentured servants.[53]

The luxurious way in which the aristocratic Jamaica planters lived was in striking contrast, as a rule, to that of their dependents.[54] On the one hand, on Sundays and court days the masters dressed in silk coats and silver-lined vests and their ladies in fashionable imported gowns; thus attired, they rode about in their smart equipages or sipped their Madeira wine on the piazzas of the one-storey but spacious plantation homes.[55] On the other hand, the field slaves, at least so it is asserted, customarily went stark naked, in many cases

---

[51] Governor Knowles to the Board of Trade, March 26, 1753, C.O. 137:25, pp. 312–14.

[52] D. Fenning and J. Collyer: A New System of Geography (2 vols., London, 1765), II, 686. As for the moral conditions, it was said of the clergy that they were "of a character so vile, that I do not care to mention it; for except a few, they are generally the most finished of all debauchees" (Charles Leslie: op. cit., p. 303). In 1754 there happily appeared the Moravian missionaries, bringing a spirit of great consecration. See W. J. Gardner: op. cit., pp. 199–202.

[53] Governor Trelawny to the Board of Trade, March 25, 1752, C.O. 137:25, pp. 235–8; see also H. A. Wyndham: op. cit., p. 273.

[54] L. J. Ragatz: The Fall of the Planter Class in the British Caribbean, 1763–1833 (New York, 1928), Chap. 1.

[55] See Charles Leslie: op. cit., p. 30, for a description of the planters' homes. The type of house-construction was dictated by the danger of hurricanes. For the destruction of the town of Savanna-la-Mar in the eighteenth century by a hurricane see William Beckford: A Descriptive Account of the Island of Jamaica (2 vols., London, 1790), I, 89–109.

even the women — "for they do not know what shame is" — and lived in miserable huts under the watchful eyes of a white overseer. These wretched people did the work which supported the prosperity of the island. The poorer whites might raise ginger, cocoa, pimento, and other things of less value, such as indigo, which had been rather extensively cultivated but was now neglected by reason of the superior quality of the French West India product. Yet the opportunities of acquiring wealth in these particular fields of activity on Jamaica seemed remote at that period to those white people thus engaged.

The wealth of Jamaica came chiefly from the labour of blacks utilized in the production of sugar.[56] The methods of sugar-production employed in the British West Indies in the eighteenth century followed in the main those evolved in the seventeenth. The soil in which the cane was planted varied from the ashy loam of St. Christopher and the black earth of Barbados and Antigua to the great variety to be found in Jamaica, among which was a mixture of clay and sand known as brick-mold. The land was in the first instance cleared of trees and other vegetation by the laborious work of slaves, who then were organized into gangs for the purpose of holing. This fatiguing operation, carried out almost exclusively by means of a heavy hoe at that date, resulted in the dotting of the field with holes some six inches in depth and about a yard in diameter at the top. Fifty good field hands working ten hours a day could hole a twenty-acre tract in something less than half a month — each man digging somewhat over a hundred holes a day.[57] Next — preferably between August and November, or in January [58] — two or more cane tops were laid into each hole and thereupon lightly covered with earth. After the sprouting, which customarily took place in about two weeks, additional soil was placed in the holes; the ground was also cleared of weeds and in the course of time was levelled throughout

---

[56] It is of interest to note the opposition of Governor Trelawny to the introduction of slavery into the English settlements in the logwood areas of the Gulf of Honduras, which he thought would weaken them rather than form an addition to British power. See Trelawny to the Board of Trade, April 14, 1750, C.O. 137:25, pp. 128–9.

[57] Bryan Edwards: op. cit., II, 215–16; W. J. Gardner: op. cit., pp. 176–7; and William Beckford: op. cit., I, 47–50.

[58] Beckford points out that the season in the northern part of Jamaica was as opposite to that in the southern part of the island "as are their points on the compass" (ibid., II, 286). He also greatly stresses the importance of the use of manure for fertilizing the cane.

the field. Then came the systematic cultivation of the cane until in the second year it was ready for the mill.[59]

The time of the year — early in the spring in southern Jamaica, as a rule — when the great sugar mill was set in motion, propelled by water, wind, or cattle, was the "season of gladness and festivity" on the plantation. "So palatable, salutary, and nourishing is the juice of the cane, that every individual of the animal creation, drinking freely of it, derives health and vigour of its use." [60] The loads of cane were carried to the mill on the backs of mules or were carted there. After the pressing, the juice flowed into a container called a "receiver" and from there was conveyed to the boiling-house, where it was clarified by heating and the application of white lime, and then drained off to be placed in an evaporator boiler; after being successively transferred to as many as six other boilers, in each of which it was continually stirred and boiled and the impurities were removed, it was placed in a shallow receptacle known as a "cooler," where it granulated; thereupon the mass was deposited in conical pots or other large containers from which the molasses drained off. The unrefined sugar thus obtained was then packed in hogsheads. This sugar was called muscovado. From the pressing of the cane to the completion of the process just described, the time required was from one month to three months.[61]

The fully equipped plantation in Jamaica in the latter part of the eighteenth century capable of producing 200 hogsheads of sugar by averaging the yield year in and out was, according to Bryan Edwards, one containing 900 acres of land, 300 acres of which would be suited to sugar-cane, with 600 additional acres reserved for timber, grazing, and the growing of food supplies. Upon this was to be found the planter's home, one for the overseer, a sugar mill, a

---

[59] The sugar-planter faced many hazards. His entire crop might be destroyed by a hurricane or during a period of prolonged drought. The canes might become infected with yellow or black blast. Likewise, when the cane approached ripeness, the innumerable rats on the island might begin their devastations, which, according to Beckford, amounted frequently to the loss of five hogsheads of sugar out of every hundred. Finally, there took place periodic infestations of caterpillars, which might eat down a whole field of young canes by attacking the tender leaves. See *ibid.*, I, 52–61. It should also be pointed out that the land in some parishes was much poorer than in others. In St. Elizabeth Parish little cane was grown in the eighteenth century, but it excelled in pasturage; on the other hand, Hanover Parish in the northwestern part of the island was credited with the greatest production of sugar. *Ibid.*, II, 242 and 251.

[60] Bryan Edwards: *op. cit.*, II, 226.

[61] William Beckford: *op. cit.*, II, 70–2.

boiling-house, a curing-house, a distillery, a hospital, mule and cattle stables, trash houses, shops, sheds, and the scattered huts of the slaves. For such a plantation 250 slaves were counted an adequate number, together with 80 oxen and 60 mules.[62] However, in Barbados the typical plantation was much smaller, averaging not more than 80 acres, which meant that on that island a large proportion of the planters were dependent upon the mills and distilleries of their neighbours. This situation was even more characteristic of the Leeward Islands, where the plantations, as a rule, were somewhat smaller than on Barbados.

The personnel requirements of a typical Jamaica plantation may be illustrated by an examination of the Houghton James estate. Five white men were employed: an overseer who received £140 per year, a distiller at £60, a bookkeeper at £40, a carpenter at £100, and a mason at £70. There were 249 slaves — 106 men, 78 women, and 65 children. The Negroes were divided according to the work assigned. Three of them were "drivers," who kept the rest at work; 3 were head boilers; 5 were carpenters; 3 were coopers, who set up the hogsheads and containers for molasses and rum and then headed them; 2 were in charge of the pens for livestock; 2 were fishermen, who seined for fish in the streams and inlets of the sea; 2 were doctors, who watched over the health of the other slaves; 9 were watchmen over their fellows and over the approaches to the plantation; 86, always the strongest Negroes, constituted the holing-gang; 42 were weeders; 18, the grass gang, collected the fodder for the livestock; 4 were cattle boys; 2 were sheep boys; and one, a woman, was a nurse. Of the 65 children, 37 were too young to work; among the mature Negroes 10 were described as "old and useless." Of livestock on this estate there were 18 horses, 66 mules, 80 steers or oxen, and 36 other kinds of cattle.[63]

In the opinion of the eighteenth-century Jamaicans, sugar-culture was necessarily predicated upon slavery. The writer William Beck-

---

[62] Bryan Edwards: op. cit., II, 250–5. Beckford, however, declared that on a plantation with 200 slaves and the same number of cattle not more than 70 acres should be devoted to the sugar-cane, which would produce about 150 hogsheads of sugar and 80 or 90 puncheons of rum. The cost of supplies from England for such a plantation, he calculated, would be about £200 and those from Ireland about £100; in addition, 60 barrels of cured fish would be required. William Beckford: op. cit., II, 206–7.

[63] "Abstracts of Houghton James Estate in Jamaica . . . May, 1773, Papers relating to Jamaica, 1693–1773," Library of Congress.

ford, who left Jamaica in 1777 after living there for many years, gave expression to this view in the following words:

> "To continue the cultivation of the West-India islands as they now stand, and to keep up their present extent of produce, will be impossible without an importation [of Negroes] — without an importation those slaves thereon will gradually diminish, the crops of course decline, and the population, as the produce, will necessarily be, in the course of no inconsiderable number of years, extinct and at an end." [64]

The total value of the sugar plantations in the British West Indies was estimated at £70,000,000, which provided a yearly revenue to Great Britain through import duties of at least £3,000,000.[65] The number of these estates in Jamaica alone in the 1770's was 1,061.[66] This wealth rested squarely upon the maintenance of the institution of slavery.

The lot of the obedient Negro under a kindly master was doubtless as fortunte as that of most of the white serfs in eastern Europe and Russia during the same period of history. He never faced starvation except in times of calamity. His little habitation with the garden plot about it was considered to be his own and became an inheritance of the family, with the eldest son falling heir to it under a rigid system of primogeniture. There were periods during the routine of plantation work when he could give much attention to his little property. Under the terms of a law passed by the Assembly in 1696 (8 Wm. III. c.2) [67] he was to be taught the way of a Christian and made fit for baptism. Sundays, as well as certain other holy days, were free days. He was privileged to carry his surplus maize, yams, chickens, and other garden produce to the nearest market, where he bartered for salt beef, fish, or pork in order to make his favourite dish, pepperpot. Again, many, if not most, masters and overseers sought to regulate in a sensible way his hours of labour and the type appropriate to his strength and maturity. When ill, he was as a rule given the best of care. Further, he might, if intelligent, look forward to a place in the plantation economy that would give him a measure of responsibility in the supervision of his fellow Negroes. He therefore might become, as it were, a right hand of his master or of the overseer.

---

[64] William Beckford; op. cit., II, 314.
[65] Ibid., II, 315.
[66] Ibid., II, 310.
[67] Acts of Assembly (1756), p. 63.

Nevertheless, the sugar plantation was regarded primarily as an economic unit that must yield at least a living to the owner, if not a handsome profit. With that end in mind the purchase of an African slave was not a missionary enterprise. Moreover, only too frequently the overseer — especially on a plantation owned by an absentee and casually supervised by his agent, an attorney living perhaps in Spanish Town or Kingston — might be a person forced to leave England for his misdeeds. Under such circumstances, according to a contemporary, "it cannot be wondered at . . . when raised to power [he] should prove a savage and inhuman tyrant." [68] Indeed, the first serious slave insurrection that took place in Jamaica, according to Governor Trelawny, had its beginnings on the estate of an absentee whose overseer treated the slaves with great cruelty. The revolt had thereupon spread to other plantations. [69] In addressing the Council and Assembly in 1749 the Governor declared that the influence on a plantation of the master's mere presence was greater than that of twenty or thirty white servants without him. [70]

The dread of a slave insurrection, owing to the overwhelming numerical superiority — over ten to one — of the blacks over the whites, [71] taken together with the presence of the Maroons in the mountainous northeastern part of the island and the fact that thousands of the plantation Negroes were new arrivals from the African jungles, made the lot of the average Jamaican slave not an easy one, to put it mildly. The black code, as provided by the Assembly, and its manner of application represented slave-control of the worst sort. [72]

The principal laws on the statute book regulating slavery in Jamaica in the middle of the eighteenth century were chiefly based

[68] [Charles Leslie]: A New History of Jamaica . . . stresses this point.

[69] See the address of the Governor, Council, and Assembly of Jamaica, November 28, 1749, P.R.O., C.O. 137:25, pp. 101–2.

[70] For Trelawny's address see C.O. 137:25, pp. 105–8.

[71] The Jamaica Assembly framed an address to the Crown setting forth their apprehensions concerning this disproportion of blacks to whites. See the Board of Trade Journal, 1749–1753, pp. 310–13.

In May 1760 a slave insurrection took place in St. Mary's Parish. It began on the plantation of a Captain Forrest and swiftly spread to other plantations. Before the Negroes were subdued they had killed 60 white people; between 300 and 400 slaves lost their lives. Soon afterward 600 of them were transported to Honduras. See [Edward Long]: History of Jamaica . . . (3 vols., London, 1774), II, 458, 462. In 1761 the number of Negroes was estimated to be 146,000 and at the end of the century, according to Bryan Edwards (op. cit., II, 2), it was 250,000.

[72] See R. W. Smith: "Legal Status of Jamaican Slaves," Journal of Negro History, XXX, 293–303.

upon a comprehensive act passed in the year 1696 which provided penalties for the striking of a white by a Negro, for the receipt of stolen goods by the latter, for giving poison to a person, black or white, and for compassing or imagining the death of a white person. The last-named crimes brought death; the other two offences were to be punished by two justices and three freeholders according to the circumstances of the case.[73] Another act, that of 1717, forbad the gathering of slaves by the beating of drums and blowing of horns, although they could meet together for "any innocent amusement." [74] These acts were supplemented by further legislation in 1749, when it was provided that a slave over eighteen years of age who had resided on the island for three years and who should thereafter run away and absent himself for six months might upon conviction suffer death; further, the same penalty could be visited on any slave harbouring a runaway; in short, the penalties against runaway slaves were increased in most respects.[75] Still in force in 1750, the black code of 1696 provided that no one who should kill a slave caught either in the act of stealing or running away or when found in the night out of his owner's estate or on the road should be liable to action or damage, provided it could be shown that the slave had refused to submit.[76]

Nevertheless, the slave had some protection from the cruelty of his master. Under the early code a person convicted of wantonly killing a Negro should for the first offence be guilty of felony with benefit of clergy, and for the second be deemed a murderer and suffer as such. A law passed in 1751 to clarify the earlier act provided that imprisonment up to twelve months could be inflicted by the court for the first offence, and for the second, death without corruption of blood and forfeiture of property.[77]

In putting this code into force it appears that a black who sought to rebel or who twice struck his master might be consigned to the

---

[73] "An Act for the better Order and Government of Slaves," 8 Wm. III, c. 2 (1698), Acts of Assembly (1756), pp. 57–65.

[74] "An Act for the more effectual punishing of Crimes committed by Slaves," 4 Geo. I, c. 4 (1717), ibid., pp. 113–16.

[75] Ibid., pp. 306–7.

[76] Ibid., p. 62; see also "An Abstract of the Jamaica Code Noir, or Laws Affecting Negroes and other Slaves in that Island," included in Edward Long's History of Jamaica, II, 485–92; see further W. J. Gardner: op. cit., pp. 177–9.

[77] Acts of Assembly (1756), pp 337–8. (There are many printed editions of the laws of Jamaica for this period, entitled respectively "Laws of Jamaica" and "Acts of Assembly. . . .")

flames and in a manner designed to prolong his tortures; or he might be starved to death in the presence of food. Hanging, however, was the penalty most frequently inflicted on Negroes condemned to suffer capital punishment. For example, in January 1749 a Negro named Hector was tried at the Kingston court house before two justices and three householders for the crime of stabbing his master; for this he was sentenced to lose his left hand and then be hanged, which sentence was immediately carried out; and in the same month a black named Ben, of Old Harbour, was hanged for stealing.[78]

One may assert that the conditions of life generally imposed upon the slaves had the effect of preventing any natural increase in their number, in spite of encouragement given them to propagate. Therefore, to keep up the supply of labour on the plantations, it was necessary to import thousands of blacks from Africa each year. During the eighteenth century an average of at least 4,000 were sold annually by slavers at Kingston, the chief port of the island.[79] In 1752 Governor Trelawny reported that from 1702 to 1752 the total number of Negroes imported was 307,744; in 1739 the number imported was 3,008 and in 1748 it reached 10,483, of which number 2,426 were sold abroad to the Spaniards. The total imported during the decade before 1750 amounted to 69,140, of which number 14,677 were reexported. Thus, between 1702 and 1752, the average importation was something over 6,000 a year.[80]

In sharp contrast to the cruelty of the slave code were the liberal provisions made by the Assembly from time to time for those of Negro blood who were, it was believed, entitled to special consideration and were the objects of peculiar regard on the part of some planters. Solicitude for these individuals appears in repeated private acts of the Assembly.

The first of the private acts to give special privileges to Negroes by name came in 1707/8, when two distinct acts provided that no evidence given by slaves against Manuel Bartholomew and John Williams — each classified as a "free Negroe" — would be received. In 1716 this special protection was now extended to the wife and

---

[78] Jamaica advices in the *Maryland Gazette*, April 5, 1749.

[79] See Newcastle Papers, B.M., Add. Mss. 33029, folios 182–97, for the importance of Kingston as a slave mart.

[80] "An Account of Negroes Imported and Exported, July 1739 to July 1749," C.O. 137:25, p. 87; see also T. Southey (*op. cit.*, II, 314) for the number of Negroes imported in 1752 and 1754.

sons of Williams. The first private act to give a Negro "the Rights and Privileges of Englishmen, born of white ancestors" was passed in 1733 in favour of John Golding, Sr., a planter, and his family. This set the pattern of many such acts. For example, in 1739 William Cunningham the Younger, reputed son of William Cunningham of Westmorland Parish by a free Negro woman, was given this status. In the same year Jane Stone, a free mulatto woman, her children, and others related to them by blood or marriage, some sixteen in all, were accorded the same standing. In 1747 six such private acts were passed.[81] In 1746 a special act was passed in favour of Anne Johnson, reputed daughter of the late John Johnson, planter, and her son Thomas of St. Catherine's Parish, which came before the Board of Trade the following year; [82] in 1748 the Board had up for consideration three acts entitling at least nine people of Negro blood, children of Jane Augier and Elizabeth Rogers, to these privileges; [83] and in 1750 an act similarly provided for Richard Furnell, the reputed son of Peter Furnell, a Kingston merchant, by "a free Negro woman." [84]

The standing of some of the Jamaica mulattoes was apparently high, as a result, doubtless, of their own qualities as well as the prestige of their putative fathers. Take the case of the mulatto Dr. Robert Halhead, who was a surgeon and whose sister, Elizabeth, was the wife of Thomas Pierce of London, Gentleman. When the question of legitimatizing Halhead came before the Jamaica Assembly in 1752 it was voted that he should be granted *all* privileges enjoyed by a native-born Englishman, which led the legal adviser of the Board of Trade, when the special act providing for this came before him, to declare: "I have not known any act of that kind passed

---

[81] See *Acts of Assembly* (1756), pp. 5, 7, 13, 15, 16, 17, 19, 20, 22, and 26. According to Mathew Lamb, legal adviser of the Board of Trade, the mulatto thus legitimatized acquired all rights of a natural-born Englishman except those of sitting and voting in the Jamaica Council or Assembly or holding the office of magistrate. See P.R.O., C.O. 137:25, p. 362. Actually his rights were more circumscribed. A law passed in 1732 that was on the statute books in 1750 declared that no person who was not three degrees removed in a lineal descent from a Negro ancestor was allowed to vote in elections. *Acts of Assembly* (1756), p. 181.

[82] Board of Trade *Journal*, 1741–1749, p. 257.

[83] *Ibid.*, p. 360.

[84] Board of Trade *Journal*, 1749–1753, p. 140. With reference to the condition of sexual promiscuity prevailing in Jamaica in the eighteenth century see R. B. Cunninghame Graham: *Doughty Deeds: An Account of the Life of Robert Graham . . . 1735–1797* (New York, 1925), Chap. 7; see also Edward Long: *op. cit.*, II, 350, *passim*.

before."[85] By this process, it goes without saying, racial amalgamation was given legal sanction on the island of Jamaica; also the manumission of slaves, the offspring of these unions with whites, proceeded. By 1790 it was estimated that there were 10,000 free Negroes and those with Negro blood living on the island, an average of 500 to every parish.[86] Moreover, some of these people of colour became heirs of sugar estates and estates devoted to cattle-raising and thereby became the masters of slaves.[87] Doubtless to prevent the rise of an aristocracy of color, the Assembly in 1761 passed a law making void any bequest of over £2,000 in value to a Negro or mulatto not born in wedlock, and any purchase such a person should make exceeding this amount.[88]

Before closing this chapter it is necessary to turn our attention to what may be called a political dependency of the government of Jamaica, although located in Central America and long considered to be a part of the great Spanish New World Empire: the swampy logwood area about Honduras Bay and the fertile region to the south of it, known as the Mosquito Coast or Shore, where soil conditions were considered favourable for the establishment of plantations for the production of indigo, cocoa, and vanilla.

As early as 1638 English ships had resorted to the coasts of Yucatan in search of the logwood that carries the botanical name of *haematoxylon campechianum* and that produced a dye highly esteemed for centuries by the makers of woollen and silk goods. At first the English simply plundered the native logwood-cutters. Later they went to the region to harvest this valuable dyewood by their own labour, for the Spaniards, with so much good land to exploit in the

---

[85] C.O. 137:25, pp. 362–4. For a discussion of the above point see W. J. Gardner: *op. cit.*, pp. 171–2; Bryan Edwards: *op. cit.*, I, Chap. 1; and H. A. Wyndham: *op. cit.*, pp. 279–81.

[86] William Beckford: *op. cit.*, II, 324. In 1774 an act was passed (15 Geo. III, c. 18) placing restrictions on manumission. There was no such number of free Negroes in any North American British colony. Virginia probably had the largest number of free Negroes in the eighteenth century. In 1782 the number was put at 2,800. See St. George Tucker: "A Dissertation on Slavery in Virginia" in his *Blackstone's Commentaries* (5 vols., Philadelphia, 1803), I, Appendix, p. 66; see also J. H. Russell: *The Free Negro in Virginia, 1619–1865* (Johns Hopkins University Studies, Baltimore, 1913), pp. 10–11.

[87] W. J. Gardner: *op. cit.*, p. 172. In 1751 the Board of Trade recommended for confirmation an Act of the Jamaica Assembly preventing Maroon Negroes from purchasing slaves. See Board of Trade *Journal*, 1749–1753, p. 189.

[88] See 15 Geo. III, c. 8 (1761); see also Edward Long: *op. cit.*, II, 823.

"The Island of Jamaica, Divided into its
Principal Parishes, With the Roads, etc."

(From the *Atlas Minor* by Herman Moll, 1736)

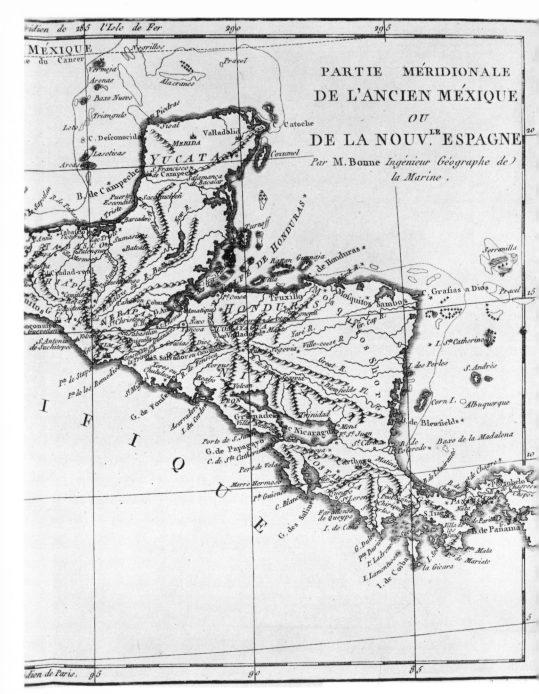

"Partie Méridionale de l'Ancien Mex-
ique . . ." by M. Bonne, showing the
logwood areas of the Gulf of Honduras
and the Mosquito Shore.

(From *Atlas de Toutes les Parties Connues . . .*, 1736)

western hemisphere, were not drawn to the region, most of which was deeply inundated during the rainy season. As a result, settlements of English, Indian, and Mestizo logwood-cutters were in time established. There they laboured strenuously at the harvest, and — after the harvested wood had been sent down the rivers at flood-water time on barges and had been placed on ocean-going vessels — they engaged just as strenuously in wild dissipation during the slack season of the year. By 1715 the number of British subjects living about Honduras Bay and along the Mosquito Coast, especially on Black River in what is now Nicaragua, was estimated to be about 1,500.[89] They and those who followed them seem to have been drawn largely from the northern English colonies and were, as a rule, restless men unsuited to live in an orderly settled society. Nevertheless, by the middle of the century they were cutting logwood to the value of £160,000 sterling, which was carried away to England principally by New England, New York, and Pennsylvania ships.[90]

It would not have been expected that the successive Kings of Spain would willingly recognize the right of these subjects of a rival monarch, regarded as intruders, to exploit lands that the Spanish claimed as their own. But other New World areas with overlapping claims were at stake between England and Spain, as in the case of English Carolina and Spanish Florida. Therefore in 1670 an Anglo-Spanish treaty was signed at Madrid, the seventh article of which reads as follows: "The King of Great Britain shall hold and enjoy all the lands, countries, etc. he is now possessed of in America." [91] Again, in 1713, as a part of the general peace settlement at Utrecht, the two powers entered into a solemn compact to "renew and confirm all treaties of peace . . . concluded between the crowns of Great Britain and Spain . . . ," [92] which had the effect of reaffirming the treaty of 1670. The British, on the one hand, took it to mean the recognition of their right of possession to those portions of Central America where they were in physical control before 1670; this position was

---

[89] Board of Trade Journal, 1708–1715, p. 588.

[90] Archives of British Honduras (ed. J. A. Burdon, 3 vols., London, 1931–35), I, 77. For a scholarly account of the early contacts of English buccaneers with Honduras and the gradual creation of settlements in the logwood regions and on the Mosquito Coast to 1750 see S. L. Caiger: British Honduras, Past and Present (London, 1951), pp. 1–73.

[91] Charles Jenkinson: A Collection of all Treaties . . . between Great Britain and Other Powers . . . 1648 to . . . 1783 (3 vols., London, 1785), I, 197.

[92] Ibid., II, 75, for Article 15 of the Treaty signed July 18, 1713.

supported by the Board of Trade in 1717 in a representation to the Privy Council under King George I.[93] The Spaniards, on the other hand, took the position that all that the logwood-cutters could claim was an "indulgence" to frequent the coast of Central America over all the lands whereof their King was sovereign. In fact, they succeeded in exerting such pressure upon the English established about the Bay of Campeche, lying north of the Yucatan Peninsula and the Gulf of Honduras, that by 1735 the English had quite withdrawn from it.[94] But they clung tenaciously to the coast of Honduras and the Mosquito Coast, the Indians of which were as friendly to them as they were hostile to the Spaniards.[95] Further, to prevent harrassment of the logwood-cutters by the Spanish *guarda costas*, they built a fort on the island of Roatan (called Rattan at that period by the English) located in the midst of the Gulf of Honduras. But their tenuous legal hold on the area is indicated by the fact that when the Treaty of Aix-la-Chapelle was signed in 1748, providing for a mutual restoration of conquered territory between Great Britain, France, and Spain, this fort was evacuated. The settlers, nevertheless, remained along the Honduras and the Mosquito coasts.[96] They continued to live there, in fact, without any settled form of government, although it is true that in 1740 Governor Edward Trelawny of Jamaica, who was expected under the terms of his instructions to exercise some sort of supervision of these British settlements, had sent a certain Captain Robert Hodgson to the Mosquito Coast to maintain friendly relations among the whites, Indians, and Zambos (those of mixed Indian and Negro blood).[97] Hodgson's powers on the Coast were given added recognition by the British government when in

---

[93] See the Board of Trade representation of September 25, 1717, P.R.O., C.O. 137:46.

[94] Board of Trade *Journal, 1734–1741,* pp. 57, 59.

[95] An attempt to Christianize the Indians of the Mosquito Coast was made by the Society for the Propagation of the Gospel in Foreign Parts after their ruler, with the Christian name Edward, had appealed to the English for ministers and teachers in 1739. It is of interest that the only missionary sent to them who accomplished anything in their behalf was the Moravian German-speaking Christian Frederick Post, who for years had laboured among the Delaware Indians in Pennsylvania and who was supported on the Coast by the Society for many years after 1765. See F. J. Klingberg: "The Efforts of the S.P.G. to Christianize the Mosquito Indians, 1742–1785," *Historical Magazine of the Protestant Episcopal Church,* IX, 305–21.

[96] Governor Trelawny of Jamaica to the Board of Trade, October 7, 1748, P.R.O., C.O. 137:25, p. 39.

[97] Richard Pares: *War and Trade in the West Indies, 1739–1763* (Oxford, 1936), pp. 98–9.

1749, in answer to Trelawny's appeal, the Duke of Bedford, at the time Secretary of State for the Southern Department, provided the Captain with a commission "to regulate and superintend the settlement upon the Mosquito Shore, which has been subsisting several years, under the protection of Our Friends and Allies the Mosquito Indians." [98] At the same time he was made dependent upon the government of Jamaica by being placed under the general direction of the Governor, from whom he was to receive his salary of £500 a year.[99] Hodgson, it may be added, had at his disposal a small body of troops. His authority, at least in all civil matters both on the Coast and along the Gulf of Honduras, was quite shadowy, if it existed at all. For all practical purposes the colonists lived by a set of customs that were adapted to their peculiar mode of life and that evolved during the period from the first English settlement in 1662. Only upon the visit of Admiral Sir William Burnaby to the Bay in 1765 were these customs given recognition by the Crown and, after being codified, were thereupon known as "Burnaby's Laws." [100] It may be added that whatever government they enjoyed in the middle of the eighteenth century centred around an informal public gathering of the free inhabitants at which decisions were made and at which some five (later changed to seven) magistrates were chosen to act without pay, with one of them selected to superintend the others.

Doubtless the most important thing about the Gulf of Honduras logwood settlements was the fact that these by their continued existence ultimately gave to the British a valid claim to the area in the eyes of international law — not by right of conquest, but by that of occupancy of the land. In 1763, in the Treaty of Paris, while Great Britain seemed to recognize that that area was still "of the territory of Spain" and agreed to demolish all fortifications erected within it, Spain at the same time recognized the right of British subjects to continue to abide unmolested in their settlements and to engage in their customary activities.[101] While all British claims to the Mosquito

---

[98] Bedford to Hodgson, October 5, 1749, Shelburne Papers, 74:153–6, Clements Library.
[99] Bedford to Trelawny, October 5, 1749, *ibid.*, 74:159–60.
[100] For Burnaby's Laws see *Archives of British Honduras*, I, 100–6; see also the *Annual Register*, 1765, pp. 99–101; *Acts of the Privy Council, Col. Ser., Unbound Papers*, p. 401; and A. B. Keith: *Constitutional History of the First British Empire* (Oxford, 1930), p. 173.
[101] For Article 17 of the Treaty of Paris of 1763 see Charles Jenkinson: *op. cit.*, III,

Coast were given up in 1786 by the Convention of London, this was not the case with the Gulf of Honduras.[102] Ultimately the region lying along the northern shore of the Gulf, where the town of Belize is located, became the recognized dependency of British Honduras through the process of undisturbed occupancy. A Crown colony in 1871, it was still tied to Jamaica, and not until 1884 was it made quite independent of that island.

But, to return to events in the logwood area in the middle of the eighteenth century, the British hold there, as suggested, was most precarious. In 1751 four Spanish ships appeared in Honduras Bay, where thirty-three vessels, most of them from the northern colonies, were at anchor, engaged in loading logwood. Two of these vessels were captured, one of them from Rhode Island, despite the fact that "brave Captains Belchier, Littlejohn and Griffin manned their ships out of the fleet and defended it until January 9," when the Spanish vessels, having news of the appearance of a twenty-gun British ship, departed.[103] But greater trouble was to follow. The Marquis de la Enseñada, Spanish Minister of State for the Marine and the Indies, had sent out orders to uproot the British settlements.[104] In May 1754 a force from Guatemala, having cut a path through the forest, suddenly descended upon one of the logwood settlements, captured some eighty slaves, looted the homes, destroyed what logwood it could, and then departed. Later in the same year warning was sent to the cutters at Belize that a fleet was sailing from Havana to complete the work of destruction. At this, some five hundred of the cutters fled to Black River on the Mosquito Coast. Nothing happened, and, thinking that they had been misled, they returned in open boats to the Bay. To their astonishment, they found there thirty Spanish warships. While busy resisting the Spaniards they beheld a still larger Spanish fleet about to enter the Bay. Those who could escape again retreated to Black River with the conviction that "they

186–7; for the French official version see European Treaties bearing on the History of the United States and its Dependencies (eds. F. G. Davenport and C. O. Paullin, 4 vols., Washington, D.C., 1917–37), IV, 95, and G. F. Martens: Recueil de Traités . . . (7 vols., Göttingue, 1801–17), I, 114–15.

[102] For a discussion of the British-Spanish Convention of London see S. L. Caiger: op. cit., pp. 91–6.

[103] For an account of this episode see The Scots Magazine, May 1752.

[104] Captain Hodgson to the Earl of Halifax, February 22, 1752, P.R.O., C.O. 137:48.

had lost the Bay for Good." [105] However, after burning the huts at Belize and some of the logwood, the intruders retired from this forbidding region and the path was once more open for the return of the cutters. The issue of their presence there became one of the high points in Anglo-Spanish relations of this period with a resort to diplomacy rather than to force.[106]

[105] Letter from Bristol, B.M., Add. Mss. 33029, folios 152–5.

[106] See the article by the author: "British Diplomacy in the Light of Anglo-Spanish New World Issues, 1750–1757," *American Historical Review*, LI, 627–48; see also S. L. Caiger: *op. cit.*, pp. 74–6, and *Archives of British Honduras*, I, 80–4.

CHAPTER VIII

Islands of Cane.
Islands of Contentment.
Home of the Old Buccaneers

BEFORE Jamaica became part of the British Empire in the seventeenth century, the English had succeeded in colonizing a number of other islands in the Caribbean Sea and had also acquired the Bermudas and subsequently the Bahamas in the South Atlantic. While the economic importance of the British West Indies was out of all proportion to their size, the same cannot be said for the South Atlantic islands in the middle of the eighteenth century. Nevertheless, as British possessions colonized by subjects of the British King, they could demand the protection of the mother country in time of war. Furthermore, in an age of sailing-ships they were deemed to have considerable strategic significance. All these colonies had certain common features as small islands or geographical groups of islands, yet each in its civilization was set apart by other characteristics that made it distinctive.

ISLANDS OF CANE

Barbados and the Leeward Islands had in common the fact that they were all producing one staple — sugar — and that the output of this article was declining in all. Moreover, they alone of all the British plantations were subject to the 4½-per-cent duty on the exportation of all dead commodities that seemed to them so inequitable, and, further, they experienced the serious effects of absenteeism, as was true of Jamaica.

Far to the eastward of Jamaica and seventy-eight miles beyond its nearest neighbour, St. Vincent, lies the little island of Barbados, the most eastern of the Caribbean group. Of all the British possessions, none had been more profitable and more extensively exploited for over a century before 1750.[1] Although it is but twenty-one miles in length and hardly more than fourteen in breadth, with scarcely over 100,000 acres of land mostly given over to sugar-cane, it contained by the official report sent early in 1748 some 15,250 people descended from English, Scottish, and Irish ancestry, with a sprinkling of Dutch, French, Portuguese, and Jews,[2] and at least 47,000 blacks. The total number of these settlers made it one of the most densely populated portions of the British Empire. Even so, the numbers here given represent a decrease from the year 1740 of some 2,500 whites and some 3,300 blacks,[3] while in 1646 it had boasted a white population of 21,000.[4] It was calculated that to keep up the supply of labour, slave importations to the number of 75,000 every thirty years were required, which meant that an average yearly supply of some 2,500 was sought.[5] The figure on the annual supply after 1749 and before 1753 must greatly have exceeded the one given if there were in the latter year on the island a total of 69,870 Negroes.[6]

Colonized in the first instance by the English a century and a quarter earlier, Barbados in the middle of the eighteenth century had been continuously in the possession of the British Crown — more

---

[1] The unknown author of *American Husbandry* (2 vols., London, 1775) calculated that between 1660 anl 1760 Barbados produced sugar with a total value of £24,000,000, with an average annual value of £240,000. See *American Husbandry* (ed. H. J. Carman, New York, 1939), p. 438.

[2] Jamaica also had many wealthy Jews.

[3] Governor Henry Grenville to the Board of Trade, February 7, 1748/9, Shelburne Papers, 45:37–51 Clements Library. For other figures see H. A. Wyndham: *Problems of Imperial Trusteeship* (Vol. II): *The Atlantic and Slavery* (London, 1935), pp. 276–7. The author of *An Account of the European Settlements in America* (2 vols., London, 1757), which has been attributed to Edmund and William Burke, stated (II, 67–8) that in 1676 "the whites were computed to be still much about fifty thousand, but their negroe slaves were increased so as to be upwards of one hundred thousand of all kinds. They employed four hundred sail of ships, one with another of an hundred and fifty tons in their trade; [and] their annual exported produce . . . amounted to upwards of three hundred and fifty thousand pounds. . . ." But in 1692 the island was decimated by a terrible contagion.

[4] For Governor Atkins's report of 1676 see Sir Robert H. Schomburgk: *History of Barbados* (London, 1848), p. 82.

[5] Governor Grenville in his report to the Board of Trade in 1749 gave the figure used above. Shelburne Papers, 45:37.

[6] R. H. Schomburgk: *op. cit.*, p. 146.

than once escaping conquest by England's rivals as the result of its inaccessibility because of the existence of dangerous rocks and coral reefs along the shores except on the south and west, where some thirty small forts and batteries afforded the necessary protection. The climate and living-conditions generally were considered the most advantageous of any of the British West Indies and there was much to delight the senses "in the bloom and fragrance of orange, lemon, lime, and citron trees, guavas, papas, aloes, and a vast multitude of other elegant and useful plants" growing about the fields of sugar cane and the plantation homes.[7]

At this period Bridgetown, the capital, on Carlisle Bay, contained some 1,200 buildings and was perhaps the finest of the English towns of the West Indies and also one of the most attractive within the Empire, with lofty, elegant, and "magnificently furnished" homes constructed of stone and brick with glazed windows. These residences together with places of business lined either side of the broad thoroughfares, the most fashionable of which, Cheapside, exacted rentals all but equal to its London namesake, with shops that vied with the best in England.[8] An impressive Anglican church edifice, almost as large and handsome as some of the cathedrals of the mother country, also graced the town, as did Codrington College, the only institution of higher education in the British West Indies.[9] "The Pilgrim," famed among the residences of colonial governors for its elegant and delightful if somewhat languid social life, added a further note of distinction. There the Hon. Henry Grenville, "by the splendour and magnificence with which he supported his rank," maintained the dignity of government.[10]

---

[7] D. Fenning and J. Collyer: A New System of Geography (2 vols., London, 1765), II, 701.

[8] [John Oldmixon]: The British Empire in America . . . (2 vols., London, 1741), II, 79. The Bridgetown of the year 1750 was largely destroyed as the result of the great fires in 1756 and in May and December of 1766.

[9] In 1702 Christopher Codrington, Governor-General of the Leeward Islands, made a bequest of two plantations on Barbados to the Society for the Propagation of the Gospel in Foreign Parts, for the purpose of erecting a college on the island. The period of the greatest activity of the College in the eighteenth century was from 1745 to 1775. While called a college, it was really a grammar school, and the students were all of tender age. See Codrington Chronicle . . . 1710–1834 (ed. F. J. Klingberg, Berkeley, Calif., 1949), Chap. 6, written by Jean Bullen and Helen E. Livingston; see also J. H. Bennett, Jr.: Bondsmen and Bishops: Slavery and Apprenticeship on the Codrington Plantations of Barbados, 1710–1838 (Berkeley and Los Angeles, 1958).

[10] John Poyer: The History of Barbados . . . (London, 1808), p. 316. It may be mentioned that Grenville's predecessor, Sir Thomas Robinson, "either for his personal

The administration of Grenville was a model, in fact, by which others were later measured. "His candour, integrity and impartiality removed all cause of party disputes, and silenced the clamours of factions." [11] At the height of his popularity he decided to resign his office and return to England. As an expression of their gratitude the members of the Assembly voted funds to pay the expense of his return home. This, however, he refused to accept. Whereupon it was voted to erect a marble statue of him to grace the town hall of Bridgetown. This was done.[12] In contrast to this intimate accord between the Governor and the Assembly one need only turn to the unhappy relations between Grenville's predecessor, Sir Thomas Robinson, and that body. After four years of almost constant friction the King — upon the basis of a petition to him from the Assembly in which were enumerated various abuses of the prerogative and violations of the rights of the people — decided to recall Robinson, apparently much to the satisfaction of almost everyone on the island.

Probably nowhere within the Empire did men generally cultivate more fully the amenities of life. "The Truth is," declared a contemporary, "the whole Community is like a single Family. Each Individual is Known to the Rest . . . so by a constant Intercourse of Business and Pleasure, there is an opportunity of conversing almost at once with Men of every Condition and Circumstance of life." He then affirmed that "In that Island (which has been for near a Century more fully inhabited and better cultivated than any Part of England except about London) the true characters of Persons are soon discovered . . . partly owing to the Hospitality of those already settled, which . . . receive and entertain strangers in the kindest and most generous manner, provided they bring any Recommendations or can give a tolerable account of themselves; always laying out how they may forward the Interests and encourage the Undertakings of such as propose to reside among them." [13] Mer-

---

convenience, or to justify his taste in architecture, . . . precipitately pulled down one of the best and largest apartments at Pilgrim, and made several expensive alterations and repairs without consulting the assembly." This led to a protest on the part of this body as a very irregular proceeding and it refused to order payment of the debt until the matter was accommodated, when Robinson made a proper apology. *Ibid.*, p. 303.

[11] *Ibid.*, p. 316.

[12] *Ibid.*, p. 317.

[13] *Caribbeana* . . . (2 vols., London, 1741), I, Preface. These volumes are extracts from the *Barbados Gazette* of an earlier date. George Washington, who went with his ailing brother Lawrence to Barbados in 1751, seemed to have dined almost every day —

chants, planters, clergy, lawyers, and physicians, as a rule, had numerous household servants in fine liveries, and the equipages in which these gentlemen travelled to and fro were rich in appearance. As the climate was too hot for hunting or such pastimes, the gentry gave great attention to cards, dice, backgammon, quoits, bowling, balls, and concerts. "There is in general," declared a contemporary, "a greater appearance of order and decency than in any other colony of the West Indies." [14]

One magnificent harbour cared for the trading interests of the entire island — for Carlisle Bay was spacious enough to allow 500 ships to ride at anchor and the wharves and quays of Bridgetown were the scene of great activity, especially during certain periods of the year. In 1748 over 220 vessels entered the port exclusive of those owned by Barbadians; in 1751 it was 511, and in 1754 it reached 650, after which there was a decline to 246 in 1760. [15] According to statistical tables prepared by Bryan Edwards, the export of sugar during the 1740's averaged annually 13,948 hogsheads of fifteen hundredweight apiece, and of rum 12,884 puncheons of 100 gallons each; [16] but little molasses ever left the island. The value of the produce of Barbados was, in spite of this impressive showing, declining. "The additional Duty, the attending charges on shipping [commodities] home, and the Low Value, to which we are all now reduced," declared Governor Henry Grenville in 1748, "will make the next [figures] that shall be seen, fall extreamly short of those which heretofore appeared." [17]

In explaining this decline in the economic importance of Barbados, the Governor declared:

---

outside of the period when he was afflicted with smallpox — with leading people of the island. See J. M. Toner's edition of *The Daily Journal of Major George Washington, in 1751–2* . . . (Albany, 1892); see also J. C. Fitzpatrick's *Diaries of Washington, 1748–1749* (4 vols., Boston, 1925), I, 22–6, and D. S. Freeman: *George Washington* (7 vols., New York, 1948–57), I, 252–8.

[14] Fenning and Collyer: *op. cit.*, II, 701.

[15] Governor Grenville's report to the Board of Trade on the "State of Barbados," February 7, 1748, Shelburne Papers, 45:37–51, and F. W. Pitman. *The Development of the British West Indies, 1700–1763* (New Haven, 1917), p. 97.

[16] Bryan Edwards: *A History . . . of the British Colonies in the West Indies* (3 vols., London, 1793–1801), I, 352.

[17] Governor Grenville to the Board of Trade, February 7, 1748, Shelburne Papers, 45:37–51. As Bryan Edwards shows in his tabulations, Barbados rapidly lost ground in the eighteenth century. In 1736, 22,769 hogsheads of sugar were produced and by 1784 the total had fallen to 9,554. Bryan Edwards: *op. cit.*, I, 352.

"The French Settlements [in the West Indies] have a worse effect upon his Majesty's Island than can be easily described; they Produce, besides others more valuable, the same Commodities as we do in much greater abundance, and at much less expence, and they pay lower Duties whereby they can afford to undersell us in every foreign Market in Europe; they permit and encourage an extensive & clandestine Trade with all the British Colonies in North America . . . ; it is to be feared the effect of their Increase of Riches, Power and Territory . . . will be soon felt in the Decay, if not the whole loss of that Valuable trade the Nation hath hitherto carried on to the West Indies." [18]

Grenville might also have stressed the great weight of public burdens in this connection.

From 1741 to 1748 there was raised £101,416.10.3½ [19] and in addition there was paid annually to the Crown 4½ per cent in specie [20] "on all dead commodities, the growth of the Island, shipped to any part of the world," a contribution levied ever since the days of Charles II and, according to the planters, amounting to 10 per cent on the clear profits of their estates. What is more, the ordinary expenses of government had gradually increased from £4,310.14.10½ in 1742 to £17,268.10.9½ in 1746, and amounted to £11,458.7.2¼ in 1747, without accounting for the extraordinary charges which averaged £5,435 per annum during this seven years because of the fortifications and the care of prisoners of war.[21] A contemporary, writing of conditions in Barbados in the 1760's, has some comments that were equally applicable to the island in the middle of the eighteenth century:

"The plantations of Barbados oppressed by taxes, impoverished by mismanagement, loaded by great and necessary expenses of their management, yield not now the profits they formerly afforded: notwithstanding the high estimation Europeans may set upon West India estates, yet . . . the landed interest of Barbados (that is throughout the whole island) does not clear *communibus annis* four per cent. Estimating the principal at what the land usually sells for. . . ." [22]

---

18 Shelburne Papers, 45:37–51.
19 *Ibid.*
20 The equivalent in kind, however, was accepted.
21 Shelburne Papers, 45:37–51.
22 [George Frere]: *A Short History of Barbados* . . . (London, 1768), p. 105. Frere asserted that "notwithstanding the uncertainty of profit, the unavoidable expense

It is probably true that no one of the other colonial establishments, at least outside of New England, was so elaborately equipped with officials, great and small, as was Barbados, and, considering its diminutive size, the impression is gained that the machinery of government was top-heavy. Some officials held office by letters patent, others by appointment of the Governor with the approbation of the Council, and still others, such as the excise waiters, were appointed by the Treasurer. There was the Governor with his council of twelve, who also constituted the court of chancery and the court of errors as well as the upper house of the legislature.[23] In addition, there were an assembly of twenty-two deputies, two masters in chancery with a register, a chief clerk and sole examiner in chancery who was also clerk of the Crown and peace by patent; a court of exchequer with a chief baron and four puisne barons; a remembrancer appointed by patent; five courts of common pleas for the five precincts with a chief justice, four assistants, and a clerk for each of them; a court of vice admiralty with a judge and a register by patent; an attorney-general by patent, a solicitor-general, a secretary of the island by patent, a court of oyer and terminer with a judge, assisted by the justices of the peace, a court of escheats with an escheator-general and a jury; a court of quarter sessions of the justices of the peace; a court of two justices and three freeholders for the trial of Negroes; a provost marshal-general by patent, a naval officer by patent, a clerk of the market by patent, a treasurer, a comptroller of the excise, and a storekeeper. In addition there were a surveyor-general, four collectors and four controllers of customs, together with the minor officers of the eleven parishes such as eleven coroners, the vestries chosen annually by the freeholders of the parishes, and the parish constables ap-

---

attending an estate is certain, and is inconceivably great." To illustrate this point he takes an estate of 250 acres. To work it properly there must be 170 Negroes, 100 horned cattle, 12 horses, 40 sheep, 3 tenants, who are militia men, with their families, a steward or manager with a salary of £100 to £150, a driver with 2 apprentices whose salaries may total £45 a year. Added to this were the salaries of a town agent and a book-poster, each receiving £15 or £20, an apothecary at £30 or £40, a farrier at £15 or £20, and the commission of an English agent entitled to 2½ per cent for the disposal of the sugar, together with the freight of it and the duties paid on it. Further, there were the taxes on the estate, with the costs of the repair of buildings; and, finally, the maintenance of the proprietor and his family with 8 or 10 servants. *Ibid.*, pp. 106–8.

[23] George Frere, a resident of Barbados writing in 1767, has the following to say about the Council as the upper house in the legislature: "The governor always sits in council, even when acts are passed; a practice that seems to have been established by custom only; for it appears to be unconstitutional. It is not a custom adopted by all the colonies" (*A Short History of Barbados* . . . , pp. 92–3).

pointed by the justices of the peace.[24] All this machinery of government had been developed to protect the interests of a population no larger than dwells in a town of moderate size today and occupying a region no larger than many American cattle ranches and virtually the same size as the Isle of Wight!

The legislation of this period in Barbados, far from disclosing any significant problems, leaves one struck by the absence of issues of great importance. By an act passed in the year 1744 a penalty of £5 was provided for anyone permitting apprentices or servants to game upon his premises.[25] A law in the year 1748 struck at "the inconveniences and mischiefs arising from lotteries, raffling and gaming whereby many of his majesty's subjects have been ruined and others impoverished." By this act a penalty of £500 was to be levied upon any person who should set up a lottery for the disposal of valuables such as lands, houses, slaves, and jewelry.[26]

But even more important than the discouraging of gaming was the question of the proper control of the Negro population, which, as has been made clear, vastly exceeded that of the whites. It would appear that frequent disorders were occurring in various parts of the Barbados as the result of quarrelling and fighting among the slaves "openly carried on in the public streets and highways," which had in some instances been encouraged by the masters of those slaves. As there was apparently no law covering this or for preventing cursing or obscene speech on the part of slaves or the use of insolent language or gestures toward white people or the setting off of fireworks by the blacks, it was determined to take the matter in hand in 1749, with the result that an act was passed providing that all Negroes duly convicted of such offences should be whipped by the constable or common whipper not exceeding thirty-nine lashes according to the offence and state of health of the offender.[27] Further, all con-

---

[24] Shelburne Papers, 45:37–51. The disposal of royal patents for offices in Barbados and in other of the British West Indies as well as the abuses attending this system are dealt with by J. H. Parry in his "The Patent Offices in the British West Indies," *English Historical Review*, LXIX, 200–25. As noted above, a number of the public offices in Barbados were held by patentees or their deputies.

[25] *Acts, Passed in the Island of Barbados. From 1643, to 1762, inclusive* . . . (London, 1764), p. 337.

[26] *Ibid.*, pp. 350–1.

[27] It may be noted that in Governor Grenville's instructions of November 10, 1746, the 41st instruction reads as follows: "To endeavour to get a Law passed for restricting of inhuman severities & the wilful killing etc. of Indians and Negros [whereby the guilty] may be punished." Commenting on this instruction on December 14, 1752,

stables were called upon to prevent the congregating of Negroes at huckstering-shops or tippling-houses and were authorized to muster a sufficient guard to disperse any such gatherings.[28]

The commission of the Governor of Barbados[29] was framed to include St. Lucia, Dominica, St. Vincent, "and the rest of our Caribbean Islands lying and being to the windward of Guadeloupe." Governor Grenville in his report for 1748 was, however, compelled to admit that the English claims to these islands at this juncture were vague. In referring to the activities of the French in this region he wrote that

> "within these late years they have begun to settle and fortify the Islands of Dominico [Dominica] and St. Lucia and [have] made considerable progress therein; they have a Governor at each of these, said to be Commission'd by the General at Martinique. At St. Vincents they have been long endeavouring to cultivate a Friendship with the Indian and Black Inhabitants, and [as] a great many French Famillies (are now settled) there is Reason to fear from the ascendancy that they obtain over the said Island; at the Island of Grenado, they are settled in great numbers under a regular Government and the place is strongly fortified. . . . [They] have very lately landed an Armed Force on the Island of Tobago in order to take Possession thereof and for the defence raised a Battery of Eighteen Guns in one of the Bays."[30]

Grenville indicated that there seemed to be sufficient provision in the laws to restrain inhuman severities used by masters or overseers against servants or slaves, "but no provision has been made in any Law that the wilful killing of Indians, or Negros, shall be punished with death. . . ." He went on to say that there had been few instances of this and that the legislature had been deterred in enacting such a law for fear of the dangerous effects it might have on the spirits of the Negroes "by lessening that Awe in which they ought to stand to their Masters, & perhaps inciting them to Insurrections . . ." (L. W. Labaree: *Royal Instructions to British Colonial Governors, 1670–1776* [2 vols., New York, 1935], II, 839–40).

[28] *Acts . . . of Barbados, 1643–1762* (1764), pp. 354–7. It should be pointed out that some efforts were made by Church of England clergymen, with the encouragement of the Society for the Propagation of the Gospel in Foreign Parts, to bring the Negroes into a Christian way of living. For example, the Rev. Arthur Holt, who served in three parishes one after another between the years 1725 and 1733, met with some success in converting slaves, among them his own. But the planters by and large looked on this practice with jaundiced eyes. See J. A. Schutz: "Arthur Holt, Anglican Clergyman, Reports on Barbados, 1723–1733," *Journal of Negro History*, XXXI, 444–69.

[29] For Henry Grenville's commission as Governor of Barbados, dated September 25, 1746, see P.R.O., C.O. 5:200, pp. 219–35; for his general instructions, dated November 10, 1746, see *ibid.*, pp. 239–301.

[30] Shelburne Papers, 45:37–51.

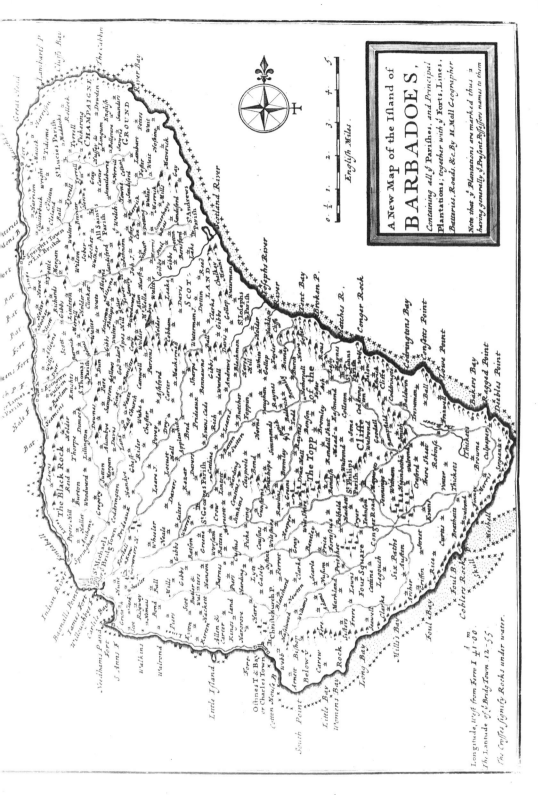

"A New Map of the Island of
Barbadoes" by H. Moll.

(From *The British Empire in America* [by John Oldmixon], 1741)

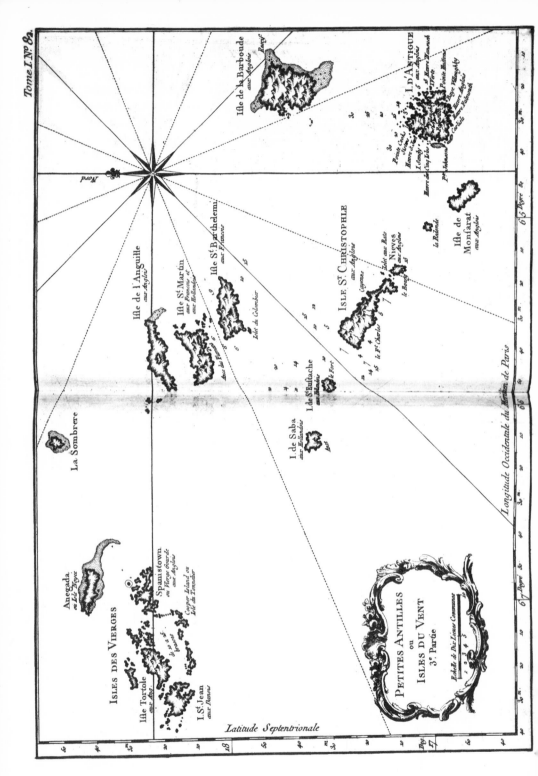

"Petites Antilles ou Isles du Vent" by
J. N. Bellin, 1764.

St. Vincent, Dominica, and St. Lucia, it may be pointed out, had been claimed by England since the reign of Charles I, by whom they were granted to the Earl of Carlisle; under Charles II they went to Lord Willoughby and in 1722 to the Duke of Montagu, who attempted, but without success, the colonization of St. Lucia and St. Vincent. In 1750, as Grenville's report indicated, the French had the upper hand in these three islands.[31]

To the north and west of Barbados in the Caribbean Sea, and lying to the leeward of the course generally followed by the Spanish flota in its annual visit to Porto Bello, is a group of islands called for geographical convenience the Leeward Islands. The British possessions in this area were, among others of less importance and size, Antigua, St. Christopher, Nevis, and Montserrat.[32] All were under one Governor, who was William Mathew in 1750 and who carried the title of "Captain General and Governor in Chief of all the Leeward Caribbean Islands from Guadeloupe to Porto Rico," and whose post was valued at £3,500 a year.[33] His residence was at St. John in Antigua and he was assisted by Lieutenant Governors in the other principal islands.[34] These officials in 1750 were Francis, Lord Hawley, of Antigua; Gilbert Fleming, Esq., of St. Christopher; Lancelot Story, Esq., of Nevis; and Benjamin Carpenter, Esq., of Montserrat.

On all these islands, as well as elsewhere in the British West Indies, the Church of England was established and supported by public taxation. Under the provision of a law passed in 1705 by the General Assembly of the Leeward Islands, before a separate Assembly was set up in each of the four islands, every minister presented by the Governor to a benefice was entitled to receive a yearly salary of 16,000 pounds of muscovado sugar, to be raised by the vestry acts of each island. This was the law in 1750.[35]

---

[31] For a treatment of the so-called neutral islands of the West Indies see Volume V of this series, Chap. 7.

[32] The lesser possessions in 1746 were Barbuda, Anguilla, the conquered French half of St. Martin, and Tortola, all of which were settled, as were such little islands as Green, Long, and Vernon's near Antigua and, among the Virgin Islands and beyond, Anegada, Peter's Island, Beef Island, Cayman Islands, and Salt Island. See "General [Governor] Mathew's Answer to the Board's General Querie to the present State of His Majesty's Leeward Charribee Islands in America Received 10 July 1746," Shelburne Papers, 45:156–86.

[33] For Governor Mathew's commission issued in 1733 see P.R.O., C.O. 5:195, pp. 465–84; for his general instructions see C.O. 153:15, pp. 143–224.

[34] The Leeward Islands were no longer federated in 1750.

[35] Laws of the Leeward Islands, p. 19. These laws, covering the years 1690 to 1705,

The island of Antigua was discovered and named by Columbus in 1493, but not until 1632 was the settlement of it begun by the English coming from the neighbouring island of St. Christopher. In 1663 it was patented to Lord Willoughby of Parham by Charles II, and in 1680 Christopher Codrington made it the seat of his government as Captain General of the Leeward Islands. With an area of something over a hundred square miles of fairly level country, it was peopled in the late 1740's with about 3,500 whites and about 28,000 blacks.[36] In contrast to most of the other Caribbean islands, it had neither springs nor streams, a circumstance that somewhat retarded its settlement. But the soil of clay and marl was quite fertile, and by the utilization of rain-water empounded in small reservoirs it was possible to secure abundant crops. However, the yield of the plantations varied greatly from year to year, on account of the liability of drought. During the 1740's the exports consisted of over 15,000 hogsheads of sugar, almost 10,000 casks of rum, between 3,000 and 4,000 bags of cotton, and some 7,000 bags of ginger.[37] By 1751 the amount of sugar produced had dropped to about 14,000 hogsheads.[38] In September of that year "the most violent hurricane every known here" wrecked many of the plantations so that the sugar crop was greatly reduced over that of the preceding season.[39]

Though the Antigua authorities in 1736 had uncovered a plot of the slaves to exterminate their masters and set up a Negro government and had punished those deeply implicated in it in the most terrible manner, by the middle of the century the island had become the scene of the humane efforts of the Unitas Fratrum or Moravian Brethren, who with great zeal and no little success were labouring

are appended to the *Acts of Assembly, Passed in the Island of St. Christopher* . . . *1711–1769* (St. Christopher, 1769).

[36] The figure for 1744 was 3,538 whites and 27,892 slaves. See Governor Mathew's Answers to Queries, 1746, *loc. cit.* Not only was Antigua the residence of the Governor of the Leeward Islands but a regiment of troops was quartered there; it also possessed the only commodious port in the British Lesser Antilles suitable for sheltering, cleaning, and refitting His Majesty's ships stationed at Barbados and the Leeward Islands. See *Acts of the Privy Council, Col. Ser., 1745–1766,* p. 75.

[37] Shelburne Papers, 45:156–86. In 1728 Antigua exported to England 187,260 hundredweight of sugar, in 1736 it was 149,106, in 1744 it was 127,787, and in 1750, 131,289. See P.R.O., Treas. 64. 274.

[38] See "Letters of a Sugar Planter in Antigua, 1739–1758" (ed. R. B. Sheridan), *Agricultural History,* XXXI, No. 3, 3–23.

[39] *Ibid.*

to Christianize the benighted blacks.[40] That the very great disproportion of whites to blacks in Antigua at this period was, however,
still a matter of deep concern to the inhabitants is indicated by the
fact that the Board of Trade was persuaded in 1754 to represent to
His Majesty, "in consideration of the decrease of the white inhabitants and great increase of the negroes," that the regiment stationed
in the island should be augmented to 700 soldiers, under the condition that the additional expense should be borne by the local government.[41]

It may be mentioned in passing that among the repercussions of
the futile attempt of the Stuarts to regain the English throne in 1746
was the passing of a law by the Antigua Assembly in that year directed against Roman Catholics who might seek to reside in the island. Such newcomers, if over eighteen years, were to depart within
ten days or be committed to gaol. Further, it was provided that
should any resident of the island hire "papists" or purchase them as
servants or provide them with lands on which to dwell, he should
suffer a month's imprisonment and pay £50 for the first offence, and
for each subsequent offence the imprisonment should be for six
months and the fine, £100. The act, when submitted to His Majesty
in Council, was found to be objectionable from a number of points
of view and was therefore repealed.[42]

To the northwest of Antigua lies St. Christopher, more commonly
known as St. Kitts, second largest of the English possessions in the
Leeward group. In contrast to Antigua, it is a narrow mountainous
island some twenty-five miles in length by less than seven in breadth,
embracing about sixty-three square miles, and capped by lofty Mount
Misery. The arable portion of it was still of marvellous fertility in the
middle of the eighteenth century.[43] It was the first of the Leewards
to be colonized. Captain Sir Thomas Warner began the work of settlement in 1623, but was soon confronted with the presence of the
French. The island thereafter witnessed a series of conflicts between

---

[40] The success of the Moravians among the Antigua Negroes is indicated by the fact
that in 1787 the number listed among the converted was 5,465; in St. Christopher it
was but 80. See Bryan Edwards: op. cit., I, 455.

[41] Acts of the Privy Council, Col. Ser., 1745–1766, p. 267.

[42] Ibid., pp. 73–4.

[43] Bryan Edwards (op. cit., I, 429–30) indicated that some land on St. Christopher
would yield as much as 8,000 pounds of sugar per acre and that the average yield per
acre was higher than in any other island.

the English, French, Spaniards, and natives; but in the Peace of Utrecht the claims of Great Britain were given full recognition.

St. Christopher has been noted for its beauty; writers of the eighteenth century represented it as one of the most delightful spots of the world. "Its mountains, notwithstanding there are dreadful rocks and thick woods between them, rise one above another and are adorned by rows of trees that wear a perpetual verdure intermixed with handsome houses covered with shining slate," declared a contemporary.[44] The capital of the island, Basse-Terre, which had been built by the French, was considered an attractive town with houses of good brick, freestone, and timber.[45] As evidence of the prosperity of the people there was to be found in each of its six parishes an impressive Anglican church edifice with an interior not only wainscotted but furnished with pews and pulpit of ebony, cedar, redwood, brazil, and other precious sorts of wood "curios for Colour and delightful for Scent."[46]

This prosperity of St. Christopher was supported by the annual exportation of over 157,000 hundredweight of sugar, 85,000 gallons of rum, and 33,000 of molasses. In fact, in 1750 the planters shipped to England as much sugar as did Antigua and Nevis combined,[47] although the white population of the two islands last named was almost twice that of St. Christopher, which was less than 2,400 in 1745. Moreover, the slaves of Antigua and Nevis in that year totalled almost 35,000 as against less than 20,000 in St. Kitts,[48] which indicates a wide difference in the cost of production of the principal staple, sugar. To defend the island three forts and six batteries had been erected, among which the fort at Brimstone Hill was held to be almost impregnable. In spite of these defences, in the recent war with the Spaniards and French the enemy had succeeded in penetrating the island in connection with certain plundering forays in the West

[44] D. Fenning and J. Collyer: op. cit., II, 691.

[45] Sandy-Point, which had been established by the English in the seventeenth century, was the only other important settlement.

[46] [John Oldmixon]: The British Empire in America . . . , II, 263.

[47] P.R.O., Treas. 64. 274. It should be pointed out that local circumstances would greatly affect the amount of sugar produced in any one of the islands. According to tables presented in American Husbandry (1939 edn., pp. 445–8), in the 1770's St. Christopher was exporting 10,000 hogsheads of sugar while Antigua was exporting 15,500 hogsheads and Nevis, 6,000.

[48] Shelburne Papers, 45:156–86. In 1756 the white population had increased to 2,783 and the Negro population to 21,891. Governor Thomas to the Board of Trade, February 20, 1756, C.O. 152:28.

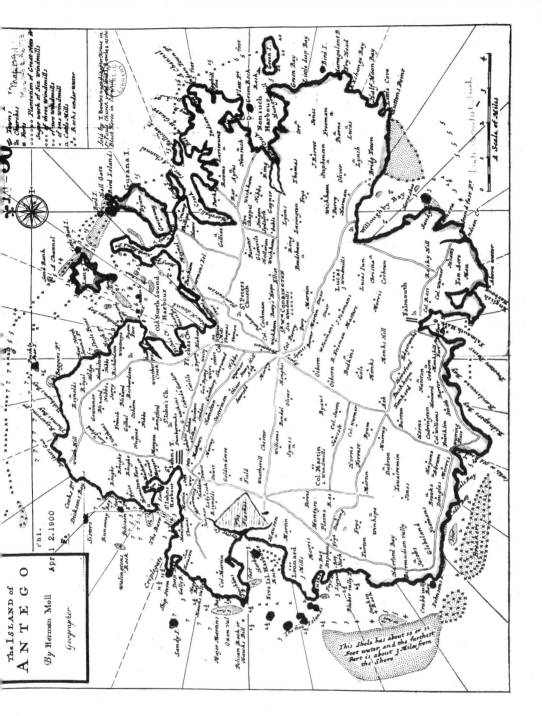

"The Island of Antego."

(From the *Atlas Minor* by Herman Moll, 1736)

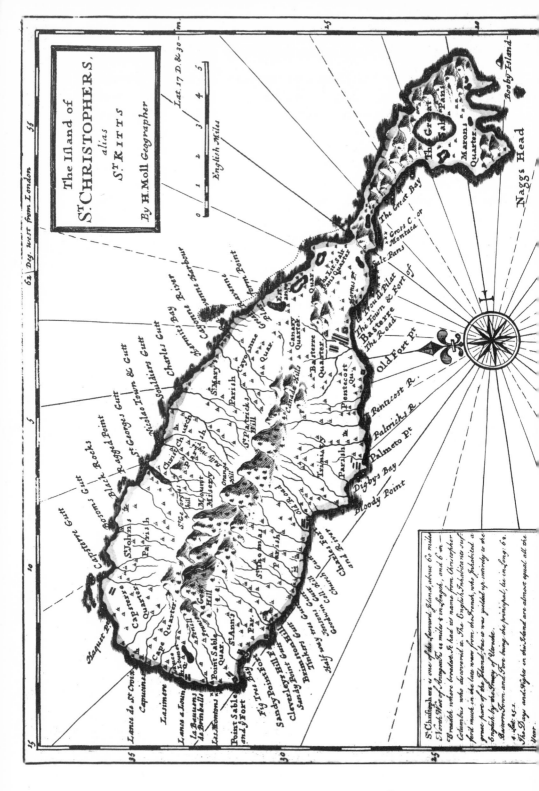

"The Island of St. Christophers, alias St. Kitts."

(From the *Atlas Minor* by Herman Moll, 1736)

Indies. This led the local Assembly to pass a law in 1746 providing for the reimbursement not only of those who had suffered but also of those who might suffer in the future by reason of these hostile expeditions.[49]

Even at Basse-Terre, the capital and the most important shipping-centre, the island was possessed of nothing resembling a harbour at this period. For the surf so continuously beat upon the shallow sandy shore as to prevent the construction of either quay or wharf. As a result, the landing and shipment of goods was inconvenient and frequently quite hazardous. To facilitate the loading of the hogsheads of sugar a small boat, especially constructed and called a "moses," was employed. This was laid upon the sands so that a hogshead could be rolled into it, after which it was righted by the sailors. However, barrels of rum, bags of cotton, and other products of the island that could bear the water were generally floated to the waiting ship.[50]

The activities of the inhabitants of the British West Indies were regulated by Parliament through the trade and navigation acts and, in addition, by many local laws. Some of the acts of the St. Christopher Assembly may help to illustrate their way of life. In 1728 a law was passed setting up markets at Basse-Terre, Old Road, Sandy-Point, and Deep Bay for sales of cattle, sheep, hogs, and turtle. In each a clerk of the market was in charge, who received all animals to be slaughtered and who turned these over to the butchers. The sale price of each type of meat was designated — such as beef, which was to sell for not more than 7½ pence per pound, and mutton, veal, and pork for not more than 9 pence per pound. Further, the law provided that from every bullock slaughtered a cut of six pounds should be taken for the use of the poor.[51] In 1739 another act, apparently to prevent the sale of stolen articles, forbad under penalty the retailing of goods by hawking them in the towns, parishes, or plantations.[52] Further, to guard against defrauding and delays in justice in cases involving those who had come to the island to trade and who

---

[49] The Act of 1746 indemnifying those who had suffered from the depredations of the enemy was confirmed in 1748. It was founded upon the same principle as was an act of the old Leeward Islands Assembly, passed in Nevis in 1701 and confirmed in 1733. See Acts of the Privy Council, Col. Ser., 1745–1766, p. 74.

[50] Thomas Jefferys: The West India Atlas or a General Description of the West Indies (London, 1780), Introduction, p. 21.

[51] Acts of Assembly, St. Christopher (1769), pp. 86–9.

[52] Ibid., pp. 102–3.

were about to depart, a court merchant was established by a law passed in 1740. It had summary powers to decide disputed claims within four days. Under its terms, a legal tender for the settlement of all such debts could be sugar, rum, molasses, cotton, ginger, indigo, tobacco, or other merchantable commodities which were the produce of the island and which had been brought to any "legal paying-place" — provided that such commodities were tendered at a price approved by the jury of the court merchant, which was presided over by the chief judge of the island court.[53]

It is of interest to note in passing that a spirit of religious toleration was abroad in St. Christopher. According to the testimony of the agent of the island before the Board of Trade in 1751,[54] the numerous Roman Catholics were allowed to vote in elections and were otherwise, it appears, placed on the same footing as the King's other subjects. During this period when the chief executive power was in the hands of the Governor of the Leeward Islands, William Mathew, there was little to disturb the calm of public affairs in the island. In 1748, however, an issue arose over the inclination of the Governor, living in Antigua, to shower favours upon his relatives living on St. Christopher, three of whom were appointed to the local Council. In this connection it was charged that he was guilty of gross nepotism by bestowing upon his nephew, the Hon. William Pym Burt, the offices of Chief Justice of the Court of King's Bench, Treasurer, and Judge of the Court of Admiralty while the latter was at the same time acting as liquor officer, powder officer, governor of Brimstone Hill, colonel of the forts of the island, and member of the Governor's Council.[55]

Not far removed from St. Christopher to the south is Nevis, another beautiful spot which really consists of nothing more than a single mountain with its slopes gradually approaching the sea.[56]

---

[53] Ibid., pp. 110–12.

[54] Board of Trade Journal, 1749–1753, December 10, 1751, p. 240.

[55] The issue involving the appointment of Burt to the Council came before the Board of Trade in June 1748. The complainant was a Mr. Jessop, who charged that to make way for Burt he was dismissed from the Council under accusation of being a Roman Catholic. This he did not explicitly deny, but stated that he had taken the oaths and "that the oath of Supremacy cannot be taken by a Roman Catholic without Perjury nor the test subscribed without his being guilty of the greatest insincerity." In this connection it is interesting to note that Jessop, while on the Council of St. Christopher, sat also as a member of the Assembly of Nevis. See ibid., 1741–1749, pp. 302–13.

[56] Bryan Edwards, a Jamaican, in describing Nevis, refers to the inhabitants of it living "amidst the beauties of an eternal spring, beneath a sky serene and unclouded,

Colonized in 1628 by Warner after he had begun the settlement of St. Christopher, it enjoyed a steady growth until 1689, when — in its opulence and with a population estimated at 10,000 whites and 20,-000 Negroes [57] — it was visited by an epidemic that swept it with terrible effects. This was followed the next year by a most violent earthquake. But its trials were not over. In 1706 it was invaded by the French, and in the following year a hurricane, the most devastating in all its history as a British colony, took a frightful toll of life and property.[58] The little island never succeeded in recovering its former prosperity after this series of calamities, but continued to decline. In 1728 it exported to England over 50,000 hundredweight of sugar; by 1736 this had dropped to less than 39,000, in 1744 the amount was less than 35,000, and by 1750 hardly more than 25,000.[59] In fact, Nevis, in the words of Mr. Martin, legal adviser for the island in 1751, was not a paradise, as it appeared to be, but an unhealthy, unpleasant place.[60]

During the period under consideration there were less than 900 white people and some 6,500 blacks on Nevis.[61] For the purpose of encouraging immigration the local Assembly repealed an earlier act of 1701, passed not only by the local Assembly of Nevis but also by the General Assembly of the Leeward Islands, designed to prevent Catholics from settling in those parts.[62] The earlier act had provided that persons coming to the island should within ten days take the required oaths on pain of forfeiture of property, and imprisonment,

---

and in a spot inexpressibly beautiful (for it is enlivened by a variety of the most enchanting prospects in the world, in the numerous islands which surround it)" (*History of the West Indies*, I, 436).

[57] [John Oldmixon]: *op. cit.*, II, 236–44, 253.

[58] *Ibid.*, II, 254–5.

[59] P.R.O., Treas. 64. 274.

[60] Board of Trade *Journal*, 1749–1753, p. 239. The student interested in the exploitation of the resources of Nevis in the eighteenth century should consult the scholarly work by Richard Pares: *A West-India Fortune* (London, 1950), which provides a history of the Pinney family from the latter part of the seventeenth century to well into the nineteenth. In the middle of the eighteenth century John Frederick Pinney was an absentee planter, the owner of two estates which taken together comprised 273 acres (*ibid.*, p. 83). The Pinney home in St. John's Parish was apparently one of the finest on the island and an inventory of its contents in the year 1722 is presented by Pares (Appendix).

[61] Governor Mathew's Answers to Queries, 1746, Shelburne Papers, 45:156–86.

[62] The Act of 1701 carried the title "An Act to prevent Papists and reputed Papists from settling in any of these His Majesty's Charribbee Leeward Islands in America." The General Assembly of the federated islands met that year in Nevis. See *Acts of Assembly, Passed in the Island of Nevis, From 1664 to 1739, inclusive* (London, 1740), pp. 35–7.

and that, should they be seen at mass subsequent to the taking of the aforesaid oaths, they were to be declared "recusant convicts" and as such were to be deprived of their property in favour of the nearest relative merely by act of a justice of the peace without jury trial and without appeal.[63] As a matter of fact, Roman Catholics had played little part in the colonization of the island either preceding or following the Act of 1701. One of the great Nevis planters, John Frederick Pinney, who was also a member of the House of Commons, declared in 1751 that there were not more than five or six residents there who professed this religion.[64] It was therefore the increase toward the close of the seventeenth century of those of this religious persuasion in the other English Leeward Islands that seems to have unnecessarily excited apprehension in Nevis. Indeed, until 1751 the laws against Roman Catholics were harsher there than in any of the other British West India possessions. As a result the Board of Trade was led to authorize the seal of the island to be affixed to the repeal act and this was thereupon confirmed by the Privy Council.[65]

The history of Nevis for this period discloses an excellent example of how the home authorities were compelled to guard against abuses that inevitably occurred from time to time as the result of the misuse of powers conferred upon royal colonial officials. In April 1752 a Spanish ship, *La Santa Rosetta*, bound from the Spainsh Main to Martinique with a cargo, ran into heavy storms and, after springing a leak, and in need of water, wood, and other supplies, entered the open road at Nevis and sought permission of the President of the Council to take on supplies and to repair the leak, which was granted. In spite of this, the ship was boarded by the searcher of the custom house, John Scholes. The crew, vessel, and cargo were then seized, and the schooner condemned in the vice-admiralty court of the island "for having imported sundry merchandise contrary to law." As a result the commander of the vessel appealed from the decision to the Privy Council, which decided in committee that the searcher should not only restore the value of the ship and cargo but pay costs amounting to £100 sterling.[66]

Lastly, among the principal Leeward Islands belonging to England and lying to the southwest of Antigua is Montserrat. In spite of its

---

[63] Board of Trade *Journal*, 1749–1753, p. 239.
[64] Ibid., pp. 240–1.
[65] Acts of the Privy Council, Col. Ser., 1745–1766, p. 806.
[66] Acts of the Privy Council, Col. Ser., 1745–1766, pp. 223–6.

"Map of Nevis."
(From the *Atlas Occidentalis* by Thomas Jefferys, 1777)

limited area of less than thirty-three square miles — two thirds of which is either mountainous, "a cluster of rugged volcanic peaks," or barren — it was esteemed a possession of great importance to England in the middle of the eighteenth century. It was another veritable treasure island. Nevertheless, in common with the other British West India possessions exclusive of Jamaica, its output of sugar by 1750 was much reduced from that of the earlier part of the century. In 1728 it sent to England over 50,000 hundredweight of sugar; in 1738 the amount was slightly over 47,000; in 1744 it was less than 39,000, and in 1750 somewhat over 36,000.[67] It was, however, better off than Nevis; for it was exporting to England in 1750 more than one million pounds beyond the amount of sugar sent by the latter, although the two were producers of approximately the same amounts in 1728.[68] Nevis, moreover, was employing over 500 more slaves than was its neighbour at the same time to achieve this result. The population of Montserrat in 1746 was hardly over 7,000, with blacks numbering five to one.[69]

In contrast to Nevis, where Catholics had always been insignificant in numbers, Montserrat had possessed from the beginning a large element of people of this faith from Ireland, who were, moreover, the leaders in its colonization. In 1751, according to the legal adviser of Montserrat, they numbered four fifths of the white population.[70] Whereas the Assembly of Nevis at this period, as has just been pointed out, proceeded to repeal the harsh laws against Catholics, the Montserrat Assembly passed an act in 1749 to regulate the election of its members which, among other things, required the oaths of abjuration and supremacy of all voters.[71] This was done with

---

[67] P.R.O., Treas. 64. 274.

[68] Ibid.

[69] Governor Mathew's Answers to Queries, 1746, Shelburne Papers, 45:156–86.

[70] Board of Trade Journal, 1749–1753, p. 235. To prevent public commotions and promote peaceful relations among the English, Scottish, and Irish inhabitants of the island a law was passed in 1668 which was still unchanged in the middle of the eighteenth century, against the use of "opprobrious Language." It recited that Montserrat was settled by "subjects of His Majesty's Three Nations" and that to preserve harmony among them it was provided no one, "as well in drink as sober," should use the terms "English Dog, Scott's Dog, Tory, Irish Dog, . . . and many other approbrious, scandalous, and disgraceful Terms" for that person "of what Quality or Degree soever" under penalty of a fine of 5,000 pounds of sugar if used against an officer or government, and 500 pounds if used against a member of the Council or Assembly. See Acts of Assembly, Passed in the Island of Montserrat, 1668–1740, inclusive (London, 1740), pp. 11–13.

[71] The title of the act was "An Act to regulate the Assembly of this island, and the elections of the members thereof." It provided that the Assembly, which consisted of

the purpose of excluding not only incoming Roman Catholics but also those who had previously exercised the right of franchise in spite of the Act of 1701 of the federal Assembly of the Leeward Islands. However, when the law came before the Board of Trade, after full discussion that body decided to direct a representation to the King proposing its repeal, which was done.[72]

The legislature of Montserrat at this period was composed of twelve members, an increase of four members over that of the period preceding the year 1748 when Governor Mathew issued writs to the towns of Plymouth and Kinsale empowering each to send two members to the Assembly. This body felt constrained in 1749 to pass a law ratifying and confirming the step taken by the Governor, although by his commission he was authorized to proceed in this fashion without their advice or concurrence. It further enacted in this measure that forever after there should be twelve and no more members, and that no assembly should last for longer than three years, when a new one should be called. Finally, it provided that the treasurer of the island should not vote, or even sit in the chamber, under heavy penalty.

The law in question when submitted to the Privy Council was also disallowed upon the basis of a Board of Trade representation to the effect that it, in many respects and in a manner highly unbecoming, encroached upon His Majesty's just prerogative.[73]

The 4½-per-cent duty that Barbados and the Leeward Islands were obliged to pay in perpetuity into the receipt of the King's exchequer was at a heavy cost to these possessions, slowly declining to a state of economic exhaustion as they were at this period. The history of this levy is part of the history of the islands themselves, which, together with other Caribbee Islands, were granted by royal letters patent in 1627 to James Hay, Earl of Carlisle. His claims were resented by the settlers, especially in view of the fact that he made no real contribution to their settlement or protection when colonized but only desired to profit by them. At the time of the Restoration, to be freed from this hated overlordship, the Assembly of Barbados in 1663 passed a law which, by granting in perpetuity to the Crown

---

eight members, should be increased to twelve and thereafter remain at this figure; further that the life of any Assembly be limited to three years and that all voters should take the oaths of abjuration and supremacy. *Ibid.*, pp. 234–7.

[72] *Acts of the Privy Council, Col. Ser.,* 1745–1766, pp. 101–3.
[73] *Acts of the Privy Council, Col. Ser.,* 1745–1766, pp. 101–3.

an export duty of 4½ per cent on the value of all dead commodities —
to satisfy the Carlisle and other claims — permitted the island to become a royal colony.[74] The following year the Governor of the Caribbee Islands, Lord Willoughby, paid a visit to the Leeward Islands,
and the Assembly of each of the four islands agreed to the same plan
to be freed of proprietorial control.[75] It may be added that this onerous tax levy, in the words of Professor Charles M. Andrews, "was to
prove one of the greatest, if not the very greatest grievances in the
years to come. . . ."[76]

The weight of the obligation to pay the 4½-per-cent export tax is
indicated by the account of John Eckersall, Receiver-General of all
these duties for the years 1744–8, who paid into the Exchequer a
total of £50,406.10.2 for the period from March 1745 to and including March 1748,[77] or for a period of three years, which was an average annual payment of £16,802.3.8 sterling.[78] As a rule this duty was
paid by the exporter in commodities rather than in specie. For example, during the fiscal year of 1745–6 the planters of St. Christopher
paid in duties at Basse-Terre 393,014 pounds of sugar, 5,644 pounds
of cotton, 1,684¾ gallons of molasses, and 5,944 gallons of rum, with
sugar rated at twenty-two shillings per hundredweight, rum at a
price that varied from two shillings threepence to two shillings per
gallon, molasses at one shilling threepence per gallon, and cotton
at one shilling per pound.[79]

Who, then, were the beneficiaries of this export tax? In the first
place, it should be emphasized again that the chief purpose of Barbados and the Leeward Islands in granting this export tax to the
Crown was to be freed from the distasteful proprietorship of the Earl
of Carlisle and his heirs.[80] Further, the desire to be relieved of some

---

[74] See "An Act for settling an Impost on the Commodities of the Growth of this
Island," passed on September 12, 1663, Acts . . . of Barbados (London, 1764), No. 36.
This is given in full by Bryan Edwards: op. cit., I, 343–6.

[75] Sir Alan Burns: History of the British West Indies (London, 1954), p. 302.

[76] C. M. Andrews: The Colonial Period of American History (4 vols., New Haven,
1934–8), II, 268. For a chart indicating the amount of payments into the English exchequer secured by the 4½-per-cent duty covering the years 1700–66, see F. W. Pitman:
The Development of the British West Indies (New Haven, 1917), opposite p. 302.

[77] P.R.O., Pipe Office, Declared Accounts, Customs, Roll. 1263.

[78] P.R.O., Treas. 30. 11.

[79] Shelburne Papers, 45:156–86.

[80] During the Great Rebellion Carlisle leased half of the returns from his proprietary
to Lord Willoughby, and upon the death of the former, before the consummation of the
transferral of his rights to the Crown, the Earl of Kinnoul succeeded and secured for

of the burden of protection against their powerful enemies was also a motive in the voluntary laying of the tax by the assemblies of these islands.[81] However, an analysis of the disbursement of the income derived from the 4½-per-cent tax shows that the older sugar islands were being called upon to bear a substantial portion of the expense of supporting the more undeveloped or weaker parts of the Empire. For example, in 1750 the fund raised amounted to £18,662.14.11. Out of this sum £750 was paid to the assigns of George, Earl of Kinnoul, as beneficiaries of the Carlisle interest, who were entitled in perpetuity to £1,000 per annum; the Governor of Barbados received £2,000; that of the Leeward Islands, £1,200; and the Lieutenant Governors of Antigua, St. Christopher, Nevis, and Montserrat, sums amounting to either £200 or £300. The Governor of the Bahamas, the Governor of the Bermudas, and the agent for the islands of Newfoundland and Cape Breton and the Governor of the island of Jersey were also beneficiaries. To the Governor of South Carolina was assigned £800, while a certain sum was set aside to answer bills of exchange drawn against the royal exchequer by the Governor of Georgia. Finally, payments from this fund were made to Horatio Walpole, Surveyor and Auditor General of all His Majesty's revenues in America, and to Sir Thomas Robinson, late Captain General and Governor in Chief of Barbados.[82]

One final aspect of civilization in the sugar islands that was common to all and that was not without effect upon their economy was the prevalence of absenteeism, especially on the part of the great plantation-owners. It was calculated in 1774 that three fourths of the

himself and heirs a perpetual revenue. See J. A. Williamson: "The Colonies after the Restoration, 1660–1713," Cambridge History of the British Empire (8 vols., Cambridge, 1929–58+), I, 241–2, and G. L. Beer: The Old Colonial System, Part I (2 vols., New York, 1912), I, 171–92.

[81] It is of interest to note that an instruction was given to the Governors of Barbados and the Leeward Islands for "applying the duty of four-and-a-half per cent in our Caribbee Islands toward the repairing and erecting fortifications and other public uses for the safety of our said islands" and for supplementing it by public levies. See L. W. Labaree: Royal Instructions . . . , I, 407. In his comment on this instruction Governor Grenville of Barbados declared in 1752: "The Duty of 4½ per cent which appears by this Instruction to have been particularly directed to be applyed towards the repairing and erecting the Fortifications and other publick uses . . . has not for a number of years past been applied to almost any of those uses, for which it seems to have been originally granted" (ibid., II, 840–1). This comment was equally applicable to the British Leeward Islands.

[82] P.R.O., Treas. 30. 11.

children of Jamaica planters were sent to England for their education, many of whom remained there.[83] In 1740 a writer declared:
"Whenever a Person has made a Fortune, he seldom fails to transport
his Family and Effects to England." [84] Many factors leading to this
practice are obvious: the unhealthfulness of the climate, the destruc-
tiveness of hurricanes, the lack of cultural advantages, the ever-
present danger of insurrection on the part of Negro slaves, and the
low moral tone on most of the plantations were chief among them.
"Home" to most of the great planters was still England, where their
relatives lived and where their forebears had been laid to rest. How
prevalent this absenteeism was in the latter part of the eighteenth century is indicated by the statement of one traveller in Jamaica to the
effect that in one northern district of the island, out "of eighty proprietors not three are to be found at this time on the spot." [85]

But absenteeism frequently meant financial ruin. No agent, no
matter how conscientious, could be expected to take the personal
interest in a plantation that a resident owner would bestow upon it.
Indeed, the proprietor in many cases was systematically fleeced of
his profits. The author of *American Husbandry* in commenting upon
this point in 1775 stated "that greater extortioners are hardly to be
met with than West India agents, attornies and overseers." He illustrated the point by an account of a small plantation of 110 acres on
the island of St. Christopher. It was purchased for £3,200; in addition the buyer paid £2,914 for forty-seven Negroes (at an average
price of £62), £640 for the livestock, and £113 for implements and
other things. The plantation yielded annually £900 in sugar and
£234 in rum, giving a total yield of £1,134. Out of this total £343
was paid out as interest on the purchase money and £655.10 as
charges presented by the agent, including his commission. This left
the owner but £135.10, or two per cent profit on his investment.[86]
On the other hand, with good management a resident owner, the
same writer affirmed, would be able to realize 25 to 35 per cent on
the money invested.[87] Yet these financial inducements of residence

[83] Edward Long: *The History of Jamaica* (3 vols., London, 1774), I, 438.

[84] *Importance of Jamaica to Great Britain* (London, [1740]), p. 56, cited by F. W.
Pitman: *The Development of the British West Indies* (New Haven, 1917), p. 35.

[85] Daniel McKennin: *Tour through the British West Indies . . .* (London, 1804),
p. 108.

[86] *American Husbandry* (1939 edn.), pp. 446–7.

[87] *Ibid.*, p. 447.

on the sugar islands were not enough to persuade most of the great planters and their families to forego the innumerable advantages offered by living in the mother country.

ISLANDS OF CONTENTMENT

Far to the north of the Lesser Antilles and almost 600 miles to the east of the Virginia coast lie what was then called the Bermudas — a group of some 400 coral islands made up of Great Bermuda, surrounded by Watford, Boaz, Ireland, and Somerset north of the Great Sound and by St. George, Paget, Smith, St. David, Cooper, and Nonsuch in a semicircle about Castle Harbour.[88] These islands are themselves fringed with islets. Most of the smaller islands were either quite uninhabited or very sparsely so in the middle of the eighteenth century, for the majority of the people were concentrated on the main island in an area but fourteen miles long by one in width. St. George, the chief town at this period, with its state house, its handsome church, and its public library, was and still is located on the island of that name.[89]

For about 150 years the Bermudas — Bermuda, as it is now called — had been in the possession of England and were numbered among the royal colonies, although during most of the seventeenth century the archipelago had constituted a proprietary controlled by an offshoot of the Virginia Company under its charter of 1612. The first settlers had designs for making the colony a tobacco plantation, but that industry had gradually declined in importance, and the population — which in 1749 was somewhat under 10,000 and made up of about 5,290 whites and 3,980 blacks living within the limits of St. George's Parish and the eight so-called "Tribes"[90] — was engaged in the building of sloops from Bermuda cedar,[91] in whale

---

[88] For the Bermudas, see H. C. Wilkinson: *Bermuda in the Old Empire* (London, 1950); an older work, T. L. Godet's *Bermuda: its History, Geology, Climate, Products* . . . (London, 1860), is still of value. For an important contribution to the history of the island covering the revolutionary period see W. B. Kerr: *Bermuda and the American Revolution, 1760–1783* (Princeton, 1936).

[89] For a description of St. George see D. Fenning and J. Collyer: *op. cit.*, II, 680–1. "A List of Inhabitants for the Year 1749" confines the entire enumerated population to the Eight Tribes and St. George's Parish. See Shelburne Papers, 45:52–9.

[90] The names of the eight tribes were: Hamilton, Smith, Devon, Pembroke, Paget, Warwick, Southampton, and Sandys.

[91] See the "State of the Bermudas, 1749" in Governor Popple's answers to the Board of Trade, Shelburne Papers, 45:52–9. William Douglass in his *A Summary, His-*

fishing,[92] and in small farming and gardening,[93] as well as in trading with North America and the West Indies in their own ships, which numbered about ninety at this period. In other words, here was a group of islands that, unlike the British West Indies, lacked an important export staple and a plantation system to produce it which could provide steady employment for the numerous slaves — apparently originally imported at the time the islands had been envisaged as tobacco plantations. Since many of the Bermudians were seafaring people who made their livelihood by trade, they employed a good many slaves on their vessels.[94] But most Negroes could, it would appear, be profitably employed only part of the time. They therefore became idle people who lacked discipline, and, as a result, they instilled a fear of slave insurrection in their white masters and mistresses. Nevertheless, no family seemed disposed to part with its slaves, as social standing was measured largely by the number of Negroes possessed and tradition against such traffic forbad their sale. Indeed, it was said that for a Bermudian to sell a slave was a

---

torical and Political, of the British Settlements in North-America (2 vols., London, 1760 edn., I, 148) stated correctly that the cedrus Bermudiana is harder than the cedar on the North American continent and of a different species. Their sloops, while mainly of cedar, were furnished with wales, beams, and keels of oak and the masts were of New England white pine. These sloops were durable and were known as "light runners."

[92] Until 1729 the practice was established of granting licences to local Bermuda companies to engage in whaling. Under Lieutenant Governor Benjamin Bennett such licences were granted to two companies upon the basis of which the Governor was allowed one third of the catch, free of all charges. After the date above, the whale fishing of the plantations was thrown open. See Board of Trade Journals, 1741–1749, pp. 286–7.

[93] The Bermuda Council estimated in 1749 that the annual value of the commodities produced on the island was £2,000. See Shelburne Papers, 45:52–9. These were largely wooden utensils (such as plates made from palmetto), livestock, onions, cabbages, and potatoes. There was also an abundance of citrus fruits growing wild. It was hoped at this period to make the islands a centre for the production of Madeira wine. See Board of Trade Journal, 1741–1749, pp. 205–25.

[94] With respect to the manning of Bermuda vessels with Negro slaves, this seemed to be in direct conflict with the instruction given to all colonial governors which specified that three fourths of the mariners of a vessel owned by the people of a colony must be British or British colonials. Governor Popple in 1754, in writing to the Board of Trade, admitted that the "navigating of vessells with negro slaves is certainly an evasion of some part of this [the Navigation] Act, which requires that 3/5 [really 3/4] of the mariners be British or of the Plantations. . . .' In this connection he pointed out that in time of war when sailors might be needed "negro slaves cannot be pressed without security given for their value in case of their loss." He therefore asked that his instruction on this head (No. 3 of his Instructions) be so altered as to clarify the matter. Despite this fact, the instruction was not changed. See Popple's "Observations on the Instructions of Trade," L. W. Labaree: Royal Instructions . . . , II, 765–6 and 878–9.

matter of reproach equal to what the sale of a son would have been elsewhere.[95]

Although the importation of Africans to the islands had been forbidden for over a century, the natural multiplication kept increasing their numbers until from close to 4,000 blacks in 1748 there were almost 6,000 in 1761.[96] However, instead of enriching their owners, as was generally the case with slaves in the West Indies, they actually impoverished them, in view of the fact that not a little of their food as well as raiment had to be purchased from abroad.

The problem of finding for the population of the island proper productive employment at home that could enrich them came to occupy the minds of some leading Bermudians. In 1765 a society was formed with this laudable objective in mind as well as for promoting a broad and ambitious program of social service. The members engaged themselves "to form a library of all books of husbandry, in whatever language they have been written; to procure to all persons, of both sexes, an employment suitable to their dispositions; to bestow a reward on every man who has introduced into the colony any new art, or contributed to the improvement of any already known; to give a pension to every daily workman, who, having assiduously continued his labour, and maintained a good character for forty years, shall not have been able to lay up a stock sufficient to allow him to pass his latter days in quiet; and, lastly, to indemnify every inhabitant of Bermuda who shall have been oppressed, either by the minister or the magistrate." [97] Unhappily, this forward-looking proposal did not bring results.

The Bermudas were protected by their isolation, the dangerous hidden rocks about the coasts, their comparative unimportance in the eyes of England's rivals, and also by the existence of the King's castle and some seventeen small forts at strategic points. About a thousand men were enrolled in the militia. Even at this period the islands had become a resort for those living in the less salubrious plantations who were seeking to mend their broken constitutions. Here it was, in these in many respects idyllic surroundings, that Bishop Berkeley had hoped earlier in the century to set up his in-

---

[95] See H. C. Wilkinson: Bermuda in the Old Empire, Chap. 9, for an excellent treatment of slavery in the Bermudas.

[96] Ibid., p. 244.

[97] Captain Thomas Southey: Chronological History of the West Indies (3 vols., London, 1827), II, 383–4.

stitution for the training of ministers for the Anglican church in the New World.[98] As there was no possibility of acquiring great wealth, the people, in the words of a contemporary writer, "seem to content themselves with the plenty and pleasures of their country and with enjoying a safe and quiet retreat from the troubles and cares of the rest of the world." He then observed: "The Bermudas have been remarkable for the integrity, simplicity, and honesty of the people." [99] Still another writer declared that "the Inhabitants here at Bermudas live some to an hundred Years, and some upwards. . . . And when they die, Age and Weakness are the Cause, and not any Disease that attends them. . . . The Air is here very sweet and pleasant. Our Diet is but ordinary: The People are generally poor, and I observe that poor People are most healthful." [100] In harmony with this view, the seventeenth-century poet Edmund Waller, wrote of the Bermudas:

> "So sweet the air, so moderate the clime,
> None sickly lives, or dies before his time."

Well might they have been called in most respects the Islands of Contentment!

However, in the realm of provincial politics there was no extreme placidity on the islands. The Bermudas enjoyed a representative form of government in common with most of the other British colonies, and the trend of local politics was not unlike that in some of the prov-

---

[98] In 1725 there was granted a royal charter which provided for the erection of St. Paul's College in Bermuda. This was to consist of a President and nine Fellows. Berkeley, then Dean of Derry, Ireland, was appointed the first President. The college was to educate not only the youth of the English plantations but also "children of savage Americans." By this means American churches could be supplied with ministers and the Indians civilized. For the "Proposal" see *The Works of George Berkeley* . . . (ed. A. C. Fraser, 4 vols., Oxford, 1871), III, 213–31. Dr. William Douglass (*op. cit.*, I, 149–50, n.) was very critical of Berkeley's plan to erect his university college or seminary in the Bermudas for the education of the youth of "British America." He argued that the islands were difficult of access, they did not produce enough food for even the permanent inhabitants, they were too confined in area, and the colleges on the mainland were better adapted to the youth of North America. Harvard College, for example, he cited as having a good health record, where "not exceeding one or two percent per annum die."

[99] D. Fenning and J. Collyer: *op. cit.*, II, 680.

The population of the Bermudas had a reputation for turbulence in the seventeenth century. See, for example, Deputy Governor Coney to the Earl of Nottingham, October 21, 1684, *Calendar of State Papers, America and the West Indies, 1681–1685*, pp. 704–5.

[100] [John Oldmixon]: *op. cit.*, II, 454.

inces on the mainland of North America.[101] The chief political issues
in the middle of the eighteenth century had to do with questions
of the purse, especially as to the amount of the Governor's salary.
Governor William Popple, like some of his contemporaries occupying
the chief executive post in an American plantation, had come to the
New World in 1747 with high anticipations as to the settlement upon
him of an appropriate salary; [102] in endeavouring to fulfil these expectations he found himself involved in a lively contest with the representatives of the tribes. This was the situation in 1748 when he
received a decided, even if temporary, setback.

A new Assembly that was held in March of that year was made
up largely of Popple's opponents. To meet this situation he refused
the Speaker presented to him and adjourned the meeting of that body
from day to day. After his friends had seceded he thereupon recognized them as legally elected and, after the others had refused to
join them, issued writs for the election of seventeen new members.
With this complaisant majority he was able at last to secure his desired salary act. However, it was charged that, in order to do so, he
violated the 71st Article of his instructions by agreeing to permit
vessels to enter and clear the Bermudas at a place other than the
port of St. George.[103]

Protests to the home government over the Governor's proceedings
now led to a review of them, with the result that they were held to

---

101 Lieutenant Governor John Bruce Hope in writing to the Board of Trade on
March 20, 1724, has the following to say about the Bermuda Assembly: "When the
Assembly is summon'd it is impracticable to keep them longer together than three days;
else their familys wou'd starve for want of fish, and their negroes wou'd turn loose. Of the
36 members, perhaps most of them can read and write; But to my experience, there is
not six in their House that has any manner of notion of publick business." He went on
to remark that there was among these people little satisfaction in a well-regulated society, for "they find it in a maroon life: This is wandering from one uninhabited Island
to another (in their sloops), fishing for wrecks and trading with pyrat's . . ." (*Calendar
of State Papers, America and the West Indies, 1724–1725*, p. 68).

102 Before going to the Bermudas, Popple had acted as solicitor and clerk of the reports to the Board of Trade. See *Board of Trade Journal, 1741–1749*, p. 170. His appointment as Governor came in March 1745, and his commission was approved in April
1745. See *ibid.*, p. 155, and *Acts of the Privy Council, Col. Ser., 1745–1766*, p. 3. For
Popple's commission see P.R.O., C. O. 5:200, pp. 61–76; it follows closely that given to
Alured Popple in 1737.

103 For Popple's instructions of May 1, 1745, see C.O. 5:200, pp. 79–126. It appears that those willing to support Popple were from the western islands of the Bermudas and demanded as their price that he in turn would supply their need for ports of
entry. For an excellent account of Popple's struggle with the Assembly see H. C. Wilkinson: *Bermuda in the Old Empire*, pp. 203–13.

be illegal and Popple was instructed to dissolve the newly elected Assembly and to issue new writs for an election.[104] His opponents were promptly returned and, when they thought that he was bent upon maintaining the fruits of his temporary victory, proceeded to forward to the Privy Council through their London agent an address signed by over 200 inhabitants and containing some thirty-one articles of complaint.[105] These charges ranged all the way from that of the Governor — together with the naval officer, the collector of customs, and other friends — monopolizing an illegal trade with the French West Indies during the war, to acting "contrary to the express commands of Almighty God" and breaking through all rules of decency in playing cards and other games publicly in the fields in disregard of the Lord's Day.[105] In the following year, 1750, even the Governor's Council addressed a complaint to His Majesty that all the avenues of justice in the Bermudas had been closed with the removal or resignation of judges and justices of the peace; further, rates could not be collected, salaries of ministers paid, or laws passed. It was charged that the chief source of all these unhappy circumstances flowed from the "rash and precipitate proceedings of the Governor. . . ."[107]

As for Popple, he defended his conduct and charged that the com-

---

[104] Acts of the Privy Council, Col. Ser., 1745–1766, pp. 62–5.

[105] This is dated March 25, 1749; see ibid., pp. 83–4, and ibid., Unbound Papers, pp. 275–7, 315–19.

[106] Other charges were that Popple had neglected the defences of the islands; that he had refused to allow a French prize ship to be condemned by trial; that, acting as judge, he had wrongly discharged a Spanish prize; that the public accounts had never been laid before the Assembly, and that with a few members of the Council he had issued orders for money payments; that he had assumed the authority to appoint a clerk of the Assembly and had forcibly taken the minutes of the proceedings in January from the old clerk; that he had authorized the violation of an act of the Assembly prohibiting net fishing; that he had permitted the deputy collector to sell dry goods at the custom house; that, acting on his sole responsibility, he had turned out the West End pilot and had given this post to another; that he had retained his salary illegally obtained; that he had neglected to enforce an act for levying duties on foreign sailcloth; that he had since his arrival neither passed laws nor done anything for the service of the islands; that he had allowed questions of salvage to be settled by private persons; that he had heard matters only determinable legally by ordinary courts of law; and that he had refused to allow the remains of a wrecked Dutch ship to be sold for the benefit of the owners. For these charges see ibid., pp. 275–7.

[107] Ibid., pp. 293–4. So bitter were some of the Governor's opponents that it was charged against the Speaker of the Assembly, Cornelius Hinson, that the latter had openly offered a soldier on the parade field £10 if he would shoot Popple through the head. See H. C. Wilkinson: op. cit., p. 210.

plaints were owing solely to his unwillingness to suffer the Assembly to make large encroachments on the royal prerogative. These complaints, he insisted, moreover, were not articles of the Assembly, were not signed by the Speaker and the Clerk of that body, nor were they by the principal inhabitants; for most of the names were of the lower inhabitants, whose signatures were secured before the articles were definitely framed.[108] Late in 1751, doubtless feeling the insecurity of his situation, he secured a leave of absence and returned to England more effectively to defend himself and also, incidentally, to try to arrange to exchange his post for another. While there he sought to bring about certain alterations in his instructions which he claimed had been the chief sources of friction. These suggested changes were three in number. The first was to allow the Assembly to appoint its own clerk, as was the practice in Barbados and other colonies; the second, to permit this body to select a committee to act with the Governor and Council in settling the public accounts, as was also the case in Barbados; the third was to make it possible for vessels to enter and clear at the West End of the islands rather than at St. George.[109] He also set forth an elaborate reply to the charges both of the Assembly and of the Council and, all in all, successfully defended himself.[110]

While in the end the Privy Council held that the election of the Assembly clerk was an encroachment on the royal prerogative not to be permitted, it did agree in 1753 to alter the instructions so as to permit the election of an Assembly committee to aid in the disbursement of the public funds granted by the legislature and, in 1755, to appoint a public searcher for the West End.[111] However, it was only in 1756, with the Great War for the Empire in progress and with the French exhibiting alarming efficiency in its prosecution, that the Governor, having meanwhile returned to the islands, was at length successful in gaining his salary objective. "After many years struggling with a

---

[108] *Acts of the Privy Council, Col. Ser., Unbound Papers*, pp. 294–5.

[109] *Ibid.*, pp. 311–12.

[110] *Ibid.*, pp. 315–21.

[111] *Ibid.*, 1745–1766, pp. 230–1, 304–5. That Popple was a man of first-rate ability is indicated by his long and carefully argued "Observations on the Instructions Given to His Majesty's Governor of Bermuda . . ." that came before the Board of Trade in November 1754. That he made a convincing case for many alterations in them is indicated by the fact that the following year he received a revised set of instructions. For his "Observations" see L. W. Labaree: *Royal Instructions* . . . , II, 848–80; for the new set of instructions issued to him on May 2, 1755, see P.R.O., C.O. 38:9, pp. 52–144.

factious, turbulent people who have prevented hitherto Your Intentions in my favour, when your Grace gave me this Government," he wrote to Newcastle, "I have at length brought them to a better temper & to make a settlement upon me since my return hither." However, he was obliged to complain that "this Settlement indeed dos [does] not go so far back as it should, nor any wise compensate for my losses before."[112]

It should at this point be made clear that the basic differences between the Governor and the Assembly involved the issue of the extent of imperial control that might be exercised in governing the Bermudas. Popple — in the words of the leading authority on the history of these islands in the eighteenth century — "strove to maintain what he was pleased to term 'the just dependence which the colonies ought to have upon the government of the Mother Country.' . . . And in great loneliness through it all, he had upheld the authority of the Crown in peace and war, as he had taken an oath to do, and with constant thought and mercy for the governed, had carried its prerogatives to a height not hitherto attained."[113] It may be added that upon his death in 1764 there came home to the people the realization that while he had been a strong, unyielding governor he had been a just one who had the interests of the Bermudas greatly at heart.

In view of the foregoing, the impression may have been given that the Bermudians were writhing under heavy public burdens. The truth was quite the contrary. One might say that they were all but free ordinarily from direct taxation in the maintenance of the royal government. According to Governor Popple, there was only a tax on the sale of liquors. There was, it is true, also a small sum collected as rent for the use of unappropriated lands known as "the King's lands," from those occupying them. No quit-rents, however, were levied on appropriated lands, as these were held from the very beginning in free and common socage.[114] As for the support of local government, each of the Tribes paid the costs of maintaining its Anglican church and its other very simple parish activities as a mat-

---

[112] William Popple to the Duke of Newcastle, April 25, 1756, B.M., Add. Mss. 32864, folio 401; see also Popple to Newcastle, December 9, 1755, ibid., 32861, folio 251. In 1753 there was due Popple a balance amounting to £3,035.9. See Acts of the Privy Council, Col. Ser., Unbound Papers, p. 321.

[113] H. C. Wilkinson: op. cit., p. 224.

[114] See Popple's statement in 1749 to the Board of Trade's queries, Shelburne Papers, 45:52–9.

ter of course. The total revenue of the colony at this period amounted to merely some £600 sterling annually.[115]

Although the chief income of the people of the Bermudas seems to have come by profits on trade, this trade was neither large nor significant. To illustrate, British manufactures to the value of but some £12,000 were annually imported in ships from the mother country. As for the vessels belonging to the islands, these were accustomed to proceed to the northern colonies for provisions and lumber. They then either returned to the islands or proceeded southward to the southern colonies, where the cargoes were disposed of, the captains receiving either the local produce or bills of exchange of Great Britain, with which they returned home. Frequently, it appears, these ships, after taking on board supplies designated for the northern colonies, sailed instead to the Dutch Island of Curaçao or to St. Eustatius, where took place widespread evasion of the British trade laws. Governor Popple in 1749 also charged that European goods were extensively introduced into the Bermudas by ships resorting to the Virgin Islands. Anguilla, in particular, he declared, contributed to an illicit trade with St. Eustatius and Saba. "A small acknowledgement made at Anguilla will procure a clearance of Dutch Goods entered as English." But there appeared to be no way of putting an end to it effectively, he concluded, "unless the officers . . . do their duty." [116] Even so, enforcement of the laws, it was admitted, would be very difficult while vessels were suffered, although illegally, to make port in any part of the Bermudas. Further, in the disposal of the contraband goods thus obtained, it goes without saying that a proportion — perhaps a very considerable proportion — ultimately found a way into the continental colonies.

HOME OF THE OLD BUCCANEERS

Far to the southwest of the Bermudas and to the east of Florida lie the Bahamas, made up of 29 coral islands, 661 cays, and over 2,000 islets or protruding rocks — an area of 5,450 square miles, without reference to the nearby Caicos and Turks Islands, which are really a continuation of this chain. The soil, while shallow, is very fertile, varying from a black humus in the forest areas of Andros and

---

[115] Ibid.

[116] Ibid. For the case of the George and Elizabeth condemned at St. George in 1725 for the loading of French goods at Martinique, see Acts of the Privy Council, Col. Ser., Unbound Papers, pp. 141–5.

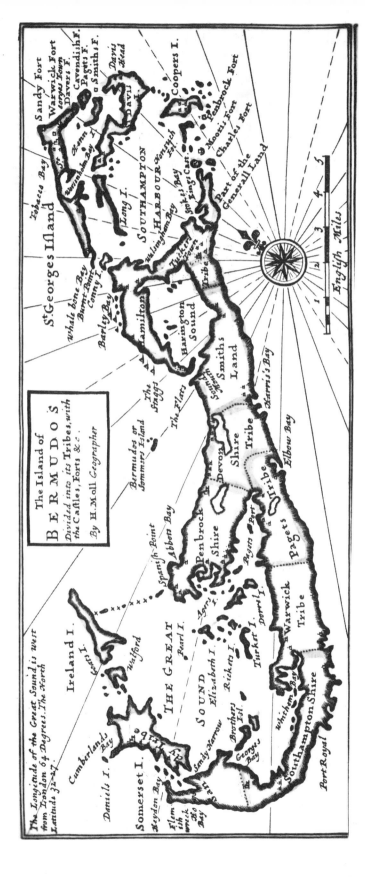

"The Island of Bermudos, Divided into its Tribes, with the Castles, Forts, etc."

(From the *Atlas Minor* by Herman Moll, 1736)

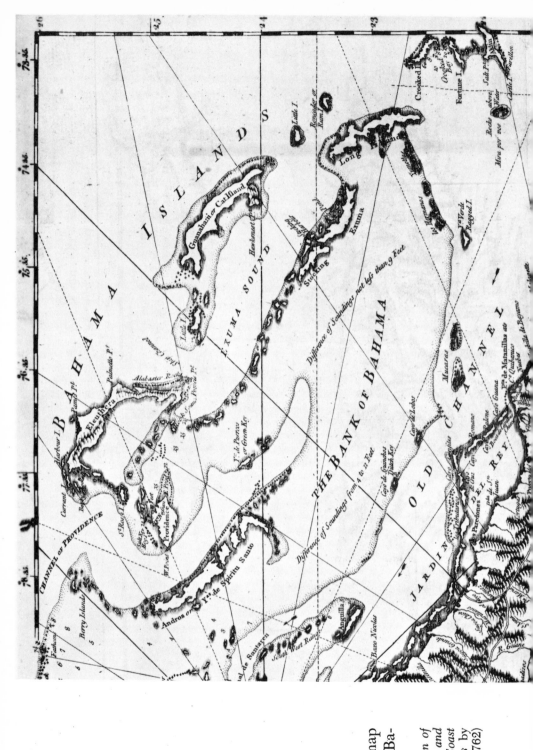

Part of the map "Cuba with the Bahama Islands."

(From *A Description of the Spanish Islands and Settlements on the Coast of the West Indies* by Thomas Jefferys, 1762) the Abacos to a reddish clay along the shore lines. On the larger islands are to be found growths of great trees — mahogany, fustic, lignum vitae, iron, and bullet. Elsewhere a larger variety of fruits and vegetables suitable to the climate can be grown.

For almost two centuries before 1750 this archipelago was the scene of wild exploits of buccaneers and pirates, although it is true that English settlers, mostly drawn from the overcrowded Bermudas, were attracted to Eleutheria (or Eleuthera) in 1646 and to New Providence in 1666[117] and that in 1670 the islands were granted to Anthony Ashley Cooper, Earl of Shaftesbury, and five other patentees of Carolina. The Proprietors experienced the greatest difficulties in contending, on the one hand, with lawlessness within these possessions, involving among other things the deportation of governors sent to rule the inhabitants, and, on the other, with the Spaniards and French, who made repeated attacks and by 1707 had apparently all but cleared the Bahamas of permanent settlers.[118] As a result, these islands again became a paradise for pirates. Thus it was not until the death of the notorious Edward Teach, called Blackbeard, in 1718 and the appointment as governor by the Crown of Captain Woodes Rogers, who arrived that year in New Providence, that the permanent settlement of the archipelago can be dated.[119]

By the middle of the eighteenth century the population of New Providence, Eleutheria, and Harbour Island numbered between 2,000 and 3,000 people.[120] According to a report sent from the islands in 1745, the number of people had much increased in that period. However, the relative unimportance of the colony's settlement may be gauged by the fact that at that date there were but 210 men reported

[117] See [John Oldmixon]: op. cit., II, 422–39, and W. H. Miller: "The Colonization of the Bahamas, 1647–1670," William and Mary Quarterly, 3rd ser., II, 33–46.

[118] See the "Petition of traders to North America and Jamaica and of the inhabitants of the Bahama Islands" of the year 1708, Acts of the Privy Council, Col. Ser., Unbound Papers, pp. 82–4; see also C. P. Lucas: A Historical Geography of the British Colonies (7 vols., Oxford, 1888–1920), II, 77–93, and particularly Sir Alan Burns: op. cit., pp. 358–62, 397–400, 425–6, 462–6.

[119] For Northey and Harcourt's opinion delivered in 1706 that, through default and neglect of the Proprietors, the Crown, in order to secure the lands and the inhabitants of the islands, could constitute a government, see "Edward Northey's Legal Opinions" (ms.), Library of Congress accessions. However, the royal interference was delayed until the year before the collapse of the proprietorial authority in South Carolina, in 1719.

[120] In 1745 Governor John Tinker gave the population of the islands, including men, women and children, both black and white, as 2,000. See Shelburne Papers, 45:153–5. According to P. H. Bruce, in his Memoirs (London, 1782), the population in 1741 was 2,300, divided about equally between whites and blacks.

as embodied in the militia of New Providence, 68 in that of Eleutheria, and 45 in that of Harbour Island. On the main island alone fortifications had been erected, with two forts, Fort Nassau and Fort Montagu, mounting 48 and 18 guns respectively.[121]

So far were the Bahamas removed from the earlier days of lawlessness that there was in operation by the middle of the century a well-established royal form of government — comparable to that of the Bermudas — of Governor, Council, and Assembly.[122] John Tinker, a capable man, occupied the chief executive post.[123] At New Providence a custom house with the proper officials for the execution of the trade laws had been established, although the means for eluding the payment of customs on dutiable articles were multitudinous.

The public finances of the Bahamas may be given succinctly. Revenues in 1751 were from the following sources: duties on imports and income on lots in the town of Nassau, £235.15; duties on exports of salt and timber, £477.3; duties on exports of Brazil wood, lignum vitae, oranges, and lemons (appropriated to the Governor's salary), £206.5; and, finally, poll taxes, £128. This provided a total revenue of £1,047.9. The charges against this fund for the ordinary expenses of government amounted to £824.19.[124]

By the middle of the eighteenth century, plantations had been established on the settled islands that, by means of slave labour, yielded sugar, pineapples, cotton, ginger, tobacco, drugs, and medicinal herbs; wood from the forests was likewise procured, such as mahogany and dye woods. The total value of these commodities was something over £7,000, which enabled the inhabitants to pay for British importations and also for their plantation provisions coming from the northern colonies.[125] Further, the ships of New Providence were accustomed to sail to Cuba and to Hispaniola, with which

121 See "Answer to the General Queries from the Board of Trade to the Governor of the Bahama Islands," July 17, 1745, Shelburne Papers, 45:153–5; Acts of the Privy Council, Col. Ser., 1745–1766, pp. 145–9; and Captain Thomas Southey: op. cit., II, 314.

122 In 1729 the House of Assembly came into existence. See Journal of the Lower House of Assembly from . . . 1729 to . . . 1786 (5 vols., Nassau, 1910–12), I, 1.

123 Tinker was appointed Governor of the Bahamas in 1740. For his commission see P.R.O., C.O. 5:198, pp. 331–43; for his instructions see P.R.O., C.O. 5:198, pp. 347–88.

124 See P.R.O., Treas. 1. 433, p. 391.

125 Governor Tinker's report in 1745, Shelburne Papers, 45:153–5. For a description in 1708 of the resources of the Bahamas see Acts of the Privy Council, Col. Ser., Unbound Papers, p. 83.

islands, at least in time of peace, there was considerable commercial intercourse. After taking all these things into account in favour of the Bahamas, it must, nevertheless, be admitted that the economic significance of the islands in no way compared, for example, to that of the Leeward Islands, although they contained a much larger area.

The inhabitants, it would appear, were disinclined to put forth any great exertion to exploit the natural resources of the islands, but rather were disposed, as in most tropical countries, to lead an easygoing life. In fact, Governor Tinker in 1749 in addressing the Assembly referred to the spirit of "Luxury and Sloth" that characterized the people of the colony.[126] It may be added that it was their good fortune to have a climate that is ideal for those of weak constitutions. Writers in the eighteenth century mentioned the fact that the tropical heats were so tempered by sea breezes that in all months of the year, even during July and August, it was possible to engage in activity throughout the day — in contrast to the West Indies. Further, the absence of swamps or marshes, it was observed, added to the healthiness of the islands. Indeed, of all the British islands in the New World, the author of *American Husbandry* pointed to the Bahamas in the 1770's as "a paradise upon earth," especially for those "whose active and variegated lives have taken off that relish for the world which once activated them; and to whom nothing appears with such charms as a prospect of a safe, easy, and agreeable retreat." [127] Moreover, during the period under consideration the islands were administered by the popular and capable Governor Tinker, upon whose death in 1758 William Shirley, another person of excellent ability, succeeded to this post. Shirley, one-time Governor of Massachusetts Bay, proved to be equally popular, and continued in office during the next decade, to be succeeded in turn by his own son.

---

[126] *Journal of the Bahamas Council* (London, 1734–53), p. 147; see also Sir Alan Burns: *op. cit.*, p. 499.

[127] *American Husbandry* (1939 edn.), p. 473. The writer contrasts the Bahamas with the Bermudas, as a place of retreat (p. 474). In the Bermudas "there is a confined society, which in the nature of things must be full of all the jars and bickerings of the world; and where the people are in too low a sphere of life to afford conversation of pleasing or satisfactory [nature] to a man of any ideas. But the Bahamas are so circumstanced that a man may live in just that degree of retirement that he likes . . . and come again into the world whenever he wishes for it."

CHAPTER IX

The Struggle for the Muscovado Markets

ALTHOUGH life in the eighteenth-century West Indies was often depicted by contemporaries as one of tropical splendour, the British colonies in 1750 shared similar hazards of earthquake and hurricane, climate and fever, war and slave rebellion, and the inadequacy of churches, schools, and presses, in a society of extremes — the wealthy aristocratic planters and the white bondsmen and Negro slaves. Perhaps even more important a similarity was the problem common to Jamaica, Barbados, and the Leeward Islands of the profitable marketing of their one great staple export, sugar.

Among the colonizing powers in America, the Portuguese first took the lead in supplying the European peoples with sugar. When at the height of their exploitation of this industry, they shipped from Brazil to Europe from 100,000 to 120,000 chests of unrefined sugar, called muscovado, which they disposed of at a price of £7 to £8 sterling per barrel.[1] The prosperity of this industry attracted the attention of the English, who introduced sugar-cane into the West Indies in the middle of the seventeenth century. The English-grown sugar then gradually supplanted that of Portuguese growth in the European markets north of Cape Finisterre. Parliament soon recognized the great potential value of this crop, and it was placed first among the enumerated articles in the Navigation Act of 1660.[2] This law provided that those specified commodities which were raised in the British plantations must be brought to the mother country before

---

[1] See Josiah Child: A New Discourse of Trade . . . (London, 1693), p. 194.
[2] 12 Chas. II, c. 18, sec. 18.

being sold abroad. Sugar was thereafter subjected to a series of imposts.

In 1661 the act of tonnage and poundage provided duties — later called the "old subsidy" — upon both dry and liquid merchandise coming into England. By it the import duty on sugar was fixed at a shilling and sixpence per hundredweight. In 1663 a 4½-per-cent export duty on dead commodities was granted first by Barbados and then by the Leeward Islands, as was made clear in the preceding chapter. The trade apparently absorbed these charges without great injury. In the first year of the reign of James II, an import duty of a farthing per pound for muscovado sugar was added, which with surcharges made the levy two shillings and fourpence per hundredweight.[3] The law provided that upon the shipment abroad of this sugar there should be a remittance of duties. However, by some oversight, refined sugar was given no such relief, which resulted in the loss of this considerable trade to the British; for the Dutch and Flemish refiners,[4] who purchased the raw sugar in England, secured not only the benefit of the remission of the duty of two shillings and fourpence, but also of other duties amounting to ninepence, which advantage allowed them to undersell the British refiners in the markets of Europe by a 12-per-cent margin.[5] This act, passed in 1685, ran for eight years, and the statement is made that it, taken together with the war which ensued with France, was so disastrous to Barbados that during the period of its enforcement over forty sugar mills were abandoned.[6] With the return of peace an attempt was made to remedy the situation in the British West Indies by dropping the tax imposed under James and by means of an act placing a duty of eight shillings per hundredweight on foreign-made molasses.[7] Nevertheless, in the face of the great financial demands caused by the European wars, sugar was again made to carry a heavy burden. In 1698, under William III, a subsidy of tonnage and poundage was granted that had the effect of raising the import duty to three shillings per

---

[3] 1 James II, c. 4; see also Sir Robert H. Schomburgk: *The History of Barbados* . . . (London, 1848), p. 299.

[4] See [G. M. Butel-Dumont]: *Histoire et Commerce des Antilles Angloises* (Paris, 1758), pp. iii–iv and 210–55.

[5] *Ibid.*

[6] *Ibid.* As Schomburgk (*op. cit.,* p. 299) points out, this heavy duty reduced the value of plantations in Barbados in view of the fact that the foreign islands had a 30-per-cent advantage over the British sugar islands.

[7] 2 William and Mary, c. 4, Par. 35.

hundredweight while conceding at the same time that the entire impost should be returned upon re-exportation provided that the sugar in question — whether raw or refined — was the product of English plantations.[8] This duty was known as the "new subsidy." Under Anne a third subsidy added sixpence per hundredweight.[9] All of this burden of taxation was designed to fall upon the English consumer by reason of the drawback features. For it is to be noticed that the last act itself gave an additional shilling per hundredweight drawback on exported refined sugar.[10] Despite these measures of relief, the sugar markets of Europe were all but lost to the English in view of the competition of their great rivals, the French. What is the explanation for this?

The French West Indies, financially a liability almost up to the end of the seventeenth century, exploited by an exclusive company, and exporting little else than ginger and indigo, had turned to sugar-production at this favourable juncture. As the result of special royal encouragement, planters on the French islands found themselves in a position to undersell those of the English West Indies, just as the latter had previously undersold the Portuguese of Brazil. The refiners of France were also able to undersell the British, as had the Dutch and Flemings done in the preceding century.[11] A Frenchman interested in the West Indies and writing in 1758 affirmed that

---

[8] 9 and 10 William III, c. 23, Par. 8 and 9.

[9] 2 and 3 Anne, c. 9, Par. 1.

[10] 2 and 3 Anne, c. 9, Par. 2.

[11] A study of the Custom House papers reveals that in 1717 a total of 754,430 hundredweight of sugar was imported into Great Britain and 290,179 re-exported; in 1727, 643,131 hundredweight was imported and 112,699 re-exported; in 1730, 1,020,770 hundredweight was imported and 167,980 re-exported; for the whole period from 1717 to 1730, 10,173,155 hundredweight was imported and 1,971,948 re-exported. In 1728 Germany took 77,960 hundredweight, but in 1731 only 19,190; on the other hand, Ireland in 1728 took 14,797 hundredweight but in 1731 took 34,885. See Custom House report, March 24, 1731, P.R.O., Treas. 64. 273.

From Christmas 1738 to Christmas 1743 there was exported for the five years a total of something over 400,100 hundredweight of sugar, or a medium of 80,000 for each year. During the fiscal year 1738–9 a total of something over 68,149 hundredweight was exported; of this 54,416 went to Ireland, only 120 to Holland, and 2,568 to Germany. In 1742–3 the total was 151,126 hundredweight, 57,242 going to Ireland, 52,721 to Holland, and 30,732 to Germany. See Custom House report, January 1744, P.R.O., Treas. 64. 273. For sugar exportations see also valuable totals prepared by F. W. Pitman in his The Development of the British West Indies, 1700–1763 (New Haven, 1917), especially Charts III, IV, V, and VI. In this connection the student should consult the thoughtful article by C. M. Andrews: "Anglo-French Rivalry, 1700–1750: The Western Phase, I," American Historical Review, XX, 539–56.

by 1740 the French were selling 80,000 hogsheads of muscovado to foreign countries, with Germany taking 30,000 and Holland another 30,000.[12]

While this trade was slipping away from the British, the exploitation of fresh lands in the West Indies was proceeding and was gradually leading to the doubling of the world output of muscovado. In the face of these circumstances the one thing that saved the sugar islands from economic ruin was the great increase in the consumption of sugar within the British Isles. In 1709 but 379,327 hundredweight of sugar was imported into England, over one fifth of which was re-exported; while in 1730 over a million hundredweight was imported — either actually produced in the British West Indies or the French production brought in illegally as if coming from those islands — of which only about 167,980 was re-exported.[13]

In view of this expansion in West India sugar-production it is not surprising that in the early 1730's the British planters found themselves facing a glutted market. The point of saturation seems to have been reached when the British consumers were unable to take care of the increase.[14] The dip in price of muscovado sugar between 1727 and 1732 is indicated by the figures of the London market, where it sold for twenty-four shillings tenpence and two farthings in 1727; in 1729 it was twenty-one shillings eightpence and two farthings; in 1730, nineteen shillings eightpence and a farthing; in 1731, seven-

---

[12] *Histoire et Commerce des Antilles Angloises*, p. 220. From 1707 to 1742, 24,445,782 hundredweight of sugar was imported into England. Of this 3,910,702 hundredweight was re-exported as raw sugar and 366,170 as refined. See "An Account of the Quantity of Sugar imported into and exported out of England from Christmas, 1707 to Christmas, 1742," Custom House, February 1, 1743, P.R.O., Treas. 64. 273. The above figures indicate that most of the sugar stayed in England to supply local needs. It is of interest to note that in the year 1752 2,147 hundredweight of sugar was imported from Holland which had previously been re-exported to that country in the form of raw sugar. Custom House report, March 28, 1753, P.R.O., Treas. 64. 274.

[13] P.R.O., Treas. 64. 273.

[14] This excess of sugar is indicated by the fall in the price of clayed sugar, which sold in 1729 at the rate of thirty-nine shillings and threepence per hundredweight as against thirty-one shillings for the same quantity in 1732. Muscovado sold for twenty-four shillings tenpence and two farthings in 1728 as against seventeen shillings tenpence for a similar quantity in 1732. See Custom House report, April 4, 1753, P.R.O., Treas. 64. 274; see also John Ashley: *Memoirs and Considerations Concerning the Trade and Revenues of the British Colonies in America* (London, 1743), pp. 6–7. Ashley had been Deputy Surveyor and Auditor-General of all His Majesty's Revenues arising in Barbados and the Leeward Islands. He declared, on the other hand, that between 1733 and 1737 the British sugar islands made from 15,000 to 18,000 hogsheads less than in preceding years.

teen shillings and tenpence; and in 1732, but sixteen shillings elevenpence and a farthing.[15]

The sugar interests now gave close attention to the great trade that had gradually developed between the French West Indies and the British northern plantations. By prohibiting this trade (which was giving an outlet, it was estimated, for at least 20,000 hogsheads of French molasses together with substantial quantities of sugar and rum), it was thought that the prosperity of the British islands might be restored. As a recent writer has made clear, the sugar-planters felt that their once strong economic position had seriously deteriorated. This had come about in part by reason of the illegal introduction of a good deal of foreign sugar into Great Britain and Ireland which, as indicated previously, was passing under guise of being the product of the British West Indies, and especially as a result of the illicit commerce mentioned above which had developed by the third decade of the eighteenth century between the French West Indies and the British plantations in North America — and, to a lesser extent, Ireland. Further, the planters were convinced that by means of combinations entered into by English sugar-refiners and grocers the price paid for their raw sugar had been kept far too low.[16]

While the problem of the illegal introduction of foreign sugar into the British West Indies for re-export to England was largely dealt with by local agencies in the island, backed by public opinion,[17] that of the direct trade between the foreign West Indies and the North American colonies and also Ireland was a matter that appeared to require the interposition of the British government. In 1730 a petition from Barbados to the King in Council set forth the disadvantages that the planters and traders there laboured under with "the French supplying the Northern Colonys, and the Kingdom of Ireland with Sugar, Rum and Molasses." [18] This petition was later supported by one from the merchants of Liverpool.[19] However, in March of the following year the complainants were premitted to withdraw their petition when they indicated that they had now

---

[15] For a table covering the sale of muscovado sugar in London between the years 1727 and 1743 see F. W. Pitman: op. cit., p. 134.

[16] See R. B. Sheridan: "The Molasses Act and the Market Strategy of the British Sugar Planters," Journal of Economic History, XVII, 62–83.

[17] Ibid.

[18] Acts of the Privy Council, Col. Ser., 1720–1745, 297–9, and Calendar of State Papers, Colonial Series, America and the West Indies, 1730, pp. 166–8.

[19] Ibid.

made application to Parliament for relief.[20] This application — in the form of a combined petition from merchants trading to the British West Indies, the planters of these islands, and other interested parties — came before the House of Commons on February 23. In it the contention was set forth that, in violation of a treaty with France of the year 1686 and of the laws of trade, "divers of his Majesty's subjects residing within his dominions in America" carried on a trade with the foreign sugar islands which, as well as being injurious to the people of Great Britain, had "greatly impoverished the British Sugar-Colonies."[21]

The issue now raised respecting the commercial relations between the continental colonies and the foreign West Indies was to become a matter of real significance in the history of the Old British Empire. Indeed, as early as 1721 the importance to the mother country of the continental colonies lying north of Maryland as a mart for the sale of goods was emphasized by the fact that they purchased from Great Britain commodities valued at some £200,000 sterling over and above the value of their exports to the British Isles — something that, under given conditions, could only be done in terms of a profitable trade with the foreign sugar islands.[22]

The planter interest in and out of Parliament took the position that the British sugar industry could be saved only by cutting off all

---

[20] Ibid.

[21] *Cobbett's Parliamentary History* (London, 1811), VIII, 856–7. It may be noted that Ireland was not mentioned in the above memorial. In fact on January 28, 1731, a petition was presented to the Privy Council from the merchants of Dublin against what they called "the misrepresentations in the petition of Barbados" concerning an alleged trade between Ireland and the foreign West Indies. See *Acts of the Privy Council, Col. Ser.*, 1720–1745, 299. This seems to have helped to clear the atmosphere as far as Ireland was concerned. At least on March 10 the plantation merchants agreed that there could be no objections to granting to Ireland the privilege of importing from the British plantations all commodities not on the enumerated list and on April 8 leave was granted by an order in council for those who had petitioned against trade between Ireland and the foreign sugar islands to withdraw their petitions. See *Board of Trade Journal*, 1728–1734, pp. 184 and 227.

[22] Board of Trade representation to the King in Council, September 8, 1721, *New York Colonial Documents* (ed. E. B. O'Callaghan, 15 vols., Albany, 1853–87), V, 614. The total annual value of the British exports to the American continent was placed at £500,000, with the colonies south of Pennsylvania balancing their imports from Great Britain with their exports. The view expressed above should be weighed in light of a contrary view enunciated by some English mercantilists: that the only value of the northern continental colonies consisted in their ability to supply the sugar colonies with certain staples England could not furnish. See C. M. Andrews: "Anglo-French Commercial Rivalry, 1700–1750," *American Historical Review*, XX, 553–4.

trade between the continental colonies and the foreign West Indies. In fact, this very thing had been proposed as early as 1714 in a bill presented to the House of Commons, but without result.[23] In April 1731 a bill to that effect moved through the House of Commons but, fortunately, failed of enactment in the House of Lords. Another bill somewhat less extreme in form — in that it permitted American main- land exports to the foreign West Indies while forbidding imports from them — was introduced in the lower house early the following year and in March was passed by 110 votes to 37 votes against. But even this bill was permitted to die in the House of Lords without action upon it — doubtless as much too drastic in the limitations that it placed upon North American commercial activities.[24]

One might have thought, in view of the later position taken by the colonial assemblies as to the limitation of the powers of Parlia- ment, that such bills as this one and its predecessor would have been strongly protested on constitutional grounds. In the words of one student of this period: "It was attacked as unwise and unjust, it was described as 'a grievous blow' . . . and an effort to make the north- ern colonies 'slaves and bondsmen' of the sugar islands, but the *right* of Parliament to enact the law was nowhere questioned." [25] The same writer adds the following statement: "In brief, until someone proves the contrary, our conclusion must be that the colonies [in 1732] did not question the authority of Parliament to pass an act that would have crushed the major part of their commerce and proved more onerous than a hundred Stamp Acts." [26]

But the supporters of the interest of the British sugar islands were not through. If trade between the continental colonies and the for- eign West Indies could not be prohibited, trade between the latter and Ireland could be; further, a revenue measure could be devised that would wipe out the advantages that the planters of the French

---

[23] For a careful survey of the background of the so-called Molasses Act of 1733 see A. B. Southwick: "The Molasses Act — Source of Precedents," *William and Mary Quarterly*, 3rd ser., VIII, 389–405.

[24] *Ibid.*, VIII, 395–8. For the debate upon the bill of 1732 see *Parliamentary His- tory*, VIII, 918–21, 992–1002; see also *Proceedings and Debates of the British Parlia- ments Respecting North America* [to 1754] (ed. L. F. Stock, 5 vols., Washington, 1924– 41+), IV, 113–53. A telling argument from the standpoint of the British manufacturers and exporters opposed to the above bill was that British exports to North America amounted in value to £5,165,936 between the years 1714 and 1726.

[25] A. B. Southwick: op. cit., *William and Mary Quarterly*, 3rd ser., VIII, 398.

[26] *Ibid.*, VIII, 399.

islands enjoyed in the North American markets and thus help to revive the prosperity of Barbados, the Leeward Islands, and Jamaica. This was accomplished in 1733 by superimposing a fiscal measure upon one that was regulatory in nature under the title "An Act for the better securing and encouraging the trade of his Majesty's Sugar Colonies in America." [27] Under the terms of this bill an import duty into the colonies of foreign-produced rum would be ninepence a gallon, the same quantity of molasses would be sixpence, and a hundredweight of sugar would be five shillings.

When the London agent of Rhode Island, Richard Partridge, became aware that such a bill was being promoted he wrote to the Governor of this colony early in 1733 that he would vigorously oppose it. His position, simply stated, was that "if such a Law takes place, . . . it will be rather worse in the consequence of it than the Bill of prohibition of last year, because of the levying a Subsidy upon a Free People without their Knowledge [and] agst their consent, who have the libertys and Immunitys granted them [of] Natural born Subjects. . . ." [28]

That he was correct in his view that Parliament regarded this bill technically as primarily a money bill and only secondarily as a regulatory measure became evident when his petition against it came before the House of Commons on March 8, 1732/3. Unlike the two earlier bills designed to prohibit all trade between the British colonies and those of foreign powers, in connection with which large numbers of petitions were received and considered, this petition was rejected upon the ground that it was directed against a money bill. In this connection the clinching argument against receiving the petition seems to have been given by a Thomas Winnington, a member representing the borough of Droitwich in Worcestershire. Among other things the petition declared that should the bill pass into law

---

[27] 6 Geo. II, c. 13; *Statutes at Large* (Eyre and Strahan), V, 616–19. See also the recent article by R. B. Sheridan: "The Molasses Act and the Market Strategy of the British Sugar Planters," cited above, and that by Dame Lillian M. Penson: "The London West India Interest in the Eighteenth Century," *English Historical Review*, XXXVI, 378–9.

[28] Partridge to Governor Wanton, 1 mo. the 3. 1732 (that is, January 3, 1732/3), *Correspondence of the Colonial Governors of Rhode Island, 1723–1775* (ed. G. S. Kimball, 2 vols., New York, 1902), I, 34. Partridge, viewing the bill as primarily a revenue measure, went on to argue that if "a British Parliam^t imposes a duty on the Kings Subjects abroad, who have no Representatives in the State here, they may from 4/ advance to 20/— to £100 . . . which is an Infringm^t on Liberty and Property and as I apprehend a violation of the Right of the Subject."

it would be "highly prejudicial to their [the Rhode Island] charter." In reply Winnington said:

> "I hope, Sir, they have no charter which debars this House from taxing them as well as any other subject of this nation; I am sure they can have no such charter. . . ." [29]

It should be added that the Molasses Act by a clause definitely excluded Ireland from the privileges of importing foreign-produced sugar, molasses, and rum and also provided that all such British West Indies products introduced into the country must be laden in Great Britain.[30]

The Molasses Act, contrary to expectations, accomplished little for the sugar-planters. What relief they received came rather in a fluctuating rise in price on the London market for muscovado from a low of 16 shillings and 11½ pence per hundredweight in 1733 up to as high as 42 shillings and 9½ pence in 1747, with a drop to 27 shillings and 9½ pence in 1750.[31] As for the North American merchants and shippers, they circumvented the Act. The planters thereupon fell back upon a proposal which had been urged years before — that of

---

[29] Parliamentary History, VIII, 1262.

[30] 6 Geo. II, c. 13, sec. 4. Ireland, it would appear, had been supplied with considerable quantities of French sugar and also rum by New England ships. See The Importance of the Sugar Plantations in America . . . (London, 1731), pp. 39–40; see also F. W. Pitman: The Development of the British West Indies, Chap. 11, for an excellent treatment of the movement that led to the passage of the Molasses Act.

[31] See ibid., pp. 134 and 186 for tables of sugar prices.

The late Professor Richard Pares, in an article entitled "The London Sugar Market, 1740–1769" that appeared in the December 1956 Economic History Review (2nd ser., IX, 254–70), makes some interesting observations based on a study of the operations of one of the leading London sugar commission firms covering the above years. The total supply of sugar in the London market during those twenty-nine years appears to have doubled, with average imports during the years of the earlier period running at 38,725 tons and during those of the later period some 70,320 tons. Almost nine tenths of all those imports were sold either to the grocers, to be distributed for sale to consumers, or to the refiners. The chief export market for the remainder was, as a rule, Ireland. The quality of the sugar received from the British West Indies differed from island to island, and also from year to year. The brown sugar of Barbados was not desired by refiners but gladly purchased by grocers; the sugars of St. Christopher were rated as fine; those of Antigua were inferior, as a rule, to those of the two islands previously mentioned, while those of Jamaica, at least during the earlier period examined, were classified as "low brown sugars" and as "weak in quality." Yet after 1763 some of the best sugar came from that island. Again, much of the sugar of Barbados came as clayed sugar — a step in the refining process secured by putting the muscovado in a large earthenware cone and covering it with wet clay — which commanded generally much higher prices and was less in bulk.

allowing a direct trade in muscovado sugar with Europe, by means of which these markets might, it was hoped, be won back again. If this could be done, the misdeeds of the northern colonies, it may have been felt, might be ignored. As a result of the renewed agitation, the Act of 1739 was passed which granted the request of the sugar islands with important restrictions.[32] In other words, licence was given to carry British West India sugar direct to European ports during a period of five years, although ships bound for points north of Cape Finisterre were expected to touch at an English port; further, it was provided that only ships built in Great Britain might participate in this trade and that the necessary papers must be secured in the mother country by those sailing to the West Indies for the proposed cargo; and, finally, that within eight months all ships engaged in this trade must return to Great Britain with the cargoes resulting from this commerce.[33] Still the expectations of the planters were not realized. In 1742 the privilege of direct importation of sugar into Europe was further extended to include all British ships;[34] and in that same year, to diminish in England the consumption of French brandy and promote that of British colonial rum, it was permitted to land the latter article in Great Britain and warehouse it for six months before paying the import duty.[35]

One thing that added to the confusion of the planters, it should be made clear, was the violent fluctuation in the price of sugar during this period. For example, it appears from the data supplied by John Ashley, late Deputy Surveyor and Auditor-General of all His Majesty's Revenues arising in Barbados, who prepared a memoir in 1743, that during the previous three or four years this commodity sold at a good price, owing to the fact that the amount imported into

---

[32] 12 Geo. II, c. 30.

[33] The licences granted under the terms of the Act of 1739 were to be issued by the Commissioners of Customs at London and at Edinburgh. All vessels used in this direct trade of less than one hundred tons were under a security of £1,000, and those of greater tonnage were under one of £2,000 for the faithful observance of this act. Masters of these ships were forbidden to take on board any of the other enumerated articles, except as a necessary provision for the voyage. A true manifest of the cargo with an endorsed certificate was to be delivered to the collector of the British port where the ship touched before proceeding to the Continent. *Ibid.*

[34] 15 Geo. II, c. 33, Par. 5.

[35] 15 Geo. II, c. 25. As a result of this encouragement the following quantities of rum entered England during the decade 1742–1751: in 1742, 473,490 gallons; in 1748, 627,283 gallons; in 1750, 808,798 gallons; in 1751, 713,684 gallons. See "An Account of the Quantities of rum Imported into England from the Sugar Colonies in Ten Years ending Xmas. 1751," Custom House, March 24, 1753, P.R.O., Treas. 64. 274.

Europe fell short of the general demand, not only because of the increased consumption of it in Russia and other parts, but on account of the decline in sugar-production in both the British and foreign West Indies as a result of the previous low prices.[36] In 1746 the Act of 1739, about to expire, was continued, permitting direct exportation to Europe.[37] These concessions represent perhaps the high-water mark in the influence that the great sugar-planting interests had upon the imperial government in the eighteenth century.

All this legislation, however, did little to weaken the force of the competition of the French sugar islands.[38] While the War of the Austrian Succession was dividing Europe, the English, it is true, enjoyed the control of markets largely closed to the French, but with the return of peace in 1748 the hope of retaining them faded away in the face of formidable obstacles.

What were those obstacles that had to be overcome in order to restore to the British West Indies their former prosperity? Malachy Postlethwayt analysed some of them in his *Considerations on the Revival of the Royal-British Asiento*, published in 1749.[39] In this connection he refers to "An Account of the Bounties, Exemptions, Privileges, and Encouragements, given by the French to the African Company," presented by the French Council of Trade to the Royal Council of Commerce, which makes clear, according to his calculations, that at this period the value of these benefits amounted to some £50,000 sterling. As a result of this, he declared that the French

---

[36] See Ashley's *Memoirs* . . . , *op. cit.*, pp. 6–7.

[37] 19 Geo. II, c. 23.

[38] In 1742 the French produced in Martinique, Guadeloupe, and other lesser islands of the West Indies 622,500 hundredweight of sugar and in French Santo Domingo or Hispaniola 848,000 hundredweight. That same year the British islands produced a total of 65,950 hogsheads or 791,400 hundredweight. In other words, the French produced 679,000 hundredweight in excess of their rivals. See David Macpherson: *Annals of Commerce* (4 vols., London, 1805), III, 262–5. In this connection it should be pointed out that Jamaica had increased the amount of her sugar exportations to England from 289,069 hundredweight in 1732 to 409,739 in 1750; in 1742, for example, this island sent 341,048 hundredweight. Barbados, in contrast, sent in 1728 238,664 hundredweight and but 88,018 in 1750. See Custom House reports of March 10 and 24, 1753, P.R.O., Treas. 64. 274. It may be pointed out again, as was done in an earlier footnote, that much of the Barbados sugar was clayed and sold at a higher price level.

[39] Postlethwayt enlarges upon the above theme in his *Britain's Commercial Interest Explained and Improved* (2 vols., London, 1757, II, 1–156) in showing how as the result of royal decrees and other measures the French islands had been placed in a favoured position.

African Company was able not only to outbid the Royal African Company in the purchase of the better types of blacks on the Guinea Coast but also to sell them to the French West India planters for less than the English planters had to pay.[40] Further to encourage their sugar-planters the French government, he pointed out, had established the practice of giving the more industrious credit for the purchase of Negroes and other plantation equipment and even lands were presented without charge to poor but ambitious people, who were also aided out of the public treasury in case of hurricanes and other unavoidable misfortunes. "Can it be any great marvel, therefore, that the French should stock their Plantations very cheaply and plentifully with their labourers, while our Planters, paying a most exorbitant Price for 'em, can't have that Plenty, and consequently can't afford their Plantation-Produce so cheap as the French, nor can they maintain the Negroes they have so cheap as they do from their greater Plenty of Labour?" Owing to these advantages, he asserted, the French were producing more than double the value of the sugar, indigo, cotton, coffee, and ginger raised by the English, "who before this time abundantly exceeded the French in these Branches."

Moreover, as was suggested by Josiah Tucker, writing in 1748 on the superior situation of their rivals,

> "the French enjoy a decisive advantage in the fertility of their islands . . . because our Leeward Islands are worn out, being originally of no Depth of Soil, and the ground more upon a Level, so more subject to be burnt up; whereas their Islands are still very good; the ground is rich, the soil is deep; And they have high Hills in Martinico, with Water and Shade; by which means Canes of 30 Years planting are still good." [41]

This, he pointed out, was in contrast to the British practice of replanting after three to five crops. Again, the French sugar-planter,

---

[40] The author of *Considerations on the Present Peace* . . . (London, 1763), while admitting that the British had carried more Negroes to their own plantations than had the French to theirs, insisted that from 1729 to 1738 the French had sent from the Gold Coast, Popo, and Whydah 15,000 or 17,000 yearly, as against 4,000 sent from these regions by the British, "which is the truest reason that can be assigned for the prosperity of the French colonies, and the main spring of the great increase of their product." These hardy, valuable Negroes the French employed as field labourers, sugar-boilers, distillers, coopers, millwrights, carpenters, masons, and smiths. See Elizabeth Donnan: *Documents Illustrative of the History of the Slave Trade to America* (4 vols., Washington, 1930–5), II, 515–16.

[41] *A Brief Essay on the Advantages and Disadvantages which Respectively attend France and Great Britain* . . . (2d. edn., London, 1749), p. 11.

free from vexatious restrictions, could charter a ship coming to the French islands with commodities from Mississippi, Canada, or Cape Breton to convey his muscovado to Europe, while his British competitor was constrained with the complicated arrangements regarding the license papers — a handicap that, according to William Beckford, a leading West India sugar-planter, was fatal, as it meant an added ten or eleven per cent on the value of the whole cargo to bring about a direct shipment to Europe. Beckford, in fact, asserted in the House of Commons in 1748 that "no English merchant or planter can pretend to send any of our sugars to a foreign market, if this restriction is continued. . . ." [42] He further pointed out the hopelessness of the English sugar-refiner in attempting to compete with the finished French product in the markets of the world with the new tax of twelvepence on the pound sterling on sugar provided for in the general bill of poundage then before Parliament and which ultimately passed into law.[43] Five hundred pounds of the best muscovado sugar, he declared, would make not above one hundred pounds of double refined; on the latter when exported there was a drawback of but three shillings on the hundredweight, while on the sugar out of which it was made, an import duty of seven shillings and sixpence would have to be paid. To sell this sugar in the open market with peace restored — in the face of foreign competition under these conditions — could not be expected. The Frenchman Plumard de Dangeul, writing in 1752, summarizes the situation succinctly: "Witness the price of the English sugars, higher than those of France 20, 30 and sometimes from 40 to 70 per Cent. quality for quality." [44] His assertions are supported by those embodied in a petition prepared by the "Sugar Refiners, Grocers, and other Dealers in Sugar," which declared that since 1749 the sugar-planters had received a much higher price for their muscovado than they did for many years before the commencement of the late war and that the foreign markets were supplied with sugar from the French islands "at less than half the Price it is here sold for, exclusive of all Duties paid here; and

---

[42] Parliamentary History, XIV, 193–5. See also a recent brief but excellent analysis of various factors that permitted the French sugar-planters to undersell their British competitors by W. E. Gordon: "Imperial Policy Decisions in the Economic History of Jamaica, 1664–1934," Social and Economic Studies, VI, 3; see also L. J. Ragatz: The Fall of the Planter Class in the British Caribbean, 1763–1833 (New York, 1928), pp. 3–4.
[43] 21 Geo. II, c. 2, par. 7.
[44] Remarks on the Advantages and Disadvantages of France and Great Britain (London, 1754), p. 4.

the Price of Sugars at the British Sugar-Colonies is more than double the Price of what it is at the French Sugar-Colonies." [45]

After the treaty of Aix-la-Chapelle there was a revival on the part of the sugar-planters of their former complaints. In justice to them it should be pointed out that, in the words of Governor Edward Trelawny of Jamaica, "They certainly had prodigeous losses by the sudden fall of sugar upon the Preliminaries being signed, and the additional tax being laid just at the same time." [46] They had won no markets back through the privilege of direct trade. In practice it had proved so complicated, especially with the requirement that the licence papers should be secured in Great Britain by exporters, that few ships ever left the sugar islands for European ports. Even Barbados, most favourably situated of all the islands for the development of a direct Mediterranean trade, hardly availed itself of the opportunity. According to Governor Henry Grenville, writing to the Board of Trade in 1748, "not above 3 or 4 Vessels were even loaded here for the Streights and none at all to any Foreign Port but to the northward of Cape Finistre." [47]

The British sugar interests, though still powerful and aggressive, were gradually losing ground in the face of what seemed great discouragements and were prepared to demand still further protection against a type of competition on the part of the French in both the Old World and the New World that they could not meet, as Beckford had predicted. In 1750 John Sharpe, London agent for Jamaica and Barbados, James Douglas, agent for St. Christopher, and Henry Wilmot, agent for Montserrat, signed a memorial which bore also the names of fifty-six planters and merchants who either lived in England or happened to be there at the time. This was placed in the hands of the Board of Trade by Sharpe on October 18. [48]

The memorialists went back to the arguments of the early 1730's and saw in that vast trade between the northern colonies and the

[45] For the text of this petition see William Maitland: *The History and Survey of London* (2 vols., London, 1756), I, 701–2.

[46] Trelawny to the Board of Trade, June 8, 1749, P.R.O., C.O. 137:25, pp. 81–4.

[47] Henry Grenville to the Board of Trade, February 7, 1748, Shelburne Papers, 45:37–51, Clements Library.
According to a report issued by the British Customs Commissioners, only forty-eight licences had been granted to carry sugar to the south of Cape Finisterre and of these but five had actually been used. See "An Account of the Number of British Ships laden with Sugars and the Quantity of Sugars exported from the British Sugar Islands to any Port in Europe south of Cape Finistre since 1739," March 24, 1753, P.R.O., Treas. 64. 274.

[48] P.R.O., C.O. 323:13, O. 59–60.

French West Indies — a trade that had continued almost unabated in spite of legal requirements of compensatory duties on foreign molasses, sugar, and rum that were systematically eluded — the source of the economic crisis facing the planters of the British West Indies. In pointing out the disastrous effects of this contraband commerce in foreign sugars and molasses they placed the inhabitants of Rhode Island under especially heavy indictment as the ringleaders, while including those of the other northern colonies,

> "who forgetting all ties of Duty to his Majesty, the Interest of their Mother Country and the reverence due to its Laws, have (as though they thought themselves independent on it) begun since the Peace [of Aix-la-Chapelle] to revive a trade (which they had but too successfully carried on before the war). . . ." [49]

---

[49] The following letter written by Governor Knowles of Jamaica is so very illuminating as to the means taken by North American merchants to defeat the Molasses Act that it is here presented in full, involving as it does some of the leading Philadelphia families:

"St. Iago de la Vega, 16 Septem.br 1752.

"A Master of a Trading Vessel belonging to Philadelphia applying to be cleared out and declaring that he was to Sail in Ballast was asked why he did not take the Commoditys of the Island in return for his Cargo, to which he answered that they would by no means answer the Market at Philadelphia and that he was then obliged to leave a considerable Sum behind him to be remitted in Specie. And he further observed that Sugar, Rum, and Molasses were Cheaper at Philadelphia when he Sailed from thence than now at this Market, and on his being Questioned how that could happen, he frankly declared that a Company of Merchants in Philadelphia who carried on a very considerable Trade to Léogan [Léogane, Santo Domingo] and Statia [St. Eustatius] always undersold the Traders who imported the same Commodities from the English Sugar Colonies and that there was a general complaint amongst the Traders at Philadelphia of the Clandestine Trade carried on by a very opulent Merchant there, in Company with a Person in the Customs and others, which put it out of their Power to take the produce of the English Sugar Colonies in Exchange for their Commodities. He also said that the general Report was, that Mr. William Allen and Company were the people who carried on that Trade, and that Mr. Abraham Taylor, the Collector, was one of the Company, and that it was notorious that their Agent always undersold every other Dealer in Sugar, Rum, and Molasses, so that in a short time that Trade must be entirely Engrossed by them. And that it is generally believed that one William Humphrys was employed by them to transact those affairs. He likewise declared that Molasses might be purchased at Leogan for 3 Dollars per Cask containing about 60 Gallon which is about 3½d per Gallon and that the Price of Molasses at Philadelphia was at 18d [.] From whence it is observable that the Consumer is not supplyed at any considerable Rate Cheaper by those clandestine than by fair Traders; they only acquire thereby to themselves an exorbitant gain and usurp a power of Commanding the Market to the prejudice of the fair Trader, and cause a drain of Money from the Sugar Islands to lay it out among and enrich our Rivals in Trade and Commerce" (Charles Knowles to the Board of Trade, September 16, 1752, P.R.O., C.O. 137:25, H. 112).

The French, the memorial asserted, had already settled a correspondence in Rhode Island, established factors there, and bought and provided vessels destined to carry on this traffic in sugar, rum, and molasses between Hispaniola and that colony. For this "is a Traffick not taken up casually or by chance but the result of a well-weighted and concerted Plan formed or at least approved by the Court of France (as may reasonably be collected from the King's Instructions to his Governors in the Sugar Islands and their conduct in consequence thereof). . . ." The vital importance of keeping at all hazards French rum and molasses out of the British colonial markets was especially urged in the memorial. For it was obvious that the French planters — forbidden to sell these two commodities in France through the influence of the French brandy interests — were dependent upon American continental markets for the successful operation of their staple industry.[50] In this connection it was pointed out that the sale of French sugar alone could not bring a profit to the growers, who also depended on the advantageous disposal of the molasses. By the process of exclusion of the latter from the British possessions, it would be possible, so the British planters reasoned, "to damp the growth of sugar in the French Islands and . . . form a means of enabling the English to beat them out of all the foreign markets in Europe and confine them to their own consumption." [51]

This memorial led to a series of public hearings by the Board of Trade, at which testimony was taken which tended to confirm strongly the charges of widespread spiriting of foreign rum and molasses under cover of British clearances on the part of North American skippers. However, when Sharpe, at the behest of the sugar interests, laid before the Board the proposal that Parliament should be called upon to forbid all intercourse between the northern colonies and the French islands, a strong protest was naturally heard from the London agents of the northern colonies and even from some

[50] It was asserted in 1753 that there were 200 sloops, brigs, and schooners of from 30 to 100 tons burden employed in this trade from the northern colonies. See Board of Trade to the House of Commons, February 22, 1753, Library of Congress accessions, No. 2413. For the systematic violation of the terms of the Molasses Act of 1733 by Rhode Island shipmasters see J. B. Hedges: *The Browns of Providence Plantations: Colonial Years* (Cambridge, Mass., 1952), p. 43.

[51] "Memorial of the Sugar Planters, Merchants and others . . . relating to the illicit Trade carried on from the Northern Colonies to the ffrench and other fforeign Sugar Coloneys," P.R.O., C.O. 324:55–6.

of the London merchants. One of them, John Tomlinson, declared that he would consider the contrivers of this proposal the greatest enemies of the sugar colonies; he further asserted that the explanation for the failure of the New England traders to secure British molasses and rum in exchange for their lumber and other supplies was that, although these commodities were desired, the British sugar-planters would not part "with a drop" on account of the great local production of rum.[52]

The above assertion was denied. John Ashley, writing in 1743, declared:

> "I have heard it objected that Jamaica and all the British Carribbee Islands cannot make Rum and Molasses sufficient to answer the necessary Demands of those Northern provinces and that they cannot take off their surplus of Horses, Lumber, and other products. But certain it is, that there is Land enough in all these islands with proper Encouragement, to raise as much Sugar, Rum, and Molasses as will answer the Demands of all Europe and America." [53]

In referring to the fact that, during the preceding seventeen years, of the 2,500 vessels to clear for northern ports from Jamaica almost one third had gone away in ballast and that most of the remainder carried but small amounts of commodities of the island [54] for the express purpose of taking on cargoes at Hispaniola, the members of the Jamaica Assembly asserted in 1752 in an address to the King that shipmasters "might have been furnished here with a sufficient quantity of these commodities to the full amount of their cargoes. . . . This trade," they further affirmed, "hath greatly Discouraged the improvement of sugar works and Retarded and Obstructed the further settling of this Island and hath been a principal means of the Surprising Encrease of the French settlements and must in the end Ruin your Majesty's Sugar Colonies and Translate the Sugar Trade to the French." In this connection they pointed to the fact that, to secure the required lumber, pitch, tar, and other necessaries from the

---

[52] See Board of Trade Journal, 1749–1753, pp. 138–9. Tomlinson had been acting as the agent for New Hampshire, but appeared in his capacity as a sugar merchant. See G. M. Ostrander: "The Colonial Molasses Trade" Agricultural History, XXX, 77–84.

[53] John Ashley: Memoirs . . . , pp. 72–3.

[54] Governor Knowles asserted in 1752, in writing to the Board of Trade, that one half of those ships that did not leave in ballast took on only from one to five hogsheads of sugar or molasses. See P.R.O., C.O. 137:25, pp. 271–80.

northern colonies, the island was annually drained each year of some £70,000.[55]

The Jamaica planter interests at this juncture favoured a parliamentary statute that would not only prohibit all intercourse between the northern colonies and the French islands but would also deprive the Americans of all excuse for refusing to take on British West Indies commodities to the extent of their needs. The Assembly insisted that the latter end could be accomplished by inserting a clause dropping the duty of a shilling and sixpence per hundredweight on all muscovado sugar exported from the island to the northern colonies, which had been provided for by Parliament in 1672 by "An Act for the encouragement of the Greenland and Eastland trade and for better securing the Plantation trade" (25 Chas. II, c. 7, Par. 2). "We are the more encouraged in hoping," they declared, "that your subjects may be eased of that Duty as the revenue arising thereby to your Majesty amounts to a very small and inconsiderable Sum when compared with the Immense Wealth it hath been the chief cause of Draining from your Subjects and putting into the purse of the Subjects of the French King."[56] Governor Knowles reinforced this recommendation by stating that in 1751 there were imported from the northern colonies commodities valued at £112,825, while the highest value of the produce sent by Jamaica in any year to North America amounted to no more than £29,222.[57]

Doubtless realizing, as the result of the discussion that took place before the Board of Trade, the hopelessness of securing the approval of the Lords Commissioners to legislation so drastic and manifestly prejudicial to the northern plantations as the absolute prohibition of commerce between them and the French sugar islands, planter interests had already submitted in January 1751 certain other definite proposals. These, if carried into effect, while allowing the sale of commodities of the northern plantations to the French islands by northern traders, would prohibit by act of Parliament the ships of the northern colonies from receiving under any pretext whatsoever foreign sugar products, with a penalty fixed involving the loss of ship and cargo. To make this more effective it was urged that the King's

---

[55] Address of the Jamaica Assembly to the King, November 20, 1752, P.R.O., C.O. 137:25.
[56] Ibid.
[57] Admiral Knowles to the Board of Trade, October 18, 1752, P.R.O., C.O. 137:25, pp. 271–80.

ships should be empowered to visit any British vessel at sea and to bring it to any port in case prohibited goods were found on board, with the privilege of prosecuting in either a local court of record or of vice-admiralty or in the Court of Exchequer in Westminster Hall. In this connection it was recommended that four sloops of war should be regularly stationed on the coast of New England to intercept and seize such vessels as were seeking to evade the law. Finally, as an additional guarantee of proper enforcement, it was urged that the customs officials in the sugar islands should be enjoined under heavy penalty not to give cockets to North American vessels without strict search of their cargoes.[58]

But even this compromise measure did not win the approval of the Board. The influence of the great planter group in the government had manifestly waned since the 1730's. In March 1752 James Crokatt, agent for South Carolina, in a letter to the standing committee of the Commons House of Assembly of that province, wrote "That the govt.ˢ of the Sugar Colonies had made no progress in their application to Parliament concerning the Trade to The French Islands and believed they could not in a hurry." [59]

Nor did the sugar interests succeed better with the draft of a bill which they presented to the Board, February 14, 1752, which in its preamble charged that under pretended cover of an act passed in the sixth year of His Present Majesty's reign (reaffirming an act passed in the twelfth year of the reign of Charles II [60]), there was being introduced into Ireland in British shipping, free of all duties, Spanish and Portuguese sugar. This, they insisted, was in express violation of various navigation acts, and especially the Act of 1696,[61] since it manifestly was not the meaning or intent of these laws, designed to encourage commerce in general with Spain and Portugal, that the sugar of these countries should be on a better footing than that of British growth, as was now the case with cargoes from those countries entering Irish ports.[62]

---

[58] For the above proposal of 1751 see P.R.O., C.O. 323:13, O. 87.

[59] Journal of the Commons House of Assembly of South Carolina, Vol. 27:569–70, South Carolina Archives. Crokatt had previously been instructed to be neutral in this dispute between the northern colonies and the sugar islands. See ibid., 27:121–2.

[60] 12 Charles II, c. 18, Par. 14.

[61] 7 and 8 William III, c. 22, Par. 14.

[62] See P.R.O., C.O. 323:13, O. 103; see also the Board of Trade Journal, 1749–1753, p. 268. The planter interests affirmed "that as the Crown of Portugal has laid an

A final futile attempt of the year 1752 was made by Governor Knowles of Jamaica to secure adoption of measures that would save the situation for the West India planters. In writing to the Board of Trade in October he strongly recommended that every merchant ship loading in any harbour within His Majesty's dominions should be obliged as soon as the cargo was aboard to have the cockets and the manifest carefully compared and attested by the principal customs officer of the port, which would thereupon be sealed and directed to the chief customs officer of the place to which the ship by its papers was bound; that, in addition, the hatches of the ship should be barred, locked, and sealed with the custom-house seal, to break which unlawfully or the seal of the manifest would entail confiscation of vessel and cargo; finally that cockets, manifest, and hatches should be opened, except in cases of necessity, only in the presence of a customs officer and that for ships bound for more than one port, duplicate cockets and manifests should be provided.[63] This plan likewise was rejected.

The truth is that the continental colonies had a case that was much stronger than the advocates of the sugar-planter interests were willing to admit. To begin with, much, if not most, of the molasses produced in the British West Indies was distilled right on the plantation, and a considerable portion of it was shipped to England. For

---

absolute Prohibition on the importation of our sugars. Such a prohibition on our side would be justified. . . ."

On February 20, 1752, a discussion took place at a meeting of the Board of Trade. Some of those interested in the West India sugar plantations as well as merchants with Portuguese interests were invited to be present. The latter urged that the proposed bill should be postponed as already "some national difficulty had broken out at Lisbon with respect to our trade." In response to the query as to the average price of muscovado at Lisbon since the war, they replied that it was twenty-two shillings per hundredweight on board ship with a deduction of one half the duties and that it had been delivered in Ireland at twenty-nine shillings Irish currency. The West India sugar-planters declared that since the war English muscovado had advanced in price in England from twenty-eight to thirty-five shillings per hundredweight, and that on re-exportation there was a drawback of but four shillings and tenpence. As a consequence, the price of English sugar at Dublin was forty-five shillings per hundredweight as against twenty-nine shillings for the same amount of Portuguese sugar, directly imported. Nevertheless, in view of the difficulties already facing the Portuguese trading interests, the Board expressed the hope, in spite of the manifest grievance of the West India planters and merchants, that the latter would for the present postpone their bill. See Board of Trade *Journal*, 1749–1753, pp. 274–6.

In 1751 there was exported to Ireland from England 34,063 hundredweight of sugar. See Custom House report of March 28, 1753, P.R.O., Treas. 64. 274.

[63] P.R.O., C.O. 137:25, pp. 171–80.

example, from the summer of 1735 to that of 1738, 873,103 gallons of West India rum was sent to England, or an average of 291,035 a year.[64] By 1750 these islands were apparently exporting to the mother country annually 800,000 gallons, and in 1760 twice this amount.[65]

Further, it was testified in 1750 at a meeting of the Board of Trade that Jamaica and Barbados were each producing 1,320,000 gallons of rum a year, that Antigua produced almost that amount, St. Christopher 660,000 gallons, and Montserrat 165,000 gallons, or a total of 4,465,000 gallons.[66] The conclusion therefore seems inescapable that the British West Indies sugar-planters were largely utilizing their molasses by distilling it. Although the planters of Nevis were still selling molasses abroad at this time, even they were preparing to turn it to rum.[67]

It is now clear to the student that by 1750 the British West Indies, outside of Jamaica, had seen their best days. Soil-depletion and French competition were remorselessly undermining the strong commercial position they had enjoyed at the beginning of the eighteenth century. As a class the planters were in debt, many of them hopelessly so.[68] They quite naturally viewed with deepest apprehension and anger the fact that their foreign rivals in the West Indies had taken their place as the chief suppliers of Europe's need for sugar and of North America's insatiable demand for molasses, and especially that this was accomplished — and the prosperity of the French sugar-planters established — only by a wilful disregard of the Molasses Act of 1733 on the part of British colonial shipmasters and distillers. They therefore called loudly upon the mother country

---

[64] Of the above total Jamaica provided 715,874 gallons, as against but 157,229 for all the other British West Indies. See "An account of what quantity of Rum has been imported from any of the British Sugar Islands . . . ," Custom House, London, April 30, 1739, P.R.O., Treas. 64. 273.

[65] See F. W. Pitman: *The Development of the British West Indies, 1700–1763,* for a chart opposite page 214 giving the quantity of rum imported yearly into England from the British West Indies between the years 1699 and 1764.

[66] The figures as presented are given in terms of puncheons of rum, each puncheon containing 110 gallons. See Board of Trade *Journal,* 1749–1753, p. 133.

[67] *Ibid.* In this connection the student should consult the excellent article by G. M. Ostrander: "The Colonial Molasses Trade," previously cited. The writer's contention is that the chief purpose of the attack of the sugar-planters against the northern colonies was to destroy the flourishing New England rum industry, rather than to be able to compete with the French sugar islands on equal terms.

[68] Richard Pares: *Yankees and Creoles: The Trade between North America and the West Indies before the American Revolution* (London, 1956), p. 56; L. J. Ragatz: *The Fall of the Planter Class in the British Caribbean, 1763–1833* (New York, 1928), p. 10.

for assistance. However, it is not too much to affirm that, had this been given on the terms of their petitions, it would have put an end to the thriving distilling industry of New England and Pennsylvania.[69] But such a favour the government of Great Britain was unwilling to grant.

If any additional evidence were needed to show that by the 1750's the British West Indies were declining, not only in influence with the home government but also in their ability to attract the investor, this was furnished by the draft of a bill which John Sharpe, representing the sugar-planter interests, placed in the hands of the Board of Trade after the failure of other efforts. The new bill re-emphasized the profound discouragements that the planters were under and then went on to affirm that many of the latter, without due regard to the interests of their country, had

> "quitted and deserted their settlements in the British Sugar settlements and removed themselves with their negroes and effects into fforeign sugar settlements . . . to the Great Prejudice and Injury of the British Sugar Islands and Trade thereof." [70]

Some British planters, it appears, were taking up lands in the Dutch and Danish islands in the region about St. Christopher;[71] they were also resorting to the mainland of South America. "Many Planters," lamented a writer in 1748, "are actually gone, irrevocably gone from Barbadoes and the Leeward Islands, and more are preparing to go, as will appear by a late Letter received from Barbadoes of July 2, 1747. I can inform you that many Gentlemen of this Island, Col G——, J——dy, G——, Mr. B——, M—— G——, Capt. B——, and many others, as well Planters as Merchants, have chose to lay out their Money in purchasing Plantations at Barbecies, and Isequebe [Berbice and Essequibo — Dutch settlements near Surinam]

---

[69] See Richard Pares: op. cit., pp. 35–6 and 55, and especially G. M. Ostrander: op. cit., XXX, 77–84.

[70] P.R.O., C.O. 323:13, O. 104; see also the Board of Trade Journal, 1749–1753, pp. 284, 286. In May the Secretary of the Board was ordered to write a circular letter to the Governors of Jamaica, Barbados, the Leeward Islands, the Bahamas, and the Bermudas, directing them to use their utmost endeavours to prevent His Majesty's subjects taking up lands and making settlements in any foreign island or colony and also to prevent the illicit importation of foreign sugar into these British possessions. See ibid., p. 321.

[71] Ibid., p. 268.

rather than in this [Barbados] or any other English Sugar Islands." [72] To combat the transference of capital to the competing islands with the destruction thereby of the British interests, the bill just referred to proposed to make this act a high crime and misdemeanour and those convicted liable to such corporal punishment or imprisonment or fine as the court should think fit, together with the forfeiture of double the value of the plantation with its Negroes and effects — one half of which was to go to the informer.[73] Again the planters were rebuffed.

The point must be stressed that the efficient production of sugar in the British West Indies involved a large amount of capital. It was estimated that no less than £30,000 sterling was needed for the purpose of purchasing the requisite amount of land and stocking it with 250 Negroes,[74] 60 mules and other livestock, as well as for the construction of the essential buildings, such as the mill, the boiling-house, the curing-house, the distilling-house, a hospital for sick Negroes, and barns for the livestock.[75] Upon such an investment one could hope to produce not more than 200 hogsheads of sugar at sixteen hundredweight per hogshead and by this process under favourable circumstances realize some seven per cent on the capital invested. Yet the hazards involved were many, and in the 1750's those with capital watched their investments with great anxiety.[76] Further,

[72] *Reason Grounded on Facts* (London, 1748), pp. 22–3. A Mr. O'Connor, in his *Considerations on the Trade to Africa* . . . (London, 1749), writes (p. 19): "For the Truth of the Case before us is, that several of our West-India merchants and Planters, have already taken the pernicious Step of purchasing Plantations in the Dutch Settlements at Barbacie, and at Isquebe, adjoining to Surinam . . . ; and that others are . . . preparing to follow their example." That these statements were not mere idle assertions is indicated by the fact that by 1762 Englishmen owned nearly one eighth of the plantations along the Essequibo River and over one third of them along the Demerara River, both lying within what was then Dutch Guiana. See Eric Williams: "British Guiana Problems," *Journal of Negro History*, XXX, 362; see also G. C. Edmundson: "The Relations of Great Britain with Guiana," Royal Hist. Soc. *Transactions*, 4th ser., 1–6, for a brief account of the settlements at Essequibo and Demerara.

[73] C.O., 323:13, O. 104.

[74] See "Abstracts of the Houghton James Estate" in Jamaica, made by the owner, Houghton James, Esq., in 1773, in "Papers Relating to Jamaica," 1693–1784, Library of Congress accessions.

[75] In the middle of the eighteenth century, according to the *"mémoire"* of Mr. Jean Baptiste Truitie and his wife, it cost 300,000 livres to purchase the land in St. Domingue for their plantation and to equip it for the production of sugar. See *Affaires Etrangères, Mémoires et Documents, Amérique,* 10:ff. 88–117, Library of Congress photostats.

[76] See Bryan Edwards, who was a Jamaican and an authority on the above point, in his *History of the West Indies* (3 vols., London, 1793–1801), II, 248–64.

many of the sugar plantations, burdened with old debts, could be retained by their owners only under favourable conditions.[77]

However, conditions at this juncture were far from favourable for the planters. As one writer asserted in 1748: ". . . the charge of maintaining Sugar Plantations is so great that if they are not kept up to the Height, if they are suffered to remain uncultivated but for one year the Planters must be ruined. For seven-eighths are deeply in debt to Great Britain and pay a large annual interest besides." [78] The truth of this statement is hardly to be questioned in light of the fact that, year in and year out, it ordinarily cost a planter some £2,500 sterling to subsist and otherwise maintain 500 Negroes.[79] The sugar plantation could therefore bear such heavy charges only when systematically and profitably exploited.

In conclusion it may be said that the British West Indies sugar-planters in the middle of the eighteenth century had to face certain problems that affected the tobacco- and rice-planters of North America not at all or, at least, not seriously. While the producers of sugar, for example, had lost the markets of continental Europe to their competitors, the French, the tobacco of Virginia and Maryland and the rice of South Carolina dominated the great markets of northern and western Europe, including those of France itself. Again, even in British North America it was French-produced molasses that by 1750 was chiefly utilized in that flourishing industry, the distilling of rum. In fact, the only thing that saved the British West Indies planting interests from virtual bankruptcy was the increased consumption of sugar and its by-products in the British Isles, where the price of this commodity (in a protected market) was much higher than that in the free market on the continent.

---

[77] For example, Richard Assheton wrote from Jamaica in 1728: "Hynes is Marryed to a Lady of Two Estates — indebted £24,000, worth about £20,000, much good may it do him!" (Jefferies Collection of Manuscripts, Bristol Reference Library).

[78] *Reason Grounded on Facts* (London, 1748), p. 7. Professor Pitman in his essay "The Settlement and Financing of British West India Plantations" has made clear the difficulties that faced the small sugar-planters. He gives figures also for a later period, which show the high percentage of business failures among planters. See *Essays in Colonial History by Students of Charles McLean Andrews* (New Haven, 1931), pp. 252–84.

[79] "An Estimate of the First Cost of 500 Negroes as also the yearly Expense of Victualling and Cloathing them.

"To the Cloathing of said Negroes four times a year with Oxen-brig Frocks and trousers at 4/6 each . . . . £ 450.

"To maintain said Negroes 52 weeks at 22ᵈ each week . . . . 2383.6.0."

See P.R.O., C.O. 137:35, p. 16.

Further, climatic conditions were far less favourable for sustained health and human survival in the British West Indies than on the North American continent. The mortality among whites and blacks was therefore much greater. One result was the need of maintaining the labour force on the islands at great expense by a constant supply of slaves drawn from Africa.[80] Another result was that sugar-planters who could possibly see their way clear to do so — even by mortgaging their estates — were apt to carry their families to England and thus become absentees.[81] Not only did England provide a climate that was very much more salubrious, but the cultural environment was vastly superior to that presented on the typical sugar plantations, where the planters' children were apt to be brought in contact with people fresh from the jungles of Africa, many of whom were of a type so warlike and dangerous — such as the Koromantyns of the Gold Coast — that outside of Carolina [82] they were not wanted in North America and were only favoured in the West Indies because of their strong constitutions and ability to endure the hardship of slave labor.

One may indeed assert in dealing with the British settlements in the New World that as one progresses northward from the tropics the dependence of the agriculturists upon slave labour and also upon the purchase of annual fresh increments of Negroes becomes less and less. Likewise was there less and less tendency for families to feel the need of deserting their homes in the colonies and to become absentee landlords in England — a practice that led only too frequently to unfortunate financial involvement and the decline in the value of the plantation left to the dubious supervision of agents and overseers.

---

[80] In the middle of the eighteenth century Jamaica imported over 12,000 Negroes, some of whom were re-exported; Barbados, Antigua, and St. Christopher each imported some 2,000, Montserrat received 500, and Nevis 200. See Elizabeth Donnan: op. cit., II, xlviii–ix.

[81] Only on Antigua was absentee ownership of plantations not the prevailing pattern among the larger planters of the British West Indies before the end of the eighteenth century. In fact, the smaller sugar-planters were gradually eliminated in Jamaica, so that before the outbreak of the War for American Independence the average planter is said to have owned little short of 1,000 acres of land. Only one carrying on large operations could easily afford to settle in England. See L. J. Ragatz: "Absentee Landlordism in the British Caribbean, 1750–1833," Agricultural History, V, 23.

[82] There was a demand in South Carolina for Gold Coast slaves, even Koromantyns, in the middle of the eighteenth century. See Elizabeth Donnan: "Slave Trade into South Carolina before the Revolution," American Historical Review, XXXIII, 804–24.

CHAPTER X

Guinea and the Empire

HE PRECEDING chapters of this volume which have to do with those portions of the old British Empire where Negro labour was an essential element in the economic and social life of the inhabitants indicate that the importance to the Empire of Guinea [1] in the eighteenth century can hardly be overemphasized — abhorrent as was the institution of slavery even to many contemporaries. Its coasts helped to maintain the New England rum industry and offered perhaps the greatest market for the profitable sale of the coarse fabrics furnished by the United East India Company to traders who exchanged these commodities for slaves, gold, and ivory.[2] It has been estimated that in the exploitation of the human resources of the Gulf of Guinea area and the adjacent parts of Africa, between the years 1680 and 1786, over two million blacks were received within the Empire.[3] These slaves were held to be an essential element in the production of the sugar of the West Indies, the rice and indigo of South Carolina, and the tobacco of the Chesapeake Bay; further, their presence in these parts guaranteed the prosperity of the provision trade of Ireland and of Pennsylvania, as well as the prosperity

---

[1] "By Guinea here, I mean all Negro-land, from about the River Senega Northward, to within a few Degrees of Cape Bon Esperance [Good Hope]; because Ships bound to any part of this extent are said to be bound to Guinea" (John Atkins: *A Voyage to Guinea, Brazil, and the West-Indies* [2nd edn., London, 1737], p. 38).

[2] Between the years 1715 and 1726 commodities of the value of £1,652,571.10.11 were sent from England to Africa, of which £914,869.10.11 worth were certified goods produced outside England. Custom House report, April 4, 1732, P.R.O., Treas. 64. 273. Between the years 1748 and 1754, inclusive, commodities valued at £1,553,994 were carried there. See Bryan Edwards: *The History, Civil and Commercial, of the British Colonies in the West Indies* (2 vols., London, 1793), II (Appendix), 201.

[3] *Ibid.*, II, 55.

of the Massachusetts Bay fisheries by furnishing a market for the lower grades of fish. To Malachy Postlethwayt, writing in 1745, the African trade was "the fundamental prop and support" of the Empire.[4]

Those portions of Africa inhabited by the Negro were, for the most part, fertile almost beyond description.[5] The inhabitants, therefore, with only moderate exertion were able to supply their basic wants and also tended under favourable circumstances to increase in numbers. For, unlike the Europeans, they were adjusted to an equatorial climate and to other local conditions such as characterized the Slave, Gold, Ivory, and Grain coasts as well as the tropical areas following the Atlantic Ocean front to the north of the Gulf of Guinea. But the slave trade, during the period under consideration, encouraged wars between the native kingdoms which in some cases resulted in a dislocation of population and the depopulation of once thickly inhabited towns and districts.

The African Negroes were sharply distinguished into categories by the experienced slaver and the master of slaves. From Senegambia and the Windward Coast to the southward were drawn the so-called Mandingoes; these blacks were known for the comparative delicacy of their features; the lips were thinner than those of most Negroes, the hair less woolly, the noses less flattened, and they were largely free from the peculiar odor of the Guinea Coast blacks; many were

---

[4] See Postlethwayt's *The African Trade, the Great Pillar and Support of the British Plantation Trade in North America* (London, 1745), pp. 4–6. For an excellent survey of the forces in Great Britain that fostered the slave trade see Eric Williams: "The Golden Age of the Slave System in Britain," *Journal of Negro History*, XXV, 60–106.

[5] See Anthony Benezet: *Some Historical Account of Guinea* . . . (4th edn., London, 1808), pp. 1–34. This book had its beginning in 1762 when Benezet published a pamphlet in Philadelphia carrying the title *A Short Account of that Part of Africa Inhabited by the Negroes*. The book itself is remarkable for the number of first-hand accounts of the western coast of Africa and its inhabitants. Among other contemporary accounts of Guinea see William Smith: *Voyage to Guinea* (London [1744]), Francis Moor: *Travels into Distant Parts of Africa* (London, 1738), and John Atkins: *A Voyage to Guinea, Brazil, and the West-Indies* (London, 1737), as well as the many reports by masters of slave vessels for the period under consideration in *Documents Illustrative of the History of the Slave Trade to America* (ed. Elizabeth Donnan, 4 vols., Washington, 1930–5), Volume II. See also W. E. Ward: *A History of Ghana* (London, 1958, first published in 1948 under title *A History of the Gold Coast*, with additions in the 1958 edition), pp. 1–146, and J. D. Fage: *An Introduction to the History of West Africa* (Cambridge, 1955), pp. 1–38. The student should also consult J. M. Gray: *A History of Gambia* (Cambridge, 1940), and W. W. Claridge: *History of the Gold Coast and Ashanti* (2 vols., London, 1915).

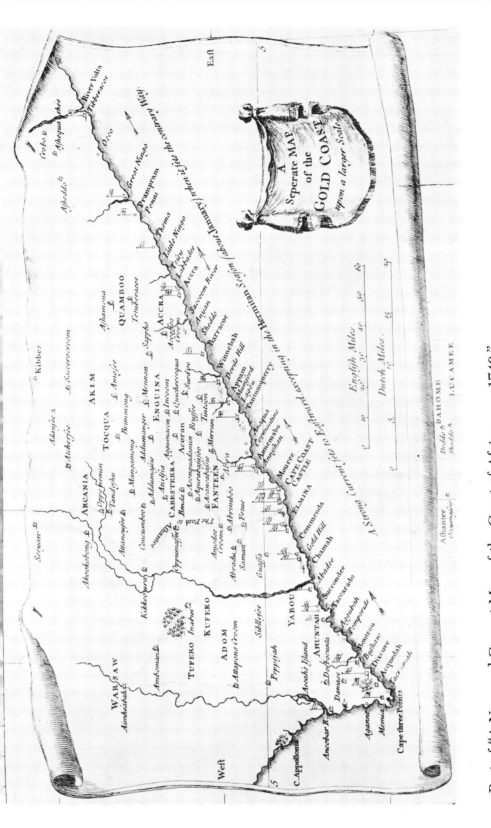

Part of "A New and Correct Map of the Coast of Africa . . . , 1746."

(From . . . *Advantages of the African Trade Considered* by Malachy Postlethwayt)

Mohammedans and some could actually write in Arabic.[6] From the Gold Coast came the Koromantyns [Cormantines], the most resolute of all those brought out of Africa, who were of gleaming black, capable of enduring hardship and pain; they were a warlike and consequently a dangerous type of slave to have in great numbers.[7] To the eastward of that region were to be found the Whydah Negroes, similar to the Koromantyns but not so fierce; there also a type of Negro was obtained differing from these, the Popows, who were inclined to be submissive and were well adapted to agricultural labour, at which many of them had been engaged as slaves before their departure from Africa. From the Bight of Benin along the Calabar Coast and that part of Africa lying directly north of the Congo, various types of Negroes were secured, but especially the Eboe, a Negro of an emotional type who became despondent unless given the most careful treatment. Finally, far to the south of the Congo were the natives of Angola.[8]

These slaves were purchased as a rule from other blacks, usually of another and hostile tribe; they might be those captured in a slaving-raid or those taken prisoner in war or those sold out of the tribe for some crime; many came from the interior, and some by the time they had made the long journey through the jungle to the coast and had reached the trading-fort or slaving-ship were unfit for sale — and that meant a massacre on the beach. The price of a good slave along the Whydah coast in the late 1730's amounted to about £16 sterling, which was higher than in nearby places by reason of an

---

[6] Bryan Edwards: op. cit., II, 60–3; see also Thomas Astley: New General Collections of Voyages and Travels (4 vols., London, 1745), II, 296, and H. A. Wyndham: Problems of Imperial Trusteeship: The Atlantic and Slavery (London, 1935), pp. 46–7. For the case of the educated Mohammedan Job Jalla of Gambia, who wrote freely in Arabic and who was carried to Maryland as a slave, see A. A. Ettinger: James Edward Oglethorpe: Imperial Idealist (Oxford, 1936), p. 148.

[7] The principal African groups that were included under the name Koromantyns were the Fantins, Akims, and the Ashantees. In 1765, after the slave insurrection, a bill was introduced into the Jamaica Assembly that provided a higher import duty upon these Negroes, but it failed to pass, owing to "the conceit of some few planters in regard to the superior strength of the Coromantins and greater hardness to support field labour" ([Edward Long]: History of Jamaica . . . [3 vols., London, 1774], II, 470–1); see also Captain William Snelgrave: A New Account of some Parts of Guinea, and the Slave Trade (London, 1734), reprinted in Elizabeth Donnan: op. cit., II, 342–61.

[8] Bryan Edwards: op. cit., II, 63–75. The slaves coming from different parts of Africa are sharply distinguished in Practical Rules for the Management and Medical Treatment of Negro Slaves in the Sugar Colonies, by a Professional Planter (London, 1803), Part I, Chap. 1.

export duty demanded by the local king; but sometimes the price was as high as £25 for a Whydah child, although a full-grown Calabar slave could generally be purchased for about £10.[9] It was maintained that it took from eight to ten ounces of gold dust to secure a real Gold Coast slave in the late 1740's, although apparently one was sometimes secured for as little as four or five ounces.[10]

In the purchase of these blacks from the slavers, the proportion of males to females seems to have been, as a rule, two to one. This was not only because of plantation demands — that is, the need for strong workers in the fields on the part of the West India and North American planters — but also by reason of the fact that fewer females of a salable type were offered for sale, owing to the prevalence of polygamy and the greater tendency of the men to commit offences that condemned them to be sold into slavery. Sometimes, however, the English slavers were instructed to secure as large a proportion of females as possible. For example, Captain Richard Prankard, who went to Angola early in 1733, was desired to purchase there, among other slaves, about one hundred boys and girls, "aiming chiefly at the females from 10 to 14 years of age. . . ."[11] As for the Negroes that were carried to the British West Indies, it was estimated that one fifth were re-exported, most of them into Spanish possessions. The disproportion of males to females, just mentioned, seems to have had the effect of combating the desire of the planters to be able to dispense with the great annual charges involved in maintaining and supplementing their supply of labour. Indeed, a state of sexual promiscuity apparently characterized the relations of the blacks on most plantations in the West Indies, and the unbridled wantonness of the women living under these unnatural conditions, it is said, made for sterility. Since it was calculated that the average life of the Negro at labour on a sugar plantation was but about seven years, therefore, on a plantation of 500 acres where at least from 120 to 140 mature blacks were constantly required, it was necessary to an-

---

[9] For extended testimony on the condition of the African slave trade by various persons involved in this traffic given to the Board of Trade, January 10–18, 1749/50, see the Board of Trade Journal, 1749–1753, pp. 6–10, 20–1, 23–5; see also H. A. Wyndham: op. cit., pp. 221–7.

[10] An ounce of gold was equal to £4.

[11] James Laroche and others to Capt. Richard Prankard, Bristol, January 29, 1732–3, Jefferies Collection of Manuscripts, Bristol Reference Library; see also Elizabeth Donnan: op. cit., II, 444–5.

ticipate the purchase of from 20 to 30 slaves every year, by reason of this lack of natural increase.[12]

The Royal African Company, the activities of which are considered in the course of this chapter, made no attempt, at least after the granting of the asiento to the South Sea Company, directly to supply the Spaniards with slaves or to meet the demands of the Empire for them, except insofar as it purchased from black factors and in turn sold to the South Sea Company or to independent traders, whose ships at this period swarmed along the African coast.[13] As a matter of fact, the merchants of Liverpool and Bristol were by 1750 the leading agencies in supplying the plantations with blacks.[14] This triangular trade — starting from England, moving to Africa, then to the West Indies or to Virginia or to South Carolina, and then homeward — involved British manufactures, East India goods, slaves, ivory, gold, sugar, rum, rice, and tobacco as the chief commodities. It attracted many of the most enterprising Englishmen. For example, one of the greatest of the financiers interested in the slaving business was Foster Cunliff of Liverpool, whose company had five ships engaged in this trade; Cunliff was also a philanthropist, making the local Blue Coat Hospital the object of his solicitude.[15] Other great Liverpool merchants who had committed their fortunes to this trade were George Campbel, John Knight, John Welsh, Richard Gildart, William Whalley, Edward Forbes, and Richard Nicholas.[16] As for

---

[12] [G. M. Butel-Dumont]: *Histoire et Commerce des Antilles Angloises* (Paris, 1758), p. 29.

[13] Eveline C. Martin: "The English Slave Trade and the African Settlements," *The Cambridge History of the British Empire* (8 vols., Cambridge, 1929–58+), I, 448–9; Elizabeth Donnan: *op. cit.*, II, xxxii.

[14] G. F. Dow: *Slave Ships and Slaving* (Salem, Mass., 1927), Chap. 5, "The Liverpool and Bristol Slavers."

[15] In old St. Peters Church, Liverpool, before its destruction, there was to be found a costly monument to the memory of Cunliff. A vase, said to contain his heart, was supported by two orphans lamenting the loss of their benefactor. The inscription read as follows: "To the Memory of Foster Cunliff of Liverpool, son of Ellis Cunliff . . . a merchant whose sagacity, honesty and diligence procured wealth and credit to himself and his Country, a magistrate who administered justice with discernment, candour, and impartiality, a Christian devout and exemplary in the exercise of every private and public duty, friend to mercy, patron to distress, an enemy only to vice and sloth, he lived esteemed by all who knew him (though few have been so extensively known) and died lamented by the wise and good in the 73 year of his age, 11th of April, 1758." See Wm. Indfield: *An Essay Toward the History of Liverpool, drawn up from Papers left by . . . George Perry . . .* (Liverpool, 1774), p. 43.

[16] *Ibid.* For a list of Liverpool ships engaged in the African trade together with the number of slaves that each could accommodate, with the names of their commanders

Bristol, it appears that all of her men of great or considerable fortune of the eighteenth century, such as William Miller, John Brickdale, Joseph Percival, Henry Hobhouse, Michael Atkins, Jeremiah Ames, Henry Tonge, John Bright, James Read, Stephen Nash, and John Curtis, were deeply involved in slaving,[17] and the first bank established in Bristol in the year 1750 was founded by a group of African Coast merchants headed by Onisiphorus Tyndale, Isaac Elton, Thomas Knox, Matthew Hale, and William Miller.[18]

Earlier in the eighteenth century Bristol had dominated the business of supplying the colonies with blacks, but by 1750 Liverpool had outstripped her, sending out seventy-five ships as against the forty-seven belonging to the former.[19] At this period six slavers were also credited to the four ports of Chester, Lancaster, Glasgow, and Plymouth, and six to London — according to figures furnished by a Mr. John Hardman, representing the Bristol and Liverpool merchants respectively before the Board of Trade in 1750.[20] In addition to these 134 ships from the mother country, it was estimated that over 20 ships came from North America, almost half of which number belonged to Rhode Island, making a total of some 155 British ships engaged in the African trade. Of the Liverpool ships, 28 con-

---

and owners, see Robert Williamson: *The Liverpool Memorandum-Book* . . . (Liverpool, 1753).

[17] "A list of the Company of Merchants Trading to Africa" is to be found among the Jefferies Collection of Manuscripts in the Bristol Reference Library. See also *Bonner's Bristol Journal* for January 8, 1785, and John Latimer: *Annals of Bristol in the Eighteenth Century* (Bristol, 1893), p. 462.

[18] See C. H. Cave: *A History of Banking in Bristol, 1750–1899* (Bristol, 1899), p. 9.

[19] Yet the total commerce of Bristol surpassed in value that of Liverpool between the years 1750 and 1757 inclusive by some £700,000. See William Barrett: *The History and Antiquities of the City of Bristol* . . . (Bristol, 1789), pp. 186–8.

[20] *Board of Trade Journal, 1749–1753*, p. 15. According to the records of the Commissioners for the Customs, in 1735 there sailed from London 22 slaving-ships with a total tonnage of 2,474 tons, from Bristol 27 ships totalling 2,440 tons, and from Liverpool 18 ships of 1,335 tons. By 1750 London was sending only 11 ships, totalling 911 tons, Bristol 24 of 2,480 tons, and Liverpool 43 of 4,075 tons. In 1751 London was sending 20 ships of 1,739 tons, Bristol 26 of 2,672 tons, and Liverpool 61 of 5,523 tons. Report of Custom House, April 19, 1755, P.R.O. Treas. 64. 274. There is, of course, a discrepancy between these figures and those given above. The table printed in Richard Brooke's *Liverpool as it was during the Last Quarter of the Eighteenth Century, 1775–1800* (Liverpool, 1853) of ships cleared from Liverpool to the coast of Africa gives the figures for 1751 at 53 of 5,334 tons. The vessels engaged in slaving were small, as indicated, but of the more than 70 registered in Bristol between 1727 and 1767 the average burden was only 80 tons. A 50-ton sloop would accommodate a cargo of about 190 slaves; on the other hand, the 100-ton *Bryce* carried as many as 414 on one trip. See C. M. MacInnes: *A Gateway to Empire* (Bristol, 1939), p. 202.

fined themselves to securing Negroes along the Gold and Winward coasts, averaging 7,040 slaves annually, with 17 Bristol ships resorting to the same regions with an average of 5,180 slaves.[21] The estimated total investment of these independent traders in 1750 in the African trade, according to Hardman, was £800,000, and the annual returns on this amounted to £1,200,000, which would serve to indicate how profitable the business was.[22] This may be further illustrated. A Captain Hill, trading out of London earlier in the century with goods valued at £12,000, secured with them 2,000 ounces of gold and a cargo of 700 slaves.[23] In the 1720's a cargo valued at £1,226 was provided for the purchase of 250 Negroes at Bonny. Of what did it consist? There were such articles as blue-flowered chintz, striped "nicconees," red-and-blue-striped handkerchiefs called "romels," blue-and-white-checkered "photaes," and "byram pauls"— all East India commodities valued at over £500. Then there were 500 muskets, 80 pistols, and 10 blunderbusses — these firearms valued at over £240 — with fourteen tons of iron valued at £230, together with two tons of lead, crystal beads, bottles, copper rods, and brandy, the latter valued at £40.[24]

A characteristic outcome of a slaving voyage is to be found in the sale of the slaves belonging to William Freke, Esq. & Co., of Bristol, carried from the Guinea Coast to Barbados in the galley *Freke* under command of John Bartlett in December 1730. Bartlett finally succeeded in disposing of the lot of 329 Negroes out of the 335 landed, for a total of £6,207.5. His own commission of five per cent on the

---

[21] Board of Trade *Journal*, 1749–1753, p. 15.

[22] *Ibid.*, p. 25. The large financial gains made by slavers is also stressed by Gomer Williams in his *History of the Liverpool Privateers . . . , with an account of the Liverpool Slave Trade* (London, 1897, Part II, Chap. 6). The defects in Williams's manner of analysing profit and loss are pointed out by Stanley Dumbell in his "Profits of the Guinea Trade," *Economic Journal*, II, 254–7, and particularly by F. C. Hyde, B. B. Parkinson, and Sheila Marriner in their "The Nature and Profitability of the Liverpool Slave Trade," *Economic History Review*, 2nd ser., V, 368–77.

[23] Board of Trade *Journal*, 1749–1753, p. 9.

[24] Isaac Hobhouse Papers, Jefferies Collection, p. 9, Bristol Reference Library. Assuming the average sale price of these slaves was but £20, this would give a total of £5,000 gross receipts for the cargo in case all of the blacks survived the voyage to America. See H. A. Wyndham: *The Atlantic and Slavery*, pp. 67–72. A good Gold Coast Negro who could be purchased in Africa for £9 or £10 would sell for £29 or £30 in the West Indies; in 1759 it took £35.11 at Charleston, South Carolina, to buy a Whydah Negro; in 1768 the price of such a slave in Jamaica was a little over £50. In that year Captain Harwood of the *Greenwich* carried to the island from Anamabo 136 Negroes who were sold for a total of £6,842. See C. M. MacInnes: *England and Slavery* (Bristol, 1934), pp. 94–5.

sales was £310.1.3; the import duty of five shillings amounted to £83.15 on the 335; the cost of maintenance before sale and the other expenses incident upon the latter (among which was an item of £25.9.3 for treating customers) totalled £66.4.6½. The net proceeds were thus reduced to £5,746.18.2½. Put up for auction were 141 men, 75 women, 65 boys, and 48 girls. The girls brought from £14 to £15 each, excepting one who sold for £29, the highest price paid for any slave at the sale; the boys sold for an average of £22, the women for an average of £23.10, and the prime men for an average of £28.10. Most of the group were disposed of on December 8, but thirty-six were left over and it was not until December 29 that the sale was terminated with some of the men going at a price as low as £18.[25]

The business, of course, had its hazards to life and property. There was always the possibility that during the weeks or months spent along the coast in completing the shipload those on board would die of confinement, or would escape, or would rise and destroy the crew when it was off guard. Isaac Hobhouse, of Bristol, and two associates, writing instructions to the commander of the brigantine *Dispatch*, William Barry, in 1725, warned him in not the most idiomatic English: "So soon as you begin to slave Let ye Knitting be fix'd breast high fore & aft & so keep 'em shackled & hand Bolted fearing their rising or leaping Overboard, to prevent wch Let always Constant & Carefull watch be appointed to wch must give ye strictest charge for the preservation of their Own Lives as well as yours & on wch ye Voy^e depends — sleeping on their Watch has been often fatall and many a good Voy^e . . . entirely ruin'd." [26]

Once the cargo was completed, there followed the matter of the voyage across the Atlantic. It is certain that in the eighteenth century extraordinary care was taken as a rule in connection with the so-called Middle Passage to bring the precious cargo to its destination with the minimum loss of life.[27] The slaves were gradually ac-

[25] See "Sale of a Cargo of Slaves," Barbados, Anno. 1730, Jefferies Collection of Manuscripts, Bristol Reference Library.

[26] For these instructions (among the Jefferies Manuscripts at Bristol), see Elizabeth Donnan: *op. cit.*, II, 327–9.

[27] For example, in 1725 the following instructions were given: "Let y^r care be in preserving so well as in purchaseing in order to wch Let their provisions be well and Carefully look'd after & boil'd & yt. its given them in due season, to see ye sailors don't abuse them wch has often been done to the prejudice of the Voy^e" (". . . Instructions from the owners to the Captain of the *Dispatch*," *ibid*).

customed to the new diet by being fed alternately on their native food and the new food, and they were generally given all they could eat, except in case of necessity when everyone on board was rationed. The men at first were chained together, but conditions were relaxed gradually. For example, a part of the day, at least in fair weather, was usually spent on deck; each slave was frequently required to bathe daily in salt water, while the sleeping-quarters were cleaned and sprinkled with vinegar. Nevertheless, with the best of treatment, usually about five per cent of the slaves did not survive the voyage, and sometimes, if a malignant fever developed on board, most of them would perish.

A news item from St. John, Antigua, in 1749, tells the grim story succinctly:

> "Capt. Perkins, in the ship —— of Liverpool, arrived Wednesday from Africa and sailed the next day for Jamaica, having had the misfortune to lose 102 by sickness." [28]

The following letter, written from Barbados in 1723 by the commander of the *Grayhound*, is also typical:

> "Sr.
>
> This with My Humble Servis to you & the Rest of the Gentlemen Owners of the Ship *Grayhound* Galley & is to certifie to you of my Arivall hear haveing seven Weeks Passage from Bony butt very Dismall & Mortall for outt of 339 Slaves I brought in hear butt 214, for the Like Mortalaty I think Never was known for Jolly Likely Men Slaves to Eatt thair Diett over Night & the Nex Morning Dead 2 & 3 in a Night for several Days after Wee came from Bony[.] As for Managementt I think itt Could Nott be Better. I always had their Victtualls in good order & Took thatt Care to Keep them & the Ship Sweett & Cleane . . . & Nott to Sufer any of them to Wett Their Foott on No Acct. . . ." [29]

The slaver, indeed, was called upon to exercise the greatest precautions in order to bring his voyage to successful conclusion. Over-severity with the blacks, or their neglect, led to great mortality and the development of a bad spirit on board; but over-indulgence led to

---

[28] Antigua advices, *Maryland Gazette*, December 27, 1749.

[29] Captain Edward Hollden to Isaac Hobhouse, April 30, 1723, Jefferies Papers, also included in Elizabeth Donnan: *op. cit.*, II, 299–300. The *Bristol Weekly Intelligencer* of October 14, 1749, carried the news that the *Southwell*, Captain Breckinridge, had arrived at Antigua on the way to Jamaica; that of the slaves who began the Middle Passage, 150 had perished; and that the remainder, numbering 301, would be up for sale.

even more tragic results from the viewpoint of slave-traders. To illustrate: the crew of the *King David*, which left the Guinea Coast in the spring of 1750, was overpowered by the slaves, who were incautiously freed of their irons and were treated in other respects with great liberality and humanity. The Negroes were encouraged to take this step after the death of a number of the whites on board and were led by a black who spoke excellent English and who had been permitted the privilege of visiting the captain in his cabin, where the arms were stored. After the captain and others had been put to death, the remainder of the crew were required by their new masters to steer the ship to land, where all on board fell into the hands of the French.[30]

According to computations made in 1750 by the slave-trading interests, the number of slaves annually required for the plantations was estimated at 10,050; of this total Jamaica took 4,780, Barbados 1,700, Antigua 1,700, St. Christopher 1,200, Montserrat and Nevis each 335; in addition to which number, it was estimated that North America required some 3,000.[31] These figures are somewhat below those of a Mr. Martin, representing the planter interests before the Board of Trade, who insisted that it took 10,750 slaves to supply the annual mortality alone among the blacks in the West Indies — not to take into account the increase of the stock on the islands for the purpose of expanding industry.[32] The sale of Negroes out of Jamaica to Spanish ports represented an additional demand. The total number of blacks then living within the Empire was placed in 1752 by one authority at 381,000, with 150,000 of these credited to the continental colonies and the remainder to the sugar islands.[33] Of those transported to the New World in the eighteenth century, three fourths, it has been asserted, had previously been slaves.[34]

---

[30] See the *Pennsylvania Journal*, September 13, 1750. The *Bristol Weekly Intelligencer* of October 28, 1749, has the following item: "The *Thomas and Ellen*, Rawlinson, of Liverpool, [was] cut off by his Negroes on the Coast of Africa"; the same paper on December 9 of that year printed the following news: "We have an account that the *Scipio* of Liverpool is cut off by Negroes on the Coast of Angola, and all Hands killed except the Doctor."

[31] *Board of Trade Journal*, 1749–1753, p. 14.

[32] *Ibid.*, p. 35. According to Mr. Martin (*ibid.*), the stock of Negroes in the British West Indies totalled 235,000, with Jamaica possessing 120,000, Barbados 60,000, Antigua 30,000, and the other islands totalling 25,000. The mortality rate, he declared, would average 105 deaths for every 100 births on these islands.

[33] James Abercromby's "Examination," May 22, 1752, Shelburne Papers, 47:38, Clements Library.

[34] W. J. Gardner: *A History of Jamaica* . . . (London, 1909), p. 175.

The year 1750 marked a change in the government policy regarding the direction and control of the slave trade and the fortunes of the Royal African Company. Under the Stuarts this trade had been made a monopoly that was first enjoyed by Sir William St. John and his associates in 1618; in 1631 the monopoly was transferred to Sir Richard Young and associated merchants,[35] and in 1660 to the Duke of York and many others of high rank. In 1672 the Royal African Company of England, which represented a reorganization of the Duke's Royal Adventurers' Company, came into existence possessed of a joint stock of £122,000.[36] It took over Cape Coast Castle on the Gold Coast, Sierra Leone, and James Fort on the Gambia from the old company and to these added other trading-stations until there were early in the eighteenth century about eighteen posts.[37] Some, however, were later abandoned, so that by 1750 but nine were being maintained: Cape Coast Castle on the Gold Coast, with Commenda, Succondee, Dixcove to the west of it, as well as James Fort on the Gambia, and Tantumquerry, Winnebah, Accra, and Whydah to the east of it.[38] The Revolution of 1689 struck a serious blow at the monopoly, and an act of the year 1698 [39] provided that any ship might freely trade along the African coast between Cape Mount and the Cape of Good Hope upon paying an export duty of ten per cent ad valorem on the goods it was carrying for this purpose, which sum was set aside for the use of the Company for the upkeep of the forts; while to trade to the north of Cape Mount a further sum of ten per cent was to be paid on all goods imported into Great Britain or the plantations, all of which duties were to be applied by the Company

---

[35] *Calendar of State Papers, America and the West Indies*, I, 1574–1660, pp. 20, 135.

[36] *Ibid.*, 1669–1674, pp. 409–13; T. Carr: *Select Charters of Trading Companies*, Selden Society Publications, XXVIII, 186–92; W. R. Scott: "The Constitution and Finance of the Royal African Company . . . till 1720," *American Historical Review*, VIII, 241–59; K. C. Davies: *The Royal African Company* (London, 1957), pp. 97–101. For a brief but scholarly account of the activities of the Royal African Company, especially in the seventeenth century, see also Eveline C. Martin's chapter on "The English Slave Trade and the African Settlements," previously referred to, *Cambridge History of the British Empire*, I, 437–59, and for a general picture, J. Gallacher's section on Africa in *The New Cambridge Modern History* (ed. J. O. Lindsay, Cambridge, 1957), VII, 566–79.

[37] For a description of the African posts in 1710 see Elizabeth Donnan: *Documents* . . . , II, 109–13.

[38] See "Abstract of the Whole Charges of the Company Forts," 1730, *ibid.*, II, 436–7. The same forts were in existence in 1750.

[39] 9 and 10 William III, c. 26; K. G. Davies: *Royal African Company*, pp. 97–122.

in maintaining forts and castles. This arrangement, according to the law, was to last for fourteen years.

It was through the above arrangement that most of the slave trade was absorbed by private merchants. The Company could not rise above financial embarrassments in spite of the fact that the duty exacted of independent traders during the period from 1698 to 1712 brought into its treasury some £75,000. For the expenses of maintaining the forts vastly exceeded this sum — some years in time of war amounting to £36,000.[40] After 1712 this public assistance ceased. Further, the following decade saw the imposition of a poll duty by Virginia on slave-importations; this practice was followed by Jamaica, Barbados, and South Carolina, all to the great irritation of the slave interests and to the disadvantage of the Company. The discouragements were so great, in fact, that had it not been for Parliament's coming to the rescue in 1730 and for many years thereafter with an annual grant of £10,000, it is likely that the Company would have gone into bankruptcy and the forts into utter ruin. Although in 1744 it was granted £20,000, in 1748 it was again memorializing the Board of Trade for £10,000 tentatively granted for its succour in 1745 but withheld as the result of public criticism of the management of its resources.[41]

In more specific consideration of the activities of the British on the African coast in 1750, we find that the nine Company trading-posts represented the beginnings of the English territorial claims in West Africa. All, of course, were fortified by means of bastions and were protected by guns ranging from two-pounders up to twenty-four-pounders. Cape Coast Castle, the chief settlement of the Company on the Guinea Coast, was held first by the Portuguese, who in 1610 built a citadel upon a large rock that projects into the sea; some years later they were dislodged by the Dutch, who in 1664 were in turn obliged to submit to Admiral Holmes of the English navy. Although De Ruyter with a squadron of thirteen Dutch men-of-war appeared off the coast the following year and ravished the settlements belonging to the English, he was unable to take the fort, which was confirmed to the possessors by the Treaty of Breda. It was sub-

---

[40] Testimony of Mr. Newland, Solicitor for the Royal African Company, January 11, 1749, Board of Trade Journal, 1749–1753, p. 22; see also K. G. Davies: op. cit., pp. 122–51.

[41] Board of Trade Journal, 1749–1753, p. 22.

sequently greatly strengthened and in the middle of the eighteenth century presented a formidable appearance with its thick, high walls of stone and brick, supported by four bastions with batteries; in all, seventy-five cannon were located at various points. Within the walls was a parade capable of accommodating 500 men. Out of the live rock beneath the platform there had been hewn a great vault for the confinement of slaves, called by one writer "an horrid dungeon," divided into cells where those who had been purchased for exportation were temporarily confined.[42] A schooner, a launch, a seventeen-hand canoe, and three that were smaller were among the equipment of the fort listed in 1751.[43] The Company's gardens lying about the walls were said to have been no less than eight miles in circumference.

Wherever along the African coasts the Company possessed forts it was naturally jealous of the trade and took steps to prevent the British independent slavers from bargaining with the natives of those localities, for the blacks that it secured were customarily sold in turn to the independents or even directly to French and Portuguese shipmasters. In connection with this latter practice, the corporation was charged repeatedly with sacrificing the national interests. One slaver, Captain Hughes, testified that in 1740 he had been compelled to leave the Gold Coast by reason of the fact that he could not compete with the high prices paid by the French to the Company, amounting to nine or ten ounces of gold per black.[44] It would appear, however, that the slaves thus disposed of were largely "refuse" and also that the independent slaver usually only resorted to the forts to complete his cargo of Negroes after he had traded at various points along the coasts.

At this period the chief slave mart of the Gold Coast was the Negro village of Anamabo, somewhat to the east of Cape Coast Castle, a place where, owing to powerful native opposition, the Royal African Company had not succeeded in maintaining a fort since the

---

[42] D. Fenning and J. Collyer: A New System of Geography (2 vols., London, 1765), I, 424–5. For a more detailed description of this fort as it was in 1710 see the Royal African Company's estimates, published in Elizabeth Donnan: Documents . . . , II, 109.

[43] See "An Account of the Castle Slaves, Canoe Men, Military Slaves, Cannon and Vessels belonging to the Royal African Company of England," Statutes at Large from Magna Charta to . . . 1761 (ed. D. Pickering, 13 vols., London [1763–1780], VII, 449–52.

[44] Board of Trade Journal, 1749–1753, p. 19.

early part of the century.[45] Anamabo, in fact, was the centre for the independent traders, who anchored their ships in front of the village; here also for many years the Company had kept a "floating factory" and had traded in gold, ivory teeth, and slaves.[46] It was asserted that more Negroes were carried from this place in one year than from all other parts of the Gold Coast, which included the forts at Cape Coast, Dixcove, and Accra.[47] Slaves, however, were not always brought even to this point in sufficient numbers to answer expectations. "The ships in General make most excessive bad voyages this year," wrote Thomas Bolter, one of the agents of the Royal African Company stationed at Cape Coast Castle, to his father in 1749. "There is now 12 sail at Annamaboe," he declared, "Captain Geddis in a very large ship, the *Saint Phillip*, belonging to Mr. Geo. Fryer here & one Captain Bemish, in a ship from London between this & Dixcove and amongst them all they don't buy 6 slaves P. diem." [48] Testimony was given in 1750 that the *St. Philip* of London, and the *Tryton* of Bristol had been for eighteen months on the Gold Coast seeking 900 slaves and that by the latest advice they were still far short of that number.[49]

The explanation of this great shortage of Negroes appears not in any lessening of the numbers brought from the interior to the coast about Anamabo, but in the presence of French ships which were also trafficking directly with the native slavers and which, after 1748, had succeeded in practically monopolizing this trade, paying nine ounces of gold as against eight ounces offered by the English.[50]

---

[45] A fort, however, was established at Anamabo about 1673 by the English and was an important asset of the Royal African Company in 1710. See Elizabeth Donnan: Documents . . . , II, 110.

[46] According to the testimony of Captain Hill before the Board of Trade, seven eighths of the returns from this Company floating factory had been in gold and ivory. See Board of Trade *Journal*, 1749–1753, p. 9.

[47] Testimony of Mr. Whitaker, January 10, 1750, *ibid.*, p. 7.

[48] This letter is is to be found in "The Merchants Hall, Book of Charters of the Society of Merchant Venturers of Bristol," for the year 1749, pp. 310–11.

[49] Testimony of Mr. Briscoe, a Bristol merchant, January 10, 1750, Board of Trade *Journal*, 1749–1753, p. 14.

[50] This is taken from the letter heretofore referred to, written by Thomas Bolter, who added in a footnote: "Note an oz of Gold is £4." See the "Bristol Merchant Venturers Book of Charters," pp. 310–11.

For a broad study of the importance of the competition between the English and French in the slave trade, as this relates to rivalry of the two nations in other fields, see C. M. Andrews: "Anglo-French Commercial Rivalry, 1700–1750: The Western Phase, I," *American Historical Review*, XX, 539–56.

According to a statement issued by the Royal African Company in 1749, the French had never visited Anamabo before 1736, but in that year some of their ships on the way to the Whydah Coast to the eastward had been invited to stop there by independent traders — probably with the idea of disposing of the "refuse" blacks in possession of the latter. The French thus discovered the economic possibilities of the village as a slave mart and proceeded to secure a grant of free trade from the local king. However, the following year several of their ships were forced to leave as the result of pressure exerted by the local agents of the Royal African Company supported by some of the free English slavers, who now realized the danger to their own interests. In 1738, as a result of a demand that the government should intervene, a British warship, the *Greenwich*, policed the waters about Anamabo, driving away the French ships. Upon its departure, the latter returned with redoubled zeal, their masters now setting up a claim to the sole trade of the place. As a consequence, in the course of the next two or three years the French succeeded in engrossing practically the whole of this trade — forcing the English, so it was claimed, to depend upon the less desirable Negroes of the Bight and of Angola for their plantations. This, of course, resulted in renewed complaints to the ministers. Two British warships were therefore sent out and again the French were driven away. When war occurred between the two nations the English were in control and remained so until after the peace in 1748. Thereupon the French again made their appearance and, as has been indicated in the preceding paragraph, in renewing their claims, offered such high prices for slaves that their rivals could not compete with them. The only solution of the problem, according to the Company officers, was to induce the local king to consent to the rebuilding of the old decayed fort which the English had earlier erected there.[51] But this was quite beyond the power of the corporation, the affairs of which were now in a truly desperate condition.

Evidence also is not lacking of the serious consequences to the Royal African Company of the competition of the slavers of other nations at places outside of Anamabo. The French African Company at this period, as has been stated in the preceding chapter, was apparently subsidized by its government to the amount of almost

---

[51] The above facts are presented in a Company memorial to the Duke of Bedford. See Minutes of the Committee of Seven, Royal African Company, August 16, 1749, 5:85–9, P.R.O., Treas. 70. 96.

£50,000 per annum;[52] its position was further strengthened by the fact that trading by private individuals owing allegiance to France was strictly forbidden, with the result that along the Gum Coast and in other regions fully under French control it was able without competition to set the price for slaves at a low figure.[53] The Royal African Company, on the other hand, owing not only to private trading on the part of Englishmen but also to the encroachments of the French and especially the Portuguese on the Whydah Coast, found that the price of Negroes there, which formerly had not been above fifty shillings, or at most £3 per head, finally advanced to almost £20, according to Postlethwayt. This meant the loss of the Whydah market to the English, who insisted that they could not dispose of Negroes at such a price with profit,[54] although at one period 6,000 Negroes had been secured annually on this coast.[55]

Indeed, to many at this period there seemed to be a very real danger that the entire African trade, held to be of vast importance to the Empire, might be lost. Not only did there exist the crisis over Anamabo on the Gold Coast and Whydah to the eastward, as stated, but in the summer of 1750 the officers of the Royal African Company received disturbing news from James Fort on the Gambia that the French were making a settlement at Albreda, above them on the same river.[56] In May of that year an attempt was also made to destroy the fort at Dixcove on the Gold Coast by natives instigated by the Dutch.[57] The French Company, moreover, had at Angola a thriving floating factory which limited the activities of the English in that region. In fact, the situation was so serious that even the

---

[52] Malachy Postlethwayt: *Considerations on the Revival of the Royal-British Assiento; Between His Catholick-Majesty and the Honourable the South-Sea Company* (London, 1749), pp. 14–17.

[53] *Ibid.*, pp. 20–1.

[54] *Ibid.*, pp. 33–4; see also, by the same author, *Britain's Commercial Interest Explained and Improved* (2 vols., London, 1757, II, 112–56), in which he deals extensively with the French African trade system, showing why the British were at so great a disadvantage in competing for supplies of slaves.

[55] Testimony of Mr. Briscoe of Bristol, January 10, 1750, Board of Trade *Journal*, 1749–1753, p. 14.

[56] *Ibid.*, p. 94. It should be pointed out that as early as 1681 the French had secured a grant of a plot of ground at Albreda from the native ruler of that region. For an account of the French activities at Albreda see J. M. Gray: *A History of Gambia*, pp. 100–4, 218–28.

[57] Extract of a letter from Wm. Husbands to John Ashley, May 10, 1750, Cape Coast Castle, Board of Trade *Journal*, 1749–1753, p. 104.

free-trading interests now considered it a matter of vital necessity to preserve the Company's forts.[58]

A very true picture of the state of the Royal African Company's affairs at this period may be secured by an examination of the minutes of its Committee of Seven annually appointed to transact the routine business. These show its broken financial condition by the late 1740's. To secure the necessary articles for carrying on the Guinea trade the Company was obliged to buy largely on credit, seeking to satisfy the clamour of its numerous creditors by means of interest-bearing bonds.[59] Its African commodities were frequently mortgaged before sale, which took place at Lloyd's Coffee House, and it was obliged in 1748 to confess, even to one in dire need of the money he had advanced to it, "that the Company's present inability is such that it is out of their Power to pay anything." [60] Its factors on the African coast were in great distress. One of their number, David Crichton, venturing to draw on the Company to supply the pressing needs of Cape Coast Castle in 1745, found himself in an English prison; [61] another, Thomas Bolter, wrote from the Guinea Coast early in 1749 that there remained little or no trading-goods at any of the out-forts except Accra and that the Whydah post had been without supplies for six months, and continued: "All I have in the world to the amount of £884 advanced into the Company's hands. . . . A great scarcity of Corn, not £1,000 of vendable goods on the whole coast, no hopes of supplies, nor any credit, for nobody will take our bills . . . nor will anybody attempt to draw again to be laid up in a prison like Mr. Crichton. . . . Unless supplies arrive in a very short time I greatly fear the Company will lose their possessions." [62]

It was generally felt that the abandonment of the posts would not only be a real disaster for the Empire but also would leave those Negro towns that had long been protected by the guns of the posts open to swift destruction by powerful native enemies. For it appears that the English at Dixcove, Succondee, and Commenda alone

---

[58] Testimony of Mr. Hardman before the Board of Trade, January 11, 1750, *ibid.*, pp. 15–19.

[59] Minutes for July 2 and September 24, 1747, "Minute Books of the Committee of Seven," 5:45–50, P.R.O., Treas. 70. 96.

[60] Minutes for December 6, 1748, 5:59, *ibid.*

[61] For the case of David Crichton see the "Minute Books of the Court of Assistants," for November 14, 1745, November 3 and December 13, 1748, *ibid.*

[62] "Minute Book of the Committee of Seven," for July 13, 1749, 5:79–80, *ibid.*

saved the Hantahs (Antees) and Commendas from the warlike Ashantees and Warsaws (Wassau); Cape Coast guaranteed the safety of the Fetues (Footoe) and Saboes from the Fanteens (Fantin); Winnebah held back the Acrans, Fanteens, and Akims from the people of the adjacent villages, while Accra had under its protection the remnant of an inland nation that differed in laws and customs from the surrounding peoples. For a number of years these weak coast towns had been in friendly relationship with the English, who had solemnly guaranteed their safety.[63]

Nevertheless, as we have seen, the affairs of the Royal African Company had reached a crisis. A memorial addressed to the Lords Commissioners of the Treasury during the summer of 1749 showed the practical collapse of the corporation in spite of the great sums of money spent in the past and the very real danger that the French would step in and take possession of the forts, which must soon be given up unless assistance arrived.[64] No time could be lost. A plan was hastily worked out by the Board of Trade whereby Henry Lascelles, a London merchant deeply interested in the slave trade, was entrusted with the £10,000 voted to the Company by Parliament in 1745 and which, as has been stated, had been held back on account of the unsatisfactory condition of the corporation's affairs. With these funds he was able to rush assistance in two ships to the forts along the Gulf of Guinea and the Gambia.[65]

It should here be pointed out that for some time the government had felt that a thoroughgoing reorganization of the African trade was imperative. In accordance with this view, the Secretary of State for the Southern Department, the Duke of Bedford, on June 30, 1749, in a communication to the Board of Trade requested that body to prepare a scheme for its improvement and extension, with the idea in mind of then submitting a bill to both houses of Parliament at the beginning of the new session pursuant to an address on June 8 by the House of Lords to His Majesty. As a result, the Board directed a circular letter to the principal merchants of London, Liverpool, and Bristol trading in Africa, to the officers also of the Royal African Company, and finally to those having an interest

---

[63] A Detection of the Proceedings and Practices of the Directors of the Royal African Company of England (London, 1749), p. 3 and note.

[64] This memorial is included in the "Minute Book" previously cited of July 13, 1749, 5:79–80.

[65] See P.R.O., Declared Accounts, E, 351, A.O. 1., Bundle 4.

in the West Indies, asking them to present their views as to the best method of promoting the trade.[66] Early in 1750 a series of conferences was held by the Lords Commissioners with the representatives of all of these groups present. The discussions that took place throw a flood of light upon certain aspects of the trade.

The sugar interests appeared, strongly favouring the idea of a reorganized joint-stock company which would include all those trading to the African coasts. Their principal spokesman was a Mr. Martin, referred to previously, who urged that such a body would have a permanent interest in the forts as the repository and bulwark of its trade, where it would always have supplies ready for all demands. He declared that, on the other hand, no open company without permanent capital could possibly furnish proper goods at all seasons; he further urged that since the later type of company inevitably would be made up of transient persons the natives would consequently turn to the Dutch and the French; finally, he argued that under permanent management, such as would exist under a joint-stock plan, it then would be possible to develop a great interior traffic in slaves by establishing factories well inland and also by making alliances with certain native groups — something beyond the power of private traders to accomplish. Out of this, he claimed, would come multitudes of Negroes. This would mean not only a greater but also a cheaper supply for the colonies without lessening the profits of those who, by buying slaves more cheaply, could sell the products of their labour more cheaply.[67]

Another thing that greatly concerned the planting interests beyond the supply of slaves was that Negroes of the right type should be secured. John Sharpe, London agent for Jamacia, asserted, in opposing the idea of an open company, that the separate traders who came to the West Indies had not for many years brought a cargo made up entirely of Gold Coast Negroes, which, with those from Whydah, were considered to be the most desirable; in fact, he affirmed that on the sugar plantations Negroes from other parts were not serviceable.[68] A Mr. Whitaker, another spokesman for the planters, in reinforcing Sharpe's position, complained that when private slavers arrived from Africa they frequently asserted that their Negroes were Gold Coast natives. Upon examination it was usually

---

[66] Board of Trade *Journal*, 1741–1749, pp. 429, 465.
[67] Testimony of Mr. Martin, January 10, 1749/50, *ibid.*, 1749–1753, pp. 4–5.
[68] *Ibid.*, p. 6.

found that only one sixth or one seventh were really of that region. He agreed with Sharpe that it was flinging money away to buy other blacks and insisted that he knew six persons, each of whom wanted at least 370 Gold Coast slaves, and had cash, but who could not secure them.[69] In this connection, he accused the traders of purchasing Windward slaves because they died sooner, which created an additional demand; finally, he affirmed that the planters would rather pay £40 for a real Gold Coast Negro than £20 for one from Calabar.[70] The explanation of this increased serviceability and hardiness of the Gold Coast Negro, according to one Maynard, who had bought slaves on the Guinea Coast and who also testified, was that they found in the West Indies the same kind of food and general living-conditions to which they had been accustomed in their native country.[71]

Thus, the planters were thoroughly convinced, it would appear, that a joint-stock company would succeed better than an open company in securing the most desirable types of Negroes; that it would be responsible and dependable, whereas the independent slaver was

---

[69] Ibid., p. 7. John Jones, writing from Jamaica in 1728 to Isaac Hobhouse, stressed the importance of sending to him and his partners, acting as the agents for Hobhouse and other slaving merchants, a constant supply of Gold Coast Negroes: "My Partner W. T. intends for England very shortly, say some time this year, when I hope he'll settle matters so as we shall be certain of 2 or 3 Gold Coast men yearly, when we shall be on as good footing as our neighbours" (Jefferies Collection of Manuscripts, Bristol Reference Library).

[70] Board of Trade Journal, 1749–1753, p. 7. As for Calabar slaves, the following item is of interest: "The John & Betty arrived here the 4 Instant, with one hundred & fifty bright Negroes, she purchased two hundred & fifty, and have buried eleven or more since her arrivall. They are the worst Cargo of Negroes [that] have been imported for several Years past. Our day of Sale was the 10th Instant. They were so bad Could not sell them to the planters. We yesterday sold One hundrd & five to Messers Lamego & Furlado at Eighteen pounds ten shilling pr. head. . . . The remainder are so very bad cannot gett £8 pr head for them" (Tyndall & Asshlon to Messrs. Hobhouse [& Co]., Jamaica, November 13, 1729, Jefferies Collection of Manuscripts, Bristol Reference Library).

It cannot be denied, however, that there was a demand for other than Gold Coast slaves. Thomas Morris writing to Hobhouse from Barbados early in 1730, declared: ". . . there was not a Cargo of Ebbo Slaves sould here a long time, and many People are Enquiring for them" (ibid.). In 1749 Bristol sent 47 ships to Guinea; 17 of these went to the Gold Coast and took on board 5,180 slaves, 23 went to the Bight of Benin, Bonny, and the Calabar Coast and took on board 8,110 slaves, and 7 went to Angola and took on board 3,350 slaves. See W. E. Minchinton: The Trade of Bristol in the Eighteenth Century (Bristol, 1957), pp. 34–5.

[71] Board of Trade Journal, 1749–1753, p. 8.

not; finally, that it would open up a greater supply of slaves, which would mean lower prices.

The assertions of this group, however, were not allowed to go unchallenged. A Mr. Ord, representing the London merchants — who favoured an open trade, as did those of Bristol and Liverpool — insisted that the slave trade had increased under the independent trading. He laid before the Board a statement of the Negroes imported into Jamacia between the year 1702 and 1749 which showed that when the trade was in the hands of an exclusive company the supply was very meagre; that when the trade was opened upon the basis of the ten-per-cent duty, it increased; and that at the expiration of the fourteen-year period, when the duties lapsed, it so flourished that in 1747 upwards of 10,000 Negroes were imported into Jamacia alone. Further, he denied any shortage of Gold Coast blacks under the prevailing system. In this connection, he asserted that in 1748 the *Phoebe* with 230 Gold Coast slaves could not sell them at Barbados and had to sail to Jamaica; that in 1749 the *Alexander* with 350 Negroes also from the Gold Coast, with the exception of about 60 purchased "to the Windward," offered them for £24 sterling per head at St. Christopher, but that no one would give the price; that also in 1749 the *Jamaica Packet* with the same number of blacks, half Gold Coast and half Windward, offered its cargo there for the same price, also without success, nor did the *Jenny* with 470 Negroes, 350 of whom were Gold Coast, find a market at Barbados.[72]

Mr. Ord, it is interesting to note, also challenged the desirability of Gold Coast slaves. While admitting that they were better fitted for labour, he insisted that they were of a dangerous, rebellious disposition which promoted disturbances and, therefore, for the sake of security, it was necessary to have others. In this connection he declared that he had managed two sugar plantations and had never purchased any Gold Coast blacks. The others, he found, had done very well and had not contracted any distempers.[73] He was supported in his contentions by a Mr. Hardman, who asserted that no Gold Coast Negroes were wanted by the northern colonies, where some 3,000 blacks were required each year.[74] Finally, Richard Smith,

---

[72] *Ibid.*, pp. 11–13.
[73] *Ibid.*
[74] *Ibid.*, p. 15.

for many years a slave merchant at Barbados, testified in support of Ord's position that between the years 1739 and 1748 he had sold about 30,000 Negroes, and that the planters had shown no such prejudice as had been asserted against other than Gold Coast Negroes. He declared that in 1739 he disposed of a cargo of Gold Coast slaves at £20 per head; in 1740 a cargo of Calabars brought the same price; in 1741–2 another cargo from the Gold Coast brought £22, and in 1743 one from Angola brought £25 and another from the Gold Coast, £27; in 1744 one from Benin averaged £25 and in 1745 a cargo from Angola, £28; after this year, with England at war, the slaves rose in value to about £30 per head. Finally, with respect to the genuine Koromantyns, he confessed that he had never known more than twenty in any cargo of Gold Coast slaves.[75] The free traders, in spite of this latter admission, clearly had the better of the argument.

During the discussion over the reorganization of the slaving activities, a plan was brought forward by the Company itself through its solicitor, Mr. Newland, and urged by two other members, that Parliament be prevailed upon to grant £20,000 per annum to support the African trade and that a new stock of £200,000 be raised out of the profits of the enterprise with which the creditors might be satisfied. They asserted that if Parliament would grant the above sum for thirty-two years, transferable stock amounting to £300,000 might be provided for, with £100,000 in so-called trust stock, and that the affairs of the Company could be then placed upon a firm basis, since its total indebtedness, exclusive of sums due the directors, was £50,000, and with the latter amount totalled only £107,-000.[76] The independent traders, however, characterized this scheme as one which had as its sole ends the procuring of £20,000 per annum from the public and the raising of the price of Negroes fifty per cent, and they asserted that the separate traders would be able

---

[75] *Ibid.*, p. 23.

[76] *Ibid.*, p. 22. In 1749 a Mr. O'Connor in his *Considerations on the Trade to Africa* (London, 1749) proposed (pp. 41–4) that the capital stock of the Royal African Company be raised to £800,000; that the present stock of £300,000 be cancelled and the owners of it be entitled to £100,000 of the new stock at £50 per hundred; that the creditors of the company in lieu of their demands be entitled to subscribe for £200,000 of said capital, likewise at £50 on the hundred; that new subscribers be entitled to subscribe for £500,000 at £40 on the hundred; and, finally, that Parliament provide an annuity of £20,000 for twenty-one years to the new company to support the new trading stock.

to afford the same protection to the business at half the cost to the public. In other words, they favoured a regulated company.

The views of the independent traders ultimately prevailed and were reflected in the Act of 1750 "for extending and improving the Trade to Africa." [77] By it the trade of Africa from Cape Blanco to the Cape of Good Hope was thrown open and those British subjects who traded there were incorporated into "The Company of Merchants Trading to Africa." All the forts, settlements, factories, stores, castle slaves, canoe men, and merchandise of the Royal African Company were thereby vested in it. Nevertheless, it was forbidden to trade in its corporate capacity or to hold any joint or transferable stock or to borrow money. Its management was entrusted to the Committee of Nine chosen annually — three by the London merchants and three by those of Bristol and of Liverpool, respectively — which was given power to maintain the forts and factories and for that purpose to appoint governors and to make the necessary regulations. In this connection the law provided that no one should serve more than three successive years on the Committee. To be entitled to participate in the activities of the new Company, traders were expected to pay a fee of forty shillings for its freedom. By another act passed in 1752 the affairs of the old corporation were wound up. To its stockholders Parliament granted the sum of £112,142.3.3 as a complete satisfaction of all assets, with the understanding that certain specified sums should be paid out to various creditor groups. [78]

This reorganization of the Guinea trade met the immediate needs of the situation excepting at Anamabo. With respect to it the government took a very firm stand, for it was felt that large imperial interests were at stake. Early in 1752 Commodore Buckle was or-

---

[77] 23 Geo. II, c. 31, *Statutes at Large* (Eyre and Strahan), VI, 497–503. It may be noted in passing that among the Liverpool slave ships that went to Africa in 1752 at least 30 resorted to the Windward and Gold coasts, 13 to New and Old Calabar, 10 to Bonny, 8 to Portuguese Angola, 5 to Gambia, and 3 to Benin. The destination of 4 vessels was not given. See Williamson's *Liverpool Memorandum Book*, 1753. For the Liverpool slaving activities in 1750 and the opposition of the local populace to this traffic, see Averil Mackenzie-Grieve: *The Last Years of the Slave Trade: Liverpool, 1750–1807* (London, 1941).

[78] 25 Geo. II, c. 40. For a recent study of the slave trade subsequent to 1750 see R. B. Sheridan: "The Commercial and Financial Organization of the British Slave Trade, 1750–1807," *Economic History Review*, 2nd ser., XI, 249–63. This article is concerned not so much with Africa as with the business relations of slavers with West India merchants and planters.

dered to go in the *Assistance* with two other warships to that point; he found upon arrival three French men-of-war of sixty-five, fifty-four, and twenty-four guns, respectively, at anchor, the officers of which were busy ingratiating themselves with the inhabitants by means of presents. In fact, they had even offered to the local ruler the equivalent of £15,000 sterling for the liberty to build a fort. Without hesitation, therefore, Buckle sent an ultimatum to the French commander that if the French persisted in what they were about, the British would look upon this as a breach of the peace and repel force with force. Whereupon the French thought proper to withdraw, but not until they had promised the natives to return in ten months at the latest.[79] Well might the Great War for the Empire have begun off the African coast at this juncture rather than at the forks of the Ohio two years later! *

---

[79] For an account of the above episode see *The Scots Magazine*, May 1752. "From Africa we have Advices that there are a great number of French men of war on the coasts of this continent. And that they are erecting floating Factories and Forts in several Parts where we formerly had the greatest Trade. Captain Bostock who arrived a few Days ago saw three French ships of 74, 56 and 18 guns on the Windward Coast" (Advices from Charleston, South Carolina, May 11, 1752, *Pennsylvania Journal*, June 25, 1752).

* Note: There will be a summarizing chapter at the end of Volume III, Revised, of this series. This summary will bring together and interpret broadly the significance of the British colonial system in the middle of the eighteenth century as set forth in detail in both the present volume and Volume III.

Index

Abacos, forest area of the Bermudas, 239

Abercrombie, James, see Abercromby, James

Abercromby, James, *The Examination of*, 61

Absenteeism, in Jamaica, 326; in the sugar islands, the effect of, on the economy, 228, 229, disadvantages of 229; in the British West Indies, 266

Absentees, Jamaica, the taxation of, and the British government, 188–9; people of wealth and culture, Jamaica, 193

"Abstracts of Houghton James Estate in Jamaica . . . , Papers Relating to Jamaica, 1693–1773," 196

Accomack (Accomac) County, Virginia, number of justices of the peace in, 28; number of tobacco warehouses in, 85 n

Account of the European Settlements in America (1757), by Edmund and William Burke, 182 n

Accra, slave post of the Royal African Company, 277; English protection of, 283–4

Acroan Negroes, the, threaten the Winnebahs, 284

Adams, the Rev. Alexander, of Maryland, protests the act reducing the church benefice, 55

Addison, the Rev. Henry, on the condition of the Maryland Anglican Establishment, 51

Africa, human resources of, 267; see Chapter 10 on the slave trade in

African trade, value of the, to independent traders, 266; see Slave Trade

Agriculture, see Indigo, Livestock, Rice, Sugar, Tobacco

Aix-la-Chapelle, the treaty of, as the basis for the rights of the logwood-cutters in Honduras, 255–6

Akin Negroes, the, threaten the Winnebahs, 284

Albemarle, William Anne Kepple, 2nd Earl of, Governor-General of Virginia, and quit-rents, 11; an absentee, 16

Albemarle County, North Carolina, mem-

Albemarle County (*continued*)
bers of the Assembly from, and opposition to Act of 1746, 116–17; original four precincts of, 117; representation of, 117; opposition of representatives from, to Gov. Johnston, 119

Albemarle County, Virginia, Presbyterianism in, 36; and tobacco, 82 n

Albemarle Sound, older established part of North Carolina, 116; Assembly members from the region about, oppose the Act of 1746, 116–17

Albreda, the French settle at, on the Gambia, 282 n

Alewives, importation of, to Jamaica, 185 n

Alexander, Robert, entailed Virginia estate of, 40

Alexander, the slave ship, activities of between the Gold Coast and St. Christopher, 287

Alexander, William, of New York, 186

All Saints Parish of Frederick County, Maryland, provisions for the clergy of, 51

Allason, William, Glasgow tobacco-buyer, 87; on the decrease of tobacco-production because of indigo-production in 1757, 87–9; on the independent attitude of the Virginia planters, 93; profits of, 94

Allason Papers, 88 n

Allegheny River, the, 4; and the Ohio Company grant, 6

Allen, William, Philadelphia merchant, accused of a clandestine trade in molasses, 256

Altamaha River, the, 128; as a boundary of Georgia, 154; settlement of Frederica on, 161

Amelia County, Virginia, 12; number of justices of the peace in, 28; Presbyterianism in, 36; and tobacco, 82 n

Amelia Township, South Carolina, lack of cultural facilities in, 138 n; activities of a Presbyterian preacher in, 139 n

American Husbandry (1775), the author of, unknown, 41; on the Virginia plant-

A NOTE ON THE AUTHOR

LAWRENCE HENRY GIPSON is Research Professor of History, Emeritus, at Lehigh University. After receiving a bachelor of arts degree from the University of Idaho, he entered Oxford as the first Rhodes Scholar from the state of Idaho, and gained a degree in the Oxford Honour School of Modern History. He was later a Bulkley Fellow in the graduate school at Yale, where his doctoral dissertation, *Jared Ingersoll: A Study of American Loyalism in Relation to British Colonial Government*, received the Porter Prize as the best work in literary form presented by a student in any division of the University during the preceding year; it was also awarded the Justin Winsor Prize by the American Historical Association. Since then he has written and published many works relating to colonial history (including thirteen volumes of his *magnum opus;* the final volume is in preparation). During the academic year 1951–2 he occupied the Harmsworth Chair in American History at Oxford; he also has been a member of the board of editors of the *American Historical Review,* was a founder of the Conference on Early American History, and is a past president of both the Conference on British Studies and the Pennsylvania Historical Association. He is the Honorary Consultant in American Colonial History to the Library of Congress for the period 1965 through 1967. Many prizes and honors have come to him as a result of his writing, including, in 1962, the Pulitzer Prize in History for Volume X of *The British Empire before the American Revolution* and, most recently, his election as Honorary Fellow of Lincoln College, Oxford University.

A NOTE ON THE TYPE

THIS BOOK is set in Linotype Caledonia. Caledonia belongs to the family of printing types called "modern face" by printers — a term used to mark the change in style of type-letters that occurred about 1800. Caledonia is in the general neighborhood of Scotch Modern in design, but is more freely drawn than that letter.

The book was designed by W. A. Dwiggins, and composed by The Plimpton Press, Norwood, Massachusetts. Printed and bound by Kingsport Press, Incorporated, Kingsport, Tennessee.

DATE DUE

GAYLORD   PRINTED IN U.S.A.